D0043609

What People Are Saying
about the Left Behind Series

"This is the most successful Christian-fiction series ever."
  —Publishers Weekly

"Tim LaHaye and Jerry B. Jenkins . . . are doing for Christian fiction what John Grisham did for courtroom thrillers."
  —TIME

"The authors' style continues to be thoroughly captivating and keeps the reader glued to the book, wondering what will happen next. And it leaves the reader hungry for more."
  —Christian Retailing

"Combines Tom Clancy–like suspense with touches of romance, high-tech flash and Biblical references."
  —The New York Times

"It's not your mama's Christian fiction anymore."
  —The Dallas Morning News

"Wildly popular—and highly controversial."
  —USA Today

"Christian thriller. Prophecy-based fiction. Juiced-up morality tale. Call it what you like, the Left Behind series . . . now has a label its creators could never have predicted: blockbuster success."
  —Entertainment Weekly

Tyndale House products by Tim LaHaye and Jerry B. Jenkins

The Left Behind® book series
Left Behind®
Tribulation Force
Nicolae
Soul Harvest
Apollyon
Assassins
The Indwelling
The Mark
Desecration
The Remnant
Armageddon
Glorious Appearing
Coming Soon: Prequel and Sequel

Other Left Behind® products
Left Behind®: The Kids
Devotionals
Calendars
Abridged audio products
Dramatic audio products
Graphic novels
Gift books
and more . . .

Other Tyndale House books by Tim LaHaye and Jerry B. Jenkins
Perhaps Today
Are We Living in the End Times?

For the latest information on individual products, release dates,
and future projects, visit www.leftbehind.com

Tyndale House books by Tim LaHaye	Tyndale House books by Jerry B. Jenkins
How to Be Happy Though Married	*Soon*
Spirit-Controlled Temperament	*Silenced*
Transformed Temperaments	
Why You Act the Way You Do	

The ONE YEAR® BOOK OF *Left Behind Devotions*

EMBRACING
LIVING EACH DAY WITH A HEART TOWARD HEAVEN
ETERNITY

TIM LAHAYE
JERRY B. JENKINS
FRANK M. MARTIN

Tyndale House Publishers, Inc.
Wheaton, Illinois

Visit Tyndale's exciting Web site at www.tyndale.com

TYNDALE is a registered trademark of Tyndale House Publishers, Inc.

Tyndale's quill logo is a trademark of Tyndale House Publishers, Inc.

Discover the latest about the Left Behind series at www.leftbehind.com

Embracing Eternity: Living Each Day with a Heart toward Heaven

The One Year is a registered trademark of Tyndale House Publishers, Inc.

Designed by Julie Chen

Edited by MaryLynn Layman

Left Behind is a registered trademark of Tyndale House Publishers, Inc.

Published in association with the literary agency of Alive Communications, Inc., 7680 Goddard Street, Suite 200, Colorado Springs, CO 80920.

ISBN 0-8423-7122-2

Printed in the United States of America

09 08 07 06 05 04
 7   6   5   4   3   2

To Ruthie,
my forever beautiful
bride

ACKNOWLEDGMENTS

IMAGINE HOW a rookie astronaut must feel the day his boss hands him the keys to the space shuttle, and you have a small sense of what I felt when I was hired to help with this project.

Jerry Jenkins and Tim LaHaye have taken the *Left Behind* series where no man has gone before—to the moon and back several times over. To date, it is still the fastest-selling Christian series in history, and I'm thrilled at the chance to ride around the block with them a few times. My first sincere note of thanks goes to Jerry and Tim for allowing me to tag along—particularly to Jerry for recommending me for this task.

Thanks also to the many fine folks at Tyndale, a publishing company that's truly more focused on its mission than its bottom line. Jan Stob, Ken Petersen, MaryLynn Layman, and so many others worked to make this book the best it could possibly be—and were a joy to work with throughout the process.

To Ruthie, my beautiful wife and best friend in the world. For being my number one fan, my most honest critic, and my silent editing partner. And to my kids for once again allowing me to tell so many of our little family secrets in order to make a point.

Finally, a huge note of thanks to my good buddy and go-to theologian, Tim King. If I had a nickel for every original thought I've had, I might have enough to buy a book like this, but I certainly couldn't scrape together enough material to write one. Tim was there on so many dry days with fresh ideas and a new look at some very old and familiar passages. Thanks for the help.

Frank M. Martin

LIVING IN THE LIGHT OF CHRIST'S RETURN

THE LEFT BEHIND series of novels is fiction at its dead-level best. The writing is fast paced, the characters engaging, and the plots suspenseful, all wrapped up in a story line that's as timely as it is gripping. It is a crash course in edge-of-your-seat storytelling. But is that all the series has to offer? A good read on a lazy Saturday afternoon? A brief escape from an otherwise busy life?

Obviously you and I know better. At its core, the Left Behind series is a clarion call to higher living—a plea for passion in a sometimes passionless world. It is a reminder that God is in control and you and I are here for a reason. It is an invitation to see the Bible as more than a tale of remote characters from days gone by, but as an inspired book about the here and now—a book that is real and relevant and reliable.

And exciting!

Lives have been changed as a result of this series. Souls have been saved, and saved souls have been drawn into a deeper relationship with Jesus. People who were once followers of God are now friends of God. And more Christians than ever are living each day with their identities wrapped up in eternity. And that is a very good thing.

It's nice to know all those trees didn't die for nothing.

So what does it mean to live in the light of Christ's return? In short, it means grasping each breath as if it could be your last, living life moment by precious moment, with your feet planted firmly on earth but your heart aimed squarely toward heaven. It means learning to embrace the role of dual citizenship—living in one world while belonging to another. It is a lifestyle of living like there's no tomorrow and then dying so that your real life can finally begin.

It is said that Winston Churchill planned his own funeral. It took place in the great Saint Paul's Cathedral and ended with a lone bugler playing taps from a balcony high above the crowd beneath the massive dome. Taps is the universal benediction, signaling the end of a life well lived.

But to the crowd's surprise, when the bugler finished, another bugler began to play—this one from the opposite balcony of the great cathedral. Only this one played the notes of reveille. *It's time to get up. It's time to get up. It's time to get up in the morning!*[1]

Winston Churchill understood that the end was only the beginning. The same holds true for you and me.

What would our life look like if we embraced this truth with the core of our being? if we truly saw life as just a precursor to eternity, simply a starting gate for the great race toward heaven? What would we do differently? How would it change our daily routine? Would we ever look at another person the same way again?

Would we ever look at *ourselves* the same way again?

These are the thoughts and questions that I woke with each morning and held with me through every stroke of the keyboard, every word, every page of the daily devotions that follow. And our prayer is that you will do the same as you walk with us through the next 365 days of your life.

Frank M. Martin
Colorado Springs, Colorado (Psalm 39:4)

JANUARY

TODAY'S READING
John 14:1-4

HIS PROMISE TO RETURN

When everything is ready, I will come and get you, so that you will always be with me where I am.   John 14:3

AS A CHILD, George Tulloch was fascinated by stories of the *Titanic*. Some might call it an obsession. As a boy he imagined himself sailing the ocean in search of the doomed vessel, maybe even salvaging pieces of it. Then after years of hard work and good fortune in business, George finally had the resources to chase after his dream. So in 1996 he put together a team of the best scientists and sailors and set out to the exact spot where the *Titanic* sank in 1912. He and his crew were able to recover numerous artifacts from the ship—eyeglasses, jewelry, dishware, some coins, and the like. But the most exciting thing they found was a large piece of the hull resting several hundred yards away. Tulloch immediately saw the opportunity to actually rescue part of the ship itself.

> "Buck had already fallen in love with God. That had to be his passion until Christ returned again."
>
> *Tribulation Force*, 34

The team did its best to raise the twenty-ton piece of iron, but to no avail. At one point the team almost had it, lifting it just below the surface, but a storm blew in and broke the ropes. The Atlantic reclaimed its treasure. Then Tulloch did something surprising before they were forced to retreat. He descended into the deep once more in a small submarine, and using a robotic arm, he attached a small handmade placard onto the section. It said, "I will come back. George Tulloch."

It was a symbolic act, not a practical one. It wasn't like anyone was going to steal a piece of iron two miles below the surface of the Atlantic. It was just a useless piece of iron. But somehow George felt the need. Two years later he made good on that promise.[1]

For a lot of the same reasons, Jesus left us with a similar message. "I am going to prepare a place for you. . . . When everything is ready, I will come and get you" (John 14:2-3). Some may wonder why he cared in the first place. Why would he even want to reclaim us? What good are we to him? In many ways we're just as worthless and cumbersome and unyielding as that lazy piece of iron in the Atlantic.

But Jesus doesn't see us that way. He's dreamed of this moment since the beginning of creation, and now that the time is near he can't help but leave his mark on our hearts. "I'm leaving now. But don't worry, I'll be back." We may not understand why he wants to come back to redeem us, but we can be certain that he will. Jesus always makes good on his promises.

REFLECTION
In what ways do you still struggle with a "troubled heart"? And how should that change in light of Jesus' promise to return?

LOVING THE LEAST

I tell you the truth, whatever you did for one of the least of these . . . ,
you did for me. Matthew 25:40, NIV

I REMEMBER a poster on a dorm-room wall during my days in college. The poster was a picture of a homeless man lying in a dirty gutter holding a bottle in a paper bag by his side. The inscription on the bottom was a quote from Mother Teresa. It read, *"You love Jesus only as much as the person you love the least."*

For all that we don't understand about the life of Jesus and the true nature of God, there is one truth that he made completely clear. The Christian faith is about service and humility. It's about helping those who can't help themselves. It's about loving others more than we love ourselves—even the most unlovable among us.

When the disciples found a few minutes alone with Jesus outside the Temple, the question they posed is the same one that you and I probably would have asked. "Will there be any sign ahead of time to signal your return and the end of the world?" (Matthew 24:3). But his answer had more to do with us than it did his return. Through parables he showed his disciples the basis on which people will be chosen on that day. "I was hungry, and you fed me. I was thirsty, and you gave me a drink. I was a stranger, and you invited me into your home. I was naked, and you gave me clothing. I was sick, and you cared for me. I was in prison, and you visited me" (Matthew 25:35-36).

What is the sign of true followers? Is it the amount of knowledge that we have? Is it the money we give to missions? the degrees we've earned? the number of people we've preached to? the hours we've spent worshiping in church? the books we've read or written?

According to Jesus, the sign of the saved is their love for the least.

It is said that when Francis of Assisi left his wealth behind to seek God, he stripped naked and walked out of the city. The first person he encountered on his journey was a leper on the side of the road. He first passed him, then turned back. He embraced the leper in his arms before continuing his journey. A few steps down the road he turned and saw that the leper was gone. Until his dying day, Francis of Assisi was convinced that the leper was Jesus. Even if he was wrong, he was right.

REFLECTION
As you reflect on this parable, try to think of one person in your life who would be considered "one of the least." What is your responsibility toward that person? What would Jesus have you do today to help him or her?

NO FEAR OF JUDGMENT

Then everyone will see the Son of Man arrive on the clouds with power and great glory. So when all these things begin to happen, stand straight and look up, for your salvation is near!   Luke 21:27-28

WHAT IMAGES come to mind when you think of "end times prophecies"? What thoughts or fears does the idea conjure up within you? Most people, if they were honest, would admit that their view of the end times is a frightening one. They've heard stories of fire raining from the skies, of mountains sinking into the seas, of the moon turning bloodred, of earthquakes and death, and bodies rising from the grave. They imagine an angry and vengeful God hovering high above it all, bent on destruction and raining terror on all who have rejected him.

> "[Rayford] wanted to investigate, to learn, to know, to act. He started by searching for a Bible. . . . Would there be some guide? An index? Something that referred to the Rapture or the judgment or something?"
>
> *Left Behind,* 121

Not a pretty picture. And certainly not what we would imagine from the loving God described in Scripture.

Have we missed something? In many ways I think we have. God didn't reveal these graphic images of the coming judgment to express his wrath or even to frighten us into believing. He revealed them to show us his wonderful grace and mercy in the midst of our sin and unworthiness. The story isn't about pending gloom and doom, but it's about a loving Father who will do anything he can to help people escape the consequences of evil.

Bible prophecy isn't intended to frighten us, but it's to prove beyond a shadow of a doubt that God is real and omnipotent and active in our lives; to warn us of the very real danger lying ahead for those who reject his love and mercy; and to encourage us to accept his gracious and free offer of salvation through his Son, Jesus.

In his first letter to Timothy, Paul tells us that God "wants everyone to be saved and to understand the truth" (2:4). Peter gives that same message in his letter. "The Lord . . . is being patient for your sake. He does not want anyone to perish, so he is giving more time for everyone to repent" (2 Peter 3:9). Time and again in Scripture we are told that God longs for his people to be with him in heaven. The Bible is not a story of wrath and judgment but of unconditional love and redemption. God longs to be with us and wants desperately for us to accept his hand of salvation. What we do with that offer is up to us.

REFLECTION
What is Jesus trying to tell us through the parable of the fig tree? How does the knowledge that the Kingdom of God is near affect what you do today?

TRUSTING JESUS

I will not abandon you as orphans—I will come to you.   John 14:18

MANY OF US remember the devastating earthquake that shook the foundations of Armenia in 1989. It lasted four minutes, and when it was finished, more than thirty thousand people had lost their lives. It was one of the greatest catastrophes of the century. But there's one story from the event you may not have heard.

Just minutes after the last tremor a father raced to a nearby elementary school to save his son. He arrived to see nothing more than a mountain of twisted steel and rubble. But he remembered a promise he had made to his young boy: "No matter what happens, I'll always be there for you." So he began to dig. Against all hope and better judgment, he dug. Other parents helped but soon gave up trying. "It's too late," they told him. "You know they are dead. You can't help." But the father didn't listen. All day and night he dug. His hands were raw and bleeding, and his energy completely gone, but he refused to give up. He'd made a promise, and he intended to keep it. Finally, after thirty-eight grueling hours, he pulled back a large boulder and suddenly heard a faint voice beneath him. He called his son's name, "Arman! Arman!" And beneath the rubble, his boy answered him. "Dad, it's me!"

The boy's next words were the most priceless. "I told the other kids not to worry. I told them if you were alive, you'd save me. And when you saved me, they'd be saved too. Because you promised, 'No matter what, I'll always be there for you.'"[2] The father had kept his promise.

Jesus has made a lot of promises to us as well. And you can believe that he plans to keep them. His disciples struggled with some of the same fears and doubts that you and I often have, but Jesus was always quick to reassure them.

You can almost sense their concern when Jesus says he would be leaving soon. "Lord, we don't know where you are going, so how can we know the way?" (John 14:5, NIV), Thomas asks him. Jesus didn't get angry; he understood Thomas's confusion. "I will not abandon you as orphans," Jesus says. "I will come to you." In effect he was saying, *I know you don't understand, Thomas, but don't worry. Trust me. I'll always be there for you.*

You and I have a lot of questions as well, and Jesus understands our confusion. His words to Thomas could be directed at us. *Trust me. I'll always be there for you.* And we can know that he'll keep that promise.

REFLECTION
What does Jesus mean when he says, "The world will not see me anymore"?
And what does it mean to be "in" Jesus as Jesus is "in" the Father?

A DAY OF REWARD

If the master returns and finds that the servant has done a good job, there will be a reward.   Matthew 24:46

THERE ARE as many ways to look at the return of Jesus as there are opinions about how it will happen. This shouldn't surprise us, since the Bible describes it with a wide range of terminology—numerous nouns, verbs, and adjectives, each bringing to mind a host of differing scenarios.

To the Romans, Paul calls it the "day of God's wrath" (Romans 2:5, NIV). This seems to be the favorite among too many preachers. In his first letter to the Corinthians, Paul refers to it as the "day of the Lord" (1 Corinthians 5:5, NIV). And in his second letter to the same church he calls it the "day of salvation" (2 Corinthians 6:2). Both are a bit more positive and encouraging. To the Ephesians he calls it a "day of redemption" (Ephesians 4:30). And he encourages the church at Philippi to stand strong until the "day of Christ Jesus" (Philippians 1:6, NIV). Jude doesn't even try to describe it—he simply calls it the "great Day" (Jude 1:6, NIV). Jesus refers to his coming in a number of ways, including the "day of judgment" (Matthew 12:36, NIV), the "last day" (John 6:40), and even simply "his day" (Luke 17:24, NIV).

> "My prayer for you is that you would continue his ministry . . . , that you would, as the Scriptures say, 'not grow weary in doing good.'"
>
> *Nicolae*, 317–18

Each of these phrases suggests a unique and different view of the second coming—and each is as significant as it is accurate. But of all the ways to describe Jesus' return, there's one that I like the best. For followers of Jesus, it will be a day of reward.

James tells us, "God blesses the people who patiently endure testing. Afterward they will receive the crown of life that God has promised to those who love him" (James 1:12). Paul tells us, "The Lord will reward each one of us for the good we do, whether we are slaves or free" (Ephesians 6:8). In his second letter to Timothy he expands on those thoughts further. "Now the prize awaits me—the crown of righteousness that the Lord, the righteous Judge, will give me on that great day of his return. And the prize is not just for me but for all who eagerly look forward to his glorious return" (4:8).

But it is Jesus himself who says it best: "Be happy about it! Be very glad! For a great reward awaits you in heaven" (Matthew 5:12). As Christians, we have a lot to look forward to!

REFLECTION

In what ways are we to "keep watch" for the day of the Lord's return? How does it comfort you to know that it will be a day of reward?

THE PROBLEM OF SUFFERING

Yet what we suffer now is nothing compared to the glory
he will give us later.   Romans 8:18

ON MY SHELF is a little book that asks a big question. It is titled *Does God Care When We Suffer?* and was written by Randy Becton. Randy is a good friend and a cancer survivor who has spent much of his life ministering to people with terminal illnesses. Randy writes:

> Of the hard "why" questions, "why is there suffering?" may be the hardest. This is probably because it not only attacks us personally, but also because whenever the question is raised, the question of God's part in suffering follows close behind. . . . We are desperate for the meaning behind all this. We seek someone to blame or deliver us, and that always leads to our view of God.[3]

For many, the problem of suffering is perhaps their single greatest obstacle to putting their faith in God. *How could a loving and powerful God sit back and watch while people suffer?* David cries out to God in his distress. "Have compassion on me, Lord, for I am weak. . . . I am sick at heart. How long, O Lord, until you restore me?" (Psalm 6:2-3).

Doesn't God care when we suffer? Of course he does. *Then why doesn't he do something about it?* He did. Becton sums it up this way:

> The answer is the cross of Jesus Christ. . . . From now on all human suffering must be understood in the light of his suffering; it is the source of meaning, hope, and new life for sufferers. When someone cries out, "He doesn't care. He's immune to pain," they are brought to the foot of the cross to see for themselves. . . . The cross and resurrection hold the key to the mystery of suffering."[4]

On the cross, Jesus settled the question of suffering once and for all. It was at Calvary that our Savior "broke the power of death and showed us the way to everlasting life" (2 Timothy 1:10). His death and resurrection ushered in a new day of hope and life for all believers. And with it, he brought about the end of all suffering for those who would put their faith in him. Until Jesus comes, pain will always be a part of life on earth. But the glory awaiting us in heaven far outweighs the afflictions of the day.

REFLECTION
Why is God's creation in "frustration"? In what ways have you
allowed suffering to distract you from God's will for your life?

THE GIFT OF SALVATION

Now God in his gracious kindness declares us not guilty.   Romans 3:24

LAST SUMMER my wife and I spent a Saturday morning going to garage sales, and an interesting thing happened. Around noon we came to a house that had closed up shop for the day. The driveway was cleared, except for a small card table next to the curb with a sign hanging from the front of it. The sign read: Free. Please Take. On top of the table was a stack of neatly folded hand towels, all white and clean. We noticed a woman and her daughter staring down at them. "We could use those," the daughter said, but the mother remained silent. You could see in her eyes that she wanted to take them, but something kept her from doing so. Was it pride? Would people think she was poor and needy? Maybe she didn't trust what the sign said. *Surely there's some kind of catch*, she might have thought. *No one gives away perfectly good towels for free!* Or maybe she decided she didn't need them after all. For whatever reason, the two walked away and left the towels on the table. I couldn't help but wonder why.

> "Most were just like [Rayford Steele] was, having been on the edges of the truth . . . but never fully accepting the truth about Christ."
>
> *Left Behind, 220*

I'm sure that Jesus wonders the same thing when people reject his free offer of salvation. What could possibly be keeping them from simply reaching out and taking it? Jesus stands holding out the free gift of eternal life—a reprise of the unspeakable pain and sorrow of judgment—and all we have to do is accept it. How could anyone turn down an offer like that?

Although it's hard to imagine, their reasons are usually similar to those of our two friends at the card table. Sometimes pride gets in the way—no one wants to look needy. Or maybe they're convinced that there's a trick to the deal, some fine print in the Bible that someone will point out later. Or, worse yet, maybe they don't think they need it. *I'm a good person*, they tell themselves. *Why would I need Jesus to cover my sins?* It's the oldest lie in the book—Satan's greatest victory since the "fruit in the garden" episode.

Make no mistake; if we could save ourselves, Jesus wouldn't have needed to die in our place. And when God holds out a free ticket to paradise, we'd be crazy not to take it. "What makes us think that we can escape if we are indifferent to this great salvation?" asks the author of Hebrews (2:3). That's a question each one of us should consider.

REFLECTION
How does righteousness come to us? What are some of the ways we try to "work" our way to heaven? How does God view these efforts?

DEALING WITH UNANSWERED PRAYERS

My gracious favor is all you need. My power works best
in your weakness.   2 Corinthians 12:9

Just last week we came home to a wonderful message on our answering machine. A woman from our church—my wife's good friend—called to say that her tumor was benign. She didn't have cancer after all. We'd been praying for such a miracle, and now those prayers had been answered. "God is so good," she said excitedly. We agreed aloud and thanked him for his kindness.

Answered prayers have a way of lifting us all a notch or two. We love sharing stories of God's miraculous intervention in our life—and that's a good thing. Yet even as I write these words this morning I wonder to myself, *What if God had chosen not to heal her? Would he be any less wonderful? Would we still be praising him for his power and goodness?* Is God still good and merciful, even when our prayers go unanswered? Paul wrestles with that question in his letter to the Corinthian church. "I was given a thorn in my flesh, a messenger from Satan to torment me and keep me from getting proud," Paul confides in his brothers and sisters in the Lord. "Three different times I begged the Lord to take it away" (2 Corinthians 12:7-8). Paul didn't just pray for help, he pleads for it, begging repeatedly.

And what was God's response? "My gracious favor is all you need" (2 Corinthians 12:9). In a word, God's answer was no to his most faithful and trusted servant. God wouldn't even heal a simple problem? *Unbelievable!* That's what I would think. But Paul has a different response: "So now I am glad to boast about my weaknesses. . . . For when I am weak, then I am strong" (2 Corinthians 12:9-10).

In the midst of suffering and unanswered prayer, Paul continues to preach about God's goodness and power. God refuses a simple request, and Paul still praises his name. He still has the thorn but glorifies God in spite of it. What does Paul understand that so many of us seem to have missed?

Paul knows that grace is all he really needs. He knows that answered prayers are nice, but they have little to do with the big picture. He knows that God has already given him more than he ever deserved—more than any of us dare ask for. And he knows that thorns are just diversions from our real purpose—temporal problems that won't even be remembered in eternity. It's great to praise God for miracles. But let's not forget to praise him in his silence.

REFLECTION
Why was Paul given a "thorn in the flesh"? What allowed him to "boast
in his weaknesses"? Is there a "thorn" that keeps your mind off
of God's purpose for you?

STUDYING BIBLE PROPHECY

God blesses the one who reads this prophecy to the church, and he blesses all who listen to it and obey what it says. For the time is near when these things will happen. Revelation 1:3

MOST OF US have noticed an increased interest in Bible prophecy over the last few years. It wasn't so long ago that only a handful of authors dealt with end-times theology, but today's bookstores often devote entire sections to the subject. The amazing success of the Left Behind series of novels only serves to underscore this truth. There are some who might wonder whether this new interest in eschatology is healthy or important. "What real difference does it make in my relationship with Christ?" they ask. "Why should I bother with it?"

The truth is, understanding biblical prophecies—those fulfilled and those yet to be fulfilled—is an integral part of the Christian faith. It is through prophecy that God revealed not only his will for the Israelites but also his plan to bring salvation to the world through his Son, Jesus Christ. It is through prophecy that he has revealed his will for the future as well. God's divine plan for his people—for your life and mine—can be readily discovered within the pages of Scripture. What could be more exciting than that?

> "What Steele had read to Buck from Revelation appeared clear. . . . It was the only theory that tied the incidents so closely to any sort of explanation. . . . Could it be true? Had he been exposed to a clear work of God?"
>
> *Left Behind,* 385

Understanding God's plan for the end times brings with it countless blessings. When we see for ourselves how God has worked in the past to preserve and care for his people, we begin to get a small glimpse of his amazing and unwavering faithfulness—even in spite of humanity's unfaithfulness. When we discover the hundreds of prophetic words and visions that were given during the days of the Old Testament and then fulfilled during the life of Christ, our faith grows stronger than ever. Any doubts we may have entertained about God and his glory quickly fade.

And when we understand his glorious plan for our future, those things of the present age start to lose their appeal. We're no longer caught up in temporal things—the lure of material possessions, the desire for fame and money, and other earthly indulgences. Instead we find ourselves focusing on what really matters, storing up "treasures in heaven," and eagerly awaiting the day that Jesus comes to take us home.

REFLECTION
What are some real blessings you've experienced through reading and understanding the prophesies of Jesus? How does this knowledge help you in your daily walk with Jesus?

THE ETERNAL QUESTION

There is a path before each person that seems right,
but it ends in death.   Proverbs 14:12

IF YOU DIED TODAY, how certain are you that you would go to heaven?

You may have been asked that question before. If you're a believer you may have posed the question to others. Or maybe it's something you don't think about much. Perhaps from time to time you lie awake at night and ponder the concept of God and heaven and hell and all that those thoughts imply, but beyond that the idea holds little value for you. Maybe you've prayed to God without even knowing what you believe about him. Perhaps you're reading this book only because you've gotten hooked on the Left Behind series and found yourself intrigued with the Christian faith.

Wherever you are on your spiritual journey, I encourage you to spend some time contemplating this important question. Because when all is said and done, it's the only question that really matters. We're all going to die; that's a certainty of life. And when that happens, life is over and our body turns to dust, but our soul goes on to another plane. There are no other options available. If the Bible is right and God is real, then heaven and hell are realities as well. If it's all fake, then there is nothing waiting for us after death. It's just that simple. One or the other is true.

I've chosen to put my faith in God and the truth of his holy Word. I've bet my future on the certainty of Scripture and have given myself entirely to God's will. It's not a blind faith, nor is it based on fear and worry. I didn't come to Jesus because I was scared of hell; I came to him because I wanted so desperately to go to heaven. When I first began reading the Bible, I was told it was God's Word—and I wanted to believe that. Today I *know* it is his Word. It's a truth that is as real to me as the air I breathe and the skin that covers my bones. Any hint of doubt about its authenticity has long since been laid to rest. I'm as certain that God is real as I am that I'm sitting in this chair this moment. Because through my faith and prayers, God has shown himself to me.

If I died this moment, I'm certain that I would go to heaven. I'm not simply "hoping" that I will; I know it. It's the single most comforting truth of my being. I live for the day that I will live forever with God.

You may not have that certainty, but you can. Jesus assured us that if we seek him, we would find him. Why not give it a try?

REFLECTION
In what ways have you struggled to believe God's promises? If you're
struggling to believe in the claims of Scripture, why not pray in faith
that God would reveal his truth to you?

DELIVERED FROM EVIL

God shows his anger from heaven against all sinful, wicked people who push the truth away from themselves. For the truth about God is known to them instinctively. God has put this knowledge in their hearts. Romans 1:18-19

WHEN WAS the last time you flipped through the channels of your television looking for something to watch? I did last night, and I wish I hadn't. My mind was tired from a long day of writing, and I was hoping to unwind with a cup of hot chocolate and some light entertainment before bedtime. It didn't work.

Channel after channel I saw nothing but evil and debased behavior: men cursing, women dancing provocatively to loud music, people screaming and fighting on talk shows, TV programs about murder, vampires, adultery, witchery, and the like. My plan to unwind had quickly turned into an exercise in spiritual combat. To escape it all I finally settled on CNN to watch the news, and that became an even deeper look into the dark side of humanity—rape, murders, thieves, pedophiles on trial. It made me wonder if I shouldn't install new deadbolts on all the doors before morning.

And we wonder why God is angry?

God's wrath may be misunderstood, but it is certainly not misplaced. What kind of father could sit back and watch his children hurt themselves without getting a little angry? The book of Habakkuk reminds us that God's "eyes are too pure to look on evil; [he] cannot tolerate wrong" (1:13, NIV). Our God is a holy God, and our sins are a direct affront to his holiness. He loves us deeply, but he hates the evil we do. That's why he sent his Son. Jesus lived a sinless life because you and I were incapable of it. He died a painful death so that the sin we commit could be covered. He did for us what we could never do for ourselves, and because of it, you and I can live forever in God's arms.

> "Horror was not a good enough word for it. . . . Rayford could not keep from staring at the devastation below. Fires had broken out all over. . . . The bloodred moon . . . 'Nicolae,' Rayford said, . . . 'You have just seen the wrath of the Lamb!'"
>
> *Nicolae*, 405, 413

Is that the act of a vengeful God bent on wrath? You and I know better. It's the action of a loving and patient Father who would do anything to save his children from self-destruction. That's the kind of God that we worship. And that's why heaven will be nothing like a frustrating evening of channel surfing.

REFLECTION
What are some of the ways that God's truth has been made plain to us? Why is Paul's language so severe in this text? Who is the one person you need most to pray for in light of this warning?

THE PROBLEM OF SIN

For all have sinned; all fall short of God's glorious standard.
Romans 3:23

YOU AND I HAVE a problem. It's not a little problem, and it's not something we can cure on our own. It's something we don't talk about much and might like to deny in front of others, but that doesn't make it less true.

The problem is, we're sinners. We do things we know are wrong, and we can't help ourselves. Even though our sins hurt others and heap guilt on our heart, we still sin. We lie, we gossip, we bicker, we lash out, we think impure thoughts. Sometimes we lose our temper and say things we don't mean—things that are neither true nor fair but are biting enough to hurt, so they serve their purpose. Other times we deceive in order to get our way. We tell half-truths in hopes that it's better than a whole lie, but in our heart we know it's still wrong. We can no more stop ourselves from sinning than we could keep the sun from rising. It's a universal problem that every man and woman has to live with.

And this problem leads to a much, much bigger problem. Sinners can't go to heaven. The Bible is clear about that fact. Paul tells us, "The wages of sin is death" (Romans 6:23), and the kind of death he is talking about is a spiritual one. God cannot allow sin to corrupt heaven the way it has corrupted earth. In fact, he can't even look at our sin. It is a direct affront to his holiness. Our sin has driven a wedge between us and God, and there is nothing we can do about that fact. We are all destined for hell from the moment we commit our first sin. And let me stress again, there is absolutely nothing we can do about that.

But there is something that God could do to fix it. He knew a way to bridge the gap—the one and only way. Someone sinless and pure would have to take our punishment for us, would have to die in our place, would have to become a sacrifice to pay for the things we've done. Someone free of sin. Someone holy and pure, just like God. And so he sent his Son. The incarnation of himself. He sent Jesus.

Jesus came to earth for only one purpose and with only one appointment: to die in our place. To be a sacrifice for our sins. To forever bridge the gap between God and us and create a way for every person to get to heaven. They call it "the greatest story ever told." Is it part of your story? You can accept Christ and make it so today.

REFLECTION
Have you known all along that your sin has driven a wedge between you and God? What is the way that God has provided to overcome that problem?

GOD ON A CROSS

For God made Christ, who never sinned, to be the offering for our sin, so
that we could be made right with God through Christ.   2 Corinthians 5:21

I REMEMBER IT as if it happened yesterday. I was ten at the time. That was nearly thirty-five years ago, yet the event is fresher on my mind than this morning's breakfast. I was sitting in a cold metal chair in an even colder Sunday school classroom, listening intently as my favorite teacher retold the story. The story of Jesus' death. A story I'd heard a thousand times, yet at this moment I was hearing it as if for the very first time. The teacher's name was Marty, and behind him stood a huge wooden cross.

A group of us boys had helped him make it the previous day. Marty rounded us up in his pickup early Saturday morning, and we went to his uncle's farm. We picked the tree, and Marty cut the lumber down to size. Then we tied the crossbeam with ropes, nailed spikes through the middle, threw it into the bed of his truck, and carried it back to the church. Between ice-cream breaks and cutting up it turned into an all-day project, and at the end of the day Marty took us all home one by one. "We're having a special class tomorrow, so don't miss it," he told us. None of us did.

 Sunday morning came, and we all sat at Marty's feet as he told the story. He brought three steel spikes and passed them around the room. He took out a crown of thorns he had made and held it in front of us as we each fingered the sharp edges. Then he laid the cross on the ground and let us take turns hammering the spikes deep into the wood, right where Jesus' hands and feet would have been positioned. Afterward we all sat in a circle as he visually re-created the entire scene, adding dialogue as he went. And for the first time in my young life I sat face-to-face with the reality of Jesus' death.

God's Son came to earth in the body of a man and lived a life free of sin. He proved his divinity through the countless miracles he performed. He brought supernatural power and healing into the natural world in order to show us the authenticity of his claim. Jesus was the Messiah who was prophesied about in the Old Testament. The King they had waited so long to crown. But the Jews rejected him and killed him instead. Even that had been prophesied, yet still they didn't see it.

The spikes that were driven into the hands and feet of Jesus were meant for you and me. The pain he felt should have been ours. We are the ones who put him there. God on a cross. The Creator dying for his creation. The Savior paying the ultimate price for the unsaved. His death was the only thing in heaven and on earth that could atone for our sins, so he willingly laid down his life. And that was only the beginning of the story!

REFLECTION
Have you ever come face-to-face with the life and death of Jesus? What has that meant for you?

MAN OR MESSIAH?

This prophesy was speaking of Jesus, whom God raised from the dead,
and we all are witnesses of this.   Acts 2:32

HAD THE DEATH of Jesus been the end of the story, we would no longer be talking about him today. I would be off writing a pulp novel right now, and you'd probably be reading a business book. Neither of us have any time to waste on fairy tales or life theories that don't hold water. But that wasn't the end of Jesus' story. His life didn't end like every other person who claimed to be a guru or a god. His death wasn't the final word. If it had been, we would know for sure that he was a fake.

Just weeks before his death Jesus said to his disciples, "The Son of Man is going to be betrayed. He will be killed, but three days later he will be raised from the dead" (Matthew 17:22-23). Jesus laid out a claim that no mortal man could possibly fulfill. He put the ultimate nail in the coffin of his movement. What he said was certain to prove that he was nothing more than another good man with a few good ideas. And ultimately it would prove him a liar and a counterfeit savior. He said he would rise from the dead. He promised to conquer the grave. He promised the miracle of miracles.

> "Woe unto you who would take the place of Jesus Christ of Nazareth, the Lamb of God who takes away the sin of the world!"
>
> *Desecration, 55*

I dare you to find another self-help guru or religious leader who would be willing to make such a claim. Muhammad wouldn't have dared it. Buddha couldn't have done it. L. Ron Hubbard knew better. No man would spend his life claiming to have all the answers and set up a religion in his name only to ruin it all at the last minute with a promise that he couldn't possibly keep. But that's exactly what Jesus did. And he did it because he knew who he was.

Jesus died a horrible and definitive death. He was taken from the cross as limp and lifeless as any person who has ever been killed. He was embalmed and buried in a tomb carved out of rock. His followers scattered and ran, sure that their mentor was gone and their movement was over. Had the story ended there, the Bible would have stopped at Malachi and been nothing more than a well-documented history of Israel. But it didn't.

Just as he said he would, Jesus rose from the grave. And he did it right on schedule, three days after his death. Jesus said that death had no hold on him, and now he had proven it. He had said he was divine, and the Resurrection proved it. Jesus *is* God's Son! God, come in the flesh!

REFLECTION
Have you considered the implications of Jesus' claim to be able to conquer death? What about the implications of his accomplishing that promise?

WHAT DO WE DO WITH JESUS?

There is salvation in no one else! There is no other name in all of heaven
for people to call on to save them.   Acts 4:12

"SO WHAT do we do with this Jesus?"

The question came from a man named Landon Saunders and was aimed at an auditorium brimming with people. Some were believers, many were die-hard skeptics, most came simply because they were curious. I was there on a high school mission trip, seated near the front row. The room grew deathly silent. Uncomfortably silent. But Landon let it linger just the same.

"If Jesus conquered death, then Jesus is God. There is no other way around the issue. The question of his identity has already been settled. The only question left is this: 'What are we going to do with him?'"

Again he paused to let the words sink in. Some rustled in their seats while others sat motionless. A few in the back walked out in anger. At one point I was certain I heard a pin drop across the room, but I kept my gaze forward. An eternity came and went within those few seconds of silence, yet still Landon remained staid and quiet, while we pondered the question.

So what do we do with Jesus? God's prophets said he would come, and he came. They described how he would live, what he would do, and how he would die, and he fulfilled every word. Jesus said he would rise from the grave, and that's exactly what he did. He said he was God, and then he proved it. And now you and I are left with the single most important question of our lives: *What do we do with this Jesus?*

We do the only thing left to be done. We believe in him. We put our faith in his promises. We put our hand in his and trust him with our future. He said he bridged the gap between man and God, so we believe that the gap has been bridged. He said he conquered death forever, so we believe that death has been forever conquered. He said he was our Savior, so we allow him to save us. It's just that simple.

You and I are the ones who make it complicated. We think we know all the right answers, but on our own we can't even come up with the right question. Salvation isn't about what we can do; it's about what Jesus has already done.

So what are *you* going to do with this Jesus?

REFLECTION
How have you been trying to save yourself? What keeps you from trusting Jesus to save you?

RAISING THE WHITE FLAG

If you confess with your mouth that Jesus is Lord and believe in your heart that God raised him from the dead, you will be saved. Romans 10:9

CHRISTIANS CALL IT the "Believer's Prayer," but it's so much more than that. It's not so much a prayer as it is a spiritual white flag. It is an act of surrender, a willful giving of ourselves to another. It is you and me finally admitting that we've run out of reasons not to believe in Jesus, and that we've given up trying to make it to heaven on our own. So we come before God and ask him to show us how. We want more than a better way to die; we want a better way to live. So we kneel before the throne of God, raise our white flag, and surrender.

If you haven't done that, I encourage you to do so today. If you have, then pray the words anyway, as a statement of continued faith. There is no magic in the words. Words mean little to God, but the condition of our heart means everything. The following prayer is simply a guide to follow. Make the thoughts your own, and say it only if you really mean it.

"For years skeptics have made fun of the evangelist's plea, 'Do you want to be saved tonight?' and yet that is what I ask you right now."

Desecration, 232

Dear Father, I turn from my sins. Please forgive me for all the wrong things I've done. I believe that Jesus Christ is your Son, and that he came to earth in the form of a man. I believe that he died on a cross and was raised after three days. I believe that his death paid the price for my sins. And I know that Jesus is the only path to eternal life. I trust in the promises and claims of Jesus, and I put my life in your hands. I submit myself to the lordship of Jesus from this day forward and to the power of the Holy Spirit. I pray that the Holy Spirit will come into my life and dominate every part of my being, and that he will deliver me from those things in my life that are displeasing to you.

Thank you, God, for sending Jesus to die on the cross for me. I know that my sins are forgiven because of Jesus. I commit myself to your Spirit and give myself over to your will for me. Thank you for loving me. Show me what you want me to do next. I love you, God!

If you just prayed that prayer for the very first time and don't feel any different, don't worry. God has promised to save those who put their trust in Jesus, and God always honors his promises. You can believe with all your heart that God heard your words and that he has saved you. Your relationship with God is sealed!

REFLECTION
If this is your first confession of faith, how does it feel to finally put your trust in God? Why not spend some time in praise and worship to him?

BAPTIZED WITH WATER

Those who believed what Peter said were baptized and added
to the church.   Acts 2:41

A YOUNG MILITARY COUPLE began attending a Baptist church in Greece. The couple was new to the Christian faith and didn't understand many of the teachings, but they wanted to be obedient. And they wanted their children to grow up knowing the Lord. So they took their little girl forward during the child dedication service.

They gave a friend their camera and asked him to take pictures for them. Then they told the little girl to be sure and look at the pulpit while the preacher was speaking so that the pictures would turn out right. The young girl agreed. But for some reason, during the entire dedication the girl faced the baptistry. She never took her eyes off of it.

After the service her father asked her why she didn't obey. "I did," protested the little girl. "I looked at the pool pit, just like you said to do!"

Obviously the little girl misunderstood. But maybe she had the right idea all along. Too often we spend a lot of time focusing on the "pulpit" and forget to give any credence to the "pool pit." The baptistry sits week after week filled with water but gets far too little use or attention.

When Jesus was ready to begin his ministry, his first stop was to visit John at the water's edge. John was baptizing in the name of the Messiah to come, and he immediately recognized Jesus as God's Anointed One. "I am the one who needs to be baptized by you," John told Jesus. But Jesus insisted. "After his baptism," records Matthew, "as Jesus came up out of the water, the heavens were opened and he saw the Spirit of God descending like a dove and settling on him. And a voice from heaven said, 'This is my beloved Son, and I am fully pleased with him'" (3:14-17).

It was more than a symbolic act on the part of our Savior; it was a lesson in humility and obedience. And it was an example for believers to follow. The baptism of Jesus stands as a testament to the kind of life that pleases our Father. It was an act of submission—a physical statement of faith on the heels of a spiritual one.

REFLECTION
What example was Jesus setting when he came to John to be baptized?
What does the dove in verse 16 represent?

A GLORIOUS REUNION

No eye has seen, no ear has heard, and no mind has imagined what
God has prepared for those who love him.   1 Corinthians 2:9

IT HAPPENED in 1948, just a few days before Christmas. A flash flood ravaged a small town, leaving a gaping hole in the wall of an old church building—right behind the pulpit. The young pastor knew there was no time to fix the damage and decided to make the best of it. But providence was in his favor. The next day he stumbled upon an old lace tablecloth at an auction and bought it for $6.50. His intent was to hang it on the wall to cover the hole—not perfect, but adequate for the occasion.

The next day, while unlocking the building, he noticed an elderly woman on the curb and invited her to come inside for warmth. She nestled into a comfortable pew while he set to work covering the hole. She gasped as he unfolded the worn tablecloth. "That's mine," she exclaimed. "It's my banquet cloth!" And she rushed to the front to show him her initials engraved in one corner. The minister listened as she retold the story of her days in Vienna, Austria, before the war. She fled from the Nazis, but her husband was captured for crimes of treason. She hadn't seen him since. Although the minister offered her the cloth, she refused. It looked pretty hanging behind the altar, the woman insisted.

After the Christmas service the following Sunday morning, an aging gentleman lingered behind to talk with the young pastor. The cloth behind the pulpit brought back painful memories for him. "Many years ago my wife and I owned such a tablecloth," he told the pastor. "We lived in Vienna then." Something told the pastor that this was more than coincidence, so he took the man with him to seek out the woman. Calls were made, and before long the two men were standing on the front steps of her apartment. As the woman opened the door, the young pastor witnessed a reunion more touching than he ever imagined possible—a husband and wife, together again after years of separation.[5]

Some stories are harder to believe than others, and this one ranks at the top of that list. Yet it happened. And even better, it is just a small glimpse of the magnificent reunions awaiting us all on the day of salvation. Of all the things heaven has to offer, this may very well be the most poignant—the reunions of husbands and wives, brothers and sisters, fathers and sons, mothers and daughters, long since separated on earth, once again embracing for an eternity together with Jesus. No earthly reunion, no matter how sweet, can compare with the glorious gathering of the saints in heaven.

REFLECTION

What was the "great multitude" that John witnessed in this vision?
How does his account of this reunion make you long for heaven?
Who is the one person you most long to see on that great day?

THE *BEMA* OF CHRIST

For we must all stand before Christ to be judged.   2 Corinthians 5:10

SCRIPTURE IS CLEAR when it comes to grace. Our sins are covered by the blood of Jesus, and nothing we've done will be held against us. Salvation is as free as it is irrevocable. But that doesn't mean our deeds won't be evaluated and our faithfulness rewarded accordingly.

"So our aim is to please him always, whether we are here in this body or away from this body," Paul writes in his letter to the Corinthians. "For we must all stand before Christ to be judged. We will each receive whatever we deserve for the good or evil we have done in our bodies" (2 Corinthians 5:9-10). The word Paul referenced in his letter was *bema*—a seat of judgment. And in his words, "we must all stand before" it to be judged by Christ. And what will Jesus judge? The "good or evil we have done in our bodies."

"But doesn't Calvary cover it all?" people sometimes ask, and the answer is a resounding yes! If we could earn our way to heaven, Jesus wouldn't have needed to die. But that doesn't negate the overwhelming evidence in Scripture that we believers will be judged for our actions after putting our faith in Christ. Works done in selfish pursuits will be destroyed; those done out of pure heart and motives will be rewarded. It is one of the most overlooked and under-taught elements of the Christian faith, yet you can't get around it. In the words of Jim Elliff, "Such warnings virtually bleed from the pores to Scripture."[6]

> "The cost is great but the reward greater. . . . You may not survive the journey to safety. But you will spend eternity with God, worshiping the Lord Christ, Messiah, Jesus."
>
> *Desecration*, 232

So what is this *bema* of Christ? The theories are as scattered as they are confusing, but a few facts seem clear enough. It's a ceremony of judgment reserved for believers, and Jesus himself will preside over the occasion. And I'm convinced that it's an integral part of the victory dance awaiting us at the last day. For those who fought well, the day holds great honor and anticipation. Rewards and privileges will be given to those who selflessly served Christ in the body. For believers, it will be a day of unparalleled joy and commemoration—unlike anything we could possibly imagine on earth.

But there's another sobering truth to the day that we can't ignore. Although we stand before Christ knowing that our salvation is secure, our deeds will be judged. Both good and bad. What we do today will echo into eternity whether we like that thought or not. And eternal "crowns" will signify our level of reward.

REFLECTION
What are some "works" in your life that you hope will please Jesus at the bema seat? What are some things you'd rather not have exposed? How does this concept change your view of judgment?

STRIVING FOR HEAVENLY REWARDS

We will each receive whatever we deserve for the good or evil
we have done in our bodies.   2 Corinthians 5:10

"THERE WILL BE no tears in heaven," my mother used to say. And yours probably did too. But that doesn't mean there won't be remorse. When the works of believers are judged by Jesus—works both good and bad—there are bound to be feelings of regret.

It is at the *bema* of Christ that Jesus will judge the works of the saints, and many will no doubt wish they could have a chance to do it all again. Thoughts of what-if are bound to be there. Images of those who were left behind because of our indifference or procrastination will no doubt haunt us. Visions of the things that could have been accomplished had we only prayed more, accumulated less, or lived with greater passion and zeal. When life is over, we all will look over our life. And what we'll see is what Jesus sees.

Most Christians give little thought to this teaching. "I'll just be content to be there," said one believer when faced with the Scriptures about heavenly rewards. And he has a point. Even a small corner of heaven is better than a passing glance of hell. But have we ever thought about what a "backseat in heaven" means to God? In a word, that row is reserved for those who disappointed him. They trusted in Jesus for salvation, but didn't do much to thank him for it, and now that their days are over, they wish they could do it again. God loves them as they are, but he longs to see them as they could have been.

Writer Jim Elliff rightfully observed that many Christians profess to be content with a "little shack in heaven," as long as they get to strive for a mansion on earth.

It's a sad dynamic but not an inevitable one. You and I can be different. We still have time to ponder the what-ifs of life and to do something about it before it's too late. Today can be the day that you decide to begin living for eternity—to put aside earthly treasures in deference to heavenly ones. To begin living in such a way that at the end of your life you can say with Paul, "I have fought a good fight, I have finished the race, I have remained faithful" (2 Timothy 4:7).

REFLECTION
Have you made it your goal in life to please him? Reflect on Paul's
words about the bema of Christ, and try to imagine the event.
How does it look for you—with your deeds in question?

THE CROWN OF LIFE

God blesses the people who patiently endure testing. Afterward they will
receive the crown of life.   James 1:12

IF YOU'RE from Utah and a basketball fan, you've probably heard of John Stockton. He's been a regular face with the Utah Jazz for longer than most people can remember. John is no Michael Jordan or Larry Bird, but fans will tell you that he gets the job done. He's seldom in the spotlight but always on the court during critical moments. Most were somewhat surprised in 1996 when John Stockton was selected as one of the 50 Greatest Players in NBA History. They were shocked to learn that he had just scored his 13,000th career point, putting him in an elite and select group of players. At the end of 2002 he had finished the season with a league record for the most years playing for the same franchise—18 seasons. At

> "God had rewarded them and compensated them for centuries of persecution."
>
> *Left Behind,* 9

this writing he has scored over 18,000 career points, well on his way to an even greater NBA record.

When asked about his amazing achievements, John simply smiled and remarked, "It's like my dad always says, 'You put a monkey at a typewriter long enough, and he'll come up with something good.'" Exactly what you might expect from a man like John Stockton. But there's an ounce of truth in his response. It isn't always the most talented person who comes home with the big prize. Sometimes it's the most persistent.

Charles Spurgeon once said, "It was perseverance that got the snails to the ark." Funny, but true. You and I often think that great rewards are reserved for the ones at the head of the class—the ones who got more than their share of talent and luck and good looks. But James reminds us that it is those who patiently endure testing, who will receive the coveted "crown of life"—an extra measure of reward on the day of salvation (James 1:12). The ones who were laughed at, overlooked, scorned, shunned, disrespected, and ignored, yet remained faithful just the same. Those who lived and toiled under the radar for years, often without notice or acknowledgment by other believers—the prayer warriors, the nursery workers, the people who visited hospitals and retirement homes, even though they hated the smell of Ben-Gay.

We may all be surprised at the judgment seat of Christ to see the most unlikely people fitted with the most glorious crowns.

REFLECTION
In what ways have you persevered in your faith? What are the "good and perfect" gifts that James speaks of (1:17)? What gifts has he given you?

THE CROWN OF RIGHTEOUSNESS

*Now the prize awaits me—the crown of righteousness that the Lord,
the righteous Judge, will give . . . all who eagerly look forward
to his glorious return.*   2 Timothy 4:8

YOU'VE NO DOUBT heard of Rin Tin Tin and Lassie, the faithful "wonder dogs" of Hollywood. But I'll bet you've never heard of Hachi, the white Akita. He lived in Japan in the early 1900s, and his loyalty puts the others to shame.

Hachi was owned by a professor at the Tokyo University, Eisaburo Ueno. Every morning Hachi would accompany his owner to the train station, then make his way home. In the evening he would return to the station to greet his master as he stepped off the train. Passersby were always warmed by these daily reunions. But one day the train arrived, and Ueno wasn't there. He had suffered a heart attack at school and died. Hachi waited patiently, then walked home alone. The next evening he returned again to the train station, looking for his owner. When Ueno didn't arrive, Hachi again found his way home. For the rest of his life—another ten years—Hachi faithfully returned to the station every evening to wait for Ueno's return. He never once failed to meet the evening train, always hopeful that one day his beloved owner would be coming home. When Hachi died, he was standing at the station waiting for Ueno.

> "The last half of the seven years is called the Great Tribulation, and if we are alive at the end of it, we will be rewarded by seeing the Glorious Appearing of Christ."
>
> *Left Behind,* 309

Today a statue of Hachi sits outside of the Shibuya station. Locals often put wreaths around the statue's neck and leave small gifts as a sign of respect and admiration. In 1987 Japanese filmmakers made a feature length movie about Hachi, to honor the faithful dog that has become a national symbol of loyalty and devotion.

Paul writes to Timothy, "Now the prize awaits me—the crown of righteousness. . . . And the prize is not just for me but for *all who eagerly look forward to his glorious return*" (2 Timothy 4:8, italics mine). Of all the precious crowns that will be awarded on the day of Jesus' return, this one may be the most distinguished. It is for those who faithfully watched and waited for the Master's return—the ones who patiently and longingly dreamed of the day when Jesus would come and take them home.

REFLECTION
*What did Paul mean when he said he was being "poured out as an offering
to God"? How much time do you spend longing for Christ's return?*

THE CROWN OF GLORY

*Be shepherds of God's flock. . . . And when the Chief Shepherd appears,
you will receive the crown of glory.*   1 Peter 5:2, 4, NIV

WE'VE ALL HEARD that teachers and spiritual leaders will be judged by a different measure than the rest of us. James tells us, "Not many of you should become teachers in the church, for we who teach will be judged by God with greater strictness" (3:1). People who are given positions of authority and leadership in the body of Christ are expected to live as examples and mentors to those who are younger and weaker in their faith. God expects more from them and more *of* them. Because of this, they can also expect a greater measure of respect during their days on earth. Paul tells Timothy, "Elders who do their work well should be paid well, especially those who work hard at both preaching and teaching" (1 Timothy 5:17).

It makes sense, then, that on the day of salvation, such people will receive a special reward from Jesus. Those who were given great responsibility on earth and carried out their duties well will receive the crown of glory.

Peter exhorts such people this way: "Care for the flock of God entrusted to you. Watch over it willingly, not grudgingly—not for what you will get out of it, but because you are eager to serve God. Don't lord it over the people *assigned to your care*, but lead them by your good example. And when the head Shepherd comes, your reward will be a never-ending share in his glory and honor" (1 Peter 5:2-4, italics mine).

The reason we appoint certain people as elders and teachers is because that's what *God* wants them to be. They are of his choosing, not ours. They are serving his church, not their own. They are to be examples of his love and goodness, not the world's. And they will be judged by God's standards, not ours.

Being called to such a position is the greatest honor a person could ask for this side of heaven. And if done well, can lead to one of the greatest honors a person could ask for on the other side of it as well.

REFLECTION
*As you read through Paul's list of desired character traits for overseers,
think about how your life reflects these qualities. Do you have the traits God
is looking for in a leader? If not, what would he have you do to prepare
yourself for greater responsibility?*

AN EVERLASTING CROWN

Run in such a way as to get the prize . . . to get a crown that will
last forever. 1 Corinthians 9:24-25, NIV

THERE IS a story told of a European princess who had everything she could ever want. Her husband was a wealthy man who adorned her with jewelry at every occasion. But the princess was a fervent Christian, and God put a burden on her heart to start an orphanage. Having no money of her own, she begged her husband to let her sell her jewels so that she could help the children.

"Don't you appreciate the jewels I give you?" he would ask in frustration. "Of course," she would answer him. "But there are so many homeless children we could help." Finally he relented, and she set out to sell her jewelry. With the money she gained, she was able to build a beautiful orphanage, and each day workers would bring in orphan children from the streets to be fed and clothed. The more children who came, the greater joy she found in showing them love and affection. One day the princess returned to her husband and said excitedly, "I found my jewels today. I found them in the bright and happy eyes of the children who were rescued from the streets. I found my jewels!"[7]

> "Do not feign modesty, my young friend. God has used you. Oh, he has used you so mightily! Ah, the rewards that await you in heaven."
>
> *Armageddon,* 134

In his Sermon on the Mount, Jesus implores us to "store your treasures in heaven, where they will never become moth-eaten or rusty and where they will be safe from thieves" (Matthew 6:20). Peter explains why this is so important. "The day of the Lord will come as unexpectedly as a thief. Then the heavens will pass away with a terrible noise, and everything in them will disappear in fire, and the earth and everything on it will be exposed to judgment" (2 Peter 3:10). The jewels of this world, precious as they may seem at the moment, are as temporal as the days. They hold no value in the eyes of God.

I heard a minister once tell of a flood that ravaged his town and flooded his basement. As he stood on the stairway surveying the damage to his possessions, watching helplessly as the things he had accumulated throughout the years were swallowed up in water, he struggled with feelings of anger and remorse. Suddenly he heard the Lord speak to his spirit. "Don't worry about all that stuff," the Lord said. "I was planning to burn it all up anyway." There is a crown waiting for those who hold possessions loosely, and its value is not only priceless but eternal.

REFLECTION
What does it mean to "run with purpose"? What does Paul do to assure that he is not disqualified for the prize? How can we emulate this practice?

THE CROWN OF THORNS

The soldiers made a crown of long, sharp thorns and put it
on his head.   John 19:2

SCRIPTURE IS FILLED with strange and confusing dichotomies.

"Many who are first will be last, and the last first" (Mark 10:31, NIV). "It is more blessed to give than to receive" (Acts 20:35). "A prophet is honored everywhere except in his own hometown" (Matthew 13:57). Jesus' Sermon on the Mount begins with a collection of mixed messages. The people he calls the most blessed are the ones we envy the least—the poor in spirit, the mourners, the meek, the hungry, the persecuted, the insulted (see Matthew 5:3-12). God clearly has a different perspective on life than we do.

But nowhere is this truth more evident—and sobering—than in these words of Jesus to his disciples: "If you try to keep your life for yourself, you will lose it. But if you give up your life for me, you will find true life" (Luke 9:24). In effect, Jesus is telling us, "If you want to be like me, you have to die like me." The secret to living in the shadow of Jesus, is to cease living for self.

> "Hattie stood shaking. . . . 'I can't believe he died because of me! I don't know what to say! I hope he's gone to his reward.'"
>
> *Assassins,* 61

Explaining his source of strength and faith, Paul tells us, "I myself no longer live, but Christ lives in me" (Galatians 2:20). His effectiveness began the day of his spiritual execution. The same holds true for you and me.

There is one more crown that will be associated with reward on the day of salvation. Only this crown won't be one that we gain but one that we exchange for another. For those who bore the crown of thorns with Jesus during their days on earth, he will be there to take it away and replace it with one of dignity and joy. For those who lived in the shadow of the cross, heaven holds a special place of honor and reward. Their crowns will be the most beautiful of all.

When describing what he saw in heaven, John said, "I saw the Son of Man sitting on a white cloud. He had a gold crown on his head and a sharp sickle in his hand" (Revelation 14:14). The crown of gold Jesus wears in heaven is a far cry from the crown of thorns he wore on earth. What a glorious sight that will be!

REFLECTION
What does it mean to "die to the law"? How is it possible to "no longer live"
so that Christ can live in us? In what ways are you still living for yourself
and your own pleasure?

AT THE FEET OF JESUS

And they lay their crowns before the throne and say, "You are worthy,
O Lord our God, to receive glory and honor and power."
Revelation 4:10-11

THERE IS DEBATE about the meaning behind the many crowns awarded to the saints at the *bema* of Christ. There are some who believe that these awards will be physical crowns, though most would agree that the term is figurative. I'm convinced that these crowns are simply symbolic of the degree of honor and special privileges that we will be given for our faithfulness in serving Christ on earth. How those privileges manifest themselves we won't know until we get there. Based on my understanding of certain Scriptures, I believe that some will be given greater degrees of responsibility than others, but I can't know for sure. It is fun to dream and speculate, though. Perhaps that's why God didn't tell us—to encourage us to use our imagination.

But whether these crowns are literal or figurative, I'm convinced that one particular event will literally happen as it's described in Scripture. At the end of the ceremony, we will all face the throne of Jesus, prostrate ourselves before him, and lay our rewards at his feet. Along with the twenty-four elders, we will come before him with tears in our eyes and joy in our heart, worshiping him in one voice and one heart. When we finally come face-to-face with our Redeemer, we won't be able to contain our love and appreciation. We will gladly lay our crowns before the throne.

There at the feet of Jesus will lay thousands upon thousands of precious jewels—crowns of life, righteousness, glory, and gold—all cast before him in a symbolic and simultaneous gesture of holy reverence.

It is this kind of scene that Paul envisioned in his letter to the Philippians:

> Because of this, God raised him up to the heights of heaven and gave
> him a name that is above every other name, so that at the name of Jesus
> every knee will bow, in heaven and on earth and under the earth, and
> every tongue will confess that Jesus Christ is Lord, to the glory of God
> the Father. (2:9-11)

However you envision the day of our salvation, and whatever you believe about the form it will take, you have to acknowledge this one truth: It will be a day like no other in the history of the world. And it will likely be typical of eternity in heaven.

REFLECTION
Who are the "living beings" that John speaks of? It is widely held that
the twenty-four elders represent the whole of the saints in heaven.
Reflect and imagine how this scene might look. What crown do you
hope to lay at the throne of Jesus?

A NEW BODY

He will take these weak mortal bodies of ours and change them into glorious
bodies like his own.   Philippians 3:21

JONI EARECKSON TADA was rendered a quadriplegic in a diving accident as
a teenager. She's spent the last few decades bound to a wheelchair, unable even
to feed and clothe herself. In her many books she has often shared the frustration
of having to live as an invalid, depending on others to take care of her needs. But
Joni is a unique, Spirit-filled Christian with a perspective that few could comprehend. She writes, "Somewhere in my broken, paralyzed body is the seed of what I
shall become. The paralysis makes what I am to become all the more grand when
you contrast atrophied, useless legs against splendorous resurrected legs."[8]

> "He raised Christ
> from the dead and
> gave him glory so
> that your faith and
> hope are in God."
>
> *Armageddon,* 139

Joni understands the temporal nature of our existence,
and her hope is in something much grander. Instead of
mourning her lot in life, she chooses to focus on her future
glory. That's where she finds her strength and resolve. And
through that strength, she has been able to touch the lives of
countless people with similar disabilities.

No matter who you are, you have to find comfort in
Paul's words to the Philippians: "We are citizens of heaven,
where the Lord Jesus Christ lives. . . . He will take these weak
mortal bodies of ours and change them into glorious bodies
like his own" (3:20-21). I still have several decades of living ahead of me (Lord
willing), yet I already feel the strain of wear and tear on my body. Often my
bones ache in places where I didn't know I had bones, and the print in my Bible
appears smaller by the day. I can only hope that the Lord will take me before my
body completely falls apart. But I don't worry too much about it because I know
that God has greater plans for us all. And Joni Tada knows it even better than I:
"I'm convinced that if there are mirrors in heaven, the image I'll see will be un-
mistakably 'Joni,' although a much better, brighter Joni. . . . I will bear the likeness of Jesus, the man from heaven."[9]

To be like Jesus! How much sweeter could heaven possibly get?

REFLECTION
What awaits those who live as "enemies of the cross"? Why is it important
to think as "citizens of heaven"? How does that change our perspective
of life on earth?

OUR STORY

The Lord gave this message to Jonah.   Jonah 1:1

WE ALL have a divine calling before God. Even those who don't understand their role in the Creator's greater plan know instinctively that they have certain gifts and strengths and that these qualities play a role in defining who they are and what they do. Like Jonah, we are called to a purpose. Jonah was a prophet of God. I am a writer. My wife is a teacher and a homemaker. You have a job before God as well.

Regardless of these differing gifts and vocations, we can all see ourselves in the story of Jonah. You don't have to be a prophet to ignore God's calling and run from him. Jonah's story is our story.

The book of Jonah is broken into four chapters, like four separate acts of the same drama. It's almost as if the translators outlined the lesson for us. In chapter one Jonah *runs away from God*. In chapter two he *runs back to God*. In chapter three Jonah *runs with God*. And in four he *runs ahead of God*. The reason we can so readily relate to his story is because we've all been at these four stages at one time or another. In fact, you're at one of these stages now, depending upon where you are in your relationship with God.

We've all run away from God. We've all felt his hand on our shoulder and his voice in our ear, only to turn away and pretend not to hear. *Later, God. I'm busy right now.*

We've all run back to God. In a moment of trial or desperation, we've all fallen to our knees and cried out for help. We've asked for deliverance, provision, justice, mercy, forgiveness, or protection. *I know I haven't been faithful, Lord, but please help me!*

> "If the Bible teaches one thing about God, it is that he is for us. He is not against us."
>
> *The Remnant,* 230

We've all run with God. We see him moving and we follow, step for step, working alongside him to fulfill a need. *Use me, Lord!*

And we've all run ahead of God. Sometimes God moves slower than we'd like, so we take things into our own hands. We decide what's best and then work to drag God into our plans. *I'm doing this for you, Lord, but I need you to cooperate.*

Jonah's story is our story.

REFLECTION
When is the last time you felt the Lord calling you?
What was your response?

RUNNING AWAY FROM GOD

Jonah [ran] . . . away from the Lord.   Jonah 1:3

WHEN GOD commanded Jonah to travel to Nineveh and warn the people of his wrath, Jonah drew a line in the sand. It was the one thing he refused to do. It wasn't as if he didn't know God's power. Jonah was a prophet—a man who had seen God's glory *and* God's wrath. He feared the Lord, but he hated the Ninevites more. Nineveh was a key city of Assyria, and Jonah was from Gath—a Jew. He'd lost count of the number of times Assyria had ravaged his homeland, terrorizing his people. Jonah not only feared the Ninevites, he hated them. And so when God asked him to warn them of his coming judgment, he refused and ran.

What is the one thing in your life that you couldn't imagine God asking you to do? Surely he wouldn't ask you to give up a career that you've worked so hard to develop or a business that you've sweated blood and tears to build. You can't imagine that he would ask you to do mission work in Africa—not with your aversion to heat and mosquitoes. Do you think he'd ever take you away from your family? Or worse yet, take your family away from you? Be careful how you answer, because if we learn anything from the story of Jonah, we learn that God is interested in our devotion, not our comfort. The one thing that you most despise may be the very thing that God calls you toward. Not because he enjoys making us miserable, but because he sees the bigger picture. As we read through the story of Jonah we have to ask ourselves, *Who received the greatest degree of deliverance— Nineveh, or Jonah?*

While running from God, Jonah hitched a ride with some Gentile sailors. God sent a storm that threatened to capsize the ship, so the sailors began to wonder about their Jewish stowaway. "'What have you done to bring this awful storm down on us?' they demanded" (Jonah 1:8). When they discovered that Jonah was running away from God, their eyes lit up with fear. "'Oh, why did you do it?' they groaned" (Jonah 1:10). Even Gentiles knew about the Hebrew God, and these guys had no interest in finding themselves on the business end of his wrath. They knew the risks of harboring a fugitive from the God of Israel. They fell to their knees and pleaded for mercy, then threw Jonah overboard.

Before running from God, ask yourself, *How much is my sin going to cost those around me?* Because it is usually those near us that suffer the greatest harm for our mistakes.

REFLECTION
What is the one thing you most fear God may ask you to do or to give up? How do you think you would respond if he did?

RUNNING BACK TO GOD

Jonah prayed to the Lord his God from inside the fish.   Jonah 2:1

HAVE YOU EVER found yourself so steeped in sin and disobedience that you can't imagine God wanting to see your face? Have you ever been so far from God that you wonder if you should even bother trying to talk to him? *He would never hear my prayers,* you think, so you bury your head in your pillow and cry.

Jonah found himself farther from God than he ever imagined possible. Lying in the stench-filled belly of a great fish, he must have wondered if God had given up on him. His only hope was to cry out in desperation and pray that somehow God might hear. "I cried out to the Lord in my great trouble," he says (Jonah 2:2). "O Lord, you have driven me from your presence. How will I ever again see your holy Temple?" (Jonah 2:4).

"I know you probably can't even hear me Lord," Jonah was saying. "But if you can, please forgive me." It was a cry from the depths of a man who had hit rock bottom, from the very pit of desperation. Jonah was at the end of himself, barely alive and spiritually dead, and with his last breath he called out to God for help. God heard his prayers and answered them. "Then the Lord ordered the fish to spit up Jonah on the beach, and it did" (2:10).

> "Dear God, I know I am a sinner. Forgive me and pardon me for waiting so long."
>
> *Apollyon, 68*

Are you longing to come back to God? Have you found yourself so far from the Lord that you don't even bother to pray to him? *How could he love me after all I've done?* you ask yourself. If so, then maybe it's time to come home.

Not only does God hear your prayers, but just look at the lengths he's willing to go to bring you back. He'll not only accept you, but he'll provide the means for you to travel. When Jonah found himself in the middle of a storm in the ocean, God sent a fish to get him. Don't you think he'd do as much for you?

Just look what God is telling us through the story of Jonah. He's saying, "I don't care how far you've run. I don't care what you've done. Wherever you are, all you have to do is call my name, and I'll send a limousine to your doorstep to bring you home. You may be able to run from me, but you can never run from my love." If there was ever a message that prodigals needed to hear, it's this one. If you are a person who thinks God won't take you back, then take comfort in the story of Jonah. Don't run from God any longer. Just call on him today, and see his faithfulness for yourself.

REFLECTION

When is the last time you cried out in desperation to the Lord? Did he hear your prayers? Do you need to come home today?

TODAY'S READING
Jonah 3

RUNNING WITH GOD

Jonah obeyed the Lord's command and went to Nineveh.   Jonah 3:3

FOLLOWING GOD'S WILL can often feel as dangerous as running away from him. Jonah came back to God, but now he faced the wrath of Nineveh. In many ways it was like sending a wounded chicken into the foxes' den to convince them to become vegetarians. Jonah was delivered from the belly of one beast, only to be thrown into the belly of another.

But he was faithful, and so was God. "When the king of Nineveh heard what Jonah was saying, he stepped down from his throne and took off his royal robes. He dressed himself in sackcloth and sat on a heap of ashes" (Jonah 3:6). Not only did the king repent, but he issued a proclamation commanding that every living being in Nineveh be covered in sackcloth and bow down to Jonah's God. No one, not even the animals, were to eat or drink. This was more than a twinge of remorse; this was a wholesale commitment to God on the part of the Ninevites.

> "I feel such a compulsion to plead with my fellow countrymen to give their lives to Messiah. . . . I must get there, and I must preach."
>
> *Armageddon,* 314

But something in the story doesn't quite fit. According to my seminary training, Jonah did it all wrong. Wasn't he supposed to give them a three-point sermon on the dangers of sinful living? What happened to his box of Sunday school tracts? Didn't he know he should have gone over the *Four Spiritual Laws* or the six steps to salvation? He should have passed out copies of the Ten Commandments with notes in the margin. Somehow Jonah made it to Nineveh without his Manual of Evangelism, yet still the Ninevites dropped to their knees in repentance.

And what did Jonah say that convinced them? He told them to repent. That's it. That was the whole of his sermon. And in the end, that's all it took to bring an entire city under conviction. As complicated as we like to make it, God's message is a simple one: *Repent, and God will forgive you.* Jonah simply relayed the message that God gave him, and God did the rest.

It doesn't take an eloquent sermon or an anointed speaker to bring people to their knees before the Lord. The power of God's Word lies in the fact that it originated with God himself. The Bible is more than God's Word; it is the very manifestation of his glory and wisdom and authority. It has power far beyond what you and I can imagine.

REFLECTION
Has God given you a mandate to reach out to someone in your sphere of influence? What's keeping you from doing so today?

FEBRUARY

RUNNING AHEAD OF GOD

This change of plans upset Jonah, and he became very angry.   Jonah 4:1

DOES THE STORY of Jeffrey Dahmer bother you as much as it does me? Not so much what he did before going to prison, but what he did just months before his death? He had the gall to repent.

In his trial Dahmer was displayed as a monster without a hint of conscience. He had brutally murdered seventeen people, keeping eleven of them in his apartment for fun. It wasn't enough to kill his victims. If any man on the planet redefined the boundaries of distaste and terror, it was this small-framed monster from Milwaukee. And then, after all he had put his victims and their families through, Dahmer had the audacity to say he was sorry—not just to the families but to God. He gave his heart to Jesus. More than that, he asked to be baptized, began reading his Bible, and even started attending chapel. *Just who does he think he is, anyway? How could he possibly think he deserved God's forgiveness?*

If you struggle to understand how God could forgive Jeffrey Dahmer, then you know a little about how Jonah might have felt when God chose to have mercy on the people of Nineveh. These were cruel and brutal people, and Jonah had seen the unspeakable evil they were capable of. He would rather die than see Nineveh prosper (see Jonah 4:3). So when God forgave them, Jonah pitched a fit. He was insane with anger. Once again God stepped in and rebuked Jonah. "Nineveh has more than 120,000 people living in spiritual darkness, not to mention all the animals. Shouldn't I feel sorry for such a great city?" (4:11).

If you think God's wrath is hard to understand, try comprehending his mercy. The next time you wonder if God really cares, just look at his response to Jonah. If you think he isn't forgiving, look how quickly he forgave Nineveh.

It's easy to get ahead of God and think we know better than he who should and shouldn't be saved. We've all fallen into the trap. The Jeffrey Dahmers of the world make us all want to play God at one time or another. But grace defies human logic, and so does God's goodness. As long as he holds the gavel, pardons will flow freely as water. And that's something we should all be thankful for. Will Jeffrey Dahmer be at the banquet table in heaven? Only God knows, but according to his Word, if Dahmer's confession was sincere, his soul is secure.

REFLECTION
In what ways do you struggle with death-row conversions? How does it force you to stretch your view of God's grace? The next time you find yourself judging others, pray that God will soften your heart and mind.

OVERCOMING OUR SINFUL NATURE

When the Holy Spirit has come upon you, you will receive power and will tell people about me.   Acts 1:8

HOW DO WE, as Christians, keep our integrity intact in a world bent on compromise and corruption? How do we prevent ourselves from caving in to the constant pressure to sin? What does it take to maintain our passion for Christ and become the kind of Christian witness that he desires for all of his children?

If Scripture teaches us anything, it shows that people have an undeniable predisposition toward sin and selfishness. When left to our own devices, we will almost always fall into Satan's web of lies and deceit. Even a cursory study of the Bible and the history of Israel will reveal humanity's unfaithfulness to God, in spite of his love and devotion toward us.

You and I have been given a gift that the children of Israel didn't have—the miraculous indwelling of the Holy Spirit. It is through the power of the Holy Spirit within us that we find the strength to overcome our sinful nature. Paul tells us that "the Holy Spirit helps us in our distress" (Romans 8:26). The apostle John reminds us that the ability to shun evil and do good comes from the Holy Spirit within us: "The Spirit who lives in you is greater than the spirit who lives in the world" (1 John 4:4).

> "If you accept God's message of salvation, his Holy Spirit will come in unto you and make you spiritually born anew."
>
> *Left Behind*, 215

When we as followers of Christ fall into sin, it is not because we lack the ability to overcome it, but it is because we have chosen our will over the Father's. Although we have the power to resist, we choose to indulge.

If we want to change this damaging pattern of behavior, we do it by unleashing the power of the Holy Spirit in our life. And that is done through a lifestyle of daily reading and meditating on God's Word, and praying for strength, wisdom, and purity of heart. We put the past behind and look only to the future. And we believe Jesus' promise of power through the Holy Spirit.

We will never obtain a life free from sin this side of heaven. But we can get to a point where sin seems ugly and where we long for God's presence more than we struggle against Satan's snares.

REFLECTION
In what ways does the Holy Spirit help us? Is there hidden sin in your life that you need the Spirit's help in overcoming? How will you begin allowing him to do so—starting today?

PRAYING EFFECTIVELY

*I urge, then, first of all, that requests, prayers, intercession and thanksgiving
be made for everyone.*   1 Timothy 2:1, NIV

THERE IS MORE than one type of prayer for believers to lift up to the Father, and in his letter to Timothy, Paul covers several of them specifically. He urges Timothy to lift up "requests, prayers, intercession and thanksgiving." This admonition is for you and me as well.

A *request* is a need, a deep desire for something we don't have—something that only God can supply. We acknowledge our helplessness before the throne and call upon God to fulfull his promise of provision.

A *prayer* is a word of praise and adoration. A more accurate translation of this word from the original Greek might be to "worship in earnest." We glorify God and acknowledge his majesty and glory, both in heaven and on earth.

Intercession is praying on behalf of others. Throughout Scripture we are encouraged to put the needs of those around us ahead of our own. Our prayers should regularly reflect this kind of selfless lifestyle.

Thanksgiving involves remembering those past prayers that have already been answered, acknowledging that we not only trust God's supremacy and involvement in our life but also see how his hand has moved and guided us in the past. We thank him for his love, his faithfulness, and his mercy, and for all that he is and does.

Developing a complete and fulfilling prayer life demands that we not only understand our need for God's wisdom and direction in every area of life but that we also desire to interact with the Father on many different levels—and in many forms. Human nature will often cause us to focus on ourselves and our earthly wants and wishes, but God wants more from us. And he wants more *for* us.

When we pray effectively, we do more than communicate with God—we commune with him. We become one in mind and spirit and purpose. Today, let the focus of your prayer time be to connect with God in a very real and personal way, not as a slave would petition his master, but as a son would enjoy the company of a loving and gracious father.

REFLECTION
*What kind of prayers does God reward? In what way is Jesus' prayer
a model for us in our own times of prayer?*

PRAYERS FOR KINGS AND AUTHORITIES

*Pray this way for kings and all others who are in authority, so that we can
live in peace and quietness, in godliness and dignity.*   1 Timothy 2:2

LET'S CONSIDER for a moment those people who hold positions of authority around us. Regardless of who we are or what we do, we all have "kings" to answer to—people who make rules and decisions that have a marked impact on our life.

Our state and national leaders come to mind first, beginning with our country's president, and including elected and appointed officials. Our city and county leaders qualify, as well as those who enforce the laws—judges, police officers, and the like. The pastors and elders of my church hold positions of authority. Scripture clearly confirms that I am to submit to their leadership (see Hebrews 13:17). Many of us have a boss at work that we answer to. Although I am a grown man with a family of my own, I still submit to the authority of my parents. Scripture commands me to "honor" my father and mother, and I do so by seeking their counsel and wisdom—by acknowledging their headship in the family.

There is a reason Paul commands us to consistently pray for all of these people. The decisions they make have a direct, sometimes lasting, impact on our life. When the leaders of my country make good decisions, my life goes better. When the laws they pass are sound and just, my family sleeps better at night. When my church leaders make godly, spirit-directed decisions, my soul is in better hands. When my boss makes wise choices, the company grows and my job is secure. When my parents handle their affairs well and stay in God's will, I can depend on the counsel they give to be solid and sound. The strength of their character will affect our family for generations to come, so I fervently pray that God will grant them wisdom and godliness in all they say and do.

> "All Rayford felt was an overwhelming hunger and thirst for the Bible and for instruction. He wanted to pray like this from now on, to constantly be in touch with God."
>
> *The Indwelling, 72*

We pray for those in authority over us because it helps us live in "peace and quietness." And because it develops within us the traits of "godliness and dignity." In many ways these simple qualities sum up the whole of our Christian witness on earth.

We are called to be peaceful people—to be at peace with God, with our salvation, with our situation on earth, and with those around us. And we are to live holy and dignified lives—to "put aside the deeds of darkness and put on the armor of light" (Romans 13:12, NIV). It is through consistent and deliberate prayer—for others, as well as ourselves—that these qualities are obtained.

REFLECTION
*What should be our primary thought and purpose when we pray for leaders
(see 1 Timothy 2:4)? How should this change the way we view
our prayers of intercession?*

CONFRONTING HELL

*The smoke of their torment rises forever and ever, and they will have
no relief day or night.* Revelation 14:11

C. S. LEWIS once wrote: "There is no doctrine which I would more willingly remove from Christianity than [hell], if it lay in my power. . . . I would pay any
price to be able to say truthfully: 'All will be saved.'"[1]

Can you relate? I certainly can. As a young man in my early twenties, I spent
over a year of my life struggling through a deep crisis of faith. It very nearly shattered my belief in God altogether, and my dilemma pivoted squarely on the doctrine of hell. Hard as I tried, I could not seem to understand how a loving God
could allow people to suffer eternal condemnation. I had no problem with
heaven. Heaven was perfectly consistent with my beliefs about God. But hell was
another story. *How could hell exist? And if hell didn't exist, was heaven a myth as well?*
It was not an easy crisis to overcome, but through it God showed me some things
that not only laid my doubts to rest but actually strengthened my faith. As much
as I resisted the idea, I finally saw that without the reality of hell, God could not
be a loving God. Confused? So was I. But let me try to explain.

If there is no hell, God is not just. If sin is not punished, then God is apathetic
toward evil. If God is neutral on the subject of evil, then what does that say to the
rapists and murderers and adulterers? What does it say to Satan and all he stands
for? More important, what does it say to those who strive to be faithful servants
of Christ? To say that hell does not exist is to say that God has turned his back on
those who serve him. And in the end, it is to say that God and the teachings of
Scripture are untrue. That question is resolved by simply looking at the abundance of evidence that proves the accuracy of God's Word. The question is not
whether hell exists, but why we struggle so much to resist the idea.

Jesus didn't shy away from the hard teachings about hell. More than half of
his parables speak about God's judgment of sinners, and 13 percent of his teachings deal with the subject of hell. No one in Scripture speaks more about the consequences of sin than Jesus. And that truth shouldn't surprise us. God isn't
obsessed with wrath; he's simply consistent with his nature. Hell is critical in the
grand scheme of God's justice and plan of salvation. God loves us dearly. That's
why he gives us the choice between accepting his love and rejecting it. He doesn't
send people to hell—they choose to go there. He simply honors that choice in
spite of the pain it causes him to do so.

REFLECTION
*What do we learn about hell from the parable of the rich man and Lazarus?
Have you struggled in your own life with the concept of hell? Pray that God
would reveal his purpose for hell through today's reading.*

A RADICAL TRANSFORMATION

*Don't copy the behavior and customs of this world, but let God transform you
into a new person by changing the way you think.*   Romans 12:2

FRANK LAUBACH was a missionary during the early 1900s. He spent much of
his life teaching people to read, so that they could study the Scriptures for themselves. At the age of forty-five, he found himself feeling dissatisfied with his spiritual life and resolved to do something about it. He recorded this commitment in
his daily journal on January 30, 1930:

> Can we have that contact with God all the time? . . . Can we do His will
> all the time? Can we think His thoughts all the time? . . . Can I bring the
> Lord back in my mind-flow every few seconds so that God shall always
> be in my mind? I choose to make the rest of my life an experiment in
> answering this question.[2]

Over the months to come, Laubach continued to chronicle this journey of
transformation, sharing both the joys and the struggles of the task. On June 1,
just five months after beginning his experiment, he wrote:

> Last Monday was the most completely successful day of my life to date,
> so far as giving my day in complete and continuous surrender to God is
> concerned. . . . I remember how as I looked at people with a love God
> gave, they looked back and acted as though they wanted to go with me.
> I felt then that for a day I saw a little of that marvelous pull that Jesus
> had as He walked along the road day after day "God-intoxicated" and
> radiant with the endless communion of His soul with God.[3]

What would it be like if you and I took Frank Laubach's adventure and made
it our own? What would the world think if every follower of Christ made such a
radical commitment to living each day as if Christ himself were shining his love
through us? as if nothing on earth mattered except discovering a complete and
unbroken communion with the Father?

Perhaps that's what Paul had in mind when he encouraged us to no longer
conform to the "behavior . . . of this world," but to instead let God transform us
by "changing the way [we] think" (Romans 12:2). In a word, he was telling us to
surrender. To give up. To change—not only our way of thinking but also our way
of living. To allow the Holy Spirit to mold and shape us until our heart and mind
are wholly devoted to the things of God. Sound a bit radical? That's because it is.
But does Jesus deserve any less?

REFLECTION
*What does it mean to offer our body as a "living sacrifice to God"? How is
this act of worship different from other types of worship? What commitment
should you make to Jesus in light of today's lesson?*

SECURE IN OUR SALVATION

For his Holy Spirit speaks to us deep in our hearts and tells us that we are God's children.   Romans 8:16

I HEARD the story of a polar bear and her young cub living in the northern part of Alaska. One day the cub came to her mother and said, "Mom, are you sure I'm a polar bear?"

"Of course you are," assured the mother. The cub went away satisfied.

But the next day the cub asked again. "Are you sure I'm 100 percent polar bear?"

The mother seemed confused. "I promise. You're absolutely 100 percent polar bear. But why do you keep asking?"

"Because," said the cub, "I'm freezing out here!"

"Please join me on your knees, heads bowed, hearts in tune with God, secure in his promise."

Desecration, 404–5

I know a lot of Christians who can relate to that little cub, don't you? Maybe you're one of them. We know we're saved because Jesus promised we would be, but too often we don't feel like it. We do all the things we know that saved people are supposed to do, yet somehow we don't seem to fit in. We read our Bible, we pray, we serve, we go to church, yet somehow our heart continues to wander. We love Jesus, but we struggle to stay *in love* with him. If you can relate, then know that you're not alone.

What we are experiencing is one of Satan's greatest weapons against believers. His strategy is simple but effective—and it's a three-fold one: (1) to make us feel alienated from Christ; (2) to cause us to sin; and (3) to keep us from reaching the lost. If he can succeed in the first two, the third will usually fall into place as well. It is a strategy that is as potent as it is transparent, and too many Christians are taken in by it.

Combating this problem can often be as simple as meditating on the promises of God, beginning with Paul's words in Romans 8:38: "I am convinced that nothing can ever separate us from his love. Death can't, and life can't. The angels can't, and the demons can't. Our fears for today, our worries about tomorrow, and even the powers of hell can't keep God's love away." The Lord's blessings are sure and irrevocable, in spite of what the enemy would have us believe.

REFLECTION
What is a "spirit of fear," and how have we been released from it? What are the rewards and implications of being "God's children"?

JESUS LOVES ME

*Moved with pity, Jesus touched him. . . . Instantly the
leprosy disappeared.*   Mark 1:41-42

AS A CHILD I remember a portrait of Jesus that hung in the middle of our living room. It was an old painting, typical of many you would see in early twentieth-century America. He was wearing a white robe, with long, curly hair and a handsome face. His gaze was friendly enough, stern and strong. But it was the eyes I remember most. They were cold eyes. Serious and contemplative. And they had a way of following you around the room, glaring, watching. Trying to catch you doing something you shouldn't be doing.

I remember standing once staring at the painting, trying to imagine if this was the Jesus that we learned about in Sunday school. Is this what he looked like? Is this what he wore? Was his hair long? Was he watching me now?

We all have our images of Jesus. We all have a picture in our mind of what he might have looked like, how he might have acted, how his voice sounded, how he looks at us. And that picture often says a lot about the nature of our relationship with him. How we picture Jesus is usually how we picture God, for they are really one and the same.

Scripture paints only one picture of Jesus—a man filled with compassion and love for others. Just before he raised Lazarus from the dead, Jesus began to weep. Those who saw him said, "See how much he loved him," (John 11:36). A short while later Jesus said to his disciples, "I have loved you even as the Father has loved me. Remain in my love" (15:9). There are so many references to the love of Jesus and his Father in Scripture that it would take the rest of this book to talk about them. It's impossible to come away from the Bible without seeing it. If you want to see pure love, just look into the eyes of Jesus.

Today I have a different painting on my wall. It's a picture of my own father, a charcoal drawing that I commissioned from an artist shortly after his death. It hangs in my office above my desk. He's smiling at me now. I'm still in awe at how accurately the artist captured his image, especially his eyes. They are kind and compassionate and loving. Just like my father, whose gaze gave only one expression—pure love! When I look at my father's eyes I see Jesus. And I can only hope that others see the same in me.

REFLECTION
*How can we "remain" in the love of Jesus? What does it take
for others to see Jesus through our eyes?*

MAKING HIS LOVE OUR HOME

All those who love me will do what I say.   John 14:23

VICTOR HUGO'S *Les Miserables* is a beautiful tale of love and redemption. It is set in nineteenth-century France and is the story of a reformed thief, Jean Valjean. Valjean learns that a young woman named Fantine has been fired from her factory job because she has an illegitimate daughter. Fantine is forced to work as a prostitute in order to care for her young child. When Fantine becomes deathly ill, Valjean takes pity on her and tries to nurse her back to health. "When you are better, I will find work for you," he tells her.

"But you don't understand," says Fantine. "I am a whore, and Cosette has no father."

"She has the Lord," Valjean tells her. "He is her Father, and you are his creation. In his eyes you have never been anything but an innocent and beautiful woman."

After Fantine's death Valjean takes her daughter, Cosette, to raise as his own. And years later Cosette, now a young woman, says about Valjean, "My father is a very good man. I grew up in his love. His love was my home."

The story paints a beautiful picture of redeemed love and faithfulness, even in the midst of sin and sorrow. In many ways the story is ours. In our unworthiness we turned away from God and sold ourselves to sin, only to have him send a Savior to buy us back. In spite of our sin, he declares us worthy and clean, and in the end he brings us back to the Father. We grow up in his love, and make his love our home.

Jesus said to his disciples, "All those who love me will do what I say. My Father will love them, and we will come to them and live with them" (John 14:23). When Jesus looks at us, he doesn't see homeless sinners, unclean and unworthy. He sees only lost souls in need of a Savior. He sees cold and hungry children longing for a father's embrace. All we have to do is accept that love and bask in the Father's redemption.

Valjean told Fantine that in God's eyes she had never been anything but an innocent and beautiful person. When we come to Jesus, he says the same to us.

REFLECTION
What does this passage say to you about the unconditional love of Jesus?
What does it say to him when we willingly disobey?

THE GOSPEL OF GRACE

God saved you by his special favor when you believed. And you can't take credit for this; it is a gift from God.   Ephesians 2:8

I SPENT MUCH of my early life as a Christian convinced that I understood the grace of God, only to find out that I knew nothing about it. Many of my days were spent in agony and self-loathing, struggling with sin and guilt and shame. At the time it was beyond my comprehension that God could no longer see my sin through the veil of Christ's blood. My faith was a longing to somehow earn God's love, and behind my mask I was miserable with the knowledge that I couldn't do it.

Through a series of events and people who God put into my life, I began seeing just a glimpse of the true gospel of grace. Little by little I started to understand, but still I struggled to feel worthy. About this time a friend gave me a copy of a book entitled *The Ragamuffin Gospel*, by Brennan Manning. Manning's view of grace was like a foreign language to me. I read through the book twice in the first few months and still didn't get it. A year later, almost by accident, I again began reading through his book, and suddenly the concepts started to come alive. Several times I had to set it aside to wipe the tears from my eyes. For the first time in my life I had come face-to-face with the true magnitude and significance of God's wonderful grace. Manning writes:

> "It also says that we are saved by grace through Christ, not of ourselves, so we can't brag about our goodness."
>
> *Left Behind*, 201

> Too many Christians are living in the house of fear and not in the house of love. . . . Though the Scriptures insist on God's initiative in the work of salvation . . . our spirituality often starts with self, not God. . . . Sooner or later we are confronted with the painful truth of our inadequacy and insufficiency. . . . Our scrambling for brownie points . . . [is] a flat denial of the gospel of grace.[4]

Manning goes on to explain that in spite of ourselves, God accepts and loves us as we are—that there is nothing we can do to make God love us any more, and there is nothing we can do to make him love us any less. His love is never in question, only our acceptance of it. "I will forgive their wickedness and will never again remember their sins," the Lord says (Jeremiah 31:34).

The gospel of grace is one of the most difficult concepts we will ever face. And it is the most pure and beautiful gift that we have ever received.

REFLECTION
What does it mean to be "dead because of your many sins"? Why is it so important to understand God's grace? How does it change the way we view ourselves?

43

BROKEN BEFORE GOD

Haughtiness goes before destruction; humility precedes
honor.   Proverbs 18:12

A MAN WALKED into a doctor's office complaining of a splitting headache. "Tell me," asked the doctor, "do you drink a lot of liquor?"

"Liquor?" said the man indignantly. "I never touch the stuff." The doctor thought for a minute and then asked him if he smoked. "I think smoking is disgusting. I've never in my life touched tobacco."

Again the doctor contemplated his answer. "Do you do any running around at night?"

"Of course not," said the man. "What do you take me for? I'm in bed every night by ten o'clock at the latest!"

The doctor leaned back in his chair and said, "I think I know your problem. You have your halo on too tight."

Simon the Pharisee had a similar problem. When dining with Jesus he was appalled at the sinful woman who bowed before Jesus and bathed his feet in perfume. "If God had really sent him, he would know what kind of woman is touching him," Simon said to himself (Luke 7:39). Like many of us, he equated sin with the sinner. Simon's religion had taught him that the best way to escape guilt was to instead focus on the shortcomings of others. You can always find someone more needy than yourself. How often do we do the same thing?

Being broken before God is an uncomfortable place to be, but it's the only place to find true peace. In the end it was the woman at Jesus' feet who found grace and forgiveness. She was the one who went away from the dinner with God's anointed blessing (see Luke 7:50). It was her heart that most warmed his.

Jesus says, "Come to me, all of you who are weary and carry heavy burdens, and I will give you rest. Take my yoke upon you. Let me teach you, because I am humble and gentle, and you will find rest for your souls" (Matthew 11:28-29). If we think our sins are hidden from God, we are mistaken. Denying them is only a vain effort to hide them from ourselves. Only when we lay them at the feet of Jesus will we find the rest we need.

REFLECTION
What was Jesus saying to Simon through this parable? What message should we gain from it?

EXPLORE THE WONDER

The heavens tell of the glory of God. The skies display his marvelous craftsmanship.   Psalm 19:1

THE STORY is told of a remarkable rabbi named Abraham Heschel. Several years before his death he suffered a massive heart attack, and he was sure he would die. His best friend sat by his side. Rabbi Heschel whispered to his friend, "Sam, I feel only gratitude for my life, for every moment I have lived. I am ready to go. I have seen so many miracles during my lifetime."

Exhausted, the old rabbi leaned back in his bed to catch his breath. "After a long pause, he said, 'Sam, never once in my life did I ask God for success or wisdom or power or fame. I asked for wonder, and he gave it to me.'"[5]

When was the last time you were truly moved by God's handiwork? Have you ever wept at a sunset or the majesty of a mountain range? Have you stood at the edge of the ocean and marveled at its expanse? Have you tried to count the stars at midnight? Have you felt the miracle of a newborn's tiny hands, or gazed into brand-new eyes? Do the words to old hymns still stir something deep within your heart? Have you cried as you envisioned Jesus on the cross, naked and thirsty and bleeding, longing for his Father's embrace?

Everything about God and creation screams out thoughts of wonder and amazement. Any person who can stand before it and yawn is either dead and buried or might as well be. With God, boredom is not an option. King David cries out to God in song, "I look at the night sky and see the work of your fingers—the moon and the stars you have set in place . . . the birds in the sky, the fish in the sea, and everything that swims the ocean currents. O Lord, our Lord, the majesty of your name fills the earth!" (Psalm 8:3, 8-9).

"Look up into the heavens. Who created all the stars?" asks the prophet Isaiah. And the answer resounds throughout all creation, just as it whispers in the heart of every man and woman on earth: "the Creator of all the earth" (Isaiah 40:26, 28).

I'm one who believes that there are no atheists in the world, only stubborn insubordinates. God's creation is his greatest evangelist. How sad that we so seldom stop to acknowledge its wonder.

REFLECTION
How do the skies "make him known"? How does this change the way you see the world around you?

OUR NEED FOR CONFESSION

Pray for each other so that you may be healed.   James 5:16

A PREACHER once came to his friend and said, "Our church has just experienced its greatest revival of repentance and brokenness." The friend was excited for the preacher. "So how many members did you add to your congregation?"

"None," said the preacher sadly. "We lost three hundred."

There is something inside of us that resists opening up about our struggles. We're inherently uncomfortable with the idea of sharing our failings with others. Sometimes pride gets in the way; other times it is simply embarrassment. And for some it may be the fear of vulnerability—of knowing that our exposure could be used against us. It's a sad dynamic, but a very real one. People who most need the support and acceptance of others often have no one to turn to in their time of need.

> "Rayford sat with his head in his hands, his heart pounding. . . . He was alone with his thoughts, alone with God. . . . 'Dear God, I admit that I'm a sinner. I am sorry for my sins.'"
>
> *Left Behind*, 215–16

The body of Christ should be the one place where sinners can go for help and understanding. Too often, though, it's the place we're least likely to find it.

It's like the sinner standing outside the locked church door, crying out to God, "Why won't they let me in?" God answers him, "Don't feel bad. They won't let me in either."

Dietrich Bonhoeffer once wrote of this dilemma: "He who is alone with his sins is utterly alone. . . . Pious fellowship permits no one to be a sinner. So everyone must conceal his sin from himself and from their fellowship. We dare not be sinners. . . . So we remain alone with our sin, living in lies and hypocrisy."[6]

Some years ago I witnessed firsthand what can happen when a spirit of brokenness comes upon a church. People who had buried their sins beneath a facade for years finally opened up and confessed to each other, asking for prayer and support. Their openness quickly fueled the flames of repentance within others, and before long the congregation was finding healing it had never dreamed possible. Decades of hurt and resentment rose to the surface, and the Spirit of God moved mightily among them. And it all started with a simple act of humility from one broken brother. Spiritual healing is critical to our Christian walk. And it begins with honest confession.

REFLECTION
In what way is healing and forgiveness contingent on confession?
What happens when we confess our sins to each other?

HEAVENLY REFLECTIONS

Let heaven fill your thoughts.   Colossians 3:2

A FEW DAYS AGO my wife told me about a dream she'd had the previous night. In the dream she found herself in a large backroom warehouse filled with beautiful decorative items. The room was overflowing with fine furnishings—lamps, tables, chairs, paintings, crystal bowls, candleholders, and the like. All the things that women love to adorn their houses with. Several dozen women were buzzing around the room, collecting items as they went. She suddenly realized that everything in the warehouse was free for the taking.

Wanting to take advantage of her good fortune, she began looking about the room, trying to find things she needed. But each time she picked something up it was chipped or broken. She couldn't find anything worth keeping.

Suddenly she began to wake up but still found herself in something of a dream stage. The feelings of frustrations lingered, and she thought to herself, *Why couldn't I find any good pieces?* Within seconds she was awake, and the irony of this idea hit her. She had to laugh. "I realized that even if I had gotten the best things in the room, it wouldn't have mattered," she told me later, "because I wouldn't have been able to bring them with me."

It was at that moment that the Lord spoke into her spirit. Through the experience he was showing her the futility of trying to fill our life with earthly treasures. No matter how many precious things we collect on earth, we can't take them with us. Although my wife has never been one to struggle with materialism, the message convicted her just the same.

> "'Can you imagine, Rafe,' she exulted, 'Jesus coming back to get us before we die?'"
>
> *Left Behind,* 4

There will come a day when earth will seem like nothing more than a dream we had long ago. We'll look back on our time here and wonder why we allowed ourselves to get caught up in such pettiness. We'll look at the time we spent shopping and accumulating, and we'll see the futility of it all. We'll wish we had loved people more, argued less, worked more reasonable hours. And we'll shake our head in amazement at the hours we spent worrying about things that were out of our hands. *God was in control all along,* we'll think. *Why did we have such a hard time believing that?*

Paul tells us, "Let heaven fill your thoughts" (Colossians 3:2). That's the only way to keep from getting wrapped up in futile pursuits on earth.

REFLECTION
In what ways have we been "raised to new life with Christ"? In what ways does heavenly reflection keep you humble and content?

FOCUS ON JESUS

We do this by keeping our eyes on Jesus.   Hebrews 12:2

LAST NIGHT my ten-year-old daughter was practicing ballet in the den while I was in a chair reading. She was jumping and running and doing pirouettes with grace. At one point I looked up to see her standing on one side of the room with her gazed fixed on the far wall. Then she began moving toward it with a series of twirls and steps, each time trying to keep her head facing forward. Her body would circle, but her eyes remained focused toward the wall. It was a typical ballerina's dance. "Do they teach you to do that because it looks pretty?" I asked her.

"No," she answered. "It's because it keeps you in a straight line and also keeps you from getting dizzy." Then she excitedly demonstrated the move again. "What you do is pick out a spot on the wall and focus on it. That keeps you from stumbling or getting out of line. If you don't have something to aim at, you get dizzy and you might fall."

Her explanation reminded me of a time during my high school days when I spent a Saturday helping a friend install an irrigation line. The two of us were using a backhoe to dig a three hundred yard trench between the street and his house. After the first hundred yards or so his father showed up and began laughing at the job we'd done. "It looks like a drunk snake dug it," he said. The trench was winding and bending in all directions. My friend's father took a stick from the field and stuck it into the front grill of the backhoe. "Now line that stick up with one corner of the house and keep it steady," he said. "Hold your head straight, and don't take your eyes off of it. That'll keep you straight." We were amazed at the difference it made.

The writer of Hebrews understood this principle. "Let us strip off every weight that slows us down, especially the sin that so easily hinders our progress. And let us run with endurance the race that God has set before us. We do this by keeping our eyes on Jesus" (12:1-2). The Christian walk is a path that Jesus has laid out for us—a race for the prize. And any good track coach knows that in order to run fast and straight, you have to stay focused on the finish line. Runners who fall behind or stumble are those who get distracted or glance over their shoulders. The ones who lose their focus.

So how do we keep from stumbling in our Christian walk? How do we keep from falling into sin and getting distracted by guilt and shame and remorse? We "fix our eyes on Jesus, the author and perfecter of our faith" (Hebrews 12:2, NIV).

REFLECTION
What distracts you most from the race you are running with Christ?
What concrete steps do you need to make in order to stay focused?

PERFECT FAITH

Let us fix our eyes on Jesus, the author and perfecter of our faith.

Hebrews 12:2, NIV

IN 1882 the renowned Spanish architect Antoni Gaudi began work on what he envisioned would become his greatest architectural masterpiece—the Sagrada Familia Cathedral in Barcelona: the "Great Cathedral of the Poor." Although he had built numerous buildings and churches throughout Spain, this was to become his crowning achievement. Work on the cathedral consumed him, so much so that he took up residence in a small room near its base. For the next thirty-four years, Gaudi agonized over his creation, often becoming impossible to please and demanding perfection from every worker and craftsman on site. His passion slowed down construction, running costs far over budget. Yet he was relentless in keeping the project alive.

> "Salvation belongs to our God who sits on the throne, and to the Lamb!"
>
> *Apollyon, 49*

Several other buildings were begun and completed by Gaudi over the years that he worked on the cathedral, yet his heart and mind were always consumed with his grandest project. Sadly, he never lived to see its completion. By the time Gaudi died in 1917, only one of the four main towers was erected. Workers continued on and off but without direction. Gaudi's vision had died with him. Today, work has again begun on the great structure, even though architects continue to squabble over what their predecessor intended his masterpiece to look like. The best they can do is to piece together the mystery one stone at a time and do their best to finish the massive cathedral.

Gaudi's vision was a grand and noble one, but it fell short just the same. He was the author of a great work but never got to see its completion.

Jesus, on the other hand, not only authored our faith but completed it. The writer of Hebrews tells us he is "the author and pefecter of our faith, who for the joy set before him *endured the cross,* scorning its shame, and sat down at the right hand of the throne of God" (Hebrews 12:2, NIV, italics mine). The true beauty of Jesus' life was not simply that he envisioned the redemption of man but that he saw it through to completion. He "endured the cross," and because of it, our faith has been made perfect—the masterpiece that God envisioned. Jesus continued to trust his Father until the last breath of his life, when he could finally close his eyes and say, "It is finished" (John 19:30).

You and I can rest in the knowledge that our destiny is in perfect hands. Our redemption is long since completed. And the one architect who knew what his masterpiece was supposed to look like laid every stone.

REFLECTION

It is the Cross and the Resurrection that set Christianity apart from all other religions. Spend time reflecting on the consistencies between the way Jesus lived and the way he died.

TEACHABLE MOMENTS

One day as the crowds were gathering, Jesus went up the mountainside with his disciples and sat down to teach them.   Matthew 5:1

AS A YOUNG MAN I worked in a bakery and had to be at work by 3 A.M. I'm not a morning person, so more often than not I straggled in a few minutes late. Thankfully, I had an understanding boss. His name was Alton, but everyone called him Sandy (though I never learned why). Many mornings I would drag in half asleep at 3:15 A.M. and see Sandy shaking his head, half smiling. He'd turn to me and say, "You know, son, any old fool can go to bed. But it takes a real man to get up in the morning."

Wise words. So much so that to this day I often find myself telling my son the same thing as he drags himself out of bed. I also give him advice on efficiency when we work in the yard together. "While you're working on a task, always be planning what you're going to do next," I tell him. "That way you don't have any downtime." That's something else I learned from Sandy during my years at the bakery. What most sticks in my memory, though, are the many days I finished work early to go with Sandy on his afternoon deliveries. I enjoyed it because his last delivery was a truck stop, and we'd stop for lunch and a slice of pecan pie. Sandy was a deeply spiritual man, and it was during these times that I gleaned the most from his words of wisdom. At the bakery he taught me how to work, but away from it, on our own time, he taught me about life. Somewhere along the way my boss had become my mentor, and to this day many of my thoughts and views—on faith, as well as life—can be traced back to Sandy.

One of the traits we learn from Jesus is to look for those teachable moments that come into our life, and then take advantage of them. As you walk through the Gospels, following the steps of Jesus, you begin to see a clear picture of a man in tune with his surroundings. He looked for people with needs and then stopped to fill them. Not only did he mentor his disciples moment by moment, but he took every opportunity to teach and heal others along his path. In doing so, he was showing us all what a true teacher looks like. Jesus instinctively knew when people were watching—people who were open to his truth. And he never passed up the opportunity.

One such teachable moment came when he sat down on a mountainside and began speaking to a crowd that had gathered to see him. His words that day still stand as one of the most encouraging and enlightening sections of Scripture. We call it the Sermon on the Mount, and it is perhaps the greatest glimpse we have into the heart of Jesus.

REFLECTION
Name a person God has put into your life for you to mentor. Ask him to help you actively look for opportunities to teach him or her. How might you find someone to mentor?

THE POOR IN SPIRIT

Blessed are the poor in spirit.   Matthew 5:3, NIV

THERE IS probably no living man through whom God has worked more mightily than Billy Graham. Dr. Graham has reached more people with the gospel of Jesus than perhaps any person in history. Yet those who know him best don't usually talk about his accomplishments or the number of people he's led to Christ. They talk of his unbelievable humility.

Several years ago Dr. Graham was interviewed on *PrimeTime Live*. He was sitting somberly in a chair when the last question came his way: "What do you want people to say about you when you're gone?" His response took many by surprise. "I don't want people to say anything about me. I want them to talk about my Savior. The only thing I want to hear is Jesus saying, 'Well done, my good and faithful servant.'" Then he bowed his head and said softly, "But I'm not sure I'm going to hear that." It was a rare but honest look into the true nature of Billy Graham's heart. In spite of all he's done for the work of the Kingdom, he still sees himself unworthy of God's commendation.

Do you want to see what Jesus looks for in a true servant? Do you wonder what he expects from those who claim him as Lord and Savior? Are you curious about the kinds of people he glories to glory in? Jesus tells us in his first words on the mountainside: "Blessed are the poor in spirit, for theirs is the kingdom of heaven" (Matthew 5:3, NIV).

> "He was humbled to the point of shame. He felt suddenly unworthy."
>
> *Nicolae, 197*

Did you catch his words? Did you understand the significance? He's telling us, "These are the kind of people that heaven was created for. The ones who don't think they deserve to go there. The people who understand the glory of God enough to know they don't belong in his presence. The ones who long to hear God say, 'Well done' but can't imagine that they deserve to hear it."

The highest honor in heaven is reserved for those who least expect it. The first in line to receive his blessing will likely be the ones who were content to stay at the back of the line on earth. If you want to know the true strength and power of Billy Graham's life, look at his heart, not his crusade attendances. God doesn't save us because of who we are or what we've done but because of our faith in accepting his gift of salvation.

REFLECTION

Why is humility such a critical trait for a servant of God? Have you ever felt God "setting himself against" you because of your pride? Ask him to show you areas of your life in which you need humility.

THOSE WHO MOURN

Blessed are those who mourn.   Matthew 5:4, NIV

THE FIRST TIME I met Nicky Cruz I was a bit apprehensive. I'd seen *The Cross and the Switchblade,* the movie that chronicled his life as a dangerous young gang leader in the streets of New York. I knew of his conversion through the ministry of David Wilkerson. I'd seen newspaper articles about his ministry to gangs across the country, complete with a photo of him on a dirty sidewalk wearing a weathered leather jacket. In preparation for our meeting, I bought a copy of *Run Baby Run,* his autobiography, and read it cover to cover. I would never have thought a man could experience what Nicky Cruz went through and come out the other end normal—or even alive.

But sitting across from him, I had a hard time believing that this was the same man I'd heard and read about. He was nothing like I expected. He was gentle and warm and unpretentious, with eyes as kind as I'd ever seen. I was there to discuss a book that he and I were writing together, but he spent more time asking about my family than talking about his past. Some weeks later I saw him preach to over six thousand inner-city kids. Hundreds responded to the invitation to receive Christ as their Savior. Later, Nicky stood to one side, staring down at a handful of gang leaders, trying to convince them to accept Jesus. I couldn't remember the last time I'd seen someone proclaim the gospel with such boldness and confidence.

But one on one, when it was just Nicky, me, and a tape recorder, his words and demeanor took on a completely different tone. "Sometimes I wish God would just let me forget my past," he told me once. "It's so painful to remember." He leaned back in his chair and gazed down at the table in front of us. A tear glinted from the corner of his eye. "So many people have been hurt by the things I've done," he said softly. "I wish I could forget."

"Blessed are those who mourn, for they will be comforted" (Matthew 5:4, NIV). Of all the people on the mountainside that day, I think that this group most needed to hear Jesus' words of reassurance—especially those with sorrow rooted in regrets and past mistakes. They mourn, not for themselves, but for those they've hurt. For damage they wish they could undo and years they wish they had back. Their reward in heaven will be especially sweet. Jesus himself will be there to wipe away their tears. And maybe he'll wash away the memories as well.

REFLECTION
*What is the sorrow in your life that you long for God to take away?
How does God use your mourning to help you minister to others
who need comfort?*

THE MEEK

Blessed are the meek.　　Matthew 5:5, NIV

WORDS OFTEN have a way of changing their connotation over time. Some words may mean one thing to one generation, yet elicit entirely different thoughts to another. *Meekness* is one of those words. Today, when you call a man meek, it tends to conjure up images of a limp-wristed, cowering doormat. A man who refuses to take up for himself. I've heard preachers use illustrations that back up this notion. But that's far from what Jesus had in mind. Lack of backbone would never have impressed a man as bold as Jesus—a man who just weeks later turned the Temple upside down in righteous anger.

The kind of meekness Jesus had in mind is best described by an event that happened several years ago when Ronald Reagan was president. One of our navy cruisers, the USS *Vincennes*, made a terrible mistake by shooting down an Iranian airliner, and 290 people were killed in the accident. President Reagan came under fire when he announced plans to pay compensation to the victim's families. The Iranian hostage crisis was still fresh in the minds of most Americans, and many saw no reason to reward a country that brutalized several of our soldiers. An indignant reporter asked Reagan at a news conference, "Wouldn't such a payment set a bad precedent?" Without pause, Reagan answered, "I don't ever find compassion a bad precedent."[7]

> "He is so delightful, so bright! . . . Almost illiterate. But what a sweet, gentle spirit! What a servant's heart!"
>
> *The Mark*, 138–39

Dr. Lynn Anderson[8] describes meekness as "power under restraint." He uses the illustration of a mighty Thoroughbred racehorse, fully bridled and waiting at the gate. When the gun sounds, the horse unleashes the fury of his strength as he gallops toward the finish line. He is anything but weak and helpless.

In his letter to the Corinthian church, Paul compares himself to Jesus by saying, "By the meekness and gentleness of Christ, I appeal to you" (2 Corinthians 10:1, NIV). In the next sentence he calls himself "timid." Then, through much of the balance of his letter, Paul sets about chastising the church for its defiant behavior. And there is no contradiction in these two actions. In the flesh, Paul was broken and weak—a man who had died to self and lived only in the shadow of Jesus. His strength and confidence came from the authority of Christ. Like Jesus, Paul was a powerful man under divine restraint.

REFLECTION
Who is the person in your life that most defines meekness to you? What is it about him or her that you most admire? How can you work to obtain a spirit of meekness?

THIRSTING FOR RIGHTEOUSNESS

Blessed are those who hunger and thirst for righteousness.

Matthew 5:6, NIV

IT HAPPENED on December 7, 1988, at 11:41 in the morning. People from the Soviet Republic of Armenia never knew what hit them. The earthquake came with no warning, and when it finished, it left more devastation than any quake in the country's history. Susanna Petroysan suddenly found herself buried beneath tons of concrete and steel at the basement of her collapsed, nine-story apartment building. Her sister-in-law lay dead just a few feet away. But to Susanna's surprise and joy, her four-year-old daughter, Karine, was still alive and breathing. The two were trapped beneath the rubble. In time her daughter became thirsty. "Mommy, I need a drink," she said. Susanna could do nothing. Hours later, her daughter's cries came again. "Mommy, I'm so thirsty. Please give me something." Groping through the darkness, Susanna somehow found a small bottle of jam and fed it to her daughter in rations. By the next day it was completely gone.

Because of the darkness, Susanna lost all track of time. Days came and went, and still there was no sign of help. She found herself slipping in and out of consciousness, but she would remember her daughter and fight to stay coherent. Her daughter's cries haunted her: "Mommy, I'm thirsty. Help me!"

Eight days passed, and Susanna was convinced that she would die. But she wanted her daughter to live. So she did the unthinkable. She gave her daughter her blood. Slicing her finger with a piece of glass, she gave it to her daughter to suck on. And when no more blood flowed, she sliced another one. Susanna has no idea how many times she cut herself during the ordeal. She only knows that her blood was her daughter's only chance for survival. The rubble was eventually cleared, and by the grace of God both mother and daughter survived to tell their story.[9]

"Blessed are those who hunger and thirst for righteousness, for they will be filled" (Matthew 5:6, NIV). There is a thirst in the heart of every man and woman. It is a hunger that lingers deep and long within the depths of our soul and yearns to be satisfied. Worst of all, it's a thirst that nothing within our grasp can quench. We long to live, but we know we're going to die. So in the midst of our darkest hour, Jesus does the unthinkable. He gives us his blood.

When the rubble is cleared, and we're rescued from the basement of earth, we will take a deep breath and realize that we are still alive—but only because of Jesus' sacrifice.

REFLECTION
What does it mean to "thirst for righteousness"? How does Jesus' blood quench that thirst?

THE MERCIFUL

Blessed are the merciful.   Matthew 5:7, NIV

JESUS ONCE TOLD a parable of a king who wanted to settle accounts with his servants. One servant came before him who owed him ten thousand talents—a debt far beyond the means of a servant. When he couldn't pay, the king ordered that he and his family be sold into slavery, but the servant begged for mercy. Then the king took pity on him, canceled the debt, and set the servant free.

As the servant was leaving he ran across another slave who owed him a hundred denarii—about three month's wages. The man demanded his money, but the friend couldn't pay. "Be patient and I will pay it," the slave pleaded. But the man refused. He had his friend arrested and thrown into debtor's prison. The master heard of the ordeal and called the first servant before him. "You evil servant," he said. "I forgave you that tremendous debt because you pleaded with me. Shouldn't you have mercy on your fellow servant?" Then the king reinstated the servant's debt and had him thrown into prison until he could pay the debt.

"That's what my heavenly Father will do to you if you refuse to forgive your brothers and sisters in your heart," Jesus said, summing up the moral to the story (see Matthew 18:23-35).

I heard a lesson on this passage once that somehow reeked of rationalization. The first servant was portrayed as a man so grossly insensitive that none of us would be able to relate to him. The teacher explained how his actions were not only brutal but irrational. "How could the man's friend repay the debt while in prison?" he wondered aloud. The act was not only reprehensible but stupid and vengeful. He quoted a commentary that called the man's actions a "moral monstrosity." We all breathed a sigh of relief. *At least we're not that bad!* Or so we like to think.

Have you ever prayed for forgiveness on Sunday then demanded your way on Monday? Have you ever reflected on the cross one moment and inwardly scowled at a brother the next? Ever yelled at your kids for making you late to church? If so, then read the parable again. Jesus' point is simple: Those who have been forgiven of so much should learn to forgive. People redeemed from certain death should act like redeemed people. Those who have received the ultimate act of mercy should learn to be merciful. Anything less shows how little we understand the true depth of the Master's kindness.

REFLECTION
Do you harbor anger or resentment toward a brother or sister? What does it mean to forgive "from your heart"? Have you taken steps to do that?

THE PURE IN HEART

Blessed are the pure in heart.   Matthew 5:8, NIV

A RABBI was going through his regular ritual of preparing for the Day of Atonement. He was parading around the synagogue and beating his breast, saying, "I am nothing. I am nothing." A cantor standing nearby decided to join him. He fell in line behind the rabbi and began chanting, "I am nothing." The two marched diligently through the halls, demonstrating their humility to all who passed by. A janitor witnessed the scene and was touched. Their words convicted him deeply of his own unworthiness and sin. He bowed his head and beat his breast, praying, "Forgive me God. I am nothing." When the rabbi heard the janitor, he turned to the cantor and said smugly, "Now look who thinks he's nothing."[10]

> "'He hears you,'
> Buck said. 'He will
> not turn away
> a true seeker.'"
>
> *Apollyon, 68*

There are two ways to approach the throne of grace, and both look pretty much the same. One man stands before God with his head bowed and his hands folded, with the language of repentance on his lips. Another stands beside him in the same manner. Twin brothers of remorse. On the surface the two seem the same, but God sees a difference.

One holds secrets in his heart, treasured sins buried deep within him. His surrender is partial, sometimes sincere, but never complete. He understands that he needs God but can't quite let go of the world. *An ounce of sorrow, a cup of remorse, that's all the recipe calls for,* he thinks. *That should be enough to get me by.*

The man beside him stands broken, fully exposed, deeply sorry for the sin within him. He didn't come to appease his conscience or keep his stature in tact but to pour himself out and beg for God's mercy. He has nothing to offer but repentance, so that's all he brings to the throne.

Two men, two stories, two motives. So which one goes away clean?

"Blessed are the pure in heart, for they will see God" (Matthew 5:8, NIV). We are never further from Jesus than in the house of pretense. We are never more near him than in the pit of sorrow.

REFLECTION
When do you struggle to come before God pure and exposed? What hidden sin have you not laid on the altar before him? Pray today for a pure heart.

THE PEACEMAKERS

Blessed are the peacemakers.   Matthew 5:9, NIV

H. L. MENCKEN was a writer and magazine editor during the early 1900s. His articles on American life often drew letters of outrage and indignation. Mencken was committed to answering every piece of mail, but he had no interest in getting into fruitless arguments with people he didn't even know. So he developed a habit that stayed with him throughout his working life. He simply wrote every person back a simple note that read, "You may be right."[11]

Good strategy. It reminds me of a man I once saw who seemed unaffected by the things people did to offend him. Someone commented on his calm disposition, asking his secret. "I just don't let people rent space in my head," he answered. His words struck me as humorous at the time, but I've since come to see a lot of wisdom in them.

Scripture has a lot to say about avoiding conflict. Proverbs 26:17 says, "Yanking a dog's ears is as foolish as interfering in someone else's argument." Another proverb reads, "Avoiding a fight is a mark of honor; only fools insist on quarreling" (20:3). And an even more sobering proverb reads, "Anyone who loves to quarrel loves sin" (17:19). Paul gave a similar warning in his second letter to Timothy, "Don't get involved in foolish, ignorant arguments that only start fights. The Lord's servants must not quarrel" (2:23-24).

The God of peace puts a high priority on peacekeeping. Jesus says that peacekeepers will be called "sons of God." Quite a compliment. And something seriously worth striving for. The next time I find myself in disagreement with a brother, I hope I have the patience and wherewithal to handle it like my good friend Rick.

While teaching a class, Rick became aware of a man who constantly disagreed with him. He wasn't sure why, but it was apparent that this brother had a problem. So he went to him and asked about it. "Have I done anything to offend you?" Without warning the man tore into him. "Look, I don't like your class, I don't like the way you teach, and I don't like you!" Rick was left speechless. Over the weeks to come he prayed for guidance and wisdom. The next time he had an opportunity he asked the man if they could meet for prayer. "If I've done something to offend you, I really need God's forgiveness," Rick said. The man hesitantly agreed, and the two began meeting each week to pray for each other. Soon they became friends. What better way to honor God than with patience and humility toward each other?

REFLECTION
Think of some of the most fruitless quarrels you've been in recently. How could they have been avoided? What will you do differently next time?

THE PERSECUTED

Blessed are those who are persecuted because of righteousness.
Matthew 5:10, NIV

HISTORY KNOWS them as the forty martyrs of Sebaste. They were soldiers in the famed Twelfth Legion of Rome's imperial army, around A.D. 320. One day the captain informed his troops that Emperor Licinius had sent down an edict commanding all soldiers to offer a sacrifice to his pagan god. Forty of the soldiers were followers of Christ, and they refused. "You can have our armor and even our bodies, but our hearts' allegiance belongs to Jesus Christ," they said.

The emperor decided to make an example of the soldiers, so in the middle of winter he marched them onto a frozen lake and stripped them of their clothes. "Renounce your God and you will be spared from death," he told them. Not one man came forward. So he left them there, huddled together to contemplate his offer. Throughout the night the men stayed together, singing their song of victory: "Forty Martyrs for Christ."

When morning came, thirty-nine of the men had frozen to death. The one survivor finally relented and crawled to safety, recanting his confession of faith in order to live. The officer in charge that night had been so moved by the scene that during his watch he'd come to Jesus, so he broke rank and walked out onto the ice. Stripping his clothes he openly confessed his faith in Christ. The furious emperor demanded that he renounce Jesus, but he refused. When the ordeal was over, the Roman soldiers carried forty frozen men off of the ice.[12]

> "The Christ came from Israel, and Satan pursued and persecuted God's chosen people even to the present day."
>
> *The Indwelling,* 300

There are times in my life when I feel victimized for the cause of Christ. I've had my share of harsh words and fingers pointed in my face. Some veiled threats came my way once because of an article I'd written. I've lost work and money because of my beliefs. *That counts, doesn't it?* Then I run across stories like this and realize that I know nothing about persecution. In comparison, my life is like a long night on a soft mattress. But there may come a day when that will change. I may one day be faced with serious consequences for my faith. You may too. Will we have the strength of character and heart and faith to stand strong just the same? Jesus says, "Blessed are those who are persecuted because of righteousness, for theirs is the kingdom of heaven" (Matthew 5:10, NIV). True faith is that which has been tested, yet remains strong.

REFLECTION
When was the last time you were persecuted for your faith? Did you remain strong? What should our response be to those who persecute us (see Matthew 5:44)?

RESTORATION THROUGH JUDGMENT

I will give you back what you lost to the stripping locusts.   Joel 2:25

IF YOU ASK twenty Bible scholars to summarize the book of Joel, nineteen of them would likely say it is a message of God's judgment on his people. And they would be right, but that doesn't tell the whole story. When you discuss God's wrath without defining God's purpose, you've taken it out of context.

When you hear the word *judgment,* you may think of a man in a long black robe behind a large desk hammering down a gavel. The room echoes, and his voice bellows out the punishment that fits the crime in question. It's an "eye for an eye" courtroom that puts fear in the hearts of all who stand before the bench. A large sign on the door reads "Don't do the crime if you can't do the time." The mere thought of standing before the judge brings a cold sweat to your brow.

We read the book of Joel and try to imagine ourselves in the Israelites' shoes. The judgment is severe. Their crops are to be stripped bare by locusts and fire. Seeds will die in the ground, and food will disappear in front of their eyes. Their barns will be emptied, and their cattle and sheep will die a miserable death. "Let everyone tremble in fear because the day of the Lord is upon us," says Joel. "It is a day of darkness and gloom, a day of thick clouds and deep blackness" (Joel 2:1-2). You and I have probably never experienced anything like it, and neither had Israel, according to Joel.

But just look what the almighty Judge does in the middle of his sentencing. He stops to tell them of his love and his plan for mercy. "Return to the Lord your God, for he is gracious and merciful. He is not easily angered. He is filled with kindness and is eager not to punish you. . . . He will reply, 'Look! I am sending you grain and wine and olive oil, enough to satisfy your needs'" (Joel 2:13, 19).

You can't talk about God's judgment without spending some time discussing his mercy. You can't remove his wrath from his ultimate love. You can't think of his punishment without meditating on his purpose. God's discipline is never about retribution. It's always about restoration. When he punishes his people, he does it to bring us back to himself. God doesn't get even—he gets our attention. And when he has it, he reminds us how much we mean to him. That's the message of the book of Joel.

REFLECTION
Have you ever felt yourself under God's hand of judgment? If so, what was he trying to say to you through his discipline?

BLESSING THROUGH RESTORATION

I [will] restore the prosperity of Judah and Jerusalem.   Joel 3:1

GOD DOESN'T JUDGE to bring about waste but to bring about prosperity. His hand of discipline doesn't come to make us less, but to make us more. When God disciplines us, it is a sign of his unmatched love for us, not his wrath or retribution.

The writer of Hebrews reminds us of this truth: "My child, don't ignore it when the Lord disciplines you, and don't be discouraged when he corrects you. For the Lord disciplines those he loves, and he punishes those he accepts as his children" (Hebrews 12:5-6).

I love my children with a passion and would never do anything to harm them. As a father, much of my time is spent seeing to their needs. I want them to be happy and healthy and well nourished. I want them to be protected from harm. I watch over them, hug them, teach them, cherish them, and love them without condition. But there are times when what they most need from me is discipline and correction. I would rather hold them, but love demands that I scold them. I know the harm that can come to them when they are disobedient. I've seen what unchecked and rebellious behavior can lead to, and I would do anything to see that my children don't fall into that kind of lifestyle. My words of caution and discipline come from a heart of complete love and devotion. And they understand that truth.

> "Those are the prophets' views of God. Where do you get your view of God?"
>
> *The Remnant,* 230

God wants us to understand that truth about him as well. When God's prophets bring warnings to his people of his judgment for their sin, there is always a reminder of God's love. After bringing one of Scripture's most powerful messages of judgment, the prophet Joel promises restoration on the heels of it. "Rejoice in the Lord your God! For the rains he sends are an expression of his grace. Once more the autumn rains will come, as well as the rains of spring. The threshing floors will again be piled high with grain, and the presses will overflow with wine and olive oil" (Joel 2:23-24).

When you find yourself in the midst of God's discipline, take comfort in the knowledge that his purpose is restoration. His desire is not to harm you but to build you up and bring you even greater blessings than before.

REFLECTION
When has God disciplined you and later opened up the storehouse of his blessing on your life? Meditate on what God might be trying to do in your life today to bring you even closer to himself.

GOD OUR DEFENDER

To his people of Israel, the Lord will be a welcoming refuge and a strong fortress.   Joel 3:16

DO YOU REMEMBER the most feared bully from your days in grade school? Is there a dreaded name that comes to mind as you reflect back on your elementary school playground? When the kids were playing and the teacher wasn't looking, who was it that pushed and shoved others around, striking fear in the hearts of every kid at recess? I have a name, and I'll bet you do too.

Those who know me now have a hard time believing this, but I was rather small in my class as a child. My growth spurt didn't show up until the tenth grade, so I spent many years in fear. Carl was our sixth-grade bully, and often I was his target. He and his friends were a head taller than I was, so I avoided them like the plague.

What I most longed for during those days was a defender—someone to stand up on my behalf. At least someone to stand with me. And I found it in my friend Forest. Forest was big and intimidating, and he happened to like me, so when Carl came around, Forest came to my aid. Several times the two of us stood face-to-face with Carl and his gang, staring them down and weighing their threats. But nothing ever happened. Carl would back down, and Forest and I would go back to playing.

It's a strange and somewhat embarrassing memory, but it's one that comes to mind when I read the words of Joel: "'At that time, when I restore the prosperity of Judah and Jerusalem,' says the Lord, 'I will gather the armies of the world into the valley of Jehoshaphat. There I will judge them for harming my people. . . . The sun and moon will grow dark, and the stars will no longer shine. The Lord's voice will roar from Zion and thunder from Jerusalem, and the earth and heavens will begin to shake. But to his people of Israel, the Lord will be a welcoming refuge and a strong fortress" (3:1-2, 15-16).

Have you ever thought of God as your defender? When the armies of the world come after you and you sit defenseless as the target of their wrath, what is it that you most need? You need God by your side. And that's what he has promised. Not only to Israel in their time of need, but to you and me in our time of despair. When God's people are threatened, God comes to the rescue. Isn't that a comforting thought?

REFLECTION
In what ways have you felt threatened by God's enemies in the past? Did you feel his presence in the midst of it? How does it feel to know that he will always be there to defend you?

MARCH

LIVING IN GOD'S BLESSING

In that day the mountains will drip with sweet wine.   Joel 3:18

AFTER ALL IS SAID and done, what does it look like when God's restoration is complete? How does the blessing of God's redemption manifest itself when he's finished reinstating his people?

When we move away from God and disobey his commands, he brings us under his hand of discipline. His purpose is to keep us from harm and to bring us back into communion with him. His discipline is a sign that we are his people, and his love compels him to punish us. His punishment brings us back to our knees, and he quickly forgives our transgressions. He restores our blessings, even greater than before. And then we sit once again in the seat of his mercy. So what does that look like?

The prophet Joel described it like this: "'In that day the mountains will drip with sweet wine, and the hills will flow with milk. Water will fill the dry streambeds of Judah, and a fountain will burst forth from the Lord's Temple, watering the arid valley of acacias. . . . Judah will remain forever, and Jerusalem will endure through all future generations. I will pardon my people's crimes . . . and I, the Lord, will make my home in Jerusalem with my people" (Joel 3:18-21).

> "Behold, now is the accepted time; behold, now is the day of salvation."
>
> *Assassins,* 368

Simply put, it looks like heaven on earth: God's people living in the light of God's blessing, moving in his will, bathing in his mercy, feeling his presence, singing his praises, experiencing his glorious love. When we live the way God wants us to live, he brings blessings too great to describe. He shelters and defends us. He provides for our every need. He hears our prayers and answers them. He resides among us.

It's hard for so many of us to imagine that because we live so much of our life in rebellion. We're so busy being disobedient that we never give God the chance to give us the blessings he has in store. God doesn't want us to spend our life under his hand of discipline—he has much greater plans. If only we could learn to rest in his love and give ourselves over to his perfect will. That's when we would know firsthand that God's provision and goodness are far beyond anything we could expect or imagine.

REFLECTION
In what ways have you lived in rebellion to God? How has this kept you from receiving his blessings in your life? Why not pray that he will deliver you and restore his blessings?

LONGING FOR WEALTH

Riches won't help on the day of judgment. Proverbs 11:4

FEW WOULD DISPUTE that Muhammad Ali was one of the greatest athletes of all time. The three-time world heavyweight-boxing champion has sent more men to the mat than the Serta Mattress Company, and he's appeared on the cover of *Sports Illustrated* more times than any athlete in history. One survey showed that his was the most recognized face on the planet—more so than even the pope or the president. Today, though, you don't see Ali much. Parkinson's disease keeps him out of the public eye.

A sportswriter wanted to catch up with the former champ, so he went to his home for an interview. Ali escorted him to a barn next to his farmhouse. On the walls were mementos of his prime: photos of him dancing and punching and smiling, holding his championship belts high in the air. A poster from The Thrilla' in Manilla. Hundreds of snapshots and awards and trophies. The room was a museum of accomplishment.

Ali walked over to the pictures and noticed white streaks on them. He glanced overhead at the pigeons in the rafters. Without a word, he slowly began turning the photos toward the wall, one by one. Then he somberly walked to the door and said something under his breath. The sportswriter asked him to repeat it. "I had the world," he said, "and it wasn't nothin'. Look now."[1]

It's strange how we can hear the same sentiment so many times in so many different ways yet never quite grasp its significance. The sayings are so common that they become monotonous. "You can't take it with you." "There are no moving vans at a funeral." "Money won't make you happy." *Yeah, yeah. We know already.* You'd think we'd get the message after years of nagging, yet still we long for fame and fortune and power. We know that money won't appease, yet we continue working long hours and filling our houses with stuff. We know that fame is fleeting, yet we fill our mantels with trophies and glory in our accomplishments. We read a lonely rich man's obituary and shake our head, saying, "He never did find happiness." Yet somewhere in the back of our mind we catch ourselves thinking, *I wonder how much he was worth?*

It's not that we don't understand the dilemma. It's part of the human condition. And therein lies the real problem. We're not called to human thoughts but to heavenly ones. Our focus should be on things above, not things below. And until we internalize that truth, we are destined to spend our days in futile pursuits.

REFLECTION
In what ways have you put your faith in human pursuits?
What is God telling you through today's reading?

FUTILE PURSUITS

*How do you benefit if you gain the whole world but lose your own soul
in the process?*   Matthew 16:26

NOWHERE IS the problem of futile pursuits demonstrated more succinctly than in the story of the Roman emperor Charlemagne. According to legend, the infamous king asked to be entombed sitting upright in his throne. He asked that his crown be placed on his head and his scepter in his hand and that his royal cape be draped over his shoulder. He wanted an open Bible placed on his lap. He died in A.D. 814.

Nearly two hundred years later, the emperor Othello wondered if his predecessor's wishes were carried out, so he sent a team of men to open the tomb and find out. They found the body exactly as Charlemagne had requested. He was sitting upright in full dress with a book open on his lap. The book was a Bible, just as Charlemagne had commanded. But upon closer inspection, they noticed that the servants who buried him had taken the liberty of placing one of the emperor's hands on the book, extending his index finger toward a particular passage. It was Matthew 16:26: "What good will it be for a man if he gains the whole world, yet forfeits his soul?" (NIV).[2]

The psalmist writes, "Don't be dismayed when the wicked grow rich, and their homes become ever more splendid. For when they die, they carry nothing with them. Their wealth will not follow them into the grave" (Psalm 49:16-17).

Like the king, we all find ourselves struggling with an attachment to the things of this world. Even those who long for heaven and eagerly await the coming of Jesus find it difficult to let go of temporal treasures on earth. It's not that we don't trust God; we just find it difficult to look past the moment. Wall Street promises instant gratification, while Jesus tells us to wait for it. Madison Avenue says it can quench our thirst today, while Jesus beckons us to put our faith in the stream of "living water" (see John 4:10). We know his promises are true, but our fleshly desires are often so insistent.

Jesus says, "My nourishment comes from doing the will of God" (John 4:34). Jesus understands our desires for worldly indulgencies and our struggles to overcome them. His life on earth is a pattern for us to follow. The strength we need to forsake futile pursuits in deference for heavenly ones can be found through the words and actions of the Savior. It is possible to overcome our drive for fortune and fame and glory. We begin by letting the life of Jesus become the template for our own.

REFLECTION
*What does it mean to let our "nourishment" be the will of God?
How does that change your perspective of earthly indulgences?*

THE KEY TO PURITY

How can a young person stay pure?   Psalm 119:9

WHENEVER SCRIPTURE poses a critical question about life, it also gives the answer—often within the next few sentences. God isn't in the business of confusing us. He wants our life to be fruitful and obedient and prosperous.

The psalmist asked this question: "How can a young person stay pure?" And the formula is found immediately following. "By *obeying your word* and following its rules. I have *tried my best to find you*—don't let me wander from your commands. I have *hidden your word in my heart*, that I might not sin against you. . . . I have *recited aloud all the laws* you have given us" (Psalm 119:9-13, italics mine).

First, we *obey his Word*. We allow the Bible to become our blueprint for living. We take God's commandments to heart and make obedience our primary desire and longing.

Second, *we seek to find him*. Jesus tells us: "Love the Lord your God with all your heart, all your soul, all your mind, and all your strength" (Mark 12:30). A critical ingredient to a pure life is to seek God with every fiber of our being.

Third, *we hide his Word in our heart*. By reading and meditating on Scripture daily, we become intimately aware of God's will for us and his desire for our holiness.

> "God, please, bring to mind Scriptures you want me to hear right now. Don't let hunger or fatigue or fear keep me from remembering."
>
> *Armageddon*, 207

Fourth, *we recite his Word aloud*. When tempted in the desert by Satan, Jesus didn't attempt to develop new arguments for the enemy; he simply restated what God had already said. God's Word is complete enough to guide us through each and every situation. When faced with temptation, we, too, should quote God's Word aloud.

This is the four-step plan for pure and holy living outlined in Scripture for anyone serious about his or her Christian walk. And though the psalmist's words are aimed at the young, the advice is applicable to us all.

REFLECTION

Meditate on today's passage, asking God to speak to you specifically regarding the state of your heart. How does your life reflect the purity that God wants for you? What portions of the Word have you hidden in your heart to ward off temptation and help you discover God's will for your life?

A RENEWED MIND

Give your bodies to God. Let them be a living and holy sacrifice.

Romans 12:1

JUST AS SCRIPTURE doesn't ask questions that it can't answer, God's Word also doesn't tell us to do something without also telling us how—and usually within the next few lines.

When Paul admonishes the Roman Christians to "give [their] bodies to God," he doesn't leave them without a few words about how to accomplish that task. In the next verse he writes, "Don't copy the behavior and customs of this world, but let God transform you into a new person by *changing the way you think*" (Romans 12:2, italics mine). In other words, "If you want to please God, it's crucial to change the way you think." In this same letter Paul says, "Those who are dominated by the sinful nature think about sinful things, but those who are controlled by the Holy Spirit think about things that please the Spirit" (8:5).

The key is in the mind. The world's pattern is simple: Think about what you want, and then go after it. Let your heart decide what it desires, and then let your brain think of a way to acquire it. "If you can dream it, you can achieve it," the world's posters of success tell us.

But Christians have a different litmus test. Our desire is not to fulfill our heart's wishes but God's. Our goal is to become "living sacrifices"—to be laid bare on the altar of God's bidding. We allow his Spirit to set our agenda, and we work to set our mind on what the Spirit is telling us. A renewal of the mind is accomplished by first pouring out our own agenda and then allowing God to replace it with his. The result is a life that is holy and pleasing to God.

Like most principles of the Christian faith, this assignment sounds easier on paper than it really is. The mind is a stubborn and complex thing, and our will is often strong and unyielding. We spend most of our years struggling to get our way, and then Jesus comes along and asks us to relinquish those desires. Few of us do without a good fight. But God promises a great reward if we do: "All who are led by the Spirit of God are children of God" (Romans 8:14). How can we refuse an offer like that?

REFLECTION

It is "in view of God's mercy" that Paul tells us to become "living sacrifices" (Romans 12:1, NIV). Why does God's grace make that task desirable? In what way have you struggled with being transformed by God and "changing the way you think" (Romans 12:2)?

FULLY ALIVE

My purpose is to give life in all its fullness.   John 10:10

R. BUCKMINSTER FULLER was one of the most creative minds of the twentieth century. His list of inventions would take an entire book to discuss. In 1933 he developed the three-wheeled, rear-engine "Dymaxion Car," which became the prototype for most of today's streamlined automobiles. He created the first spherical, cartographic projection of the world ever to be granted a U.S. patent. And in 1947 he made scientific history by inventing the geodesic dome—his most famous, if not significant, contribution to society.

When asked about his inventions, Fuller credited his creativity to a freak happening during his childhood years. As a very young boy, Fuller went to bed one night and woke up blind. Medical experts were baffled. There seemed to be no reason for his sudden lack of sight. It just happened. For several years he remained blind, until one morning, to everyone's surprise, he awoke able to see. He had regained his sight just as suddenly and unexpectedly as he had lost it. To this day the event has baffled doctors and scientists alike.

Fuller later explained that when his sight came back, the world suddenly proved new and exciting to him. He saw things more clearly than ever before. Every sunrise seemed a miracle. The sky, the trees, the ocean took on a heightened level of wonder. And because of his passion for the world around him, he was able to open up a world of creativity and discovery beyond anything he had ever imagined before.[3]

For the believer, Jesus brings that same kind of wonder and passion and discovery. Instead of seeing the world through eyes of darkness and confusion, we suddenly see everything with new eyes and new hope. Where once we saw limitation, we now see possibility. Everything is new. "I am the light of the world," Jesus says (John 8:12), and through that light we are able to see beyond the here and now and into the hereafter.

When Jesus tells us, "My purpose is to give life in all its fullness" (10:10), he is telling us what we can expect if we allow him to open our eyes to the truth of God's Word. Jesus doesn't just show us a better way to die; he shows us a better way to live. Abundantly. Completely and fully alive.

REFLECTION
Are you still walking in darkness in your life? If so, what would Jesus have you do? How can you come to the light of Jesus?

AWAKE TO PASSION

I am the resurrection and the life. Those who believe in me, even though they die like everyone else, will live again.   John 11:25

RUSSIAN NOVELIST Fyodor Dostoyevsky was a revolutionist during the early nineteenth century. It was a time when challenging the czar's totalitarian regime was a dangerous preoccupation. Rebels were subjected to cruel beatings and psychological abuse. Prisoners were regularly brought before a firing squad. The commanders would slowly count down their final moments. "Ready! . . . Aim! . . . Fire!" Shots would ring out, but the bullets would never come. They were blanks. The marksmen would have a good laugh at the prisoner's expense before taking them back to their cells. To many of the prisoners, death would have been a kinder punishment. This daily torment often proved to be more than they could handle. It drove many prisoners insane with anxiety and fear.

> "I'm calling you to the truth. Your life may get worse, but your death will be the best! No matter how you die, you will wake up in heaven."
>
> *Assassins, 270*

Dostoyevsky faced this same torture during his captivity. Yet his response did nothing but frustrate his captors. In spite of their constant attempts to torment him, Dostoyevsky never broke under the pressure. In fact, he seemed to thrive on it. Through writings he later explained that their attempts only proved to heighten his awareness of life. Before being led out to each firing line, he would eat his last meal by savoring every bite. He would stand before his executioners studying their faces, wondering if they would be the last he would see. Every element of life took on new appreciation and passion. It was in the face of dying that he truly learned to live.[4]

Jesus says, "Those who believe in me, even though they die . . . , will live again" (John 11:25). When you can live in the face of death, then you are truly living. When you can experience life through the eyes of mortality—knowing that your days on earth are numbered but understanding how little that really matters—that's when you are truly free to live. For the follower of Christ, passion should be a natural extension of faith. Just knowing that life on earth is but a small precursor to the glorious existence to come should set our heart ablaze with purpose and delight.

When Jesus' disciples heard that he wanted to go back to Judea, they begged him not to go. "The Jewish leaders . . . were trying to kill you," they told him. But Jesus ignored their warnings. "Our friend Lazarus has fallen asleep, but now I will go and wake him up" (John 11:8, 11). Most people on earth go through their lives asleep. Let Jesus wake you up to the passion of living.

REFLECTION
How does the resurrection of Jesus change the way we should live?
When is the last time you felt truly alive in the face of your eternal destiny?

FOR LOVE OF THE GAME

If a soldier demands that you carry his gear for a mile,
carry it two miles.   Matthew 5:41

NBA FANS will tell you that Michael Jordan almost single-handedly revolutionized the game of basketball—all but rewriting the laws of physics in the process. His ability on the court is uncanny. He is arguably the greatest player ever to play the game. Before Jordan came onto the scene, the standard NBA contract included a clause that prevented players from playing off-season games without the approval of the team owner. Managers didn't want players to get hurt while on their own time. When the contract was offered to Jordan, he refused to sign it. He couldn't imagine going through the off-season without playing at every opportunity. The owner finally gave in and revised Jordan's contract, allowing him to play all he wanted—even on his own time. It's become known as the "love of the game" clause.

Jesus brought that same level of passion to everything he did, and because of it, many of his words baffled the believers of the day. Imagine what the crowd must have thought when he stood on a mountainside and said, "If you are slapped on the right cheek, turn the other, too" (Matthew 5:39). The very thought of allowing such injustice must have sent them reeling with confusion. But he didn't stop there. "If you are ordered to court and your shirt is taken from you, give your coat, too." *Absurd! Why on earth would we do that?* Still Jesus continues, "If a soldier demands that you carry his gear for a mile, carry it two miles" (5:40-41).

Jesus' admonition was foreign to the usual way of life. *We've always tried to be fair, but what you're asking is far above what's expected in the law!* And that was his point. He was looking for people willing to live over and above the call of duty. To raise the bar. To set aside the standard contract and demand to be able to play in the off-season. It was his "love of the game" clause. Jesus wants believers with such a passion and love for him and his words that they look for opportunities to stretch the boundaries of expectation. He wants us to be so sold out to the game that we can't imagine being bound by a set of rules. "Look beyond what's expected of you," he says. "That's how true lovers of the game play."

Today, look for ways to evoke your "love of the game" clause.

REFLECTION
How do you normally respond when people treat you unfairly? How do you
think Jesus would have you respond in the future?

SPIRITUAL APATHY

The harvest is so great, but the workers are so few.   Matthew 9:37

MOST OF US have heard the following famous line by Edmund Burke: "All that is necessary for evil to triumph is for good men to do nothing." But have we thought about the consequences of his statement in relation to the gospel of Jesus? Have we wondered what would happen if everyone bearing the key to salvation chose not to tell anyone? What if apathy reigned supreme within the Christian community? Some might say it already does.

Jesus mourned the lack of commitment as he went through towns and villages, seeing crowd after crowd longing for help. He told his disciples, "So pray to the Lord who is in charge of the harvest; ask him to send out more workers for his fields" (Matthew 9:38). Everywhere he turned he saw people in need, but so few willing to reach out to them. They were "like sheep without a shepherd," Matthew records (9:36).

The same could easily be said of the majority of people today. So many are lost and helpless, longing for a shepherd. And though they interact with Christians on a daily basis, they still haven't heard the truth of Jesus.

Several years ago two men were convicted of bombing the Federal Building in Oklahoma City. Timothy McVeigh and Terry Nichols spent years planning and preparing their monstrous crime and then carried it out in April of 1995. Over 168 people lost their lives, including many children. Just as shocking as their act of terrorism was the fact that at least one man knew of their plans and yet didn't do anything to warn us. Michael Fortier heard the pair speak of their intentions time and again, yet he didn't bother to report them. "I thought his plan would never bear fruit," he said later. On May 27, 1998, Fortier was sentenced to twelve years in prison for the crime of passivity.[5]

We reel in disgust when we hear about Fortier's apathy. Yet how is it different from Christians who know the truth of God's Word and the imminence of his coming judgment but go day after day never bothering to share that news with others? How can we know of Jesus' love and the beauty of salvation, yet keep it to ourselves? Are we not just as guilty as Michael Fortier? It's a sobering and harsh comparison, but maybe that's what we most need. "The harvest is so great," says Jesus, "but the workers are so few." Isn't that what you and I are called to do?

REFLECTION
Who are the people in your life who are "like sheep without a shepherd"?
Ask the Holy Spirit to open up an opportunity for you to share with them.

THE HEART'S WITNESS

They demonstrate that God's law is written within them,
for their own consciences either accuse them or tell them
they are doing what is right.   Romans 2:15

FFYONA CAMPBELL was listed in the *Guinness Book of World Records* for her eleven-year trek across five continents of the world. She walked more than 19,500 miles and was billed as the first woman in history to walk around the world. For over two years her name was listed in the famous record book—until 1996, when Campbell called the people at Guinness and asked that her name be removed. She admitted to cheating. During long stretches of her walk between Indiana and New Mexico, Campbell became tired and hitchhiked a ride with her support truck. Most of the journey was legitimate—she wore out 100 pairs of running shoes along the way. In fact, she only rode a few hundred miles of the trip—not terribly significant when you consider the distance she traveled. But the guilt wouldn't leave her.

"Once you've lied about your achievements," says Ffyona, "you've created a burden for yourself which you can never, never put down. My lie almost destroyed me." She found herself so ridden with guilt during that time that she began dabbling in drugs and even considered suicide. That's when she decided to confess and make things right. Her name was taken out of the record book. More than a year later she returned to Indianapolis and made the trip to New Mexico in secret. It was something of a symbolic gesture—not for the record, but for her peace of mind.

> "Where was this guilt coming from?
> He had locked eyes with Hattie numerous times, and they had spent hours alone together over dinners in various cities."
>
> *Left Behind*, 145

You don't have to give a man a copy of the Ten Commandments to convince him of his sin. You don't need to explain to an adulterer why adultery is wrong. It doesn't take a lesson in Old Testament law to persuade a thief and a liar that his actions are harmful. His heart has already done that. Paul writes to the Romans, "Their own consciences either accuse them or tell them they are doing what is right" (Romans 2:15). Our conscience is that small voice inside that speaks up whenever and wherever God's Word is assaulted and ignored.

Ever have trouble falling asleep after fighting with your spouse? Ever scramble for words to explain away a half-truth to your boss? Ever look at the ground when the preacher starts to meddle? There's a good reason for that. And it's not because your mother raised you right.

REFLECTION
What is one sin in your life that weighs heavily on your heart and regularly brings feelings of guilt? Why not deal with it today?

JOSHUA'S JOURNEY

For I will be with you as I was with Moses   Joshua 1:5

HOWARD HENDRICKS once observed, "There is no such thing as a correspondence course for swimming." There are some things in life that simply have to be experienced to learn. Trust is one of those things. We can hear a thousand sermons on trusting God to provide, but until we live and breathe the experience, seeing his hand at work day after day, hour after hour, the concept will never quite settle into our heart and soul.

The book of Joshua is a manual on trust. It reads like an educational documentary on the supernatural provision and power of God in the lives of a people on the brink of discovering Canaan—the Promised Land. From the first page to the last, you see how God literally moved heaven and earth to protect his people and see that they arrived safely home.

We can't come away from the book of Joshua without seeing five important principles at work. In the midst of their journey, God was teaching Joshua and the people of Israel to trust him. At the same time he was hammering home a critical lesson about what it takes to stay in his perfect will. They are principles that apply to anyone longing for Canaan—to all those who find themselves journeying through the desert with God, looking for home. These principles are simple but far from simplistic:

1. *Allow God to lead.* He is in control every moment, even when it seems that he isn't.
2. *Be strong and courageous.* When you're being led by the all-powerful God, you have no time for weakness and insecurity and complacency.
3. *Meditate on God's Word.* There is supernatural power in the Word of God, and reading it brings supernatural wisdom.
4. *Remember what God has done.* Looking forward gives direction, but taking time to look back builds strength and trust.
5. *Be united.* "A triple-braided cord is not easily broken," says King Solomon (Ecclesiastes 4:12), and God beautifully demonstrates that truth in the story of Joshua.

REFLECTION
Imagine yourself in Joshua's shoes as God puts his blessing on him. How do you think he felt? Have you ever felt commissioned by God?

ALLOW GOD TO LEAD

I will not fail you or abandon you.   Joshua 1:5

LISTEN TO the promises God made to Joshua: "You must lead my people across the Jordan River into the land I am giving them. I promise you what I promised Moses: 'Everywhere you go, you will be on land I have given you—from the Negev Desert in the south to the Lebanon mountains in the north.' . . . No one will be able to stand their ground against you as long as you live. . . . I will not fail you or abandon you. . . . You will be successful in everything you do. . . . For the Lord your God is with you wherever you go" (Joshua 1:2-9). We could go on if time and space permitted, but the point is simple: God ordered the Israelites' days and took care of them as clearly as the sun rises in the morning. He promised to be faithful, and he kept that promise. When God is allowed to lead, he not only leads lovingly but decisively. That truth is displayed throughout the story of Joshua.

> "How thrilling to know that God was faithful! He was there at the darkest hour."
>
> *The Mark*, 340

God has given you and me the same promise. "I am with you always, even to the end of the age," Jesus tells us (Matthew 28:20). Just as God went before the Israelites ordering their days, he is walking beside us today, guiding our every step.

Do you find that as comforting as I find it? Does it make your heart soar to learn that he cares enough to leave his throne and walk through the desert with you? Does it bring a tear to your eye to think that the God of the universe, the Creator of heaven and earth, the God of Abraham, Isaac, Jacob, and Joshua is also the God of Fred and Martha and Frank?

As you read through the story of Joshua, a clear pattern quickly arises. Whenever the Israelites followed God and remained faithful, they prospered. They won every battle with ease, ate and drank in abundance, and lived fruitful, happy lives. But when they went their own way, leaving God and his commandments behind, they failed. Without exception. Apart from God they had no chance of winning, but when following God's lead, they had no chance of losing. It doesn't take a rocket scientist to figure out the best approach.

Knowing that truth, why would we want to set out on any conquest without letting God take the lead? Why try to even start the day without first looking to God for guidance?

REFLECTION
How did God work in this passage to reveal his provision to Israel?
How has he worked to reveal his provision in your life?

BE STRONG AND COURAGEOUS

Be strong and courageous! Do not be afraid or discouraged. For the Lord
your God is with you wherever you go.   Joshua 1:9

IMAGINE THIS scene for a minute. You're a captain in Joshua's army camped a few miles outside the city of Jericho. You've seen the thick, double-layered stone walls surrounding the city and the armed soldiers guarding every entrance. You've heard tales of the fierce Canaanite army and their ability to hold their ground in battle.

In the midst of all this, an edict comes down from the upper ranks. Israel is planning to take Jericho. Actually, what the message says is that Israel has already taken Jericho, but Jericho just doesn't know it yet. The battle plan is really no plan at all. You're supposed to get your troops together and conduct a victory march around the city. Just once, then you'll head back to camp for the evening. The next day you're supposed to do it again—for six days in a row, to be exact. Then on the seventh day you're to march seven times around the city. That's when your soldiers can march in and take possession. There's a postscript at the bottom of the note. "Of course, we've already taken the city; this marching is just a formality." It's your job to relay this message to your troops. And then to make sure that their armor is shined and ready for the big parade. Suddenly you find yourself wondering what kind of army you've enlisted in.

The next day you're marching around the city, and you can't help but hear the taunts coming from inside the walls. "Hey buddy, aren't you supposed to *win* a battle before you light up your cigar?" "You there, soldier boy, your momma called . . . you forgot your helmet." You know how silly this all looks, but you keep marching just the same. Because you know that God is on your side, and you've seen what he can do.

This is why God reminded Joshua time and again to "be strong and coura- geous." God has a way of working that tends to fall outside the norm, and he needs people who trust him enough to go the distance, no matter how bizarre the game plan. Courage is important to God because courage is a natural by- product of trust. And the greater we trust, the braver we become. As long as God leads the battle, we can march in confidence, knowing that we've already won. God gave Jericho to Israel on the seventh day, just as he said he would. So, . . . what wall does he have you marching around?

REFLECTION
Why is it important to believe that we've won the battle, even before it has
begun? How have you shown courage in the face of spiritual obstacles?

MEDITATE ON GOD'S WORD

*Study this Book of the Law continually. Meditate on it
day and night.*   Joshua 1:8

GAYLORD KAMBARAMI worked for the American Bible Society in Zimbabwe, distributing Bibles to the locals. But one day he ran across a man who refused to take one. The man was extremely hostile toward Christians. "I'll only roll the pages and use them to make cigarettes," the man told him. But Kambarami was a persistent man. "I understand that," he told the man, "but at least promise to read the page of the New Testament before you smoke it." The man agreed, somewhat confused, and the two parted ways.

Fifteen years passed, and Kambarami didn't think much more about the incident until by coincidence he ran across the man again—this time at a Methodist convention in Zimbabwe. The man was now a full-time evangelist and one of the speakers at the gathering. During his speech the man gave his personal testimony, recalling for the audience the day that Kambarami gave him his first New Testament. He told the audience, "I smoked Matthew and I smoked Mark and I smoked Luke, but when I got to John 3:16, I couldn't smoke anymore. My life was changed from that moment."[6]

There is power in the Word of God far beyond what you and I can comprehend. The mere words elicit a level of authority and muscle that no other text can possess. Just reading what the Creator has written brings supernatural insight and wisdom to the mind of the reader.

The Lord tells Joshua, "Study this Book of the Law continually. Meditate on it day and night so you may be sure to obey all that is written in it. Only then will you succeed" (Joshua 1:8). One key to following God is to meditate on Scripture and then to let those words flow from your mouth at every occasion. To let the promises of God seep into the pores of your heart and mind. To drink of God's wisdom by devouring his Word.

Maybe our friend from Zimbabwe was on to something. Maybe you and I should get into the practice of smoking God's Word—not literally, but spiritually. We should first read it and then sit back and savor the flavor, allowing the aroma to linger around us and within us. Let's do more than read God's Word; let's inhale it.

> "No matter where he was in the world, regardless of what he had done during the day or evening, sometime he would be going to bed. Regardless of the location or situation, before he turned out the light, he would get his daily Bible study in."
>
> *Soul Harvest, 231–32*

REFLECTION
*Begin today making a habit to pray the words of Psalm 119:17-24
before you study. How has that brought supernatural insight
to your mind as you read God's Word?*

REMEMBER WHAT GOD HAS DONE

*These stones will stand as a permanent memorial among the
people of Israel.*   Joshua 4:7

MY WIFE THINKS my office looks like a thrift store. The walls are overcrowded with pictures and plaques, and the bookshelves are decorated with gifts and mementos and trinkets collected throughout the years. This is my favorite room in the house, because here I am surrounded by memories. To my right is a photo of our family shooting the rapids near Glenwood Springs, Colorado. Beneath it is one of my son and me canoeing on Eagle Lake, and another of my daughter and me at Sea World. There's one of our family posing with our four-wheelers on top of Granny Peak, then still another of us all on a schooner in the ocean near North Carolina. On the bookshelves are trinkets and gifts that my kids have given me. A few model cars that my boy and I built, including some pine cars that we raced when he was a Cub Scout, and a Tiger Woods beanie that my daughter gave me. Then there's a plaque that says World's Best Dad—a plastic one. I'm sure it cost them all of three dollars, but it became worth a million the moment I opened it.

These are the things I surround myself with because they remind me who I am. And they reflect how good God has been to me through the years. They also serve as symbols to my children of who we are as a family. It not only reminds them where we've been but where we are going. These things say to them, "This is a family that stays together, that loves each other, that will be there for each other forever, no matter what."

That's what God had in mind when he told Joshua and the people of Israel to take twelve stones from the middle of the Jordan River. The Lord had just miraculously parted the Jordan, allowing the Israelites to enter the Promised Land at last. He had them build a stone marker—a memorial to his miracle that day. "In the future, your children will ask, 'What do these stones mean to you?' Then you can tell them, 'They remind us that the Jordan River stopped flowing when the Ark of the Lord's covenant went across'" (Joshua 4:6-7). The memorial was for the sake of the children—for the generations to come. He knew that Israel's future was dependent upon her memory of his faithfulness in the past.

Knowing where you're going is a good thing. But there's nothing quite as comforting as remembering where you've been.

REFLECTION
What kind of "stone markers" do you surround yourself with? What message do these things give to you and your family?

BE UNITED

*Stay with them until the Lord gives rest to them as he
has given rest to you.* Joshua 1:14-15

BEFORE MOSES DIED he made a promise to two and a half of Israel's tribes. The Reubenites, the Gadites, and the half tribe of Manasseh saw that the land east of the Jordan was rich and suitable for livestock. They had many herds and flocks and asked Moses if they could remain behind and settle in the lands of Jazer and Gilead. Moses agreed but on one condition: They were to first cross the Jordan and fight alongside their brothers as they took Canaan. Then they could return and make their homes (see Numbers 32:1-27). When it came time for Israel to cross the Jordan, the tribes reminded Joshua of this promise from Moses. They also remembered their agreement to first help their brothers take Canaan. They fulfilled that promise. And God fulfilled his. Jericho was given into their hands.

> "We now come
> together in faith,
> believing. . . . We
> ask that you remove
> from this boy any
> sign of the evil one."
>
> *Armageddon,* 139–40

Could God have accomplished this task without the help of these two-and-a-half tribes? Did God need the extra fighting men to overcome Canaan? You and I know the answer. He helped Gideon slay the Midianites with only three hundred men armed with trumpets (Judges 7). God doesn't need an army to fulfill his wishes. What God desired was for the Israelites to stay together. To fight alongside each other, even though the war had already been won. To be a team, united under one God and one cause.

Unity has always been a passion and priority with God. When Jesus prayed for all believers, present and future, unity was of utmost importance to him. "May they be brought to complete unity to let the world know that you sent me and have loved them even as you have loved me" (John 17:23, NIV). And being unified is more than just getting along with each other, shaking hands as we pass by in the sanctuary. Unity means standing shoulder to shoulder in the midst of battle. Going all the way to Canaan with our brethren.

When is the last time you tried to rally a team for an outreach project? Your church leaders set their sights on Jericho and then worked to mobilize the troops. The day finally came, and your army was missing more than a few soldiers. "That's not my gift," said one. "I'd come, but I'm busy with a project of my own," said another. But God says, "When one goes to battle, we all go to battle." Unity means going the distance with our brothers and sisters, not because God needs the numbers, but because we need each other.

REFLECTION
*When have you been guilty of staying behind when your brothers
and sisters forged on toward battle? What would God have
you do differently in the future?*

GOD THE REDEEMER

You will know that I am the Lord, when I deal with you
for my name's sake.   Ezekiel 20:44, NIV

HAVE YOU EVER given God reason to be angry with you? Have you ever been so steeped in sin that you tried to hide your face from his, convinced that his wrath was imminent? Compare your sins with the sins of Israel. As you read through the Old Testament, you discover a truth that seems to shock most people: At no time in Israel's history did they ever remain faithful to God. Of course there were periods of collective obedience when they honored God with their words and actions, and he always blessed them for it. But as soon as the blessings flowed, their hearts wandered, and once again they fell into their evil ways. Their lives were steeped in a constant pattern of rebellion and unfaithful living.

Ezekiel records just one of the many times God responded to Israel's unfaithfulness. God says to them, "In this also your fathers blasphemed me by forsaking me. . . . You continue to defile yourselves with all your idols to this day. . . . You say, 'We want to be like the nations, like the peoples of the world, who serve wood and stone.' . . . As I judged your fathers in the desert of the land of Egypt, so I will judge you, declares the Sovereign Lord" (Ezekiel 20:27, 31-36, NIV). Once again Israel had provoked the wrath of God, and now they sat awaiting his judgment. If there was ever a time that Israel deserved to be wiped from the face of the planet, it was this moment. In spite of all he had done for them, they continued to rebel, and now their sentence was at hand. Hold on to your chairs because here comes the gavel!

"You will know that I am the Lord, when I deal with you *for my name's sake and not according to your evil ways* and your corrupt practices" (Ezekiel 20:44, NIV, italics mine).

And what is God's name? *Redeemer. Deliverer. Savior.* What is the judgment he hands down? *He plans to redeem them.* Again. "You will know that I am the Lord, when I bring you into the land of Israel, the land I had sworn with uplifted hand to give to your fathers" (20:42, NIV). God's judgment on Israel is to once again bring them back home. He deals with them according to his goodness, not their evil. He forgives them. Not because they deserve it but because it is God's nature to forgive.

Do you think your sins could cause God to turn his back on you? You haven't felt love and acceptance until you've disappointed God.

REFLECTION
What sin has kept you from God? Why not ask him to restore you today?

GOD'S HAND OF DISCIPLINE

The Lord disciplines those he loves. Hebrews 12:6

I KNOW a young man in desperate need of discipline. He's not even a teenager, and already he's rude and crude and obnoxious. When I try to talk to him, he won't look me in the eye, and he answers every question with a sullen "Yeah" or "I dunno" or "Huh?" I've yet to see him carry on a pleasant conversation. Often I've wondered why his parents haven't taken the time to teach the boy some basic manners. In spite of his rude behavior, though, I haven't done anything to correct him. Why? Because he isn't my child.

You treat your own children differently than you treat other children. You have a vested interest in their behavior because they belong to you. They are part of your family, and you care how they grow up. God looks at us the same way. The writer of Hebrews says, "Have you entirely forgotten the encouraging words God spoke to you, his children? He said, 'My child, don't ignore it when the Lord disciplines you, and don't be discouraged when he corrects you. For the Lord disciplines those he loves, and he punishes those he accepts as his children'" (12:5-6).

God's discipline is a sign of ownership. His paddle on our bottom demonstrates our place in his heart. He reins us in because he loves us, and he cares deeply about the kind of people we grow into. "No discipline is enjoyable while it is happening," the writer continues, "it is painful! But afterward there will be a *quiet harvest of right living* for those who are trained in this way" (12:11, italics mine).

A father who loves his children longs for them to know the peace of righteousness. He wants them to feel the security that comes from a fruitful and productive life. Unruly kids grow up to be unhappy adults, and no father wants that for his children. He does anything and everything in his power to see that they keep their paths straight and their noses clean so that when they reach maturity, they will be dignified and wise and stable.

When you feel God's hand of discipline, take heed. But also take heart. Because the pain is a sign of his love.

REFLECTION
When was the last time you felt God's discipline on your life? How did your behavior change? Does it bring security to know that you are God's child?

THE MERCY SEAT

I want the people . . . to build me a sacred residence where I can live
among them. Exodus 25:8

IF YOU FIND yourself moved by God's holiness and love and power, just spend some time reflecting on his imagery. Scripture is filled with examples of God's propensity to speak to us through symbols and metaphors. Here's one to meditate on:

In Exodus 25 God is unfolding his plans for Moses to build the Ark of the Covenant. "I want the people of Israel to build me a sacred residence," God tells him, "where I can live among them" (25:8). God explains to Moses exactly how the Ark is to be built. "Make the Ark's cover—the place of atonement—out of pure gold. It must be 3¾ feet long and 2¼ feet wide. Then use hammered gold to make two cherubim, and place them at the two ends of the atonement cover. Attach the cherubim to each end of the atonement cover, making it all one piece.

> "The Lamb is Jesus Christ, the Son of God, who died for our sins."
>
> *Tribulation Force, 70*

The cherubim will face each other, looking down on the atonement cover with their wings spread out above it. . . . I will meet with you there and talk to you from above the atonement cover between the gold cherubim" (25:17-22).

The Ark was built as God directed, with two cherubim facing each other on each end of the atonement cover. God called it the "mercy seat." It was here that God met with his people.

Now let's fast-forward to another event in history. Mary Magdalene has just discovered the stone rolled away from the tomb where Jesus had been buried. John records, "Mary was standing outside the tomb crying, and as she wept, she stooped and looked in. She saw two white-robed angels sitting at the head and foot of the place where the body of Jesus had been lying" (John 20:11-12).

Another time in history, another place, another group of witnesses. But the scene is the same. Two angels seated on opposite ends of the burial cloth of Jesus. The cover of atonement. The Savior had once again come down to meet with his people, and standing at the entrance to the tomb, Mary saw what Moses saw. What all of humanity would soon come to recognize. The mercy seat of God.

REFLECTION
As you read through the description of the Ark of Covenant,
what thoughts come to your mind about God? Do you see other
bits of symbolism in the description?

THE FINGER OF GOD

As the Lord finished speaking with Moses on Mount Sinai, he gave him the two stone tablets inscribed with the terms of the covenant, written by the finger of God.   Exodus 31:18

MOSES SPENT forty days on Mount Sinai as God laid out his laws for Israel. When he was finished, God wrote his Commandments on tablets of stone for Moses to carry back with him. The stone tablets were "written by the finger of God" (Exodus 31:18). This was the law by which men would be judged by God.

It was this same law that the Pharisees quoted in the Temple courts when they brought an adulterous woman before Jesus. "'Teacher,' they said to Jesus, 'this woman was caught in the very act of adultery. The law of Moses says to stone her. What do you say?'" (John 8:4-5). The question was an attempt to discredit Jesus. The woman was irrelevant to their agenda—just a pawn used to try and corner the elusive King. You can almost hear them taunting Jesus. "You know the law, don't you Jesus? The one that God gave to us—the law that he wrote in stone with his own finger?"

And what is Jesus' response? He bends down and begins to write in the sand. Scripture doesn't tell us what he wrote, only that he wrote with his finger. The inscription was irrelevant, but the act was as significant as Jesus himself.

God has come in the flesh, and now he stands before an angry mob. A mob that is bent on wrath and "justice." And once again God begins to write. Only this time the message is not one of judgment and condemnation but mercy. "He stood up again and said, 'All right, stone her. But let those who have never sinned throw the first stones!'" (John 8:7). The crowds are silenced, and again Jesus bends to write in the sand.

In one single act of symbolism God takes his finger and rewrites the fate of humanity. The Law that was once written in stone will now be written on our heart. The God who laid out the punishment for sin has now come to earth to take our punishment upon himself. The finger that once condemned now pardons.

"Didn't even one of them condemn you?" Jesus asked the woman. "'No, Lord,' she said. And Jesus said, 'Neither do I. Go and sin no more'" (John 8:10-11).

REFLECTION
How do you normally respond when others are caught in sin?
Based on this story about Jesus, how should we respond?

FORGIVING OTHERS

*Be kind to each other, . . . forgiving one another, just as God through Christ
has forgiven you.*   Ephesians 4:32

THROUGH A SERIES of events, a wife happened to learn of her husband's past
infidelity. The act had occurred over a decade earlier, but the husband had kept it
a secret. When the wife found out, she was devastated.

The two met with a counselor, who suggested that they drop everything and
go away for several days to discuss their future. During this fateful trip they
needed to make a decision. Would they stay together, or would they separate? It
was the most critical decision of their entire marriage. The two prayed and talked
and wept together, and for a time it seemed as if their marriage might be over. The
woman had every right to leave, and she knew it. The husband knew it as well.

On the tenth night of their trip, the husband found a small note on his pillow.
With his heart in his throat, he picked the card up and turned it over. It read: *I forgive you. I love you. Let's move on.*

Nine simple words that might as well have been a symphony of mercy. He deserved nothing, yet he received everything. He expected wrath, but he got forgiveness instead. That's what God did for us when he sent his Son to die in our place.
He had every right to abandon us, and no one could have blamed him for it. But
he chose instead to redeem us.

Paul writes to the Colossians, "You must make allowance for each other's
faults and forgive the person who offends you. Remember, the Lord forgave you"
(3:13). He doesn't say, "Forgive and you'll get the upper hand," or "Forgive because they deserve it." He doesn't even say, "Forgive and you'll get rewarded." He
says to forgive because that's what God did for us. No catch. No stipulation. No
condition. Simply forgive.

We tend to focus on what's fair and right in a given circumstance. But God
wants us to do what's merciful.

REFLECTION
*Who has wronged you that you need to forgive? Why not pray
that God would help you do so today?*

CLOTHED IN MERCY

You must clothe yourselves with tenderhearted mercy.   Colossians 3:12

IT HAPPENED during the darkest days of Europe's history. Hitler was sweeping across the land promoting his contempt for Jews and his plan to exterminate them from the planet. Too often he found little resistance for his brand of race hatred. Many countries were easily conned by his propaganda.

But Denmark had a king that wasn't so easily taken in. He received Hitler's edict concerning the armbands that Jews would be required to wear. As king it was his job to relay this message to his people. So he went out on the balcony of his palace and began reading the edict line by line. The Danes gathered beneath him, listening carefully to every word. Hitler's henchmen stood watch at a safe distance. The king read the Nazi's note aloud, describing the armband that Jewish citizens must wear in order to be easily identified. Then when finished, he tucked the note away and reached into his pocket, pulling out a small yellow armband. The king slipped it onto his coat sleeve. Many of the Danes present did the same. Over the weeks to come, thousands of Danes found ways to acquire these yellow armbands and wore them whenever they went out in public, just as the Jews were forced to do. As a result, Hitler's men found themselves in a constant struggle to separate the Jews from the non-Jews in Denmark.[7]

> "'I feel such compassion for you,' Tsion [told Hattie], 'such a longing for you to come to Jesus.'"
>
> *Apollyon,* 274

George Eliot writes, "More helpful than all wisdom is one draught of simple human pity that will not forsake us."[8] Compassion is a trait within us that is very near the heart of God. In fact, Paul says that God is "the Father of compassion and the God of all comfort" (2 Corinthians 1:3, NIV). "Clothe yourselves with tenderhearted mercy," Paul writes to the Colossian church (3:12). Make it an integral part of your wardrobe. Put it on daily, as you would a hat or a sweater. Show mercy to others because it is through mercy that others see Christ's love within us.

"[Jesus] is the source of every mercy and the God who comforts us. He comforts us in all our troubles so that we can comfort others" (2 Corinthians 1:3-4).

REFLECTION
What does compassion produce within us (see 2 Corinthians 1:6)?
In what way should Christ's compassion flow through us?

85

CLOTHED IN KINDNESS

Clothe yourselves with . . . kindness.   Colossians 3:12

A DOCTOR once stepped into a taxicab and discovered an unusually friendly driver. He'd been in cabs before and knew how unusual this was, so he asked the man why he was so cheerful. "It all started," he said, "when I heard about a taxi driver who was so kind to a passenger that the man remembered him in his will, leaving him $65,000. I thought I would try it, and maybe somebody might leave me something. But after I tried it, I found it was so much fun being good that I decided I would do it for the fun of it, reward or no reward."[9]

Wrong motive—but nice idea. The world would certainly be a more cheerful place if we all had such good dispositions. Imagine walking down the street and seeing nothing but smiling faces. Every door you come to would be held open for you, and strangers would nod and wave as you passed. Flowers would always be in full bloom, and the spring would never leave your step.

Nice dream, but that's far from reality. The truth is, the world can be a mean place, and people can be a pain to live with. Life is not a bed of roses, and most people are too happy to let you know that. That's what we tell ourselves when we want to appease our guilt on those dark and dreary days. *I'm not the only one who's had a bad day,* we think. *People are just going to have to understand.*

Maybe they do, but how does Jesus feel about it? "You are the salt of the earth," Jesus tells us. "But what good is salt if it has lost its flavor? Can you make it useful again? . . . You are the light of the world. . . . Don't hide your light under a basket! Instead, put it on a stand and let it shine for all . . . so that everyone will praise your heavenly Father" (Matthew 5:13-16).

Kindness should flow out of the life of a Christian. That's what Jesus was trying to tell us. The world has an excuse to be angry, but we don't. Redeemed people should act like they're happy to be redeemed. Paul tells us, "Always try to do good to each other and to everyone else" (1 Thessalonians 5:15).

This is what separates believers from those who haven't discovered the goodness of Christ. We have a reason to rejoice. We have a standard to uphold. We have a Savior to pattern our life after. "Clothe yourselves with . . . kindness. . . . Let it be as a representative of the Lord Jesus" (Colossians 3:12, 17).

REFLECTION
Write down some characteristics of "salt" and "light" that believers should have. What are some concrete ways you can show these qualities?

CLOTHED IN HUMILITY

Clothe yourselves with . . . humility.   Colossians 3:12

IF IT WEREN'T for one problem, Gary's life would be perfect. He's a good-looking man with a beautiful wife. He has two wonderful children—one a healthy boy who was born just a few weeks ago. He's thirty-five-years old and just started a new career as a motivational speaker. And he's good at what he does.

Gary has always had a pretty good life. He was the star of his high school track team and a first-string baseball pitcher. In college he was recruited to play football, even though it wasn't his sport. The coach noticed his speed and knew he could make a first-rate running back out of him. Out of college Gary took a good-paying job and married a wonderful Christian woman, then started to climb the corporate ladder. He's always done well for himself. His parents love him, his wife adores him, his kids admire him, his friends want to be around him. Gary has the perfect life, except for one problem.

Gary has Lou Gehrig's disease. He was diagnosed in his twenties, and now at thirty-five has only a few short years to live. His new career as a speaker was born out of necessity. He can't work, and bills need to be paid, so he travels and talks to groups about how good God has been to him. Yes, you read that right. Gary's ministry is to travel the country and speak about God's goodness.

> "But she glows with a spirituality, a humility. She has a real Christlike quality."
>
> *The Mark,* 358

I heard Gary speak at a men's breakfast two weeks ago, and I'm still in awe of his gentle spirit in the face of terminal illness. "I thank God every day for my disease," he said. "Not because I look forward to dying, but because through this, God has shown me his mercy. He has drawn me closer to him than I ever thought I could be." The breakfast was scheduled to end at 8:30, but when 10:00 rolled around, not a man had left. Gary's humility so touched us that no one wanted to leave. So we lingered. Tears flowed freely, and God's presence filled the room.

"Humble yourselves before the Lord, and he will lift you up," says James (4:10, NIV). True strength is found only through humility. Disease may beat and crush the body, but it can't touch the spirit.

REFLECTION
Describe some traits of true humility. Do you feel that you have humbled yourself before God? If not, what pride still lingers in your spirit?

CLOTHED IN GENTLENESS

Clothe yourselves with . . . gentleness.   Colossians 3:12

SANDY ALLEN is listed in the *Guinness Book of World Records* as the world's tallest woman, but she should have been recognized for having the world's biggest heart. At over seven feet seven inches, Sandy stands heads above most people. But her claim to fame was not won without a lot of heartache and pain. Sandy has spent much of her life being stared at and made fun of by others. Her childhood was an especially cruel one. The children who didn't tease her simply ignored her. Her nighttime prayers were consumed by requests to be normal, like all the other girls. Sandy struggled to understand why God would allow her to be so different.

The disorder Sandy has is called acromegaly, "Giant's Disease." Sandy simply continued to grow, long after her friends had stopped. In the seventies she appeared on the *Tom Snyder Show,* and a band was so taken by her gentle spirit that they wrote a song about her. It was called "Hello Sandy Allen"—a glowing tribute to the woman the musicians had only met once but remembered for a lifetime. That's the kind of effect Sandy has on people. But make no mistake; behind the smiles is a well of sadness. "We are all different in some way," says Sandy. And she has chosen to use her plight to help others deal with difficult situations—especially children. "What I try to do is encourage people who might be down on their lives and down on life itself," she says. Sandy has made it her personal mission in life to teach the world the Golden Rule. "So in everything, do to others what you would have them do to you" (Matthew 7:12, NIV).[10]

We live in an age where personal worth is measured largely by outward appearance. Those who are different are the lepers of society—the outcasts of the modern world. It's the young and beautiful who get all the press and adulation. But God looks on the heart, and so should you and I.

"Don't be concerned about the outward beauty that depends on fancy hairstyles, expensive jewelry, or beautiful clothes. You should be known for the beauty that comes from within, the unfading beauty of a gentle and quiet spirit, which is so precious to God" (1 Peter 3:3-4). Sandy Allen knows her worth in the eyes of God, and that is where she finds her strength. It is also the key to her gentle and kind spirit in the face of pain and rejection. "Clothe yourselves with . . . gentleness," writes Paul (Colossians 3:12). Because gentleness is the only beauty that God sees.

REFLECTION
How would you define gentleness? Do you believe you have true beauty in the eyes of God?

CLOTHED IN PATIENCE

Clothe yourselves with . . . patience.   Colossians 3:12

MOST OF US would like to have more patience, but who has the time to work at it? Our "Things to Do" box is overflowing (mostly with deadlines that were yesterday), and we don't see much change soon on the horizon. Our calendars are so filled that we're scribbling in the margins, and still we can't seem to catch up. Hurry is the curse of a society measured in productivity.

Dr. James Dobson has some sobering words about our hurried pace of life:

> It isn't easy to implement a slower lifestyle. Prior commitments have to be met. Financial pressures must be confronted. The employer seldom asks if you want to accept a new assignment. Your business would fail without your supervision. Your patients have no other physician to whom they can turn. . . . There seems to be no place to stop. . . . Thus, we live our entire lives in the fast lane, hurtling down the road toward heart failure.[11]

It's no secret that a lot of us would like to slow down and live more relaxed lives. We all long for more peace and tranquility; we just don't know how to go about getting it.

The problem with this modern-day dynamic is that it leaves little time to focus on God and his will for our life. We're so busy producing that we never stop long enough to find out what God wants us to produce. A full calendar is the natural enemy of godly priorities. "A patient man has great understanding," says Solomon (Proverbs 14:29, NIV). Patience is the trait that God needs in order to relay his desires to our heart. God begins to speak when we stop and wait for him.

"Be still in the presence of the Lord, and wait patiently for him to act," says King David (Psalm 37:7). If you want to hear God, stop rushing, he is telling us. Linger in his presence. Allow yourself the time to sit back and meditate on God. Listen for the Lord's "gentle whisper" (1 Kings 19:12).

"Clothe yourselves with . . . patience," says Paul (Colossians 3:12). It is through slowing down and waiting that we feel God's power and presence.

> "Here is the patience of the saints; here are those who keep the commandments of God and the faith of Jesus."
>
> *Desecration, 394*

REFLECTION

Reflect on the fruit of the Spirit outlined in Galatians 5:22-23. Do these traits describe your character? What would the Lord have you pray about this?

THE LION'S JUDGMENT

The lion has roared.   Amos 3:8

THE PROPHET AMOS declares, "The lion has roared—tremble in fear! The Sovereign Lord has spoken—I dare not refuse to proclaim his message!" (Amos 3:8). When God put his message on Amos's heart, he was so shaken with conviction that keeping silent was not an option. Amos could no more keep quiet than could a prey about to be devoured by a ferocious lion.

Hunters will tell you that the lion is the undisputed king of the jungle. He enjoys total dominion over every other creature. Every animal cowers at the mere sight of one.

It's also a fact that lions don't roar until they have their prey. The purpose of their roar is to freeze the victim in its tracks. And when you hear a lion roar, you know that his prey has no chance of escape. When the prey is so near that it can't possibly get away and so frightened that it can no longer move, the lion roars, then pounces. The end is not only real—it's imminent.

Amos knew that God meant business. "The lion has roared—tremble in fear!" he says. He knew that God's wrath was so near that escape for Israel was no longer an option. They had avoided God's wrath in the past, but this time it was imminent.

Have you ever heard God roar? Has he ever sent warning flags so large that you cowered in fear and trembled in your tracks? Have you ever felt his breath on the back of your neck? ever felt his mane brush against your skin? Has he ever pounced, bringing discipline down so hard that it leaves you licking your wounds and wondering what happened?

God's judgment is not something we should take lightly. He is a patient God who overlooks many of our transgressions, but there are times when he knows he needs to act.

Don't make God come after you. Don't make him have to roar and pounce. Don't turn a deaf ear to his message.

REFLECTION
In what ways have you felt God's hand of discipline in your life? What are you doing to see that he doesn't have to "roar" to get your attention?

A HUMBLE HEART

I hate all your show and pretense.   Amos 5:21

WHEN GOD ROARED (Amos 3:8) in the presence of Israel through his prophet Amos, what was the message he was trying to bring? What was the proclamation that Amos could no longer keep silent about? In part it's this: "I hate all your show and pretense—the hypocrisy of your religious festivals and solemn assemblies. I will not accept your burnt offerings and grain offerings. I won't even notice all your choice peace offerings. Away with your hymns of praise! They are only noise to my ears. I will not listen to your music, no matter how lovely it is. Instead, I want to see a mighty flood of justice, a river of righteous living that will never run dry" (Amos 5:21-24).

When the lion opened his mouth to speak, he spoke out against the injustice and hypocrisy of his people. The Israelites were doing all the right things in their assemblies but all the wrong things in their cities. Their worship was mighty, but their hearts were rotten.

> "Rayford knelt silently. Eventually the emotion and fervency of the prayers so humiliated and humbled him that he was powerless to hide anymore."
>
> *Assassins,* 70

One thing God makes perfectly clear throughout Scripture is that he looks on the heart. God is never fooled by religious words or solemn worship. What he looks for is an obedient and contrite spirit.

Jesus told a parable about two men who went to the Temple to pray. One was a Pharisee, the other a tax collector. The proud Pharisee prayed in a loud voice, "I thank you, God, that I am not a sinner like everyone else, especially like that tax collector over there!" (Luke 18:11). But the tax collector knew he was unworthy, and his prayers took on a different tone: "O God, be merciful to me, for I am a sinner" (18:13).

The first man had spent his life in the synagogue, studying the laws of God and checking them off as he kept them. Religion was his obsession, and he threw himself into the work of the synagogue. The second man spent his life cheating others. He probably didn't even own a copy of the Scriptures. Yet he saw himself for what he was and despised what he had become. So he turned to God for mercy.

And which man found favor in the eyes of God? As always, it was the one whose heart was humbled and repentant. Before you and I get too caught up in our acts of praise and worship in the church, we should make sure that our spirit is right before God. Otherwise we may become just another proud Pharisee praying in the Temple.

REFLECTION
What did God want to see in place of Israel's worship?
Doesn't he want to see the same thing today?

PURPOSE VS. CONTENTMENT

*How terrible it will be for you who sprawl on ivory beds surrounded
with luxury.*   Amos 6:4

WHICH IS the bigger concern for you at the moment—to be comfortable and at ease or to share the greatest story ever told? Are you more interested in personal contentment or in making sure that God's Word is spread to those in your city?

Many of us may say that God's message of salvation is the primary focus of our life, yet our lifestyle often says otherwise. Through his prophet Amos, God warned Israel against this type of priority shift. "How terrible it will be for you who sprawl on ivory beds surrounded with luxury, eating the meat of tender lambs and choice calves. You sing idle songs to the sound of the harp, and you fancy yourselves to be great musicians, as King David was. You drink wine by the bowlful, and you perfume yourselves with exotic fragrances, caring nothing at all that your nation is going to ruin" (Amos 6:4-6).

God never called us to be comfortable; he called us to be holy. To be set apart from the world. To think and act and speak differently from the rest of society. Our thoughts and priorities should transcend the physical world and be driven instead by the spiritual realities we've come to understand. Our goal should be singular and unwavering—to bring others before God's throne. Our primary purpose and passion should be to save others from the pit of hell, just as God has saved us from it. So why do we still spend so much time seeking personal comfort? Why is the bulk of our money and time and energy spent on making our own life easier? Is it because we think we deserve it?

Too often we convince ourselves that God wants to manifest his blessings on his people in the form of ease and luxury. A friend of mine once said, "If there were no problems in the world, no one would ever talk to God." Heaven would be a lonely and quiet place if God's people didn't have a little pain and discomfort in their lives. And pain is not always a bad thing. Being uncomfortable is not always a sign of God's displeasure.

If you're feeling uneasy and distressed at this point in your life, chances are good that you're right where God wants you to be. You're being pulled and shaped by him, prodded toward something greater and nobler than personal comfort. And that's a good place to be.

REFLECTION
*Why does God use discomfort to get our attention? How might
he be trying to get your attention at the moment?*

WHEN PUNISHMENT IS WITHHELD

For we are only a small nation.   Amos 7:2

THE LORD SHOWED Amos a vision. In the vision God revealed his plan to bring judgment on Israel for its sins. He saw locusts swarming over the land, devouring Israel's crops. So Amos pleaded with the Lord not to do it. "Unless you relent, Israel will not survive, for we are only a small nation," he said (Amos 7:2). God heard his cries and pulled away his judgment.

A while later the Lord showed Amos another vision, similar to the first. Israel still disobeyed, so God planned to punish them with fire—fire so consuming that it would destroy both the land and the sea. Again Amos pleaded for clemency. "Unless you relent, Israel will not survive, for we are only a small nation" (7:5). Once more God showed mercy and refrained from punishing them.

Two times God showed Amos visions of devastation and destruction, and twice Amos appealed to God's mercy. "Don't do it God, for we are so small." God's compassion came through, and Israel was spared.

So often we insist on seeing ourselves as bigger than we really are. We think we're too big to need God's help. We think we've outgrown our need for God's provision and mercy and love. Sometimes we even think our sins are too big for the blood of Jesus to cover. But God sees us as we are. We are small children in need of guidance from a big and powerful Savior. We need his mercy, whether we admit it or not.

> "Dr. Ben-Judah, how does this square with your contention that these judgments are as much about God's mercy and compassion as they are about his wrath?"
>
> *The Remnant,* 390

Last week my two children were arguing before bedtime. I wasn't sure what started their bickering. I just knew it was late and they needed to make up and go to bed. I stood in the hallway between their bedrooms, shaking my head in frustration. "If you two don't stop arguing and go to sleep, I'm going to . . . I'm going to . . ." My mind went blank, and I couldn't think of how to finish the sentence. *What was I going to do?* The infraction wasn't that serious, and they're only kids. So I let it slide. "Just say you're sorry and go to sleep," I told them. "You'll feel better in the morning." Then I hugged them and went to bed.

Sometimes you and I need to be punished. We need God to step in and change our behavior. He knows it too. But when he looks at us, he sees how small and immature we are. He reprimands us but then lets the infraction slide. A merciful father knows that sometimes kids need to be punished, and sometimes they simply need a word and a hug.

REFLECTION

Can you think of a time when you deserved God's discipline, yet it didn't come? How does that make you want to please him even more?

FORFEITING GRACE

Those who worship false gods turn their backs on all God's
mercies.   Jonah 2:8

IT'S AMAZING how you can read a passage of Scripture a thousand times in your life and then suddenly find something in it that you've never seen before. That happened last night as my wife shared something she noticed in the story of the rich young man.

In this story the young man comes to Jesus and asks, "Teacher, what good things must I do to have eternal life?" Jesus answers him, "You can receive eternal life if you keep the commandments." Then he qualifies the statement by outlining several of the key laws in Scripture. "'I've obeyed all these commandments,' the young man replies. 'What else must I do?'"

Then comes Jesus' most sobering answer: "If you want to be perfect, go and sell all you have and give the money to the poor, and you will have treasure in heaven. Then come, follow me." The man walks sadly away because of his many possessions (see Matthew 19:16-22).

We've all heard the application. The man wanted to get to heaven on his own merit, but Jesus teaches that only God's grace can save us. "I am the way, the truth, and the life," says Jesus. "No one can come to the Father except through me" (John 14:6). The young man is convinced that keeping the law is the road to salvation, and Jesus simply dispels this pharisaical belief.

So what did we see in the passage that we'd never noticed before? Look at Jesus' final four words to the young man after asking him to sell all he had: "Then come, follow me" (Matthew 19:21). I've seen it a thousand times but never caught it. They are the same words Jesus uses when he calls each of his disciples. He doesn't utter those words to everyone. To the woman caught in the act of adultery he says, "Go and sin no more" (John 8:11). After healing the crippled man he says, "Pick up your sleeping mat, and walk" (John 5:8). When Jesus ministers to people he usually sends them home with a blessing, but this time his words are different. This time he says, "Follow me."

The question begs: Just what did the young ruler give up? We know he passed on salvation, but did he also pass on the offer to be a disciple of Jesus? We can't know for sure, but the text suggests it. "Those who worship false gods turn their backs on all God's mercies," records Jonah 2:8). We will never know what good things we give up by turning our backs on Jesus.

REFLECTION
Was Jesus singling out wealthy people with his words to his disciples
in this reading? If not, what is the application? What worthless idols
do you struggle with clinging to?

APRIL

A HEART FOR ETERNITY

God has made everything beautiful for its own time. He has planted eternity in the human heart. Ecclesiastes 3:11

MARSHALL SHELLEY, an editor of *Leadership* magazine, had a child who lived only two minutes. His son Toby came into the world on November 22, 1991, at 8:20 P.M. and took his last breath at 8:22. Marshall writes:

> My wife, Susan, and I never got to see him take his first steps. We barely got to see him take his first breath. I don't know if he would have enjoyed softball or software, dinosaurs or dragonflies. We never got to wrestle, race, or read. . . . What would have made him laugh? Made him scared? Made him angry?[1]

Toby was born with a rare genetic disorder that took his life just minutes after his birth. The Shelleys were devastated, and they cried out to God for answers. None seemed to come. Then, as if life hadn't dealt the Shelleys enough tragedy, just two months later they lost their little girl, Mandy. She was only two years old.

"In my flesh I do not look forward to death. . . . But to tell you the truth, in my spirit, I cannot wait."

Armageddon, 259

In the wake of these two excruciating losses, the Shelleys wrestled with God. *Why, God? Why did you do that? What was all that about?* Like any parent who loses a child, the Shelleys grappled to understand. How could a good God allow such pain and sorrow? It doesn't seem to make sense.

"Why did God create a child to live two minutes?" Marshall asked in his moment of deepest despair. He later answered that question, both for himself and others.

> He didn't. [And] he didn't create Mandy to live two years. He did not create me to live 40 years (or whatever number he may choose to extend my days in this world). God created Toby for eternity. He created each of us for eternity, where we may be surprised to find our true calling, which always seemed just out of reach here on earth.[2]

The wise king Solomon said, "God has made everything beautiful for its own time. He has planted eternity in the human heart, but even so, people cannot see the whole scope of God's work from beginning to end" (Ecclesiastes 3:11). When life seems completely unfair and out of control, the only place to look for comfort is toward heaven. That's what we were made for. And that's where the answer to all of life's suffering can be found.

REFLECTION
Are you struggling with a devastating loss in your life? What is the place to look to find comfort according to the words of Solomon?

FINDING FULFILLMENT

What do people get for all their hard work?   Ecclesiastes 1:3

IS THERE ANYTHING your heart deeply longs for? Maybe it's an accomplishment that you've always wanted to achieve or a promotion that you know you deserve. Maybe you want the house of your dreams or a car that's priced just outside of your budget. Is there a person that you long to know better, a child you've been trying to conceive, a book that you've wanted to write? Are you convinced that if you could just attain this special desire of your heart, you would then be happy and content? If so, you're not alone. We all desire and long for fulfillment. And we all chase after things that we're sure will fill those desires.

King Solomon made his life an experiment in personal fulfillment. He became the wisest and wealthiest man to ever live and still found that he lacked satisfaction. So he continued to pursue earthly desires, determined to find the one thing in life that would make him happy. I . . . tried to find meaning by building huge homes for myself and by planting beautiful vineyards. I made gardens and parks, filling them with all kinds of fruit trees. I built reservoirs to collect the water to irrigate my many flourishing groves. I bought slaves. . . . I also owned great herds and flocks. . . . I hired wonderful singers, both men and women, and had many beautiful concubines. I had everything a man could desire (Ecclesiastes 2:4-8).

Solomon made himself a poster boy of indulgence, acquiring things and people and wives like a boy would collect trading cards. Nothing was out of his grasp. Everything was within his vast means, and he was determined to find happiness. "Anything I wanted, I took. I did not restrain myself from any joy" (2:10).

And what did Solomon discover at the end of his experiment? "It was all so meaningless. It was like chasing the wind. There was nothing really worthwhile anywhere" (2:11). He found that it doesn't work. That fulfillment apart from God can never be obtained. That life on earth is wholly and completely meaningless apart from the hope of heaven. Our hope is found in knowing that earth is just a precursor to life's real glory and meaning. Ultimate fulfillment will be found, but not this side of heaven.

REFLECTION
Are you looking for fulfillment in the things you own or accomplish on earth?
What is God saying to you through Solomon's words?

THE PROBLEM OF INDULGING

God gives wisdom, knowledge, and joy to those who please him. But if a sinner becomes wealthy, God takes the wealth away and gives it to those who please him.   Ecclesiastes 2:26

WHEN THE KIDS were young, I would take the video camera out on Christmas morning and set it up on a tripod in one corner of the room as we all opened our presents. Often the tapes would be put away afterward, and we'd forget we had them. *Who has time to go through them?* But from time to time we'll take out our old tapes and watch them as a family, laughing at the memories we've caught on video. The kids love to see themselves toddling around in diapers, and they love to make fun of dad's funny haircuts from ten years ago.

We recently watched one of our old Christmas tapes in which both the kids were preschoolers and cute as could be. That particular Christmas we'd gone way overboard on the number of presents. As young parents are wont to do, we gave our kids everything they had asked for—and more. The tape shows paper and boxes and toys strewn all over the living room as our two children wandered through the middle of it all, playing with one toy, then throwing it aside and picking up another. Over and over we'd see them open presents that we'd forgotten they'd ever had. Most toys they seldom played with afterward, and all had long since been given to Goodwill.

I remember a sinking feeling in my heart as we watched the tape. The Lord used that time to speak to me in my spirit. *What are you teaching your children?* he asked me. *What does it say to them when you indulge their every desire?* I knew the answer before the question was asked. I quickly reminded myself that we had long since stopped overdoing Christmas the way we did when they were young, but still I knew that that wasn't what God was referring to. The number of gifts may have decreased, but still we strived to indulge.

Since that time we've made a conscious effort to point our children toward heavenly rewards, not earthly ones. By our actions, as well as our words, we want to teach them to put away earthly desires and instead look forward to "an inheritance that can never perish, spoil or fade" (1 Peter 1:4, NIV). The real rewards are awaiting us all in heaven. Everything else is just "stuff" waiting to be given to Goodwill.

REFLECTION
When do you find yourself trying to numb your desires through earthly indulgences? What concrete things can you do to reverse this damaging pattern?

A HOPEFUL FAITH

We are citizens of heaven, where the Lord Jesus Christ lives. And we are eagerly waiting for him to return as our Savior.   Philippians 3:20

THE SPANISH PHILOSOPHER Miguel de Unamuno set out to create a religion that would be both socially acceptable and intellectually respectable. He wanted a religion that was free of any sort of guilt or shame or remorse. A religion that was based on needs of the day instead of what he considered "medieval superstitions." He was tired of all the talk of "divine wrath" and "heavenly rewards," and he wanted his beliefs to be purged of all such things. No afterlife, no hell, no heaven.

He was certain he'd created the perfect religion, but first he wanted to test his philosophies to see if they appealed to the working class. He found a rather simple-minded peasant and explained his views, then asked the peasant what he thought. The peasant reflected for a moment then asked, "So what is this god for?" The philosopher was stumped.[3]

> "Keep yourselves in the love of God, looking for the mercy of our Lord Jesus Christ unto eternal life."
>
> *Desecration*, 325

The apostle Paul also discusses various religious beliefs regarding the afterlife in 1 Corinthians: "If there is no resurrection, 'Let's feast and get drunk, for tomorrow we die!'" (15:32). A religion without hope is no religion at all—it's just a way to numb the senses and appease the guilt. Try to take away the hope of an afterlife, and you've done nothing but create a hopeless philosophy of life. What good is a god that expects nothing and gives nothing in return?

"For just as there are natural bodies, so also there are spiritual bodies," Paul continues. "Just as we are now like Adam, the man of the earth, so we will someday be like Christ, the man from heaven" (15:44, 49).

Our destiny is far greater than earthly minds can conceive. Our faith is not built on superstition but on the inerrant Word of the one true God. And our hope rests not in vain philosophies, but in life everlasting.

REFLECTION
Who are the first and second Adams in this text? How do you envision your heavenly body?

DEALING WITH DISCOURAGEMENT

That is why we never give up.   2 Corinthians 4:16

I HEARD that the devil once had a garage sale. On the table before him were all the worn tools he had used for so long. The rusty hammers of harassment and intimidation, the knives of enticement and accusation, the blades of greed and envy—all were laid out with price tags. Lust was expensive, but not nearly as much as gossip. Pride was more than both combined. But one item was priced higher than all the others. It was plain but well worn. A simple tool, like all the rest, yet the cost was much, much greater.

"What is this?" asked a customer. "And why is it priced so high?"

"Ahh," the devil said, cradling the tool in his bony fingers. "How I cherish this. This is the most effective tool I've ever used. It works when no other item in my bag can do the trick. When lust and envy and greed and sloth fail to do their jobs—when pride can't make a dent—this finishes the job without fail. I have beaten more saints and sinners with this one tool than with all the others on the table."

"Well, what is it?" the customer asked in anticipation. "Discouragement," said the devil.

I'm sure this parable rings true to you. No matter who you are, you've struggled against Satan's most effective tool, because he wields it often. The apostle Paul speaks about discouragement in his letter to the Corinthian church: "We are pressed on every side by troubles, . . . crushed and broken. We are perplexed . . . hunted down. These bodies of ours constantly share in the death of Jesus" (2 Corinthians 4:8-10). Anytime you fight on the side of Jesus, Satan's wrath comes down hard on you. But the advice Paul gives to the Corinthians applies to us all: "Though our bodies are dying, our spirits are being renewed every day. For our present troubles are quite small and won't last very long. . . . For the troubles we see will soon be over, but the joys to come will last forever" (4:16-18).

The key to overcoming discouragement is to allow God to renew us inwardly day by day. And that is done through remaining heavenly minded. By focusing on eternal glory instead of temporal struggles. By letting God replace thoughts of failure with visions of heavenly rewards.

REFLECTION
How well do you handle discouragement when it comes to your life?
What can you do to thwart Satan's attempts to beat you down?

THINGS UNSEEN

So we fix our eyes not on what is seen,
but on what is unseen.   2 Corinthians 4:18, NIV

IN OUR LANGUAGE the word *fix* takes on a number of connotations. When we have a problem with our car, we take it to the mechanic and ask him to *fix* it. That's a good thing. But what if a prizefighter is caught *fixing* a fight? His name is marked forever. A junkie says he needs a *fix*. Not long ago I *fixed* my daughter's bracelet. If I didn't pay my taxes, I'd be in a *fix*.

But the word Paul uses when encouraging us to "fix our eyes not on what is seen, but on what is unseen" (2 Corinthians 4:18, NIV), has only one meaning. In the Greek the word is *skope*. It means an intensity of gaze—a determined, attentive searching out. It means to set your eyes on something and keep them there.

By Paul's definition, heaven is meant to be a total fixation with us—an obsession. Something worthy of our complete and unwavering attention. Not simply a passing thought during worship or a regular object of reflection, but a thing that is so real to us and so intensely on our mind that we lock our eyes and heart on it with total resolve. We become so heavenly minded that earth never quite feels like home.

This is the kind of focus that so endeared Abraham to God and made him the "father" of our faith (see Romans 4:16). The writer of Hebrews records, "It was by faith that Abraham obeyed when God called him to leave home and go to another land . . . for he was like a foreigner, living in a tent. . . . Abraham did this because he was confidently looking forward to a city with eternal foundations, a city designed and built by God" (Hebrews 11:7-10). Although Abraham was a wealthy man, he chose to live in tents in the desert, like a nomad in a strange land. How much more effective and focused would we be if we had that same attitude? What if we were so fixated on heaven that earth seemed no more to us than a tent in the desert?

Do you long to have the kind of faith that Abraham had? Do you want to be so in tune to God's will that obedience becomes second nature to you? Do you want to do great things for God's kingdom? Then look to Abraham's example, and fix your eyes and thoughts on heaven.

REFLECTION
In what ways do we "groan" while on earth? How does God's Spirit
help us become heavenly minded?

UNWAVERING FAITH

Be strong and steady, always enthusiastic about the
Lord's work.   1 Corinthians 15:58

JOHN HARPER was an evangelist during the early 1900s. His success in spreading the gospel in London became so widely known that Moody Church in Chicago brought him to the states to preach at a revival in the winter of 1911. The meeting went so well that he was invited back the following spring. So on April 11, 1912, thirty-nine-year-old Harper boarded a ship to America. His six-year-old daughter was with him. The ship they boarded had already made news around the globe as the most seaworthy vessel of all time. It was the maiden voyage of the SS *Titanic*.

> "God, fill me with courage, with power, with whatever I need to be a witness."
>
> *Left Behind*, 346

When the ship's fate became evident, Harper wrapped his daughter in a blanket and made sure she got onto one of the lifeboats. Then he went back to help other women and children do the same. Somewhere along the way, Harper took off his life jacket and gave it to another man. That man was later saved by the SS *Carpathia* and was able to give even greater detail about the faith of John Harper.

He said he passed by Harper several times in the water as the two struggled to stay afloat. The minister called out to him in the dark, "Are you saved?" The man admitted that he didn't know the Lord, so Harper began quoting Scripture to him. "Believe on the Lord Jesus and you will be saved," he said, quoting Acts 16:31. Before the man had a chance to respond, the two were separated by the waves. Soon afterward the currents brought them together again, and Harper continued his questioning. "Are you saved?" he yelled over the noise. "No, I can't say that I am," the man told him. Once more Harper quoted from the book of Acts before being carried away by a large wave. The man watched from a distance as Harper eventually sank to his death.

As the man later retold the story of his encounter with Harper, he said with reverence, "There, alone in the night, with two miles of water beneath me, I believed." John Harper's unwavering faith, even in the face of death, had brought the man face-to-face with his own mortality. And he called out to God for salvation. "I am John Harper's last convert," the man said.[4]

To his dying breath John Harper preached the salvation of Jesus. He gave himself fully to the work of the Lord, even to the disregard of his own life. And today countless people believe because of his tenacious faith. We can only hope that our legacy emulates his.

REFLECTION
Have you ever considered what you might do in a similar circumstance?
Does your faith hold the same level of strength and passion as John Harper's?
When have you applied that enthusiasm in your everyday life?

REDEEMED OF THE LORD

Your salvation is near.   Luke 21:28

MANY OF US have seen how the Old Testament prophesied the coming of Jesus. We've read the passages that describe the coming Messiah and his death, burial, and resurrection. The accuracy of these prophecies leaves no doubt about the authority of Jesus and the amazing authenticity of Scripture. But did you know that the Old Testament also speaks of the second coming of Jesus? If you didn't, don't be embarrassed. I've heard scholars say that the Old Testament is silent on Jesus' return. But let's look at a text from Isaiah: "The Lord has sent this message to every land: 'Tell the people of Israel, "Look, your Savior is coming. See, he brings his reward with him as he comes."' They will be called the Holy People and the People Redeemed by the Lord. And Jerusalem will be known as the Desirable Place and the City No Longer Forsaken" (Isaiah 62:11-12).

This is the prophecy that Jesus referred to when telling his disciples about his plans to return. "Those will be days of God's vengeance, and *the prophetic words of the Scriptures will be fulfilled. . . .* So when all these things begin to happen, stand straight and look up, for your salvation is near!" (Luke 21:22, 28, italics mine). The correlation is clear. And when we see it, we suddenly look at Isaiah's words with greater interest. You and I are the ones "Redeemed by the Lord." We are the "City No Longer Forsaken."

When Jesus comes, there will be judgment. There's no mistaking that truth. For those who have rejected his love, the day will be filled with distress and turmoil. But that's not the purpose of his coming. His purpose is for you and me. He's coming to redeem his people.

It's so very critical that we see Jesus' return the way that he sees it. Not as a day of wrath and judgment but as a day of love and salvation. A day of redemption. A day when the loving Savior of all humanity is coming to take his bride home. For those taken to heaven it will be a day of reward, and for those left behind it will be a day of second chances. Where is the wrath in that? God has only one purpose in mind. He wants "everyone to be saved" (1 Timothy 2:4).

REFLECTION
How have you viewed the second coming of Jesus? Does the thought of it bring you fear or comfort? Are you able to call Jesus your Redeemer?

WHITE AS SNOW

I can make you as clean as freshly fallen snow.   Isaiah 1:18

I HAVE A THING about seeing kids with food on their faces. It's become something of a running joke in our family. I can't stand to see babies—or anyone else, for that matter—with ice cream or spaghetti sauce or pizza smeared all over their faces and dripping from the corners of their mouths. I'm not sure where this aversion came from (probably a high chair long, long ago), but it's very real. And my kids think it's funny.

They had a good laugh at my expense a few weeks ago when we were watching one of the many funny home video shows on television. During one segment, the show highlighted a series of videos depicting kids with food on their faces. It was one of the most disgusting things I'd seen on TV, and my kids laughed aloud as I squirmed. During one such video, a child stood in his kitchen with his face, hands, legs, and feet all covered with chocolate sauce. Then, as if the scene weren't nauseating enough, a man walked over and kissed the kid on the mouth. My kids thought it was hilarious, but I had to look away.

> "The Bible is clear that all our righteousnesses are like filthy rags. . . . All have sinned and fall short of the glory of God."
>
> *Nicolae*, 314

What would make a man do such a thing? I thought to myself. *What kind of man would kiss a filthy kid on the mouth?* I knew the answer before the question even formed in my mind. A loving father, that's who. A man who doesn't even see the mess; he sees only his child. A man who is so totally in love with his boy that he'd wallow in the mud with him for an ounce of affection.

The prophet Isaiah describes the condition of humanity in words that each of us can understand: "We are all infected and impure with sin. When we proudly display our righteous deeds, we find they are but filthy rags" (Isaiah 64:6). Through the eyes of righteousness, you and I are like kids covered in sin from head to toe. Our unfaithfulness is so vile and disgusting that even we can't imagine someone wanting to come near us. But God doesn't see us that way. "No matter how deep the stain of your sins, I can remove it. I can make you as clean as freshly fallen snow" (Isaiah 1:18). That's how a loving Father sees his children.

REFLECTION
What is the correlation between these two passages?
Do you see yourself as God sees you?

NO FEAR OF DYING

Precious in the sight of the Lord is the death of his saints.
Psalm 116:15, NIV

HOW WOULD IT change your view of death if you saw it as God's gain? What if you understood your mortality as a treasure in the eyes of the Lord? your death as something he is looking forward to?

There is no greater fear in the hearts of men than the fear of the unknown. And there is nothing we know less about than death. We fear death because we don't understand it. Yet God says that the thing we dread the most is something he treasures deeply.

If you heard today that you had only three weeks to live, how would you feel? Would it make your heart sing? Would you rejoice? Would you call up your friends and family to share your good news with them? Probably not. Even those of us who eagerly long for heaven tend to cringe at the thought of dying. We know we have a glorious home waiting for us, yet we still hang on to earth. The comfort of the known outweighs our anticipation of the unknown. So we fight against death and hold on to life with all our might.

> "If you survive until the Glorious Appearing . . . imagine!"
>
> *Assassins, 270*

But let's look at it from God's perspective. How does he react when he hears that we're on our way home? *Make up the bed, get the room ready, set up the banquet table—my child is coming home!* "Precious in the sight of the Lord is the death of his saints," says the psalmist (Psalm 116:15, NIV). And why does God rejoice at an event that holds such fear for his people? Because he knows that death is just the beginning.

"O death, where is your victory? O death, where is your sting?" asks the apostle Paul (1 Corinthians 15:55). For those who put their faith in Christ, death no longer exists. There is no end to life, only a passing from one life to the next. We have nothing to fear and no reason to dread. So the next time you find yourself worried about dying, ask yourself this question: What matters most—the way I see things or the way God sees things? And remember the words of Paul: "In Christ all will be made alive" (15:22, NIV).

REFLECTION

Do you struggle with a fear of dying? What would God say to you in light of today's reading? How should salvation change our view of death?

TODAY'S READING
Psalm 22:1-25; Mark 15:34

NEVER FORSAKEN

My God, my God, why have you forsaken me?   Mark 15:34

DO ME A FAVOR and finish the following phrases. "A rose by any other name . . ." "A penny saved is . . ." "Two roads diverged in a wood and I . . ."

Did you have any trouble? I'm guessing not. The words are familiar to most of us. Which makes me wonder if we haven't misunderstood Jesus' cry on the cross, just minutes before his death.

Shortly before the Savior's final breath, he cries out, "My God, my God, why have you forsaken me?" (Mark 15:34). In the face of unimaginable pain and anguish, Jesus called out to his Father. Mark recorded the words, and I'm convinced that people have misinterpreted them ever since.

"It was the human side of Jesus," some have said. "It simply shows the degree of pain he was suffering." Maybe so, but I'm not so sure.

"When Jesus took our sin upon himself, God could no longer look at him," others speculate. "Jesus was begging God not to turn away." Once again I think the mark is missed.

I don't believe that Jesus was giving way to his humanity nor that God had turned his back on his Son. Our Savior was simply quoting Scripture. A passage that he knew from memory. A passage that those nearby should have remembered.

"My God, my God! why have you forsaken me?" begins a psalm of David. "Why do you remain so distant? Why do you ignore my cries for help?" The king's rhetorical poem asks the question, only to answer it a few lines later. "For he has not ignored the suffering of the needy. He has not turned and walked away. He has listened to their cries for help. I will praise you among all the people; I will fulfill my vows in the presence of those who worship you" (Psalm 22:1, 24-25). Jesus died with the same faith and dignity with which he lived. His pain was real, unbearable, yet he never forgot his mission. "I will fulfill my vows in the presence of those who worship you." And Jesus did just that.

REFLECTION
Have you ever felt forsaken by God? How do the words of David in this reading bring you comfort?

WHY NOT ASK?

I would have given you much, much more.   2 Samuel 12:8

WHAT IS IT that you lack in life? Is there something your heart desires—something you're convinced you will never have? Do you long for a fruitful marriage? Maybe you struggle to relate to your wife the way you wish you could. Maybe your husband doesn't look at you the way he once did, and you long to recapture his heart. Does your job fulfill you? Do your friends make you happy? Is your life all that you thought it would be? If not, then you aren't alone.

David had everything most of us can only imagine. He had wealth, power, prestige, women—and luxuries beyond what many can fathom. And on top of all that he had a meaningful relationship with God. What else could he possibly want?

He wanted Bathsheba. The bathing beauty from across the street. Although he had many wives, he longed for just one encounter with the beautiful Bathsheba. So David used his power to get what he wanted. He was blinded by his own desires and determined to get his prize, regardless of whom he might hurt along the way. Most of us know how the story ended. Bathsheba became pregnant, David had her husband killed, and his actions brought disgrace to Israel's throne.

> "There shall be showers of blessing; this is the promise of love. There shall be seasons refreshing, sent from the Savior above."
>
> *Armageddon*, 215

The web of deceit that David wove to get what he wanted would make a writer of soap operas blush. And on the heels of all this intrigue, what does God say to David when he finally gets his attention? "I anointed you king of Israel and saved you from the power of Saul. I gave you his house and his wives and the kingdoms of Israel and Judah. And if that had not been enough, I would have given you much, much more" (2 Samuel 12:7-8).

God says to David, "If you wanted more from me, all you had to do was ask." David was so busy trying to rearrange his life that he failed to think about the One who arranged it in the beginning. Who knows what blessings David forfeited by trying to find fulfillment on his own?

So let me pose the question again. What is it that you lack in life? Before taking things into your own hands, why not try asking the One who gave you life in the first place?

REFLECTION
What were the consequences David faced for his actions? What blessings might you be missing by taking things into your own hands?

THE LITTLEST WARRIOR

The Spirit of the Lord took possession of Gideon.　　Judges 6:34

IMAGINE THAT it's the last quarter of the last football game of the year. Your team is beaten and battered beyond hope, and all you can think about is sneaking away to the showers before the other guys have a chance to score another point. Suddenly, out of the locker room comes the legendary Coach "Bear" Bryant. He glances at the playbook and gathers your team into a huddle. "This ain't over yet, men," he says with a glint in his eye. "Trust me. We can still win this thing." The huddle breaks. He glares across the field at the other team, then turns to survey his wide-eyed players. *What's he going to do next?* you wonder. *Who's he going to send in?* Then just as your hopes soar, he does something that dashes them once again. He turns to your friend Mike. Little Mikey, you call him. The smallest guy on the team. The kid who couldn't catch a pass if his life depended on it. "It's all up to you, kid," the coach says as he sends him to the field.

That's how the Israelites must have felt when God sent an angel to Gideon. At the time they were so defeated by the Midianites that they lived in mountain caves and ate what little they could find on the ground. Every time they planted a crop their enemies raided the harvest. Their herds of sheep and cattle were stolen or killed. It was a dark hour in Israel's history, and time seemed to be running out quickly. And who does God call to save the people? Who does the Coach of coaches send in to turn the game around? Gideon. Little-bitty Gideon. The smallest man in the weakest tribe of all of Israel. The man who jumped at his own shadow is now expected to jump at the chance to bring victory to Israel. Imagine how that news might have lit the team up with excitement.

Gideon isn't easily convinced that he's the man for the job, but God doesn't give up easily. In spite of his doubt, Gideon slips on his helmet and goes to work. The enemy brings their forces together and camps just across the river, and suddenly Gideon starts to shine. "Then the Spirit of the Lord took possession of Gideon. He blew a ram's horn as a call to arms, and the men of the clan of Abiezer came to him" (Judges 6:34). To put an even finer point on his lesson, God dwindles his army down to three hundred, yet the enemy is still no match for his men. When the final play is over, Gideon's team is triumphant.

Do you think you're too unimportant to do mighty things for God? Do you wonder how he could ever use someone so small and insignificant? Then the story of Gideon could be yours. When God calls you to battle, just put on your helmet and go. Let him worry about the details.

REFLECTION
What happened to Gideon after God's Spirit came upon him? Have you ever felt the Spirit of the Lord come upon you? What is keeping you from doing great things with God's help?

THE SPIRIT'S HELP

When the Spirit of truth comes, he will guide you into all truth.
John 16:13

IGNACE PADEREWSKI was more than the prime minister of Poland—he was also a world-renowned pianist. Often the Polish leader would conduct live performances for the people of his country. The story is told that before one such performance, while the audience was still making their way to their seats, a young boy somehow slipped away from his mother and found his way onto the stage. In front of the spotlights, the boy crawled up onto the seat in front of the theater's polished Steinway and began picking out a song he had learned in music class: "Twinkle, Twinkle, Little Star."

> "All Rayford could do was pray. 'Lord,' he said silently, . . . 'Thank you for helping me find the truth.'"
>
> *Nicolae, 132*

The crowd laughed, and the boy's mother gasped. But before she had a chance to retrieve her young son, Paderewski appeared on the stage and stood behind him. "Don't quit. Keep playing," he whispered to the boy. The master leaned over with his left hand and began softly filling in a bass part. Then his right arm reached around the other side, encircling the child, and a running obbligato filled the auditorium. Soon the two were playing in such beautiful sync that the crowd was left mesmerized. They finished the tune, and the audience begged for more.[5]

Do you ever feel completely inadequate for the task before you? Do you sometimes feel like a young boy on the seat of a grand Steinway on the world's great stage? The people in the audience are expecting a world-class concerto, and the only song you know is "Twinkle, Twinkle, Little Star." You hear them laughing at a distance, but you're afraid to look up. You just keep your eyes forward and continue to play, hoping your mother will rescue you soon.

Jesus promises the Holy Spirit to help us. "When the Spirit of truth comes, he will guide you into all truth. . . . He will bring me glory by revealing to you whatever he receives from me" (John 16:13-14).

The Master knows that we need help, and he's standing right behind us, with his arms around our sides. What the audience hears is what he wants them to hear. Don't try to go it alone. Let the music of his life bring fullness to the music of ours.

REFLECTION
What "truth" will the Holy Spirit guide us into? In what ways does he promise to help us?

A SAVIOR OF GRACE

*The cloth that had covered Jesus' head was folded up and lying
to the side.*   John 20:7

YOU COULD READ the passage a thousand times and never catch it. You could meditate on John's account of Jesus' resurrection for hours and still not come away with this particular thought. It's so subtle that you might never find it. In fact, I'm convinced I would have never seen it had my wife not pointed it out to me. We were sitting in church while the passage was read, and she reached over and put her finger on my Bible, bringing a phrase to my attention. "I've never noticed that before," I told her. Neither had she. See if you can find the words she pointed out.

"Simon Peter arrived and went inside. He also noticed the linen wrappings lying there, while the cloth that had covered Jesus' head was folded up and lying to the side" (John 20:6-7).

Does anything stand out? Any phrase seem to jump out at you? Let me narrow it down. "The cloth that had covered Jesus' head was *folded up.*" When the disciples looked into the empty tomb of Jesus, what was the first thing they saw? They saw his head cloth "folded up" on the seat where Jesus once lay. It wasn't thrown across the room in victory, it wasn't lying in a heap on the floor; it was neatly folded and placed on the bench. Does this speak to you like it does to me? It must have made an impact on John since he took the time to record it.

Jesus comes back to life after all he's been through, and he takes the time to fold his sheets? Jesus bursts through the gates of hell, steals the key, deals Satan and his demons a fatal blow, then finishes the act by rising victoriously from the grave, and then what does he do next? Does he pump his fist in victory? Does he shove the stone away with supernatural might and claim his authority to the guards? No. He sits and folds his head cloth. He lays it on the bench and waits for the angel.

Doesn't that speak volumes about the character of Jesus? Isn't that the way you like to picture him? I know I do. Jesus was a man of unlimited power and strength, yet he lived with incredible humility and restraint. He didn't come to show us how mighty and omnipotent he is—he came to complete a mission.

REFLECTION
*How does this picture of Jesus give you comfort? How can you live daily
with the same grace and dignity with which Jesus lived and died?*

HE IS RISEN

Then the other disciple also went in, and he saw and believed.   John 20:8

IT HAPPENED in the middle of Moscow's Red Square on May Day 1990. Communism was still the reigning form of government in the Soviet Union. Mikhail Gorbachev was in power but slowly losing his grip on a nation deeply in debt and under growing dissension from the people.

Shortly before the regime crumbled, a parade was held. The route passed directly in front of the platform where the aging Soviet Leaders, including Gorbachev, sat. First came the mighty military machines that defined the Russian mind-set. The great Union of Soviet Socialist Republics and an endless procession of tanks, missiles, and troops all honored the Communist Party elite as they went by. Behind them marched a giant crowd of protestors—an uncommon and unwelcome sight in a country ruled so long by iron fists. The faces of the leaders showed no sign of worry or capitulation.

Next in line in the procession two lone priests carried a large crucifix on their shoulders. It was steadied by ropes held by a handful of parishioners marching closely behind them. The cross was large and unyielding, hovering high above the small group of followers.

Just as the throng passed directly in front of the Soviet leaders, who stood sternly in their place of honor high above the crowd, the priests hoisted the large crucifix toward the sky. From Gorbachev's platform, as he looked out over the procession, the cross completely obstructed his view of the giant posters lining the square—Karl Marx, Friedrich Engels, and Vladimir Lenin. None could be seen through the shadow

> "Will you trust a God like that? Can you love a God like that?"
>
> *The Remnant,* 232

of this mighty crucifix staring back at the Russian leader. At that very moment a voice pierced the noon air. "Mikhail Sergeyevich!" shouted one of the priests. "Christ is risen!" It was a sobering moment in time. Within months of that event, the Soviet Union was officially dissolved.[6] The truth of a risen Savior changes everything.

When the disciples peered into the empty tomb of Jesus, what they saw left them speechless. There lay the burial cloth of the Savior. Jesus was risen, and they knew that nothing would ever again be the same. "[Peter and] the other disciple also went in, and he saw and believed—for until then they hadn't realized that the Scriptures said he would rise from the dead" (John 20:8-9). He is risen indeed!

REFLECTION
Have you come face-to-face with the risen Savior?
How have you allowed it to change your life?

ALIVE IN CHRIST

You died when Christ died, and your real life is hidden
with Christ in God.   Colossians 3:3

SOMEWHERE in the night, around 1:00 A.M., eighteen-month-old Erika awoke from her sleep and began walking around the house. Maybe she was in a trance. Or maybe she wanted a glass of milk. No one knows for sure. They only knew that somehow Erika ended up outside. She walked out the back door and into the cold of night, barefoot on the frozen snow. Twenty feet from the house, Erika lay down on the ground, curled up into a ball, and died. Tiny footprints wound throughout the yard, as if she were in a strange daze.

Her mother was the first one to find her. It was around five in the morning before she noticed her little girl missing. She screamed and ran to her child, cradling her stiff and lifeless body in her arms and sprinting back into the house. She called 9-1-1, and within minutes the paramedics were there, trying desperately to revive little Erika. All the way to the hospital they tried, but to no avail. Further efforts were made in the emergency room, but no one could bring Erika back to life.

Suddenly, after hours of frustration, almost out of nowhere a nurse noticed a sign of breath. The baby's heart monitor blipped. Her eyes twitched. Erika was coming back. The doctors worked feverishly, and within a few minutes she woke up. Tired but very much alive. Before the week was out, Erika had fully recovered.[7]

One moment Erika was dead, and the next she was back among the living. Her mother was days away from burying her little girl and instead found herself embracing her child once again. It's likely that Erika and her mother will forever carry this moment of destiny with them. Her mother will retell the story in detail to anyone willing to listen.

"Even while we were dead because of our sins, he gave us life when he raised Christ from the dead," Paul reminds us (Ephesians 2:5). At one time we were all just like Erika. Dead in sin. No hope of a future among the living. Then suddenly Jesus changed all that. He defeated death and brought us back, and now we breathe again. How can we help but let it forever change the way we see our future?

REFLECTION
How often do you reflect on the gift of life that Jesus brought to you?
How should that change the way you view yourself and others?

REAL LOVE

We know what real love is because Christ gave up his life for us.
1 John 3:16

A YOUNG BOY was sitting in the waiting room of a hospital worried about his sick sister when a doctor sat down beside him. The boy's parents sat on the other side. The doctor explained to the boy that his sister needed a blood transfusion and that he was one of the few people with the kind of blood that she needed. Both he and his sister had very rare blood types, the doctor explained. And unless his sister received this transfusion, she would probably die.

"Would you give your blood to Mary?" the doctor asked. Johnny hesitated and bit his lip to keep it from quivering. "Sure, for my sister," he said, smiling to hide his fear.

Soon the two children were wheeled into the hospital room. Mary was pale and thin. Johnny was robust and healthy. Neither spoke as the nurse inserted the needles into their arms, beginning the transfusion. Johnny's smile faded as he saw the blood flow through the tubes. He laid his head back on his pillow and closed his eyes. His face never changed. When the procedure was almost done, he looked up at the doctor and with a slightly shaken voice asked, "Doctor, when do I die?"[8]

> "There's no doubt in my mind that nothing can separate you from God and his love."
>
> *Desecration, 21*

I hope someone was quick to hug the selfless child!

Jesus says, "I command you to love each other in the same way that I love you. And here is how to measure it—the greatest love is shown when people lay down their lives for their friends" (John 15:12-13).

If you want to know the depth of people's love, just look at how much they are willing to sacrifice for you. If you wonder what people think of you, look at what they're willing to do for you. When people are willing to pay the ultimate price, you no longer have to wonder if their love is genuine.

You and I may never be called on to give up our life for someone we love. But people will know just the same, because how we live says as much about us as how we're willing to die.

REFLECTION
According to today's reading, how will we know what real love is? Can you say honestly that you display the love of Christ to those around you? Can you give examples of how you do that?

THE GREATEST STORY

When we were utterly helpless, Christ came . . . and died
for us sinners.   Romans 5:6

ODESSA MOORE knew that her assignment wouldn't be an easy one, but she took it anyway. Someone needed to minister to people in prison, and Moore was committed to serving wherever the Lord sent her.

One day she ran across a juvenile awaiting trial for first-degree murder. His eyes were so filled with hate and anger that she almost passed him by and went on to the next cell, but something told her she had to try. So she sat across from the young man and began to talk. His story was a common one. His father was an addict, and his mother an alcoholic. Both parents beat and abused him. All of his life the boy had been told he was worthless. No one cared for him, and he certainly didn't care for anyone else. "There is someone who loves you," Odessa told him. The boy just turned away in anger.

"No way," he said. "Nobody!"

"You're in here for murder, right?" Odessa asked the boy, trying to keep the conversation going.

"Yes, and I'll do it again," the young man snapped.

"How would you like it if someone came in here tonight and said, 'I am going to take your place for you'? How would you like that?" Suddenly she had the boy's attention. He perked up and began to listen, and she used the opportunity to tell him about Jesus. She told him the story of the Cross and the redemption that was won there for all who accept him. By the end of the evening, the stone-cold teenager had melted, weeping tears of remorse and repentance. That night he committed his life to Christ.[9]

There's something about the story of Jesus that touches even the most sinful and hardened heart among us. His grace is something we all need. His forgiveness is something we all crave deep within our soul. We all want to believe that someone could love us enough to die in our place. To do for us what Jesus willingly did. It's the greatest story ever told, and the greatest one any of us will ever hear. We all need a Savior.

REFLECTION
How often do you reflect on the price that Jesus paid for your sins?
How should we live in light of his sacrifice? When is the last time you
shared the story of Jesus with someone else?

SAVED FOR HEAVEN

I keep working toward that day when I will finally be all that Christ Jesus saved me for and wants me to be.   Philippians 3:12

AS BELIEVERS, most of us can readily explain what Jesus saved us from, but how often do we consider what he saved us *for*?

In short, Jesus saved us *from* eternal condemnation. What he did on the cross saved all who would trust him from the certainty of spiritual death—from an eternity of endless suffering and pain. He saved us from a life of hopelessness and despair—a life of living meaninglessly, day after day, knowing that death will bring even greater misery.

Many would call that the Good News, but it's only a small fraction of it. The greatest part of the story is what Jesus saved us *for*. He saved us for a life in heaven for eternity. He saved us for the joy of getting to live with him forever, of moving past this world some day and into an existence beyond our wildest imagination. He saved us so that we could have eternal life with no more pain and heartache. He saved us so that we could one day rule with him.

"I keep working toward that day when I will finally be all that Christ Jesus saved me for and wants me to be," says Paul. "No, dear brothers and sisters, I am still not all I should be, but I am focusing all my energies on this one thing: Forgetting the past and looking forward to what lies ahead, I strain to reach the end of the race and receive the prize for which God, through Christ Jesus, is calling us up to heaven" (Philippians 3:12-14).

> "If you agree that God is using the period we now live in to get people ready for the millennial kingdom and for eternity, what will you do with your life?"
>
> *The Remnant,* 232

I once made an attempt to share the gospel with a friend, but all I succeeded in doing was to push him farther away from God. My efforts were sincere, but my brand of evangelism left a lot to be desired. I told him all he needed to know about hell but never quite got around to heaven. He left in a huff, and I was left wondering how someone could be so stubborn.

If freedom from hell is the only good news we have to share, then we won't find many people interested in sticking around for the punch line. The gospel of grace is about heaven. It's about life, not death. It's about living in eternal happiness, not just escaping eternal hopelessness. It's about what Jesus has done, not about what Satan wants to do.

REFLECTION

Is your mind set on things above? How do we go about focusing our energies on "what lies ahead"?

$3 WORTH OF GOD

*Anyone who puts a hand to the plow and then looks back is not fit
for the Kingdom of God.*   Luke 9:62

"I WOULD LIKE to buy $3 worth of God, please, not enough to explode my soul or disturb my sleep, but just enough to equal a cup of warm milk or a snooze in the sunshine. I don't want enough of him to make me love a black man or pick beets with a migrant. I want ecstasy, not transformation; I want the warmth of the womb, not a new birth. I want a pound of the Eternal in a paper sack. I would like to buy $3 worth of God, please."[10]

I have a friend with an attitude that bothers me deeply. He is a believer who attends church on a regular basis. Most of his friends are Christians, and so is his family. My friend would get upset if you doubted his faith or salvation, and he'd probably be able to recite a verse or two to prove his standing. Yet something about him bothers me. And at the risk of sounding judgmental, I'll tell you what it is: my friend doesn't remind me of Christ.

Although he professes to be a follower, I see little in his life that illustrates his faith in Jesus or his desire to be different from the world. Although I can't see into my friend's heart, I can see his actions. And I have legitimate concern for his standing before God.

Jesus had a sobering message for those who claim him in words but deny him in their deeds. "Not all people who sound religious are really godly. They may refer to me as 'Lord,' but they still won't enter the Kingdom of Heaven. The decisive issue is whether they obey my Father in heaven. On judgment day many will tell me, 'Lord, Lord, we . . . performed many miracles in your name.' But I will reply, 'I never knew you. Go away'" (Matthew 7:21-23).

Trying to buy only $3 worth of God is a dangerous proposition. And it doesn't work. Jesus is looking for followers who are wholly devoted to him and his Word, and who are willing to forsake the things of this world in deference for the next.

REFLECTION
*Are you trying to be satisfied with "$3 worth of God"? What message might
Jesus have for you in light of today's reading?*

HOLDING BACK YOUR HEART

Make sure that your own hearts are not evil.   Hebrews 3:12

WHEN TERRY became a Christian, he decided to turn everything over to God.

He gave his career to God. After graduation from college, he went into full-time youth ministry work. With his winning smile and approachable personality, Terry quickly endeared himself to the young people of his church.

He gave his marriage to God. Terry married a beautiful Christian woman who pledged to work side-by-side with him in the daily chores of his ministry. She understood the demands of church work and was willing to make the needed sacrifices.

He gave his children to God. Two precious children. He read to them from the Bible, taught them all about Jesus, and prayed with them every night before bedtime.

He gave his possessions to God. His house was always open to the kids he ministered to. On more than a few occasions, Terry opened his home and his wallet to a stranger in need. If you needed to borrow his car, all you had to do was ask.

But there was one part of Terry that he just couldn't seem to turn loose of. He tried to let go, but he couldn't. It was the part of him that wanted desperately to be liberated from the constraints of ministry, marriage, children, and responsibility. The part that wanted to be free. So one clear, sunny day, Terry decided to leave. Without notice. Without a clue as to why or where he went. His car was found on a dirt road outside of a small town in Texas, with his wallet and keys on the ground beside it. No note, no explanation, no sign of abduction. No Terry. An investigation would eventually find him in a faraway state with a different life and a different lover. Terry was finally free.

The part of Terry that he couldn't give up was the one part that Jesus most needed to change. He couldn't surrender himself. Terry gave everything to Jesus but his heart, and in the end, his heart took it all back. The writer of Hebrews warns, "Be careful then, dear brothers and sisters. Make sure that your own hearts are not evil and unbelieving, turning you away from the living God" (3:12).

REFLECTION
Is there a part of you that you haven't yet surrendered to God?
If so, why not pray today that he will help you do that?

THE PROBLEM OF GREED

For a greedy person is really an idolater who worships the things
of this world.   Ephesians 5:5

A SEVENTY-ONE-YEAR-OLD woman in West Palm Beach, Florida, was found dead in her apartment. The cause of death was malnutrition. She'd lived in the poorest section of the city's low-rent district for as long as anyone could remember. Neighbors described her as a pitiful and forgotten widow who spent most of her days digging through Salvation Army bins for clothes. When she wasn't doing that, she was begging for food at the back alley entrances of local restaurants. The woman had no family or friends to be found. She was given a pauper's grave and forgotten.

But an investigation into her death would soon prove enlightening. Two keys turned up in her apartment that led to two safety deposit boxes in different banks. The first contained over $200,000 in cash, along with a host of valuable bonds and financial securities. The second box contained only money. Lots of it— $600,000, to be exact.[11]

> "That kind of money gets a man's attention. He becomes willing to make concessions for it."
>
> *Left Behind, 296*

The woman whose life of poverty brought pity from all who knew her was in reality a millionaire widow who would rather starve than spend a penny of her monthly Social Security checks. She was completely consumed with greed.

Greed is perhaps the deadliest of the seven deadly sins. Peter calls its victims "an accursed brood . . . springs without water" (2 Peter 2:14, 17, NIV). Greed "drives us to compromise principles of justice, yield on the canons of morality, and even to lose our souls," writes Tony Campolo.[12] But it is Paul, I think, who says it best. "You can be sure that no immoral, impure, or greedy person will inherit the Kingdom of Christ and of God" (Ephesians 5:5).

Simply stated, a lust for possessions and a life in Christ cannot coexist. A person can have one or the other but not both. Either we love God or we love money. The chasm between greed and Jesus is so wide that we can't possibly have a foot on both sides at the same time. This is one fence that simply can't be straddled.

REFLECTION
Do you struggle with greed in your life? What have you done
to release your grip on the things of this world?

OVERCOMING GREED

Be rich in good works . . . give generously to those in need,
always being ready to share with others.   1 Timothy 6:18

GREED IS NOT a new concept. It has been around since the beginning of time. It was greed—the lust for something more—that brought down Adam and Eve in the Garden. The children of Israel constantly turned their backs on God in their lust for earthly treasures. And Jesus encountered its victims at every turn. When he wasn't toppling over money-changing tables in the Temple or having dinner with money-grabbing tax collectors, he was staring into the back of a rich young ruler, walking away with a full wallet and an empty soul. Ironically enough, it was greed that eventually sold him into the hands of Pilate.

Today, greed continues to rear its ugly head at every opportunity. We all struggle with it. I have to remind myself daily that the joys of sacrifice and contentment far outweigh the thrill of a new car or the status of a bigger house. I still tend to measure success in silver, and self-worth by the number of zeros at the end of my paycheck. The rivers of materialism run so deep and rampant throughout society that at times it's all we can do to keep from drowning in it.

So what do we do about it? How do we keep our lust for possessions from taking control of us? How do we keep ourselves afloat in the middle of greed's fast-rising tide? Part of the solution can be found in Paul's first letter to Timothy: "Tell those who are rich in this world not to be proud and not to trust in their money, which will soon be gone. But their trust should be in the living God, who richly gives us all we need for our enjoyment. Tell them to use their money to do good. . . . By doing this they will be storing up their treasure as a good foundation for the future so that they may take hold of real life" (6:17-19).

The most effective way to overcome greed is to begin using what we have for the good of others. And to start focusing on future treasures in heaven instead of the worthless ones we've accumulated on earth. That's how to take hold of "real life."

REFLECTION
Do you find that it appeases your desire for things when you help others?
What have you done lately to help someone else? What can you do
to actively store up riches in heaven?

AN UNFAILING GOD

I will never fail you.   Hebrews 13:5

A BATTLESHIP had been at sea on maneuvers in heavy weather for several days. Visibility was poor because the fog was thick and patchy, so the captain of the ship remained on the bridge, keeping an eye on all activities. Shortly after dark the ship's lookout reported seeing a light in the direction of the starboard bow. "Is it steady or moving astern?" asked the captain. "Steady, captain," came the reply. After further watch the captain knew that they were on a collision course with this other ship, so he called out to the signalman, "Signal that ship: We are on a collision course. Advise you change course 20 degrees."

The signal was sent, and immediately one was returned. "Advisable for you to change course 20 degrees," was the response. The captain quickly had another signal sent. "I am a captain. Change course 20 degrees."

Once again a response came quickly. "I am a seaman second class. You had better change course 20 degrees."

By this time the captain was furious, and he barked another signal. "I am a battleship. Change your course!"

Back came a simple message. "I am a lighthouse."[13] Needless to say, the captain changed his course. He knew that he could bark at the lighthouse all he wanted yet never cause it to move. Some things in life are constant and unchanging. They are the beacons that guide the rest of us throughout life.

> "To you who share my faith and are willing to be faithful unto death, remember the promise."
>
> *Armageddon, 279*

God's faithfulness is like that. It is one constant that will never change, never give way, never move. Joshua says to his people, "Deep in your hearts you know that every promise of the Lord your God has come true. Not a single one has failed!" (Joshua 23:14). That sentiment echoes throughout the universe.

"I will never fail you. I will never forsake you," God promises us (Hebrews 13:5). We can bark and complain all we want, but in the end, we are the ones who will have to adjust our course. Because lighthouses don't move.

REFLECTION
In what ways does God's faithfulness bring us confidence?
Do you find comfort in knowing that he will never fail you?

FINDING MIDDLE C

He alone is my rock and my salvation.   Psalm 62:2

AUTHOR LLOYD DOUGLAS tells of a time that he lived in a boarding house as a university student. Below him, in the apartment on the first floor, lived an elderly retired music teacher. The man was crippled and unable to leave his apartment. Douglas said that he had a regular ritual he developed, mostly as a means of keeping an eye on his infirm friend. Each morning before school, Douglas would open the front door to the man's apartment and ask in a booming voice, "Well, what's the good news?"

The old man would pick up his tuning fork, tap it on the side of his wheelchair, and say, "That's middle C! It was middle C yesterday; it will be middle C tomorrow; it will be middle C a thousand years from now. The tenor upstairs sings flat, the piano across the hall is out of tune, but my friend, that is middle C!"

A lifetime in music had taught the old man one thing upon which he could depend. Everything else may change, but one constant will always remain: middle C.[14]

If you've ever played in an orchestra, you know how important middle C is to the music. A fifty-piece ensemble could give a flawless performance on stage, but just let one lone trumpet play out of tune, and it ruins the entire concert. Orchestras depend on the constancy of middle C for the success of their composition.

Life is the same way. We need a true north on which we can depend. Something that will never change and never fail. Something constant, like God. "'The mountains may depart and the hills disappear, but even then I will remain loyal to you. My covenant of blessing will never be broken,' says the Lord" (Isaiah 54:10). God is the middle C of life. He is the one note on which all others depend for success and continuity. If we set our instruments to him, our song will ring out pure and true. If we don't, we'll always find ourselves out of tune.

In a world of false ideas and scattered voices, it's nice to be part of an orchestra that plays faithfully to middle C.

REFLECTION
In what ways is it comforting to know that God is faithful?
How can you put your trust in him completely, instead of listening to other voices promising fulfillment?

THE STAFF OF GOD

In his hand he carried the staff of God.   Exodus 4:20

IF YOU FIND yourself in awe of what God can do through the life of a person, just look at what he did with a shepherd's staff. It's just an inanimate object with no power of its own, but in God's hands it became mightier than all the kings and kingdoms of Egypt.

When Moses appeared before the burning bush, his staff was nothing but a walking stick—a branch from a dead tree. "What do you have there in your hand?" God asked him. "A shepherd's staff," Moses replied. Then God commanded him to throw it on the ground, and it became a snake. In the hands of Moses it was useless and dull, but under God's direction it became a powerful tool for deliverance. At the end of their encounter on the mountain, Moses set off toward Egypt to free God's people. "In his hand he carried the staff of God" (see Exodus 4:2-20). What was once a simple shepherding stick had now become the staff of God. The title had suddenly changed hands, and now amazing things were about to happen. It was through this staff that God performed mighty miracles in the company of Pharaoh. And with it, Moses was able to deliver Israel from slavery.

Only God can take a simple piece of wood and turn it into an instrument of redemption. The phenomenal success of the Left Behind series of novels is just one more testament to that truth. As coauthors of the books, Jerry Jenkins and Tim LaHaye have continued to claim no glory for the mighty things God has accomplished through this series. Thousands have come to the Lord as a direct result of these novels, and countless others have been brought closer to God through reading them.

If God can do such great things through a shepherd's staff or a handful of hardcover books, imagine what he can do through the life of a person fully committed to serving him. Put yourself in God's hands, and see for yourself what he can accomplish.

REFLECTION
How do you long for God to use you in his service? In what ways can you put yourself completely in his control?

GOD'S ARMY

For there are more on our side than on theirs!   2 Kings 6:16

HAVE YOU EVER felt hopeless and helpless in the face of your enemy? Have you ever found yourself so surrounded by opposition that you can't imagine getting through another day? Do you ever want to just curl up in bed and hide?

If so, then you have a small idea what Elisha must have experienced when he incurred the wrath of the mighty king of Aram. As a prophet of God, Elisha had continually disrupted the plans of Israel's most fierce enemy. At every turn Aram's king plotted to overtake Israel, yet each time God would warn them through the prophet Elisha. The Aramean army was foiled time and again.

One day the king of Aram confronted his troops in a rage, demanding to know if they had a traitor among them. "It's not us, my lord," one of the officers replied. "Elisha, the prophet in Israel, tells the king of Israel even the words you speak in the privacy of your bedroom!" (2 Kings 6:12). The king of Aram determined to flush out and kill this pesky prophet of God, so he sent his soldiers to surround Elisha as he slept.

Elisha's servant was the first to notice the Aramean army surrounding the city. He awoke early in the morning and went outside to see thousands of horses and chariots and warriors on every side. In a panic he woke up Elisha. "What will we do now?" he cried out. But Elisha was unfazed.

"'Don't be afraid!' Elisha told him. 'For there are more on our side than on theirs!' Then Elisha prayed, 'O Lord, open his eyes and let him see!' The Lord opened his servant's eyes, and when he looked up, he saw that the hillside around Elisha was filled with horses and chariots of fire" (6:15-17). What should have been Elisha's darkest hour suddenly became his moment of greatest victory. God's angels were there all along, waiting to fight his battle for him. He was never alone, and had no reason to fear.

The lesson for us is simple: God doesn't send people into battle without sending backup along with them. We can choose to fight our own battles, or we can let God fight them for us. There is no battle in life that we have to wage on our own.

> "Rayford was assured again that he was on the side of the army that had already won this war."
>
> *Soul Harvest*, 411

REFLECTION

What battles are you trying to fight on your own?
What will your prayer be to God for help?

A GARDEN TO TEND

*The Lord God placed the man in the Garden of Eden to tend
and care for it.*   Genesis 2:15

TO UNDERSTAND God's Word, it's critical that you and I see ourselves as every person in Scripture. The Bible was not only written to us but *about* us. On any given day we can easily see ourselves in the stories.

Some days we are the Jewish man who was beaten and left for dead on the side of the road to Jericho. Other days we are the priest and Temple assistant who saw him there but didn't want to be "late to church," so we hurry past on the far side of the road. Still other days, we are the Samaritan who stops and lifts the man out of the ditch. We take him home, pay his bills, and tell him not to worry anymore about it. Depending upon the day and the circumstances, you and I have the capacity to be any one of the people in the story.

At the beginning God gave Adam a beautiful garden to tend. It was filled with trees and fruits and plants, with streams running throughout. Adam's job was simply to tend the Garden. He wasn't asked to do great things that would change the world; he was simply asked to watch over the ground in front of him.

God has given you and me a garden as well. It is ours to till and to keep and to watch over. My garden consists of a wife and two beautiful children. We have a small plot of land, with a house that keeps us warm and dry. This is the garden God has given us, and it's our job to protect it, to watch it, to work it daily.

You've been given a garden as well, and God expects you to tend it, just as he expected Adam to tend to his. God has not asked us to change the world. He's asked only that we keep our garden. That we plant and toil and work the things within our sphere of influence to the best of our ability.

It's so easy to get caught up in thoughts of doing great and mighty things for God. We want to make an impact on the world, so we set our sights high and far. But God is the One who decides when it's time to expand our garden. Our role is to simply tend to the task at hand—to sow our seeds daily, water the land freely, and watch as God makes it grow and flourish.

REFLECTION
Where do you see yourself in this parable of Jesus?
Which character can you most readily relate to?

DEBATING GOD

"Come now, let us argue this out," says the Lord.   Isaiah 1:18

IF YOU DECIDED to debate with God, whom do you think would win? Let's imagine for a minute that you've found yourself standing on a podium opposite the Creator of the universe ready to debate an issue. You have your carefully typed notes in front of you, with stars in the margins beside all your best points. But the moment comes for you to begin, and suddenly you realize that there's no way on earth you could ever win.

Now imagine yourself in the Israelites' shoes when God calls them to the podium. "'Come now, let us argue this out,' says the Lord" (Isaiah 1:18). "You think you know better than I?" God says to them. God calls them to the stage for a debate. And when they stand before him, what does he want to talk about?

The depth of his love. That's what God wants to talk about. Listen to his beginning arguments: "No matter how deep the stain of your sins, I can remove it. I can make you as clean as freshly fallen snow. Even if you are stained as red as crimson, I can make you as white as wool" (1:18). Israel stood before him ready to debate their sin and unworthiness, but not God. He's more interested in talking about what he plans to do with their sins. We're waiting for judgment; God is hammering the podium with redemption.

"But Lord, I'm so guilty. You've seen what I've done."

"Of course I've seen it," says God. "But you haven't seen what I can do."

You and I will have days when we feel so unclean that we can't imagine going to God with our sins. We'll fall so hard or so often that we won't want to look in his direction. And on those days we'll call him out to debate our unworthiness. But God will never walk away from the stage without getting the last word: "I can remove it. I can make you as clean as freshly fallen snow."

If you argue with God, you're always going to lose.

REFLECTION
Have you ever felt unworthy of God's love? When you honestly consider your sins, which ones are beyond his forgiveness? Take refuge in God's message to Israel.

MAY

INSCRIBED ON GOD'S HAND

See, I have written your name on my hand.   Isaiah 49:16

THERE'S NOTHING quite as deflating as being forgotten by a friend. I once had a breakfast meeting set up with an acquaintance and he never showed. I remember being embarrassed, drinking one cup of coffee after another as the waitress checked back with me periodically. "Would you like to order now, or still wait?" she would ask. "I'm sure he'll be here," I would tell her. "Let's give him a few more minutes." I watched for his car outside the window, but he never came. Finally I paid for my coffee, thanked the waitress for her patience, and slipped away. My friend called later to apologize, and I told him it wasn't that big of a deal. He had no real excuse, he had just forgotten. I didn't hold the episode against him, but I have to be honest and say that it hurt. Somehow you hope that you mean enough to your friends that they won't forget you.

> "You can have your name written in the Book of Life! That is the good news."
>
> *Armageddon, 279*

There are times when it feels as if God has forgotten us. When life beats us down and gets the best of us, it's easy to think we've been deserted. *Maybe he's busy putting out fires elsewhere,* we think to ourselves. And our prayers begin to feel empty and distant. That's why it's so important to stay in God's Word, because it reminds us that God is always near. Especially when we feel the most neglected.

"Can a mother forget her nursing child? Can she feel no love for a child she has borne?" God asks us through the prophet Isaiah. Never! "But even if that were possible, I would not forget you!" (Isaiah 49:15).

"Although it's hard to imagine it," God says to us, "a nursing mother might just forget her baby. It's possible, though not very probable. But one thing is not possible. I could never forget you."

"See, I have engraved you on the palms of my hands" (Isaiah 49:16, NIV). Like an obsessed lover, God has had our name tattooed on his hands. He won't forget us. When you feel forgotten by God, just close your eyes and envision the hands of the Almighty. And remember his words: "I could never forget you."

REFLECTION
When was the last time you felt abandoned by God? How do you find comfort in knowing that he will never forget you?

THE SPIRIT OF GOD

The Spirit of God was hovering over its surface.   Genesis 1:2

BEFORE CREATION there was nothing. The Bible says that the "earth was empty, a formless mass cloaked in darkness" (Genesis 1:2). The human mind is incapable of comprehending complete nothingness, but that's what the universe was like. No sound, no sight, no light, no movement. Absolutely nothing. And in the midst of this nothingness, "the Spirit of God was hovering over its surface" (1:2).

You can almost picture this vast void of time and space just waiting for God to speak. Creation lingering in complete silence before the Almighty. Who knows how long the universe waited in this state of nothingness? And God hovered overhead, contemplating, planning, resting in utter silence. Then suddenly he speaks, and it all begins. From nothing comes everything.

This is the same Spirit of God that came upon the Virgin Mary. Once again God came down and hovered above his creation. He spoke into her womb, and Jesus was conceived. From nothing comes everything.

At the baptism of Jesus he speaks again. "After his baptism, as Jesus came up out of the water, the heavens were opened and he saw the Spirit of God descending like a dove and settling on him." And again God opens his mouth and speaks. "This is my beloved Son, and I am fully pleased with him" (Matthew 3:16-17).

Jesus dies on a cross, is buried in a cave, and rises three days later. And he appears to his disciples again. This time to breathe into them the Spirit of God who lives inside of him. "'As the Father has sent me, so I send you.' Then he breathed on them and said to them, 'Receive the Holy Spirit'" (John 20:21-22). The Spirit of God who once hovered above the vastness of the universe, who spoke all creation into existence, who conceived the Savior in the womb of a virgin, now comes to reside inside of God's people. God's mighty Spirit now hovers above our heart.

REFLECTION
Can you feel God's Spirit speak to your heart when you sit silently before him? What is he saying to you? How can you spend more time listening?

GENERATIONAL CURSES

As you have done to Israel, so it will be done to you.   Obadiah 1:15

THE BOOK of Obadiah is a staunch testament to the power and reality of generational curses. If you want to see how your family relationships can affect your relatives for generations to come, then take a good look at the dynamics played out in this tiny prophetic book.

The nation of Israel descended from Jacob, and the nation of Edom descended from Esau. And most of us know the story of Jacob and Esau—the two brothers who started fighting in their mother's womb before they were even born (see Genesis 25:19-34).

From these twins came two separate nations, and they would clash for generations to come. Israel's kings would suffer through constant struggles with the Edomites throughout the reigns of Saul, David, Solomon, Jehoram, and Ahaz. There seemed to be no end to the hate between these two nations.

And then we get to the book of Obadiah and see the outcome of this ancient feud between Edom and Israel—a feud that began in the womb of Rebecca. Ironically, Jacob and Esau made peace with each other in their lifetime (see Genesis 33:1-20), but the generational curse they created had already been set in motion.

The Lord told Moses, "I show this unfailing love to many thousands by forgiving every kind of sin and rebellion. Even so I do not leave sin unpunished, but I punish the children for the sins of their parents to the third and fourth generations" (Exodus 34:7). God makes it clear in Scripture that we are responsible for our sins and our own salvation, but sins carry with them consequences that affect everyone around us. Our relationships with those in our family can have an impact on our children and our children's children. Through our relational transgressions we can set in motion a pattern of behavior that can give Satan a foothold in our family for generations to come.

REFLECTION
What are the patterns of conflict and sin in your family? How can you cancel the generational curses that may afflict you and your descendants?

A HAUGHTY HEART

You are proud because you live in a rock fortress.   Obadiah 1:3

THE EDOMITES lived in a fortress surrounded by sandstone cliffs over five thousand feet high. The entrance to the city was thought to be only twelve to fifteen feet wide, and it was the only way to get in. They had created a sanctuary for themselves that was close to impenetrable. The only way an enemy could get to them would be through trickery, and the Edomites were a shrewd people, not easily succumbing to deception. For all practical purposes they were untouchable. And because of it, their hearts became haughty.

The Edomites were certain they didn't need help from anyone—not Israel, not other nations, not even God. Their trust was in their own power. Their faith was in their location, in their wealth, and in their ability to provide food and water for themselves. But God was not impressed. Nor was he happy with Edom. Listen to what he tells them:

> "'Cameron, look,' Tsion said. 'Look at all the unmarked men! They proudly parade around, beaming at each other.'"
>
> *Armageddon, 324*

"I will cut you down to size among the nations, Edom; you will be small and despised. You are proud because you live in a rock fortress and make your home high in the mountains. . . . Though you soar as high as eagles and build your nest among the stars, I will bring you crashing down. I, the Lord, have spoken!" (Obadiah 1:2-4).

Ever find yourself thinking the world can't touch you? Ever boast in your heart that you've got it all together? Ever look down at those beneath you in income or intellect or favor and think you're a bit better than they?

I have. More than once. And it's not something I'm proud to admit. In fact, it's something that I've repented of and prayed to overcome. Because haughty hearts and proud lips will always bring down God's hand of judgment.

REFLECTION
When have you struggled with a prideful heart? What are some steps you need to take to overcome this tendency?

GLOATING OVER OTHERS' MISFORTUNE

You shouldn't have rejoiced because they were suffering
such misfortune.   Obadiah 1:12

HAVE YOU EVER had someone gloat over your misfortune? Have you ever found out that a friend scoffed behind your back when you were down? Maybe you lost a good deal of money when the market turned south and later learned that your relatives laughed at your financial downturn. "I would have put the money in bonds," they said smugly. "It serves him right for being so stupid." Or maybe you lost a job that you loved and found that your coworkers said you had it coming. "He wasn't worth his paycheck anyway."

I have a friend who went through a terrible trial a few years ago. His business collapsed, and his family was in crisis, and he struggled just to keep it all together. In the middle of his misfortune a man from his church began sending e-mails and letters, gloating over my friend's calamity. The problems eventually worked themselves out, but my friend is still deeply wounded by the episode. And rumors that were set in motion still circulate.

Edom gloated over Israel's misfortune, and God let them know exactly how he felt about it. "You shouldn't have done this!" God begins. "You shouldn't have gloated when they exiled your relatives to distant lands. You shouldn't have rejoiced because they were suffering such misfortune" (Obadiah 1:12-13). "You shouldn't . . . You shouldn't . . . You shouldn't. . . ." Over and over he condemns them for laughing while Israel struggled. And it wasn't as if Israel didn't deserve their trouble—it was brought on by their sin. But it was God's business to deal with that and not Edom's to gloat about.

It's never fun to be in crisis and find that others are having a good time at your expense. The temptation is to strike back, but that never solves anything. The best approach is to step back and let God deal with them. Our Lord is the only one we have to answer to—and turn to—during times of trouble. He can fight our battles for us if he sees the need. And if the past is any indication of the future, it never sets well with God when someone gloats over another's misfortune. Trust him. And see that you don't fall into the same trap.

REFLECTION
Has anyone ever gloated over your problems? Have you tried to get even?
Or are you willing to let God fight your battle?

THE LORD WILL BE KING

And the Lord himself will be king!   Obadiah 1:21

OBADIAH ENDS with a message that you and I need to begin each day with. The last words on Obadiah's lips should be the first thing that you and I remember in each and every situation. "And the Lord himself will be king!" (Obadiah 1:21).

Those who sit in fortresses five thousand feet above the ground may think they will get the last word, that they don't need God, that they are immune to destruction, but it is the Lord who will ultimately get the glory. Those who wallow in their self-sufficiency and take pride in their own wit and wisdom may rule for a day—but only until God decides to bring them down to earth. Those who laugh and gloat at the misfortune of others may enjoy a moment or two of satisfaction, but they won't gloat for long. In the end God always gets the last word.

"The exiles of Israel will return to their land and occupy the Phoenician coast as far north as Zarephath. The captives from Jerusalem exiled in the north will return to their homeland and resettle the villages of the Negev. Deliverers will go up to Mount Zion in Jerusalem to rule over the mountains of Edom. And the Lord himself will be king!" (1:20-21).

The Kingdom of God belongs to God and no one else. It will never be overthrown, never be taken, never be overshadowed, never be mocked, never be shaken or destroyed. It will never be ruled by another.

And who are the ones who will enjoy the blessings of that truth? Those who have accepted the redemption that only Christ can bring. Those who trust in God and God alone for their salvation.

All other kings and kingdoms will fall some day. None will survive the ultimate day of God's judgment. But his people will live forever, in a city of eternal joy and wonder. "And the Lord himself will be king."

REFLECTION
What kingdom are you trusting in? Are you trusting in a kingdom that is temporal? If so, why not transfer your citizenship today?

JESUS OUR DEFENDER

No one will snatch them away from me.   John 10:28

"IT WAS NOW WINTER, and Jesus was in Jerusalem at the time of Hanukkah. He was at the Temple, walking through the section known as Solomon's Colonnade" (John 10:22-23). Do you ever wonder what he was thinking? Jesus is alone in the dead of winter, strolling through the remains of the Temple. He walks through the portico of Solomon, the only section of the Temple that survived the Babylonian captivity in 586 B.C. Is he thinking of the history attached to this sacred place? about the rebellion of God's people that led to the Temple's destruction? Perhaps he was in prayer. We don't know for sure, but we do know that the Jewish leaders chose this moment to confront him.

> "We of all people should have the boldness of Christ to aggressively tell the world of its only hope in him."
>
> *Apollyon, 49*

"If you are the Messiah, tell us plainly," they say to him (John 10:24). You can almost sense their arrogance in the way the question was posed. These are the Pharisees who have spent their careers perverting the Scriptures they were commissioned to keep, and now they surround the very Messiah they've been preaching about, taunting and teasing him. *How dare they question Jesus! Not here. And not now.*

Did Jesus pause to stare them down one at a time before answering? "I have already told you, and you don't believe me. The proof is what I do in the name of my Father. But you don't believe me because you are not part of my flock. My sheep recognize my voice; I know them, and they follow me. I give them eternal life, and they will never perish." You can almost visualize the smug detractors folding their arms and trying to look away, but he holds their gaze. Jesus could have stopped there and walked away. He'd made his point. But he didn't. Not quite yet. There was one more thing they needed to hear. "No one will snatch them away from me, for my Father has given them to me" (John 10:25-29).

The boldness of Jesus is equaled only by his protective instinct for us.

REFLECTION
Do you find comfort knowing that Jesus will always defend you?
What can we learn from his resolve in the face of opposition?

THE BOLDNESS OF JESUS

Jesus stood and shouted to the crowds.   John 7:37

THE JEWS had many traditions, and one of the more sacred was the Feast of Tabernacles. For seven days the Jews would celebrate. Each day the high priest would draw water from the pool of Siloam with a golden vessel and ascend with it toward the altar in the Temple. Shouts of joy and praise would fill the air as the priest poured the water out before the altar of the Lord.

The seventh day of this feast was the most sacred and celebrated of all. The festival would climax with the priest walking toward the altar as he had on previous days, but the anticipation was much greater. It was the final and greatest day of the Festival of Booths, and was not an event taken lightly by the Jews.

It was at this moment that Jesus stood and shouted before the crowd, "If you are thirsty, come to me! If you believe in me, come and drink! For the Scriptures declare that rivers of living water will flow out from within" (John 7:37-38).

His words didn't confuse the crowd the way they often confuse us. They knew what he was saying. They understood the significance of the festival and the meaning behind the "living water" that the priest carried before the Lord. The stranger's declaration may have taken them off guard, but his comparison wasn't lost on them. He was telling them he was the Messiah, and they knew it.

Some believed him, others despised him, many wanted him arrested for blasphemy. But none doubted the boldness of his testimony. That's why the Pharisees immediately tried to capture and kill him. When you rock the boat as hard as Jesus did, someone's bound to get angry. Jesus wasn't afraid to speak his message. Maybe you and I could learn to speak boldly of Christ to others.

REFLECTION
*How do you display boldness in your faith? What lesson can
you take from the life of Jesus?*

YOUR HEART'S DESIRE

Take delight in the Lord, and he will give you your
heart's desires.   Psalm 37:4

A LOT OF MY childhood memories are vague and scattered, but some remain clear in my mind. I have one vivid memory of sitting on the ground behind our small home in Texas, writing a story about two men who built a spaceship and then traveled around the galaxy searching for aliens. It was only one of many stories and poems and songs that I wrote as a child. For as long as I can remember, I've been finding comfort in the joy of writing.

Even though my high school teachers encouraged me to take up journalism as a career, I couldn't see myself as a professional writer. I opted instead to go into business, and that's where I spent the first twenty years of my career. Throughout that time, writing remained a passion and a hobby but not much more.

> "We are his highest creation, but we are weak and selfish and too easily tempted by Satan to forget our purpose in life."
>
> *The Remnant, 288*

Thankfully, God had other plans. He had gifted me with an ability and a desire to write, and he never let go of the dream he had in store for me—even if I had. Over the last few years, God restored that dream in my life. Today I make a living doing what I've always longed to do. My heart's deepest desire is being realized. I'm not the best writer in the world; I'm not even sure I'm the best writer in my house, but I'm a writer. And just knowing that truth fills my heart with joy.

Has God planted a desire in your heart? One that you have yet to realize? Maybe one that still rises to the surface of your consciousness as you lie awake at night, dreaming of the future? Has God given you a gift but not a chance to use it yet?

"Take delight in the Lord, and he will give you your heart's desires" sings the psalmist (Psalm 37:4). God doesn't plant dreams to simply sit back and watch them die on rocky soil. Delight in his love and presence, and just see if his promises aren't real.

REFLECTION
What desires has God placed in your heart? What obstacles in your heart
or life are getting in the way of that dream being fulfilled by God?

A SPIRIT OF FEAR

For God has not given us a spirit of fear.   2 Timothy 1:7

IF YOU WANT to know where people are most gifted, look at where they have been the most wounded. If you want to discover their purpose, ask them about their fears. If you want to see what God has planned for them, look at where the enemy has attacked their lives and hearts most fiercely.

The apostle Paul says, "Put on all of God's armor so that you will be able to stand firm against all strategies and tricks of the Devil. For we are not fighting against people made of flesh and blood, but against the evil rulers and authorities of the unseen world" (Ephesians 6:11-12). Satan's primary obsession is to keep God's people from living in God's perfect will, and one of the ways he accomplishes that task is by weaving thoughts of fear and doubt within our mind. He instills fear where God instills gifts.

Do you want to know what gifts God wants to develop and use within you? Then note where you've been the most attacked and wounded. Do you want to know what God wants you to accomplish for his Kingdom? Then look at what you've come to fear the most.

I believe God intended me to write, and he placed that desire in my heart at an early age. It took me forty years to realize that dream, and as I look back on my life, I can see why. I have vivid memories of being laughed at as a young boy for my attempts at poetry and songs. The pain soon turned to doubt, and doubt to fear of further cruelty. The enemy hit me where it hurt the worst.

"Fan into flames the spiritual gift God gave you when I laid my hands on you," Paul told Timothy. "For God has not given us a spirit of fear and timidity, but of power, love, and self-discipline" (2 Timothy 1:6-7). There is no room in the child of God for fear. There is no reason for doubt. There is no place for intimidation in the heart of a person devoted to finding God's great and perfect will. Don't let anything or anyone deter you from finding your gift from God and fanning it into a raging fire of purpose!

REFLECTION
*Do you know which gifts God has given you? Have you claimed
victory over the enemy's attacks on that gifting?*

A CONSUMING FIRE

Fan into flames the spiritual gift God gave you.   2 Timothy 1:6

PAUL TELLS TIMOTHY, "Fan into flames the spiritual gift God gave you when I laid my hands on you" (2 Timothy 1:6). The gift that Timothy was given was from God. This commission from the church, his spiritual gift, and his spiritual walk with the Lord were all Timothy needed to live a fruitful and triumphant life before God.

God has given you and me a gift as well, and his desire is to see us use and grow it until it becomes a fire of passion within our spirit. He wants our gift to develop into a full-blown purpose and vision. And he is there to help that happen.

When God's anointing falls on a believer, it is a powerful force to reckon with. When we fan into flames the spiritual gift God places within us, we are fanning a fire that can literally turn the world upside down. God has equipped us with everything we need to live a glorious and victorious life, and all we have to do is tap into that power.

> "God daily refreshes me and allows me— expects me— to exercise all the gifts he has bestowed on a pastor-teacher."
>
> *The Remnant,* 123

That's why the enemy works so frantically to neutralize that passion. He will do everything in his power to keep us from finding and fanning God's divine and holy destiny for us. His sole desire is to quench our spirit. And we cannot afford to let him.

Before the foundations of the earth were laid, God envisioned his divine destiny for your life. He knew your purpose long before you were born. And then he placed his supernatural gifting for that purpose within your spirit. It's been there since the beginning of time, waiting for you to accept it—to embrace his vision and let him fulfill his purpose for you. Without it you are just another Christian struggling against Satan, doing the best you can to make it through another day. But with it, you are empowered by the Spirit of God for a purpose that reaches to eternity.

REFLECTION
What is your purpose before God? What is keeping you from embracing the gift God has placed within your spirit? Pray today for the power to fan that flame into a raging fire!

PRAYING FOR GIFTS

I have filled him with the Spirit of God, giving him great . . .
skill in all kinds of crafts.   Exodus 31:3

GOD COMMISSIONED Moses with the task of building the Ark of the Covenant and the Tabernacle and all the other things needed for worship and sacrifice, and many in his camp were probably wondering how they were going to pull it all off. Who among them was qualified for such fine craftsmanship?

The minute God finished his instructions, he empowered Moses' people to complete them. He filled Bezalel with his Spirit and gave him the skills he needed for cutting and setting gemstones and in carving wood. Then he appointed Oholiab to be Bezalel's assistant. God said, "I have given special skill to all the naturally talented craftsmen so they can make all the things I have instructed you to make" (see Exodus 31:1-6). Our Lord thinks of everything.

I know a man who was just naive enough to think that maybe, just maybe, if God gave a skill to Bezalel and Oholiab, then he might give him one as well. So he set his heart to pray.

His name is Mark, and at the time he was recuperating from a construction accident. He had slipped on a roof and landed twenty feet below on his back, fracturing his leg in several places. Doctors didn't hold much hope that he could ever return to his same job. So he prayed for a skill—a specific one. Mark wanted to be a sculptor. He had never done it before and had no idea how to begin, except to pray. He clung to the story of Bezalel and Oholiab and believed God for a miracle.

Today, Mark is a gifted sculptor—undoubtedly the most talented one I've ever run across. We have three of his pieces in our home. He's won national and international awards for his art, and his bronze sculptures grace the halls of some of the finest buildings in the world. Mark never took a lesson, never took a class; he didn't even practice much. He simply prayed for skill, picked up a lump of clay, and started molding. God anointed his hands with power.

Do you believe that God has done great things in the past? Why not believe that he can do great things today?

REFLECTION
What is keeping you from praying a bold prayer for God's supernatural
gifting? Why not believe today that he can do so?

BELIEVING GOD

Abram believed the Lord.   Genesis 15:6

HAVE YOU EVER wondered why Abram was chosen to receive a covenant from God? Why was he set apart among all the people of the world to become the father of our faith? Was it his trust in God? Was it his boldness in the face of opposition?

If so, then you have to wonder about the Lord's standards. Within days of Abram's leaving his homeland and following God to Canaan, his knees started to buckle with fear. Before entering Egypt he says to his wife, Sarah, "You are a very beautiful woman. When the Egyptians see you, they will say, 'This is his wife. Let's kill him; then we can have her!' But if you say you are my sister, then the Egyptians will treat me well because of their interest in you, and they will spare my life" (Genesis 12:11-13). Abram's trust was shaken, his boldness was nonexistent, and his integrity was compromised. And he'd barely begun his journey.

So if that isn't why God chose him, then what could it have been? What was it about Abram, later called Abraham, that so intrigued the Creator of the universe that he would handpick him for greatness? According to Paul, it was this: "Abraham believed God, so God declared him to be righteous" (Romans 4:3). In spite of his many faults and shortcomings, even in spite of himself, Abraham believed what God told him. And he obeyed whenever God gave him an assignment. Because of Abraham's faith, God made a covenant with him.

"Now this wonderful truth—that God declared him to be righteous—wasn't just for Abraham's benefit," declares the apostle Paul. "It was for us, too, assuring us that God will also declare us to be righteous if we believe in God" (4:23-24). The blessing that Abraham received can be shared by us all. The righteousness that was attributed to him can also be attributed to you and me.

REFLECTION
What is the difference between believing in God and believing God?
In what ways to you struggle to believe God?

PRAYING FOR A COVENANT

So the Lord made a covenant with Abram.   Genesis 15:18

ABRAM BELIEVED GOD, and he was declared righteous because of it. He listened when God spoke to him, went where God sent him, did whatever God asked him to do, and God took notice. Abram trusted God, and God knew that he could trust Abram. So God made a covenant with him, "an arrangement between two parties involving mutual obligations."[1]

Many would say that God made a covenant *with* Abram, because that's how most translations read, but that's not how it really happened. The covenant wasn't Abram's idea, and it wasn't something he asked for. God initiated the idea. God created the covenant and then informed Abram.

"This is my covenant with you: I will make you the father of not just one nation, but a multitude of nations! What's more, I am changing your name. It will no longer be Abram; now you will be known as Abraham, for you will be the father of many nations. I will give you millions of descendants who will represent many nations. Kings will be among them! I will continue this everlasting covenant between us, generation after generation. It will continue between me and your offspring forever" (Genesis 17:4-7).

> "This strange affection for the Jews resulted in what he tells them is an eternal covenant of blessing."
>
> Armageddon, 298

In the New Testament Jesus Christ brought a new covenant through his shed blood on the cross. It is a covenant created for us, and like God's covenant with Abraham, it is unshakable and irrevocable. Have you received this new covenant? Have you accepted the promise of eternal life that God brought through his Son, Jesus? Have you given yourself over to God's precious gift? Maybe it's time for you and me to go to the mountain and meet with God to recognize his new covenant with us. If you don't have a mountain, try your prayer closet. Thank him for the new life you have in Jesus.

REFLECTION
How does it change your life to know that you are living under an irrevocable covenant with God? What are some specific things you can do to thank God for the amazing gift of eternal life?

BEWARE OF THE VULTURES

Some vultures came down . . . but Abram chased
them away.   Genesis 15:11

WHEN THE LORD told Abram that he was preparing to make a covenant for him, he asked him to make a sacrifice. God told Abram, "Bring me a three-year-old heifer, a three-year-old female goat, a three-year-old ram, a turtledove, and a young pigeon" (Genesis 15:9). Abram was to sacrifice the animals on an altar he had built. He did as the Lord asked, and soon the birds of prey came swooping down on his camp. "Some vultures came down to eat the carcasses, but Abram chased them away. That evening, as the sun was going down, Abram fell into a deep sleep. He saw a terrifying vision of darkness and horror" (15:11-12).

There is a universal law in the spiritual realm that you and I should be aware of. When God's people set themselves toward living in God's blessings, the devil's vultures will always be there to try and foil the effort. When you go before God to receive a covenant, you can expect the birds of prey to be right on your heels.

Vultures come in many forms. You may have friends and family laugh at you, scoff at your faith, roll their eyes at your prayers, plant seeds of doubt in your mind. They've read the story of Abraham, and they remind you that you are "definitely no Abraham." And the temptation will be to believe them.

Some vultures get inside your head and manifest themselves in the form of negative thinking. *Who do you think you are? Why would God take the time to make a covenant for someone like you?* They'll come to you at night and affect your dreams, bringing nightmares and visions of darkness.

And some birds of prey find it more effective to simply get in your way and blind your vision. They throw obstacles in your path and try to steal your time and keep you from praying. But don't let them do it. When you've set your heart and mind on asking God for a covenant blessing, don't allow the enemy to distract you. Stay the course and remain faithful until you hear from him.

REFLECTION
What form has the enemy's vultures taken in the past in your Christian walk?
Have you let them discourage and distract you? Pray that God will help you
chase them away as you seek his covenant.

THE GREATEST GIFT

Blessed is the man whose sin the Lord does not count against him.
Psalm 32:2, NIV

I CAN THINK of a lot of things I'd like to have from God. When I think of the blessings that I would enjoy having showered upon my family and me, I'm sure I could come up with a list much longer than I have the courage to ask or hope for. Most of those things would feel selfish and unnecessary and would likely be scratched off as quickly as they were penciled in. It's not that I don't believe that God enjoys showering his children with good things; I just want to keep my priorities in order. I want God to see that my desires are more spiritual than they are temporal.

What about you? What would your list look like? Would you ask for a deeper faith, a more meaningful prayer life, a heavenly perspective, an anointing, a soul to win? Some of us might slip in a request for a new car or a better job, and that's okay because God has told us to ask when we have a need.

All of these things are blessings that are well within God's desire and ability to give us. And yet all pale in comparison to what he has already given. In fact, not one thing we could ask for would come even remotely close to the present God laid in our hands the day we gave ourselves over to him.

"Oh, what joy for those whose rebellion is forgiven, whose sin is put out of sight! Yes, what joy for those whose record the Lord has cleared of sin, whose lives are lived in complete honesty!" (Psalm 32:1-2). Of everything you could ask God to give you, can you imagine yourself asking for this forgiveness? Could you ever muster the courage? Could you even begin to pencil such a bold and arrogant request on your wish list?

Imagine yourself praying through your list. You start out rather simply—a clean bill of health at next week's physical, patience in dealing with your children, help in budgeting for this year's vacation. And then somewhere along the way you try to slip it in. "Oh yes, if it's not too much trouble, Lord, could you please disregard every sin I've ever committed, and then forget they ever happened?" Even as the words leave your tongue, the audaciousness of the request takes you aback. And yet that's exactly what God has done for us. He took the one blessing that none of us could ever hope to ask for and laid it at our feet. All you and I have to do is accept it.

REFLECTION
*When did you accept God's gift of eternal life? If you haven't yet,
why not pray today and ask him to accept you as his child?*

PERFECT GIFTS FROM GOD

Whatever is good and perfect comes to us from God above.   James 1:17

WHY WAS EVE so easily deceived by the serpent in the Garden of Eden? How did it happen that a slithery snake could convince her to take a bite of fruit when the Master of the universe told her not to? Did she forget who God was? That's doubtful. Did she forget that he created her—that he was there to watch over her? Even more doubtful. Did she think that Satan knew more than God? Let's get real.

What Eve forgot was so basic and simple that many of us don't even recognize it. She forgot something that you and I forget every day. Something that Satan wants us to forget. Something that God wants us to remember.

> "He loves you with a perfect love."
>
> *Apollyon, 274*

Eve forgot that only God can bring good things. James tells us, "So don't be misled, my dear brothers and sisters. Whatever is good and perfect comes to us from God above" (James 1:16-17). If it comes from God, it is good; if it doesn't it is evil. It's a truth that is as simple as it is profound.

Eve would never have fallen to Satan's lies if she had internalized this one basic fact of the universe. She would have never eaten the fruit if she had remembered this principle. Adam would have never followed her into sin if he had thought of this one simple thing.

This is a truth that you and I need to settle in our heart once and for all. Nothing is good outside the realm of God's perfect will. Nothing will satisfy that he has not given us. Nothing will improve our life, make us stronger, give us hope, help us live, or bring us fulfillment outside of the things that come to us directly from God. No matter how good it looks, how good it sounds, how much it promises, or how harmless it seems, if God is not the One who brought it to us, we should refuse the offer and run. In the end it will only lead to sorrow and sin.

Embrace this truth, and you won't be deceived. Settle it in your heart, and Satan won't be able to touch you.

REFLECTION
When was the last time you were deceived by Satan? Would he have been successful if you had internalized the truth that only God can bring good things?

WAITING ON GOD

A day is like a thousand years to the Lord, and a thousand years is like a day.   2 Peter 3:8

FOR A BELIEVER there's nothing quite as hard—or frustrating—as waiting on the Lord. We believe God's promises when he says that our prayers will be answered, and many of us have felt a specific calling on our life. God has set us toward a task that he wants to accomplish through us, and we work daily to see it to fruition. We're convinced we've heard the Lord correctly, and even though it seems at times that we're all alone on the journey, we continue on in faith. We remind God often that we haven't forgotten our mission. And we work to rally others to help in an effort to fulfill our commission. Sometimes we even go to God in doubt, wondering if maybe he's forgotten us. Or worse, we fear that he's given up on us.

I have several tasks before me that I'm convinced God commissioned me to accomplish. I prayed about each one, over long periods of time, and I clearly felt God leading me to carry them forward. Each time I saw confirmation from trusted friends, family, and Scripture. And each time I set my hand to the plow and began tilling the soil and planting the seeds.

But I'm not always right in my assessments. Sometimes in the past I've moved forward on things I was convinced God wanted me to do, only to be stopped in my tracks and forced to abandon the task. What I was sure was a mandate from God proved to be of my own making. So I admitted I was wrong and set my sights on finding a new mandate. I move forward in faith, praying for guidance and direction, all the while waiting for God to answer. I'm sure you can relate.

It's easy to get impatient with God. We all do at one time or another. But we need to remind ourselves that God is not on our timetable. When you're doing business with the God of the universe, you quickly learn that time has no meaning to him. Peter tells us, "You must not forget, dear friends, that a day is like a thousand years to the Lord, and a thousand years is like a day" (2 Peter 3:8). God doesn't wear a watch, and he has no intention of getting one. He does things in his way and in his time. Our job is to pray steadily, work diligently, believe mightily, and know that he is in control. Even when it seems he isn't.

REFLECTION
What task has God commissioned you to do? Have you confirmed that this is God's mission and not yours? If so, remain patient and keep moving.

A DISOBEDIENT SPIRIT

It is a message to obey, not just to listen to.   James 1:22

I KNOW SEVERAL people in the church whose lives are one crisis after another. They always seem to be in some sort of trouble. They go from one sickness to the next and always say they feel poorly. They lose jobs as quickly as they find them and seem to be in constant financial need. Each new crisis appears to get worse as time goes by, and as soon as it looks like they're coming out of it, another shoe drops, and again they're in some kind of trouble.

These people appear to be terribly unlucky. Their constant afflictions keep them at the top of their church's prayer list, and they're usually not much fun to be around. I've watched as these people go through separations and divorces, as they struggle with rebellious children, as they get passed over for promotions, as their houses get robbed, and their cars get stolen. There always seems to be something, and it never seems to end. If you didn't know better, you'd think they were under some kind of a curse.

> "Receive him into your life and then live in obedience to him. He wants you."
>
> *The Remnant, 232*

And maybe they are. But more likely, they may be under God's judgment.

It is not our place to judge, and none of us should do that. If we did, we would often be wrong. There are many people who go through hardships because God is trying to mold them into something better than they are. Some suffer as a result of their obedience to God's calling. It would be a critical error for us to assume that they are out of God's will because of the bad things that happen to them. But it is true that some people suffer because God's hand of judgment is on them.

James warns us to "get rid of all the filth and evil in your lives, and humbly accept the message God has planted in your hearts. . . . It is a message to obey, not just to listen to" (James 1:21-22). Paul tells us why it is so important to obey. "Don't be fooled by those who try to excuse these sins, for the terrible anger of God comes upon all those who disobey him" (Ephesians 5:6). Believers who live in a state of disobedience to God will not go without feeling the judgment of God on their lives. God will not allow them to wallow in sin while professing to follow Christ.

Maybe this truth hits a little too close to home for you. Maybe you're the person who lives from one affliction to the next, always wondering why you can't get a break. If so, then examine your heart and life diligently. And set the matter to prayer. See if God is trying to tell you something.

REFLECTION
Do things seem to be going wrong in your life? What might be the reason?

HEAVENLY LONGINGS

We long for the day when we will put on our heavenly bodies.
2 Corinthians 5:2

C. S. LEWIS called earth "the Shadowlands." It was a brilliant observation and an analogy that was lost on many. Yet he knew what he meant. To Lewis, earth was a land of nothing but shapes and shadows. No beauty or joy truly satisfied. Even the most ecstatic moments eventually turned to sorrow. Even in the happiest moments of life there was always a sense that something was missing, that something was not quite right. He explains this view in one of his writings:

> Creatures are not born with desires unless satisfaction for those desires exists. A baby feels hunger: well, there is such a thing as food. A duckling wants to swim: well, there is such a thing as water. Men feel sexual desire: well, there is such a thing as sex. If I find in myself a desire which no experience in this world can satisfy, the most probable explanation is that I was made for another world. If none of my earthly pleasures satisfy it, that does not mean the universe is a fraud . . . earthly pleasures were never meant to satisfy it, but only to arouse it, to suggest the real thing.[2]

It makes no sense that we would miss something we've never had. If I lost an arm, I'm certain I would mourn the loss and wish I could have it back. Yet I've never longed to have a third arm. The thought has never crossed my mind. The death of my wife would bring immense sorrow and pain, but what if I'd never been married to her? What if I'd never met her? Her passing would go unnoticed. You can't miss something you've never had. Yet we all have a deep longing within our heart. A longing for a place we've never been. A yearning for a life we've never known. A desire that burns within our heart and often leaves us feeling cold and empty.

Paul explains the source of this desire: "We know that when this earthly tent we live in is taken down—when we die and leave these bodies—we will have a home in heaven, an eternal body made for us by God himself. . . . We grow weary in our present bodies, and we long for the day when we will put on our heavenly bodies" (2 Corinthians 5:1-2).

We long for heaven because that's where we will live with God forever. Our longing is for intimacy with God, not for the streets of gold, and not even for life eternal. What we want is what we were created to have. To be who we were created to be. To live and laugh and love with the One who created us to do all of that—and more!

REFLECTION
Take a moment to reflect on heaven and your desire to see God one day.
Can you sense his presence? How does that give meaning to your day?

EMBARRASSING GOD

They deny him by the way they live.   Titus 1:16

NOT SO LONG AGO I saw a man shopping in a grocery store while his young son ran up and down the aisles. The boy was unleashed and hyper, making a complete nuisance of himself. The father kept calling his son's name, but the boy only ran faster—up one aisle and down the other.

Just as the father caught up with him, the boy reached out and grabbed a handful of candy bars. The father tried to take them away, but the boy held on tightly. Then he started to scream. It was a high-pitched, piercing scream that reverberated throughout the store. Clerks and customers turned to look from every direction as the frustrated father tried his best to squelch his son's cries. The boy only screamed louder and started to kick. Finally the father let him go, and once again he ran down the aisle with all his might, chocolate still clutched in his greedy little grip.

At that moment I caught a glimpse of the father's face. Earlier he had tried to hide his frustration, but now he seemed oblivious to the dozens of people standing nearby. His shoulders dropped, and his head sagged. He took a deep breath and then let it slowly escape. His eyes were closed, and his head shook back and forth. It was the look of complete and total embarrassment. Although I'm sure he loved his son dearly, at this moment he was ashamed to be his father.

Do you think God ever feels that way with his children? Do you think he's ever been embarrassed by the way we act in front of others? Do you think he's ever ashamed to be our Father? Imagine how he must feel when we become so earthly minded that we run through life, ignoring his voice and oblivious to his warnings, grabbing things as we go and holding them tightly. He tries to get our attention, and we only fight harder to get away. "I opened my arms to my own people all day long, but they have rebelled," says God about Israel. "They follow their own evil paths and thoughts. All day long they insult me to my face by worshiping idols in their sacred gardens" (Isaiah 65:2-3).

Do you think God doesn't get embarrassed by the way his children act? Our life is a reflection of his authority. And when we disobey, he is the One the world scoffs at.

REFLECTION
How have you embarrassed your heavenly Father lately?
Has this become a pattern of behavior with you?

THROWING OFF WEIGHT

Let us strip off every weight that slows us down.   Hebrews 12:1

IN HIS CLASSIC NOVEL *The Mysterious Island*, Jules Verne tells the story of five men who escape a Civil War prison camp by hijacking a hot-air balloon, and the wind carried them over the ocean.

The hours pass, and the balloon begins to drift downward, closer to the surface of the ocean. The men have no way of heating the air in the balloon and realize that their only hope is to lighten their load. Shoes, overcoats, and weapons are discarded, and quickly the balloon again rises. But not for long. Soon they again find themselves drifting dangerously close to the waves. This time they begin tossing their food overboard. Better to be alive and hungry than to drown on a full belly! They know it is only a temporary fix, but it is their only hope. In time, the balloon again drifts downward.

> "Do you feel like you just spent the devil's money?"
>
> *Nicolae, 24*

The balloon doesn't stay up much longer. Within a short while it again glides downward. But before hitting the water, the men notice an island in the distance. They jump from the balloon and swim toward it. The men's lives are spared because of their willingness to discard what they didn't need for a chance to survive. What they once considered "necessities" they couldn't live without became the very things that nearly cost them their lives.

Are we able to discern between the things we need in life and those things that are simply weighing us down? How readily can we recognize the difference between life-sustaining items and life-threatening ones? The writer of Hebrews says, "Let us strip off every weight that slows us down, especially the sin that so easily hinders our progress" (12:1). Are there things in your life that keep you from growing closer to God or even cause you to sin? Does the car you drive give you a sense of pride and arrogance? Do your television viewing habits lead to thoughts of lust or habits of laziness? Maybe it's time to do some reevaluation.

REFLECTION
*What is the thing in your life that most keeps you from doing God's will?
Is there something that's causing you to sin? Could you cut it loose?*

BECOMING A TRUE FRIEND

Love each other with genuine affection.   Romans 12:10

THE NAME on his gravestone reads *John Doe*. Just one among many. The name given to the nameless—more for the purposes of record keeping than for the sake of dignity. But this time, at least, it seemed appropriate since it was the name he asked for.

He was found on a wooded section of the road near Belle Chasse, Louisiana, with a white bedsheet knotted tightly around his neck. A farewell note lay at the foot of the tree he was hanging from. It was addressed to "Mom and Dad."

> I never did develop into a real person and I cannot tolerate the false and empty existence I have created. . . . What frustrated me most in the last year was that I had built no ties to family or friends. There was nothing of lasting worth and value. I led a detached existence. . . . I am a bomb of frustration and should never marry or have children. It is safest to defuse the bomb harmlessly now. . . . Simply cremate me as John Doe.[3]

Fingerprints were taken and sent to police across the country, but no one ever came forward to claim him. His true identity was never found. Had he not left the note, we would know nothing about him, yet the circumstances of his death force us to wonder who he was and what he was like. "There was nothing of lasting worth and value," he wrote. "I led a detached existence." Whatever else John Doe was, he was desperately lonely. Lonely and alone. In a world of hand-holding couples and family picnics, John had no one he could call a true friend. No one to laugh and cry with. No one to talk to in his time of deepest need.

Paul tells us, "Don't just pretend that you love others. Really love them. . . . Love each other with genuine affection" (Romans 12:9-10). Whatever else you believe about the Christian faith, this is one truth that can't be ignored. We are called to be a friend to the friendless. To love the unloved—even the unlovable. We are to seek out and find the John Does of the world and shower them with the authentic affection they most need. And when times get dark and lonely, when life begins to spin out of control, when they long for someone to turn to, we should be there for them.

"Don't just pretend that you love others," says Paul. "Really love them."

REFLECTION
*Think about someone God has put in your life who needs your friendship.
Have you resisted getting close? Why not call that person today?*

BECOMING REAL

Be honest in your estimate of yourselves.   Romans 12:3

THERE IS A SMALL children's book that I used to read to my children titled *The Velveteen Rabbit*. It's a precious story that speaks volumes about the virtues of true character and authenticity. In one section we are eavesdropping on a conversation between a new toy rabbit and an old skin horse. As they lie side by side in the nursery, the rabbit asks the horse:

> "What is REAL? Does it mean having things that buzz inside you and a stick-out handle?"
>
> "Real isn't how you are made," said the Skin Horse. "It's a thing that happens to you. When a child loves you for a long, long time, not just to play with, but REALLY loves you, then you become REAL. . . ."
>
> "Does it happen all at once, like being wound up," he asked, "or bit by bit?"
>
> "It doesn't happen all at once," said the Skin Horse. "You become. It takes a long time. That's why it doesn't often happen to people who break easily, or have sharp edges, or have to be carefully kept. Generally, by the time you are REAL, most of your hair has been loved off, and your eyes drop out and you get loose in the joints and very shabby. But these things don't matter at all because once you are REAL you can't be ugly, except to people who don't understand."[4]

Take a long look at yourself in the mirror. Are you a real person? Do people see the real you when you greet them, or are they merely staring at one of the many masks you choose to wear? Is your friendship genuine and your faith real?

Paul encourages us to "be filled with love that comes from a pure heart, a clear conscience, and sincere faith" (1 Timothy 1:5). "Be honest in your estimate of yourselves, measuring your value by how much faith God has given you," he tells the Christians in Rome (Romans 12:3). An authentic heart and faith is a critical element to the Christian life. The world has its quota of counterfeit people with shallow smiles and false beliefs. The world needs people who are genuine. "Real isn't how you are made," said the Skin Horse. "It's a thing that happens to you." And that's exactly what the love of Jesus can do for us.

> "I don't want our personality conflict to get in the way of what's real and true."
>
> *Nicolae, 365*

REFLECTION

In what ways do you struggle with a genuine faith? How can you allow God to shape your heart into a pure and authentic tool for righteousness?

TODAY'S READING
Isaiah 66:2-4

A CONTRITE HEART

I will bless those who have humble and contrite hearts.   Isaiah 66:2

DO YOU HAVE anything in your house that's stolen? Do you have a twinge of guilt that passes through your heart when you think back to a time when you took something that wasn't yours or said something that wasn't true? Ever cheated on your taxes? Ever padded your time sheet at work? Ever lied to your boss? your mom? your wife? If so, ever wonder why it still bothers you?

You can be sure that you're not alone. In fact, guilt is such a widespread problem that the U.S. government has had to set up a "Conscience Fund" as part of its revenue system. This is a fund for all the money that comes in unexpectedly from anonymous, guilt-ridden Americans. "I am sending ten dollars for blankets I stole while in World War II," starts one letter. "My mind could not rest." It was signed, "An ex-GI."

A man from Brazil sent fifty dollars to cover the cost of two pair of cavalry boots, two pairs of trousers, one case of K-rations, and thirty pounds of frozen meat he stole from the army between 1943 and 1946. Figures show that an average of $45,000 per year is received and deposited into the Conscience Fund, most of it in increments of one to ten dollars.[5]

The need for a clean conscience is one that we all share. It's a thread that runs deep and wide throughout humanity. We don't always understand it, but we all feel it. And that's because God intended it that way. "They demonstrate that God's law is written within them," Paul writes to the Roman Christians, "for their own consciences . . . accuse them" (Romans 2:15). Sensitivity toward sin is a trait we are all born with. But it's what we do with our guilt that makes the difference.

"I will bless those who have humble and contrite hearts, who tremble at my word," God says. "But those who choose their own ways, delighting in their sins, are cursed" (Isaiah 66:2-3). Don't ignore the voice inside that keeps you honest. Let it guide you toward a pure heart and life within God's perfect will.

REFLECTION
Have you made an effort to right the wrongs that you've done?
Ask God what he would have you do.

JESUS OUR BROTHER

Jesus is not ashamed to call them his brothers and sisters.   Hebrews 2:11

BEING A FOLLOWER of Christ is so much more than believing the gospel and reading the Bible. It's about developing a deep and personal relationship with Jesus. It's about calling God our Father, and seeing Jesus as our brother. It's about embracing the love and forgiveness that God has extended—about resting in his grace and learning to love him back.

I know Christians who have been believers most of their lives, yet they still have not comprehended this truth. Their religion is more about making and keeping rules than about accepting and extending grace. They are bitter and judgmental and unbending.

I'm still amazed that anyone could come away from Scripture with such a dim and perverted view of God. I'm even more amazed that anyone would want to. It's not only wrong, but it's a complete distortion of everything Jesus taught and stood for.

> "Truly they were brothers and sisters in Christ, and there would be no surviving without them."
>
> *Assassins,* 149

"God's law was given so that all people could see how sinful they were. But as people sinned more and more, God's wonderful kindness became more abundant. So just as sin ruled over all people and brought them to death, now God's wonderful kindness rules instead, giving us right standing with God and resulting in eternal life through Jesus Christ our Lord" (Romans 5:20-21). That's the gospel of Jesus according to Paul. And I dare anyone to find an ounce of condemnation in it.

"Let us come boldly to the throne of our gracious God," says the writer of Hebrews. "There we will receive his mercy, and we will find grace to help us when we need it" (4:16). It is God's mercy that draws men to salvation. And it is through that same mercy that we are able to call Jesus our friend and brother.

"Anyone who does God's will is my brother and sister and mother," says Jesus (Mark 3:35). To those who would follow him he offered more than a place in heaven; he offered a share in his inheritance. He extends a branch of his family tree and offers to graft us into it. A child of God. A brother of Jesus. A member of the family from now through eternity. That's what being a Christian is about.

REFLECTION
How does it feel to call Jesus your brother? to call God your Father?

A FROG OR A PRINCESS?

Live for the glory of God through Christ Jesus.   Romans 6:11

AN OLD MAN was walking beside a creek when he heard a frog call out to him. "Kiss me, old man, for I'm really a beautiful princess." The old man stopped, somewhat startled and picked the frog up. Again the frog told him, "Kiss me, and I'll turn into a beautiful princess." The man put the frog into his pocket and began to walk. After a while the frog protested, "I told you I was a beautiful princess. Why haven't you kissed me?" The old man kept walking. "I believe you," he said, "but at my age I'd just as soon have a talking frog."

Ever known anyone like that? Ever run across someone who could have had a beautiful princess but decided instead to settle for a talking frog? Ever done that yourself? I have. On more than a few occasions.

The problem with following Jesus is that he doesn't force you to follow him. He extends his salvation to all, and we can accept it and let that be enough. We can settle for his grace without ever exploring the wonders of his blessings. We can take the Holy Spirit into our heart without ever allowing him to change us. "Just as Christ was raised from the dead by the glorious power of the Father," says Paul, "now we also may live new lives. . . . We are no longer slaves to sin. . . . He died once to defeat sin, and now he lives for the glory of God. So you should consider yourselves dead to sin and able to live for the glory of God through Christ Jesus" (Romans 6:4-11).

Jesus extends the promise of a "beautiful princess," but many simply settle for the novelty of a "talking frog." Somehow it seems nice to know it's there if we ever need it, but for now it's not worth the effort. Change is hard work, and who needs that at our age?

It's a sad way to think and a loser way to live. Don't give into it. Jesus offers a life of abundance, filled with unmatchable blessing. He extends the promise of power and joy beyond our wildest dreams, and we'd be fools not to accept it. Don't let Jesus save you without asking him to change you. Especially when it's just one kiss away.

REFLECTION
In what ways have you grown complacent about God's grace and not trusted in his power to change? What is it in your life that needs changing?

A DONKEY OR A HORSE?

*Who makes the wild donkey wild? . . . Have you given
the horse its strength . . . ?*   Job 39:5, 19

HERE'S A QUESTION you may have never considered: How do horses and donkeys react differently when surrounded by opposition? If you're a farmer, you may know the answer already, but I was surprised by it. Are you curious?

When horses are surrounded by unfriendly animals, they instinctively gather in a circle with their heads toward the center. And then they begin to kick. The attacking animals are soon beaten and battered and usually leave with their tails between their legs.

When donkeys are attacked, they too gather in a tight circle and begin to kick and fight, but not in the way you would expect. They face the wrong direction. Donkeys stand with their heads toward their enemy, so their blows land on the backsides of the other donkeys in the pack. The foe has to do little more than wait until they've kicked themselves to death.

The Lord had his reasons for making both animals, but he is also quick to point out the differences. "Who makes the wild donkey wild?" God asks Job. "I have placed it in the wilderness; its home is the wasteland." But his description of the mighty horse takes on a different tone. "Have you given the horse its strength or clothed its neck with a flowing mane? . . . Its majestic snorting is something to hear! It paws the earth and rejoices in its strength. When it charges to war, it is unafraid" (Job 39:5, 19-22).

The valiant horse and the sniveling donkey. Two animals with similar frames but polar personalities. One was bred for greatness, the other for self-survival. One leads men to battle and carries them through to victory, the other runs and hides at the sight of trouble.

Neither has a choice in how they respond, but you and I do. In any given circumstance we have a decision to make. Will we be a horse or a donkey? Will we stand together and strong in the face of opposition or fend for ourselves and cowardly kick at our own pack? Will we stand against sin or give in to it? A valiant horse or a frightened donkey? You decide.

REFLECTION
*How do you react when faced with Satan's opposition? Ask God to give
you the strength of the mighty horse for future encounters.*

HOSEA'S STORY

Go and marry a prostitute.   Hosea 1:2

SOME STORIES in Scripture surprise us. They seem to reflect a side of God that confuses and frustrates us as followers until we begin to wonder if we understand our Lord at all. *God wouldn't do that, would he?* we think. Such is the story of Hosea and Gomer.

Hosea was a prophet of God. In the Hebrew his name literally means "salvation" or "the Lord saves." He was a man who lived in complete obedience to God, no matter what he was asked to do. So what does God ask him to do? He commands Hosea to take a wife. God tells him to marry Gomer, a prostitute—a woman without a shred of faithfulness in her. Hosea marries Gomer, and she gives him three children. But even that doesn't keep her heart from wandering. Gomer leaves Hosea and takes another lover, once again prostituting herself. And God tells Hosea to go and get her. To buy her back—to redeem her and forgive her and bring her back home.

> "Weak and frail and wicked as they were, unfaithful, ignorant, impatient, and dallying with other gods, the God of the universe himself catered to the children of Israel."
>
> *The Mark, 233*

What kind of God would ask a man to do such a thing? The kind of God who did that very thing for us. Hosea's story is a reflection of our story. Hosea's faithfulness symbolizes God's faithfulness. Gomer symbolizes Israel, but she also symbolizes you and me.

If you think that's too harsh an analogy, spend some time reflecting on the times you've wandered away from God. How many times have you broken God's heart by directing your attention to another? How many days have you gone without even acknowledging his presence in your life? How many things have you looked to for love and significance? Ever turned your back on God? So have I. We're the unfaithful wife whom God continues to love and care for in spite of our wayward spirit.

You can't read Hosea's story without being humbled. To read about Hosea's faithfulness to Gomer brings a deep sigh of relief and a new understanding of God's unbelievable love for his people.

REFLECTION
What significance do you find in the meaning of Hosea's name—"salvation"? Now that you know Hosea represents God and his faithfulness, how does the story take on new meaning for you?

FAITHFUL OBEDIENCE

So Hosea married Gomer.   Hosea 1:3

WE CAN'T PRETEND that the story of Hosea doesn't bother us. It's hard to fathom that God would ask a trusted servant to take a prostitute for his wife. Why would God want one of his most faithful prophets to be married to one of earth's most unfaithful women? What could God have been thinking?

The story is hard enough to believe that many scholars excuse it away as an allegory. Even the commentary in my Bible says that the story must be fictitious since God would never ask a godly prophet to marry a prostitute just to make a point. God was simply telling us a parable that reflects his love for his people, the writer maintains through two paragraphs of academic language.

Granted, the story is hard to believe, but that doesn't mean it's not literal. Hosea and Gomer were real people, just like you and me. God commanded Hosea to marry Gomer, and he obeyed. The children she bore were flesh and bone. She left him for another lover, and Hosea bought her back, just as God asked him to do.

The question is, Why do we struggle so to understand God's ways and purposes? Why do we have such a hard time believing that God is more interested in our obedience than our comfort? What makes us think that God wouldn't do anything to draw us into a deeper understanding of his love and mercy? Doubting the reality of the story shows how little we understand the temporal nature of life on earth. God sees things from a heavenly perspective, and that makes all the difference.

Maybe that's why believers often struggle to obey God's calling. I know a couple that felt called to the mission field in Africa. They put their funds together and made the trip, only to get there and decide that this calling wasn't for them after all. Africa is hot and humid and filled with mosquitoes. They assumed they had misread God's calling and abandoned their mission. Obedience always looks easier on the drafting board than it does in reality. Hosea knew that his comfort would come in the form of a heavenly reward, not earthly convenience. That's why he could so easily obey and remain faithful. Lives always take on a different perspective when we look at God's will through a heavenly perspective.

REFLECTION
What was God trying to teach Hosea by asking him to take Gomer as his wife? What applications can we draw from his example?

157

GOD THE MERCIFUL

For I am God and not a mere mortal.   Hosea 11:9

A PREREQUISITE to understanding how God works in our life is to first have an accurate view of Scripture. The stories in the Bible are not fairy-tale versions of real life, nor are they allegories; they are real stories of real people—people just like you and me. The history of Israel is packed with examples of people struggling to find God in the midst of chaos and confusion, just like we do. Had we lived at that time, our names may have ended up in the text. Picture yourself in the Bible, and then see how the stories begin to come alive for you.

The people of Israel struggled to remain faithful to God. In spite of their best attempts, their hearts continued to wander. They tried to be obedient, and for periods they succeeded, but they inevitably would fall back into their old sinful ways. Does that describe your struggle? Can you relate to their battle against the sinful nature? We all can, and that's why the stories should give us comfort.

> "How could you not love the God the prophets describe? How could you not love the God Jesus the Messiah refers to as our Father who is in heaven?"
>
> *The Remnant, 230*

The book of Hosea is one of many records of Israel's disobedience in the face of God's faithfulness. As always, they continued to fail and disappoint God. As you read through the book, you find yourself wondering: *How could they possibly continue to sin and fall away over and over again?* Then we lean back and realize that we do the same thing. We give our heart to God one minute, then turn back to our idols the next. We promise to be faithful, only to again give in to temptation. And our sin hurts God as much as theirs did.

God's words to Israel take on new levels of meaning to us when we realize that their story is ours. In spite of all they have done, God still proclaims his love for them. "My heart is torn within me, and my compassion overflows. . . . I will not completely destroy Israel, for I am God and not a mere mortal. I am the Holy One living among you, and I will not come to destroy" (Hosea 11:8-9). It is one of the most power-packed messages of grace in all of Scripture.

The words were for Israel, but the message is for us. God loves us in spite of who we are and what we've done. We will never be able to understand his mercy, only accept it.

REFLECTION
Does an understanding of God's love and mercy make you want to be more faithful to him? What are some concrete ways you can do this?

JUNE

GOD THE REDEEMER

Love her, even though she loves adultery.   Hosea 3:1

THE LANGUAGE of Hosea is as strong as the message behind it. Once again we see God's propensity for symbolism as we look to the story of Hosea.

We've learned that the name Hosea means "salvation," or "the Lord saves." But the story takes on even greater significance when we look at some of the other players.

Hosea and Gomer had three children, and God gave them names that reflected their symbolic roles in the story. Jezreel means "God scatters," Lo-ruhamah means "Not loved," and Lo-ammi, means "Not my people." All of these names describe Israel's offspring and their propensity for rebellion and waywardness. Through the names of Gomer's children, God was giving us a glimpse into Israel's cold and rebellious heart toward him.

When Gomer left Hosea to live with another lover, God commanded Hosea to buy her back. He redeemed her for "fifteen pieces of silver and about five bushels of barley and a measure of wine" (Hosea 3:2). This amount is what it might cost to purchase a common mule, far less than a good woman would be worth. I can imagine that Gomer was so despised and defiled that even her peers looked on her with shame. She was a woman without reputation, shunned by women and used by men.

Hosea was a man who epitomized love and faithfulness, yet he was given a harlot for a wife. In spite of her shameful ways, he took her in and loved her. She regarded him with contempt; he rewarded her with deliverance. She looked on him with hate; he looked on her with love and compassion. She ran from his goodness; he paid to get her back. It's our story put into perspective from the eyes of God. God redeemed us in spite of our contempt and rebellion, but the price he paid was far greater. In fact, it was unthinkable. He paid with the blood of his own Son. Is it possible to comprehend the unconditional love of God? Probably not.

REFLECTION
When you consider the price God paid to redeem us, how does it change the way you see the story of Gomer? Does it change the way you see your unfaithfulness?

DOING LITTLE THINGS WELL

Onesimus hasn't been of much use to you in the past,
but now he is very useful.   Philemon 1:11

WE ALL WANT to do great things for God, don't we? We'd all like to take on grand projects in the name of the Lord and use our faith to make a powerful impact on the world around us. New Christians are especially fervent for God's Kingdom. They are often so excited about their new faith that they stand ready to blaze new trails on the mission field. They're willing to go to the ends of the earth to reach millions with the message of God's grace. But sometimes God simply wants us to do little things better—the same things we've been doing, but with greater zeal and love.

The book of Philemon is a short but powerful testament to this truth. The book is really a letter, written by Paul to his good friend Philemon. He's writing on behalf of Onesimus, one of Philemon's slaves. Onesimus ran away from Philemon in an effort to gain his freedom and along the way was brought to Christ by Paul.

Imagine how excited Onesimus must have been about finding faith in the Lord. Think what the prospect of heaven must have meant to a man who had spent his life as a lowly slave. From sweating over a hot kitchen to living in his own mansion in glory. From the servant quarters to the streets of gold. From a cold, hard bed to the arms of a loving Savior.

You think Onesimus wasn't ready to shout from the rooftops? You think he wasn't prepared to preach about Jesus in the synagogue or to take on the whole city of Rome or even to travel to the farthest corner of the globe to share his faith? "Just tell me what to do, and with God's help, I'll do it!" he must have told Paul.

And what did Paul tell him to do? He told him to go back home and serve his former master, Philemon. He told him to take up his slave garments and go back to the kitchen. Back to his cold bed and life of thankless service. Then Paul wrote a letter for him to take with him, explaining where he had been and why he was returning. It couldn't have been the assignment Onesimus wanted, but it was the one he got. And he accepted and obeyed. We all want to do great things for God, but sometimes the best way to bring him glory is to simply do what we've been doing, but much better. To be a better friend, husband, worker, son, daughter, and neighbor than we've ever been. To do little things with greater zeal in the name of God.

REFLECTION
Are you neglecting the little things in an effort to do great things for God?
What are some tasks that he would have you do better?

GOD'S DELIVERANCE

The God whom we serve is able to save us.   Daniel 3:17

MOST OF US have heard the story of Shadrach, Meshach, and Abednego—the three men who were saved from a blazing furnace. King Nebuchadnezzar ordered everyone under his authority to bow down to the ninety-foot gold statue he had set up on the plain of Dura in the province of Babylon. All races and nationalities were commanded to worship the king's god, but Shadrach, Meshach, and Abednego refused. They served the living God of Israel and wouldn't bow to the king's idol.

"If we are thrown into the blazing furnace," they told him, "the God whom we serve is able to save us. He will rescue us from your power, Your Majesty. But even if he doesn't, Your Majesty can be sure that we will never serve your gods or worship the gold statue you have set up" (Daniel 3:17-18).

> "Whom will you serve? Will you obey the ruler of this world, or will you call on the name of the Lord?"
>
> *The Remnant,* 232

The three Israelites were thrown into the fire but didn't burn up. Even after the king had the furnace turned up seven times hotter, they walked away unscathed. And because of their faith and courage, the king worshiped and revered God. Their story is an amazing testament to the power of faith and the might of God in the face of opposition. It's the perfect Sunday school illustration. "Stand strong in your beliefs and God will take care of you" is the application. And it's a good one.

But what if God hadn't saved these three friends from the fire? Would their faith have been less admired? Would they still be seen as heroes of the Bible? Could we say with the same confidence that God still delivered them?

Shadrach, Meshach, and Abednego understood the stakes involved in their stand, yet they chose the fire anyway. They knew that God didn't have to save them and that he might choose not to. They knew that he might let them fry in the furnace, but that didn't mean they would be abandoned. Their deliverance had little to do with their physical bodies and everything to do with their spiritual ones. They were willing to be thrown into the fire and take the consequence of staying true to their faith. They knew that God had the power to protect them, but they also knew that God was God and that he would choose the outcome he wanted.

Some people are martyred for the sake of Christ, and others are saved at the last moment to live many more years. But the question of deliverance is not ever in question.

REFLECTION
How strong is your faith in the face of danger? Would you be willing to pay the ultimate sacrifice for your faith?

WHAT IS MAN?

What is man that you are mindful of him?   Psalm 8:4, NIV

A FRIEND OF MINE was once given a tour of Harvard University by one of the professors, and when they came to one particular building, he told my friend an interesting story. The building was donated by a very wealthy man who was an atheist. He gave the school an unconditional grant to erect the building. Later, during construction, the man came to them with a request. He wanted an inscription placed at the base of the building that read "Man is the measure of all things."

The builders agreed, though somewhat reluctantly. But before the building was completed the rich atheist died. The donor never lived to see the final result of his grant.

When the time came to mount the inscription, a professor stepped forward with a better idea. Today the inscription on the building reads "What is man that you are mindful of him? Psalm 8:4."

God's perspective is certainly different than man's.

Paul tells the Christians in Rome, "I plead with you to give your bodies to God. Let them be a living and holy sacrifice. . . . Be honest in your estimate of yourselves, measuring your value by how much faith God has given you" (Romans 12:1, 3). Left to our own thinking we will always see ourselves as greater than we are. We have always had a tendency to see ourselves as the ultimate beings. We dominate the earth and name the stars as if they were all our own. We claim the sea's treasures and walk on the moon, then pat ourselves on the back for our accomplishments. We're the dominant species, so why shouldn't we have a right to gloat?

That's why science and philosophy have worked so hard at eliminating thoughts of God. If God is real and we are his creations, our notch has been lowered on the board. We can no longer claim the ultimate bragging rights.

The problem is, atheists are wrong. We are not the masters of our universe; we are servants of God. We didn't come from a bucket of sludge; we were fashioned by a loving Creator. We're not "all that and a bag of chips." We're strangers in a land not our own. "What is man that you are mindful of him?" asks the psalmist (Psalm 8:4, NIV). And all creation nods in agreement.

REFLECTION
Have you ever thought your worth greater than it is? How should we measure our worth in light of God's grace and majesty?

LIFELESS IDOLS

Do not worship any other gods besides me.   Exodus 20:3

ONE OF MY all-time favorite movies is *Raiders of the Lost Ark,* the first film in the Indiana Jones trilogy. I think it's Steven Spielberg's greatest work. In the film Hitler's Nazis have stolen the newly recovered Ark of the Covenant and placed it aboard a German submarine. The Ark is housed inside a wooden crate with a large swastika, the insignia of the brutal Nazi empire, emblazed on the side. During one scene we see the crate in the dark hull of the ship with rats scurrying about. The camera pans toward the swastika as the music builds, and suddenly it begins to scorch. The rats nearby fall dead, and within seconds the Nazi symbol is completely burned away. It's a powerful scene that is meant to show God's contempt for man's evil plans. And Spielberg's theology was right on target.

> "Much as the world system tries to downplay it, our society has seen catastrophic rises in drug abuse, sexual immorality, murder, theft, demon worship, and idolatry."
>
> *Apollyon, 330*

The scene could have come right out of the pages of Scripture. In fact, it is reminiscent of one that was recorded in the book of 1 Samuel. In this excerpt from Scripture, the Ark had been stolen by the Philistines and placed in the temple of their god Dagon. To the Philistines, the Ark was simply another trophy made in honor of another tribe's god, so they put it in a tent alongside the idol of Dagon. "When the citizens of Ashdod went to see it the next morning," Samuel records, "Dagon had fallen with his face to the ground in front of the Ark of the Lord!" (5:3). So the confused Philistines set the idol back on its feet. The next morning the same thing happened, only this time the statue had been assaulted. "His head and hands had broken off and were lying in the doorway. Only the trunk of his body was left intact," writes Samuel (5:4).

God had left little doubt about his contempt for other gods.

"Do not make idols of any kind," God tells us, "whether in the shape of birds or animals or fish. You must never worship or bow down to them, for I, the Lord your God, am a jealous God who will not share your affection with any other god!" (Exodus 20:4-5).

If you want to know how God feels about the lifeless things we worship, you don't have to look very hard to find out. He has little patience for little gods and even less for those who bow down to them. And this jealousy is not misplaced or without warrant. When we, as God's greatest creation, give our affections to idols, we are heaping the ultimate insult on him. Why wouldn't he be angry?

REFLECTION
What are some idols that you've bowed down to lately? How do you think it makes God feel when we give all of our affection to people instead of to him?

BRIGHT BLUE CRAYONS

Flee from the worship of idols.   1 Corinthians 10:14

THERE WAS ONCE a man who had a son he loved very much. The boy wanted to be an artist, so the father gave him a bright blue crayon. It was the boy's favorite color. The son cuddled and held the crayon tightly, even taking it to bed with him at night. He loved his bright blue coloring tool. "Someday I'm going to be an artist," said the boy.

Then one day the father saw the boy talking to the crayon. He had placed it in the center of the desk in his room and stood gazing down at it with admiration. "I so wish I had some paper," said the boy. "O great blue crayon, please bring me something to write on." The father was grieved, but he remained silent. Over the days to come the boy stopped talking to his father, but he continued to worship the crayon. "I know that you gave me the skill to be an artist," he would say, "and someday you'll bring me some paper. But only when you think I'm ready."

Weeks went by, but still the father hadn't heard from his son. All the while he continued to watch from a distance as the boy hugged and cradled his blue crayon. He longed for even a short visit with his beloved son, but his boy was much too busy.

It's a simple and strange little fable but not as farfetched as you might think. We laugh at the young boy's antics and wonder how he could be so naïve and ungrateful. But haven't we all done the same thing?

Years ago I longed to be a writer and prayed for God's help and guidance. Then my first book was published, and I held it in my hands, admiring my name on the cover. I thanked God for his kindness, but my thoughts were mainly focused on my new career. I used the book to build a résumé and continued to approach publishers. The book became proof of my skill and ability to write, I thought. Surely it would help me procure another contract. "O great and mighty book, please bring me another book to write," I said, though not in so many words. All the while the Father who gave me the skill in the first place and opened the door for my first book, stood by wondering why I had forgotten him.

Who among us hasn't cuddled and idolized a bright blue crayon from our Father? Haven't we all bowed down to a lifeless idol or two, forgetting all about the one who really loves and cares for us? And all the while he sits by watching, wanting desperately to say to us, "I'm the one who provided the crayon. Don't you think I'd give you some paper too? All you have to do is ask!"

REFLECTION
How does Paul describe idols in today's reading? How does that change your view of the things you hold tightly?

165

GOD KNOWS YOUR NAME

Look at the lilies and how they grow.   Matthew 6:28

A GOOD FRIEND of mine once went to visit his brother during a time of deep crisis. His brother was at one of the lowest points of his life. His marriage was struggling, his business was near collapse, and his money was drying up quickly. He had just sold his home and moved into a one-bedroom apartment and had no idea how he was going to dig himself out of his financial and relational problems.

My friend listened as his brother confided in him about his deep frustration. "Some days you want to just go outside and shake your fist at heaven and say, 'God, why don't you help me?'" his brother confessed.

My friend looked his brother in the eye and said somberly, "That wouldn't do any good. He doesn't even know who you are." The two looked at each other for several seconds then burst out laughing. The two brothers had spent their lives trusting God and studying his Word, and the absurdity of the statement left them both in stitches. My friend's humor wasn't lost on his brother a bit. In fact, years later as the two were reflecting back on that episode, the brother told my friend that his joke had brought him a great deal of comfort during his trying time. Even more, it gave him renewed perspective.

"Don't worry about everyday life," Jesus tells us. "Look at the birds. They don't need to plant or harvest or put food in barns because your heavenly Father feeds them. And you are far more valuable to him than they are. . . . Look at the lilies and how they grow. They don't work or make their clothing, yet Solomon in all his glory was not dressed as beautifully as they are. And if God cares so wonderfully for flowers that are here today and gone tomorrow, won't he more surely care for you?" (Matthew 6:25-30).

We've all felt abandoned by God at one time or another. We've all wanted to shake our fist toward heaven and ask God *why*. Some of us have even done it, and God understands our frustration. But that doesn't mean he's forgotten us. God cares deeply when we suffer, and he is right there beside us all the time. Even when it seems he isn't doing anything to help, you can be certain that he is. His help doesn't always come in the form we'd expect, but it always comes in the manner we most need.

At times like these the best thing to do is to put your hand in his and trust him with your future. Because he not only knows what you're going through, he knows exactly who you are.

REFLECTION
What kind of trial or crisis have you most recently faced? Have you put your trust in God to help you through it? Why not do so today?

THE ONE THING

The one thing I ask of the Lord . . .   Psalm 27:4

IF YOU COULD ask God for one thing, what would it be? If God came to you and granted you one big wish, what would you wish for?

I asked my fourteen-year-old son that question a few weeks ago, and without skipping a beat he said, "Knowledge and chocolate." I'm sure he got his sense of humor from his dad.

God posed that very question to Solomon, and he asked for wisdom and knowledge. Solomon was young and the newly appointed king of Israel, and he knew that this was what he most needed to govern God's people well. God was pleased with his request and gave him even more than he asked. God blessed Solomon beyond his wildest dreams, making him the wisest and wealthiest man to ever live. But in the end, knowledge didn't save him. Knowledge couldn't keep his heart from straying.

> "He had never felt so vividly the presence of God. So this was the feeling of dwelling on holy ground."
>
> *Tribulation Force, 241*

Solomon should have taken a lesson from his father. David asked himself the same question, but his answer couldn't have been more different. "The one thing I ask of the Lord— the thing I seek most—is to live in the house of the Lord all the days of my life, delighting in the Lord's perfections and meditating in his Temple" (Psalm 27:4).

 David's one wish in life was to be near God. To worship him, to delight in his majesty, to meditate on his will and his Word. David didn't ask for wisdom because he knew that God had enough wisdom for the both of them. He didn't ask for knowledge, because all he needed to know was God's nearness. David's one desire was to desire God. And in the end it made him a "man after [God's] own heart" (1 Samuel 13:14).

My boy and I have both decided that David is the better model. We want God to know that the thing we most long for in life is his presence. We want to rest in the shadow of his majesty and grace. We desire wisdom and knowledge, but those are not the things that will keep us close to God. What we most want is "to live in the house of the Lord" forever. And maybe he'll throw in a little chocolate as well!

REFLECTION

What do you think of David's request from God? What does it mean to "seek" the Lord? When is the last time you delighted in "his perfections"?

A REASON TO LIVE

Can my dust praise you from the grave?　　Psalm 30:9

"WHAT WILL YOU gain if I die, if I sink down into the grave?" David cries out to the Lord. "Can my dust praise you from the grave? Can it tell the world of your faithfulness?" (Psalm 30:9).

When David found himself surrounded by enemies out for blood, he called to the Lord for help, and God answered his prayer. He delivered David from certain death, and David praised him for it.

"You have turned my mourning into joyful dancing. You have taken away my clothes of mourning and clothed me with joy, that I might sing praises to you and not be silent" (Psalm 30:11-12).

Many years ago I found myself counseling a teenage girl in the pit of despair. She was only sixteen, and her parents had just filed for divorce. It was an agonizing time in her life, and she felt she had no one to turn to. Because I was a college student and a Sunday school teacher, the task somehow fell to me, though I was completely unequipped to deal with her sorrow. "I don't want to live anymore," she said through sobs. "Why are they doing this to me? I just want to die."

All I knew to do was listen and console her as best I could. I had no words of wisdom that seemed to help. "You don't really mean that," I remember saying. "The pain will ease in time." I said what I could, but it was hardly inspired. I wish I'd thought of these words from David.

"What good would my death bring?" David was saying. "If I die and turn to dust, will that dust praise you? Will it witness to my friends? Tell me how my death will honor you, God! What purpose would it serve?" The reason we should go on living is not because life is always easy but because death is irreversible. And it's not our decision. The time will come when God will take us all home, and that will be a glorious day. But until then, we all have work to do. We have people to touch, a world to witness to, and a God to worship. Dust and bones can't glorify God, but you and I can.

If I could go back in time, that's what I would tell my friend. I hope by now she knows.

REFLECTION
Have you ever been tired of living? Ever longed for an end to life?
What would God say to you during those times?

DELIVERANCE THROUGH PAIN

We can rejoice, too, when we run into problems and trials.   Romans 5:3

GOD DOESN'T ALWAYS deliver us from our pain; sometimes he delivers us through it.

Before Jesus began his public ministry, the Holy Spirit led him into the desert to be tempted. Christ spent forty days and nights without food, and in his weakest hour Satan came to tempt him. The temptations were real, and so was his anguish, but he stood strong and resisted. God could have taken the suffering away. He could have provided food and led his Son out of the desert. But he knew that suffering served a purpose.

When Jesus went to the cross, he knew he didn't have to do it. He could have stopped the ordeal any time he wanted. As he hung in agony, with blood flowing from his body, the people below taunted him. "Well then, if you are the Son of God, save yourself and come down from the cross!" (Matthew 27:40). And the greatest irony was that their words were accurate—he was the Son of God, and he could have come down from the cross. He could have called forth a legion of angels and brought Rome to her knees, all in one fell swoop. And the Father could have done the same thing. He didn't have to watch the whole excruciating sight from heaven and allow it to go on. But he knew there was a purpose behind his Son's suffering.

"Even though Jesus was God's Son," says the writer of Hebrews, "he learned obedience from the things he suffered. In this way, God qualified him as a perfect High Priest, and he became the source of eternal salvation for all those who obey him" (Hebrews 5:8-9). The pain that Jesus went through during his early years prepared him for the cross. And the pain he suffered on the cross brought salvation to all people. Jesus knew that sometimes deliverance demands pain. And often the greater the deliverance, the more you have to suffer.

"We can rejoice, too," says Paul, "when we run into problems and trials, for we know that they are good for us—they help us learn to endure. And endurance develops strength of character in us, and character strengthens our confident expectation of salvation" (Romans 5:3-4).

Too often our prayers are dominated by requests for God to take away the pain, to stop the agony, to deliver us from our suffering. But sometimes God delivers us *through* our pain instead.

REFLECTION
When did you last go through a time of deep trial and suffering? How did you plead with God to take away the pain? How would he have you pray?

WHEN BROTHERS STUMBLE

Though they stumble, they will not fall.   Psalm 37:24

I KNOW A MAN who stumbled in sin some years ago. His sin was large, and so was his repentance. He saw the pain he inflicted on those around him, and it brought him to his knees before God and man. And now he has spent the past ten years paying for his transgression—working to rebuild the trust he lost and to repair the damage. His repentance has brought him closer to God, and it has brought his family closer to each other. And yet today there are pockets of people in his church who still condemn him. They remember his sin, and when his back is turned, they discuss it among themselves. Instead of encouraging my friend for turning back to God and remaining faithful, they choose to define him by the sin he committed years ago.

If God promises not only to forgive us of our sins but also to forget them, shouldn't we work to do the same for each other? Do we have any right to hold a man's sin against him long after he has repented and turned back to God? Of course we don't.

> "You were born in sin and separated from God, but the Bible says God is not willing that any should perish but that all should come to repentance."
>
> *Desecration, 136*

Few of us will ever sin as grandly or publicly as King David. He completely turned his back on God's commandments when he sinned with Bathsheba and then had her husband killed. He hurt more people and did more damage in that one event than many of us will do in a lifetime. And yet on the heels of his repentance, he writes a psalm to God, saying, "The steps of the godly are directed by the Lord. He delights in every detail of their lives. *Though they stumble, they will not fall*, for the Lord holds them by the hand" (Psalm 37:23-24, italics mine).

"I may have stumbled, but I didn't fall," David says. How can he think that? Didn't he fall flat on his face? But David knows that the true test came afterward. His sin could have brought him down, but it didn't. He could have allowed his stumble to make him fall away from God, but he got back to his feet. David didn't fall, he stumbled. "For the Lord holds them by the hand," he writes. When David saw himself falling, he reached out at the last minute and caught God by the hand. That's the only thing that saved him.

I heard once that a general wrote to Abraham Lincoln about a battle his troops had lost. Lincoln wrote back, "I'm aware that you've fallen. My concern is that you arise." God sends that same message to you and me. Shouldn't we send that message to others?

REFLECTION
Do you still find yourself talking about a sin committed by a brother or sister years ago? Why not focus instead on that person's repentance?

HIDING SIN

When I refused to confess my sin, I was weak and miserable.   Psalm 32:3

DOES ANYONE really get away with sin? Is it possible to sin without getting caught or suffering the consequences?

We can all think back to a time when we sinned and didn't get caught. Maybe you cheated on a test, and no one saw you. Your grade came out better than you deserved; it's now years later, and no one is the wiser. Maybe you cheated on your taxes one season. You took a deduction you didn't deserve or fudged a bit on the numbers. The transgression appeared to go unnoticed.

Maybe you lied to your wife. It was a little lie, and it helped curtail a much bigger confrontation, so you justified the act in your mind. She never suspected, and you never got caught, so it feels like you came away unscathed. But did you? Do we ever come away from sin without getting caught?

"When I refused to confess my sin," says David, "I was weak and miserable, and I groaned all day long. Day and night your hand of discipline was heavy on me. My strength evaporated like water in the summer heat" (Psalm 32:3-4).

Even when it seemed that his sin was going undetected by other people, David's heart burned with guilt and shame. David was rich and powerful enough to possibly escape the earthly consequences of his transgressions, but he couldn't get away from the heavenly ones. His sin had created a chasm between him and God, and it proved more than he could bear.

"Finally, I confessed all my sins to you and stopped trying to hide them. . . . And you forgave me! All my guilt is gone" (32:5).

Some of us may believe that we can do wrong in the eyes of God and get away with it, but we're mistaken. We may think we can fool everybody, but we can't fool God. We may be able to hide our sin from other people and curb the earthly consequences, but we can't get past the heavenly One. Our Father knows what we did, and in the end that's what matters the most.

REFLECTION
What unconfessed sin is in your heart? How is it affecting your relationship with God? Isn't it time to bring it before him?

OUR ROCK

Lead me to the towering rock of safety.   Psalm 61:2

HAVE YOU EVER noticed how people tend to flock to men and women of great wisdom and strength? We all want to be near those who epitomize stability—people who have good ideas and stand true to their convictions. They know what they believe and why they believe it, and we like to be around them in an effort to draw on their knowledge. Their passion inspires and captivates us, and just being near them makes us feel more alive.

Dr. James Dobson comes to mind as a good example of this kind of person. As president of Focus on the Family, he has spent his life championing the importance of the family and fighting for the rights of Christians. His strength and charisma have gained an enormous following around the world. Every day people flock to Colorado Springs by the hundreds to visit his ministry headquarters. Thousands come each year just to be near his campus, hoping to get a chance to meet him or to perhaps see him in the studio. He is an icon of trust and dependability among Christians, and because of it, people come in droves to try and draw from his strength.

The attraction is not without warrant. We are fascinated by people of conviction because we want to be like them. We admire their tenacity and character, and we flock to their side in an effort to grow strong ourselves.

"Lead me to the towering rock of safety," King David cries out to God, "for you are my safe refuge, a fortress where my enemies cannot reach me. Let me live forever in your sanctuary, safe beneath the shelter of your wings!" (Psalm 61:2-4).

We flock to strength because strength is what we most need in life, and God is the ultimate "rock of safety." He is our shelter from the pouring rains of doubt and confusion. Our fortress when our enemies line up against us. Our eternal sanctuary. Our tower of strength in a world crumbling beneath our feet.

There are times in my life when I've been the picture of instability. In spite of my best efforts to remain true and faithful to God and others, I've struggled to stay on my feet. I've let people down and failed to live up to God's standard. During those times, I need a rock to hold onto. Something stronger and higher than myself—something from which I can draw renewed wisdom and strength. I need a fortress—a rock. I need God.

REFLECTION
Do you look to God for the strength you need? How do we go about finding shelter beneath his wings?

GOD'S BIG PLANS

Is anything too hard for the Lord?   Genesis 18:14

WHEN GOD PROMISED Abraham a son, his wife, Sarah, was listening nearby. She was long past the childbearing years, and she laughed silently at the idea. "How could a worn-out woman like me have a baby?" she thought to herself (Genesis 18:12). God heard her scoffs and confronted her about it. "Is anything too hard for the Lord?" he asked her (18:14). Most of us know the end of the story. Sarah became pregnant and gave birth to Isaac, the son of promise.

I wonder how often we scoff at the Lord's plans. How many times have we inwardly laughed at the big ideas that God plants in our spirit?

> "My friend, if I had gone through what you've gone through and seen prayer answered the way you have, I would not be challenging God to do something so simple."
>
> *Nicolae, 199*

Have you ever found yourself dreaming of doing something great for God? Have you ever lain awake at night and imagined yourself in the midst of a task so big and powerful and overwhelming that you eventually chuckled and shook your head in embarrassment? *Who do I think I am . . . Billy Graham? I could never do that. God would never do something like that through someone like me!* You blame it on the pizza and roll over and go to sleep.

"The reason you don't have what you want is that you don't ask God for it," James tells us (James 4:2). It doesn't always occur to us that maybe the big dreams in our mind were placed there by God. He plants his plans in our heart, and we scoff at them simply because they feel much too big. And how will we ever know if we are so quick to discount the idea?

Why would we expect God to do great things through us if we don't ask? How can we accomplish big plans if we never try? How can we expect God to answer big prayers when we never ask him to?

Do you need healing—healing that only a miracle from God can bring? Why not believe that he will do it? God wants you to have a faith that is active and expectant—a faith that knows his power and believes that he is waiting to show it. God wants people who will listen to his unbelievable plans and then believe, shaking off any doubt. Don't scoff at the ideas God puts in your heart. Trust him to carry them out.

REFLECTION
When was the last time God planted a big dream in your heart? How did you respond? How would God have you pray about this now?

"I Am"

Just tell them, "I Am."   Exodus 3:14

THERE WAS ONCE a family of mice who lived their entire lives in a large piano. Every day they were surrounded by beautiful music echoing throughout the dark spaces of their world. The mice woke each morning in great anticipation of the music. It comforted them and gave them a sense of wonder and delight. They loved to imagine the Great Player high above, though they couldn't see him.

Then one day a daring mouse climbed up in the bowels of the piano in an effort to discover the source of the music. He returned somewhat thoughtful and arrogant. "It's only a bunch of wires," he said. "There is no Great Player." The mice were saddened by the news, but only a few accepted his explanation.

Some time later another adventurous mouse made the climb to the top of the piano and came back even more sure of himself. "It's not as simple as we thought," he explained. "The music is caused by great hammers clanging against the wires. They dance in unison and create the sound we love to hear." The account was more complicated but seemed to show that there really was a scientific reason for the music. It was nice to believe in the Great Player, but soon most came to consider that it was all purely mechanical. All the while the Pianist continued to play.

There will always be those who refuse to believe in the power and authority of God. Skeptics have been around for thousands of years and will be here until Christ returns. If you can't understand who God is, try bringing him down to your level. What better way to elevate your self-worth? But God is God, whether we acknowledge him or not.

"Moses protested, 'If I go to the people of Israel and tell them, "The God of your ancestors has sent me to you," they won't believe me. They will ask, ". . . What is his name?" Then what should I tell them?'

"God replied, '. . . Just tell them, "I Am has sent me to you."'" (Exodus 3:13-14).

When Moses asked God for his name, he told him "I Am." The necessary inference we can draw is that you and I "are not." Only God is God. And the music he brings to life is majestic and beautiful!

REFLECTION
*Have you ever struggled to acknowledge the existence and authority of God?
In what ways have you tried to bring God down to your level?*

FLEEING TEMPTATION

Temptation comes from the lure of our own evil desires.   James 1:14

IF A PERSON you know believes she is not vulnerable to temptation, I would stay out of her way because she is the most likely person around you to fall. Satan is already busy laying the groundwork for victory. And unless that person comes to her senses and admits her susceptibility, she is likely to be the enemy's next victim.

When it happens, she will inevitably blame her spouse or a friend or even God. But those around her should know better. James tells us, "No one who wants to do wrong should ever say, 'God is tempting me.' God is never tempted to do wrong, and he never tempts anyone else either. Temptation comes from the lure of our own evil desires. These evil desires lead to evil actions, and evil actions lead to death" (1:13-15).

Some years ago I was teaching a class of several hundred people. I was speaking on the subject of temptation and had just finished reading from Paul's first letter to Timothy: "But you, Timothy, belong to God; so run from all these evil things, and follow what is right and good" (6:11). I explained that the reason we should flee from temptation is because it keeps us from our greater purpose. Temptation is from Satan, and the more time we give him the less time we have to give to God. The time we waste trying to struggle against the enemy would be better spent in nobler pursuits, like evangelism, prayer and worship, or helping others. I justified my comments by reading several other similar passages in Scripture.

I made my point and was ready to move on to another passage when a man in the audience interrupted me. He angrily flipped through his Bible, looking for a passage that he never seemed to find, all the while ranting about my lesson. Most of what he said was incoherent, but his anger was visible to everyone. He finally slammed his Bible shut and exclaimed loudly, "Maybe you're afraid to go toe-to-toe with Satan, but I'm not. He doesn't tempt me anymore because he knows who I am. I'll never run from temptation, and everyone knows it!"

I was so stunned by his comments that I don't remember how I responded, but his words said volumes about why so many fall into sin. We convince ourselves that evil has no hold on us, that we are strong enough to overcome it on our own, only to learn one day how terribly wrong we were. Temptation is not a sin, but it can easily lead to one—especially for those who have little respect for its power.

REFLECTION
What is your normal response when temptation comes your way?
How would God have you respond in light of today's reading?

KNOW YOUR ENEMY

Be careful! Watch out for attacks from the Devil, your
great enemy.   1 Peter 5:8

SATAN HAS only one objective when he leads us into temptation. He wants to see us sin. His sole purpose is to oppose God, and nothing hurts God more than to see his people hurt themselves and each other. Satan is the eternal stumbling block. And he's had enough practice through the ages to be very good at his job.

His primary strategy is both simple and effective. He tempts us where we are most vulnerable. He knows those parts of our heart that are most likely to wander, and he attacks those parts often and relentlessly.

A man who struggles with infidelity can expect to be tempted by women at the most unexpected times and places and in situations most of us could never understand. Men who experience this dynamic can attest to the frustration. They commit to remaining faithful, only to find themselves in a constant battle with temptation.

> "'You don't want to negotiate with the devil,' Tsion said."
>
> *Armageddon,* 371

A woman who is trying to free herself from the grip of alcoholism will encounter liquor at every turn. She'll be offered a drink more times in a week than some of us might be offered in a year. Recovering drug addicts will experience the same problem. Satan attacks us where we are most easily tempted. It's his only hope of getting us to crumble.

It's important for us to realize this truth if we are to ever hope to combat it. If we know that temptation is inevitable, we'll be better equipped to curtail the enemy's tactics. The greatest temptations are those that catch us by surprise. The enticements that come to us when we're least on our guard. The lures that we haven't anticipated. But if we assume that they will come and have a strategy in place when they do, we will have a much greater chance of remaining strong.

"Be careful!" says Peter. "Watch out for attacks from the Devil, your great enemy. He prowls around like a roaring lion, looking for some victim to devour. Take a firm stand against him, and be strong in your faith" (1 Peter 5:8-9).

Temptation doesn't have to defeat us. We don't have to fall to sin at Satan's every whim. It is possible to stay true to God in spite of our weakness toward sin. And understanding the enemy's tricks is more than half the battle.

REFLECTION
What are some concrete strategies you use to guard yourself from temptation? Have they been effective? Are there other strategies you should consider?

VICTOR OR VICTIM?

Hold on to what is good.   1 Thessalonians 5:21

TWO LITTLE GIRLS were skipping through a field on their way to school when an angry bull started toward them. One girl screamed and dropped her books, then said to the other, "Let's stop and pray that God will protect us!" The other girl was a bit wiser. "No," she said, "let's pray while we're running!"

Some situations demand action on our part as well as trust in God. Temptation to sin is one of those things. It's important to lean on God's help and power, but overcoming temptation also requires personal responsibility.

Every temptation we encounter provides us with two possible and distinct outcomes. We can either sin or be victorious. We can either defeat Satan or fall to him. We can either grow stronger in our faith or weaker through our failure. We can glorify God or disappoint him. We can grow more focused on our purpose or be diverted from it. We can grow closer to God or draw away from him.

Temptation is an opportunity to develop power and mastery over the enemy's roadblocks. We should see it as a stepping-stone toward greater character and faith—a chance to grow in grace and love and control over our sinful nature. How we react to temptation depends on what we want to be before God. How strong we want to become. How great a weight we want our witness to carry. How mighty a warrior we want to be in God's earthly kingdom.

God understands the moral struggles we deal with daily, and he allows them because they develop strength of character within us. The stumbling blocks that Satan throws in our path become God's tools to sharpen us. What Satan would use to destroy us, God uses to give us dominion over him. We were made to be conquerors, not cowards. Victors, not victims.

"Hold on to what is good," says Paul. "Keep away from every kind of evil" (1 Thessalonians 5:21-22). Remaining faithful to God is more than an act of faith—it is a commitment of the will. Temptation will come to every one of us. More often than we would hope. And how we handle it makes all the difference.

REFLECTION
How does it help you overcome sin when you see it as God's tool for sharpening your character? What should you pray when temptation comes?

TESTING THE SPIRITS

Any story sounds true until someone sets the record straight. Proverbs 18:17

IS IT ANY WONDER why there are so many different religions and cults in the world? There are so many different views on life and death and God that it's impossible to keep up. Every day it seems that there is another self-help guru in the news promising to have found the true secret of happiness or the right path to life. It's not surprising because people are looking for answers, and when someone claims to have them, an audience is not hard to find. "Any story sounds true until someone sets the record straight," says King Solomon (Proverbs 18:17). And today it seems that few people are willing to stand up and "set the record straight."

> "When it becomes obvious who the Antichrist is, the false prophet; the evil, counterfeit religion, we'll have to oppose them, speak out against them."
>
> *Left Behind,* 420

Some of these modern day "messiahs" teach a gospel that is a direct affront to God's Word. One recent example is John Edward, star of the TV show *Crossing Over,* where people look for answers through summoning the spirits of their dead relatives. Television has embraced Edward's practices because it brings good ratings, but it is a dangerous and ungodly movement. "Do not let your people practice fortune-telling or sorcery," God tells us, "or allow them to interpret omens, or engage in witchcraft, or cast spells, or function as mediums or psychics, or call forth the spirits of the dead. Anyone who does these things is an object of horror and disgust to the Lord" (Deuteronomy 18:10-12). Scripture is very clear about how God feels about Edward's brand of religion, yet people flock to his show by the thousands to find hope. Even believers are often drawn to his message, though they should be staying clear of such things.

Today hundreds of cults exist in the name of religion. All claim to have found the truths of Scripture, and their teachings seem to make sense to many. But when you hold their doctrine up against the light of the gospel, it's not hard to see the flaws.

"Dear friends, do not believe everyone who claims to speak by the Spirit," John tells us. "You must test them to see if the spirit they have comes from God. For there are many false prophets in the world" (1 John 4:1). God holds us responsible for the things we believe. It is our role to test the things being taught—to search the Scriptures and see what God has to say about them. To pray for wisdom and discernment. And to seek the truth with diligence and good judgment.

REFLECTION
How much of your beliefs have come from what you heard others say?
Have you taken the time to "test" the spirits to see if they are from God?

THE WAY

I am the way. John 14:6

AN AIRPLANE PILOT once found himself lost in a dark cloud over the ocean. His instrument panels had malfunctioned, and his radio wasn't working. He was at a complete loss but didn't want to panic his passengers. So he came on the intercom and said, "I have some good news and some bad news. The bad news is we have no idea where we are. The instruments don't work and the clouds are so thick I can't see anything. I'm not even sure which way we're heading."

The passengers gripped their seats tightly and gasped. "But don't worry," continued the optimistic pilot. "The good news is we're making great time!"

Strange as it seems, a lot of us approach life in much the same way. How many times have we looked for happiness and personal fulfillment in those things we know can never provide them? We convince ourselves that the right job or career will give us the boost we need to feel secure. We think that the right spouse will bring contentment. We're sure that if we only had a bigger house, a nicer car, a more impressive portfolio, or a better education, everything would finally fall into place. Then when we get what we want, we find that it wasn't enough. It didn't make us happy. It didn't satisfy.

"I am the Way," says Jesus. True happiness can't be found anywhere else. Fulfillment is found on no other road. There is only one path to contentment and satisfaction—only one artery to abundant life. Jesus is the Way. He is the only north your compass needs. The only direction you'll find for life eternal.

"No one can come to the Father except through me" (John 14:6). If you want to find God, you find him through the words and life of Jesus. No one knows more about the creation than the Creator, so if you want to find your purpose, look to the One who made you. If you want to find out what it is your heart seeks, ask the One who set your heart to beating. The One who molded your heart and gave you life to begin with. And if you want to find out where you're going, ask the One who gave you wings—the One who set your life in motion.

There is no question Jesus can't answer. There is no frustration that he can't get you through. There is no quandary in life that can't be overcome by putting it in the right perspective—by looking at it through the lens of eternity. Jesus is not only the Way; he's the only Way.

REFLECTION
Have you been looking for happiness and contentment in the wrong places?
Why not ask God for the directions you need?

THE TRUTH

I am . . . the truth.   John 14:6

AUTHOR MACK STILES once witnessed to a young man from Sweden named Andreas. Andreas had heard the stories of Jesus before and was ready to commit himself to Christ. He said to Stiles, "I've been told if I decide to follow Jesus, he will meet my needs and my life will get very good."

Stiles was somewhat taken aback by the statement, and his first impulse was to quickly agree. But he couldn't bring himself to do it. He knew it would be wrong to make the Christian life on earth seem better than it is.

"No, Andreas," he told him. "You may accept Jesus and find that life goes very badly for you."

"What do you mean?" Andreas asked him, somewhat confused.

"Well, you may find that your friends reject you. You could lose your job, your family might oppose your decision—there are a lot of bad things that may happen to you if you decide to follow Jesus. Andreas, when Jesus calls you, he calls you to go the way of the cross."

Andreas stared at him for a long time before responding. Finally he asked the question that Stiles had been expecting. "Then why would I want to follow Jesus?"

Stiles cocked his head to one side and said, "Andreas, because Jesus is true."[1]

"I came to bring truth to the world," Jesus says in answer to Pilate. "All who love the truth recognize that what I say is true" (John 18:37). Jesus never promises us a life free of problems. He never says the Christian life will be easy. In fact, he usually tells us to expect the very opposite. He promises that we will be shunned and persecuted for our faith and resented by the world for our beliefs. "Everyone will hate you because of your allegiance to me," Jesus tells us (Matthew 10:22).

What Jesus brings is not a cushy life or a bigger bank account but unwavering truth. We know that his promises are real and certain. His words are solid. His teachings are accurate. His claims are real. And our faith leads to abundant and everlasting life.

REFLECTION
How does the truth of Jesus set us free? Why is it important to acknowledge that only Jesus brings real truth?

THE LIFE

I am . . . the life.   John 14:6

THE STORY is told of a group of scientists who decided to develop a fish that could live outside of water. They took a handful of healthy red herring and began to breed and crossbreed until eventually they had produced a fish that could actually breath air. It was an amazing feat. But the research director still wasn't happy. He suspected that though the fish could live on dry land, it still had a secret desire for water.

"Change its very desires," he told his team. He demanded that they continue their work until they had produced a fish that had no interest in water—one that would be repelled at the mere sight of it. The scientists persisted, again manipulating hormones and chromosomes, breeding and crossbreeding, until eventually they had it. They created a fish that would rather die than get wet. Even humidity filled the fish with dread.

The director was so proud of his triumph that he took his new fish on tour. For the sake of dramatics, he would hold conferences by the side of a lake. He'd tell of his work and then prove his accomplishment by taking the fish out and holding it over the water. Each time the fish would tremble and shake with fear until being allowed back into his dry crate. The scientist was hailed as a genius.

> "I wish more of my life had been dedicated to the one who gave his for me."
>
> *The Remnant, 259*

But during one demonstration the fish slipped out of his hand and fell into the water. It quickly clamped its eyes and gills shut in terror and slowly sank to the bottom. In horror the fish lay still, holding its breath. Every instinct told it not to breathe. But eventually it could no longer hold its breath, so it took a large gulp. Its gills filled with water, but it didn't die. Again the fish took another deep breath and open its eyes. A third time it breathed, then wriggled in delight. This time it darted away. To the dismay of the scientist, the fish had discovered water.[2]

Grace Hansen once said, "Don't be afraid your life will end; be afraid it will never begin." There are too many today who have convinced themselves that they can live without God—even that they'd *rather* live without him. Some even recoil at the thought of putting their faith in a Savior. They've never considered that maybe they were created for something much more. Maybe Jesus is the one thing that can truly set them free to live. "But we know," says Paul, "that there is only one God, the Father, who created everything, and we exist for him. And there is only one Lord, Jesus Christ, through whom God made everything and through whom we have been given life" (1 Corinthians 8:6). Without Jesus we are all just fish out of water.

REFLECTION

In what ways have you tried to live apart from God? What can you do today to more fully surrender to Jesus?

A RIPE HARVEST

The crop is ripe on the earth.   Revelation 14:15

AN INDIAN WOMAN named Alila took her tiny infant to the River Ganges one day. With tears flowing down her cheeks, she stood at the water's edge holding her baby tightly. She kissed him one last time on the cheek then threw him into the river. Alila stood crying with her head buried in her hands as her child was swept away with the current.

After some time an Asian missionary happened by and saw the Indian woman weeping at the water's edge. He asked her what was wrong.

"The problems in my home are too many and my sins are heavy on my heart," said Alila, "so I offered the best I have to the goddess Ganges: my first-born son."

The missionary began telling her of Jesus' love and forgiveness, and before long Alila responded, "I have never heard that before." The two stood face-to-face for a long time before Alila continued. "Why couldn't you have come thirty minutes earlier?" she asked. "My child would not have had to die."[3]

Though it may be hard for many of us to believe, there are still places in the world where people have never heard of Jesus. There are still people who live their entire lives never once hearing about the saving grace that Christ brings. They live in ignorance and die in hopelessness, never knowing a Savior. It's hard to imagine, but it's true.

Even harder to believe, there are people who live and die in "Christian" nations never hearing the true message of the gospel. They've heard about Jesus and have known a lot of Christians, and they've driven by hundreds of churches in their lifetime, yet they know nothing about the truth of Christ. They've heard of religion but have never been introduced to the person of Jesus.

"The harvest is so great, but the workers are so few," Jesus tells his disciples. "So pray to the Lord who is in charge of the harvest; ask him to send out more workers for his fields" (Matthew 9:37-38). As long as there are people like Alila in the world, you and I have an urgent responsibility before us. We must reach them before it is too late.

REFLECTION
What people has God put in your life who need to hear the truth about Jesus? Pray that he will give you the wisdom to reach out to them.

SELFISH AMBITIONS

Everything else is worthless when compared with the priceless gain of knowing Christ Jesus my Lord. Philippians 3:8

I OFTEN TELL people that there is nothing I enjoy more than writing, but if I were entirely honest, I would admit that I get greater joy from the praise that writing brings. As much as I enjoy the art of putting words on paper, I more enjoy the results of having put words on paper. Of seeing books in print with my name on the cover. I'm committed to giving God the glory for all I do, and I'm fully aware that I would have no writing career if it were not for God's help and grace, yet I still struggle with selfish ambitions.

For me, dying to self is a daily ritual. Each morning I begin by reminding myself once again that nothing I do outside of God's will is worth the effort I put into it. Nothing I say or think or write is of any value unless it comes from God, glorifies God, or leads others to God. Nothing I produce will last, except those things that God initiated within me. No relationship I have will succeed unless it is built on Christ. With Paul, I try desperately to remember that "everything else is worthless when compared with the priceless gain of knowing Christ Jesus my Lord" (Philippians 3:8).

> "Hattie was the only unbeliever and understandably selfish. She spent most of her time on herself."
>
> *Assassins,* 14

I don't believe I'm alone in this problem of human nature. We all struggle with selfish desires—even the most faithful among us. A. W. Tozer describes it all too well:

> Some young preacher will study until he has to get thick glasses to take care of his failing eyesight because he has an idea he wants to become a famous preacher. He wants to use Jesus Christ to make him a famous preacher. He's just a huckster buying and selling and getting gain. They will ordain him and he will be known as Reverend and if he writes a book, they will make him a doctor. And he will be known as Doctor; but still a huckster buying and selling and getting gain.[4]

How many of us set out to achieve great things for God but in the end succeed only in making a name for ourselves? Even when our motives are right our selfishness sometimes gets in the way. "I have discarded everything else," says Paul, "counting it all as garbage, so that I may have Christ and become one with him" (Philippians 3:8-9). Until we see our earthly ambitions for what they are—just pieces of garbage in the eyes of Christ—we will never fully experience a deeper life in Jesus.

REFLECTION
Where do you look for self-worth and admiration? Do you seek the praises of men or the nearness of God?

WHEN JESUS PRAYS

I am praying not only for these disciples but also for all who will ever believe in me because of their testimony.　　John 17:20

WHAT DOES CHRIST want us to be? When Jesus envisions the kind of people that he wants to represent him on earth, what kind of people does he imagine? What character traits does he want his followers to exhibit? What thoughts does he want his people to have? What makes him proud? Which actions make his heart soar with brotherly pride?

If we want to know what Jesus wants from us, what better place to look than in his prayer in John 17:

"Make them pure and holy by teaching them your words of truth," Jesus prays. "My prayer for all of them is that they will be one, just as you and I are one, Father—that just as you are in me and I am in you, so they will be in us, and the world will believe you sent me" (17:17, 21). When Jesus set out to summarize his greatest desires for his followers, his words were simple but profound.

"*Make them pure,*" Jesus says. A pure heart and mind are critical to the Christian life. We are to be innocent and childlike in the things we say and do and think. To be pure physically, emotionally, and spiritually.

"*Make them . . . holy.*" Jesus longs for his followers to be righteous and obedient. He desires that we abstain from sinful pleasures and instead look to God for personal fulfillment. We are to be faithful and virtuous people. To shun the things of this world and to be holy and consecrated.

"*Make them . . . one.*" Jesus prays for unity among believers. He desires for his people to love and care for each other, just as he loves and cares for us. He wants us to carry each other's burdens, to pray for each other, to be intimately involved in the daily struggles of our brothers and sisters in Christ. Jesus longs for his followers to be unified in both mind and spirit.

The prayer of Jesus should be our prayer as well. His wishes should be our top priority as followers of Christ. Our life should reflect the things he most desires.

REFLECTION
Does your life reflect the kind of character that Jesus prayed for?
Ask him to search your heart and reveal how he would have you change.

OUR SOURCE OF POWER

As for me, I am filled with power and the Spirit of the Lord.   Micah 3:8

DO YOU EVER FEEL as if you're living in the middle of Sodom? Do you look outside your window and wonder what God thinks of your city? Are your churches stale and your friends lukewarm?

There are godless places on earth, and many frustrated believers have found themselves deep in the middle of them, longing for strength and courage from on high. It's not an easy place to be, but if it's yours, then take comfort in this lesson from Micah. As a prophet of God, he proclaims God's judgment on the people of Israel: "Listen, you leaders of Israel! You are supposed to know right from wrong, but you are the very ones who hate good and love evil. You skin my people alive and tear the flesh off their bones. You eat my people's flesh, cut away their skin, and break their bones. . . . Then you beg the Lord for help in times of trouble! Do you really expect him to listen?" (Micah 3:1-4).

Micah found himself in the midst of a terrible generation that had no love for God and his commands. They were a people who had completely turned their backs on the Lord and who lived selfish and ungodly lives. Their hearts were as dark as their minds were corrupt.

And in the middle of this hotbed of sin, Micah stands before God and his neighbors and declares, "As for me, I am filled with power and the Spirit of the Lord. I am filled with justice and might, fearlessly pointing out Israel's sin and rebellion" (Micah 3:8).

Are you living in a place that produces no fruit? a world that shuns the light and loves the darkness? a place of corruption and evil and ungodly behavior? Then let God fill you with his power and courage and goodness. Let him be the source of your strength. Let his Spirit invigorate yours. There is no place on earth so evil that God can't reach through to fill and sustain his people. When others bring you down, he will lift you up. Jesus is all you need to live a godly life and have an unshakable faith. Even in the midst of horrible sin and corruption.

REFLECTION
When you pray for your city, what do you pray for?
Do you look to the Lord for the faith and strength you need?

WHY WAIT?

Come, let us go up to the mountain of the Lord.   Micah 4:2

WHAT WOULD a world wholly devoted to God look like? How would it feel to be in a society where every person feared and loved and worshiped the Lord? where every soul stood before him in total reverence? where every knee bowed and every lip proclaimed him as Savior? The prophet Micah described such a place. And it is what the world will look like at some point in the future.

> "I feel such boldness—not based on my own strength, but on the promises of God—that I believe I could walk alone to the Temple Mount without being harmed."
>
> *Soul Harvest,* 384

In the last days, the Temple of the Lord in Jerusalem will become the most important place on earth. People from all over the world will go there to worship. Many nations will come and say, "Come, let us go up to the mountain of the Lord, to the Temple of the God of Israel. There he will teach us his ways, so that we may obey him." For in those days the Lord's teaching and his word will go out from Jerusalem.

The Lord will settle international disputes. All the nations will beat their swords into plowshares and their spears into pruning hooks. All wars will stop, and military training will come to an end. Everyone will live quietly in their own homes in peace and prosperity, for there will be nothing to fear. The Lord Almighty has promised this! (4:1-4)

When will this event occur? I'll leave that up to scholars to speculate. I know only that it will happen. People all over the world will acknowledge God and his sovereignty. They will look to him for guidance and instruction. All will acknowledge his majesty. All will call on his name.

You and I don't have to wait until that time to know God's peace and presence. We don't have to be caught at the last moment wondering why we didn't see God's power earlier. We don't have to wait until the last days to see his wisdom or experience his majesty. We can worship him today while most of the world sleeps in ignorance. God's day will come; there is no question about that. Why not be well ahead of the game and give yourself over to him today?

REFLECTION

How can you and I honor God today in the way we live?
When you think of heaven, how do you imagine it?

WHAT DOES GOD WANT?

What can we bring to the Lord?   Micah 6:6

IF YOU HAD to get God a gift, what would you get him? What present would you lay at the feet of the Creator? Let's say you wanted to make up for the things you've done to hurt him. You've ignored his requests, you've cheated on him, you've gone months without acknowledging his existence, and now you want to say you're sorry and try to make things right. What would you give him to show him you're sincere? The prophet Micah poses this same question to the people of Israel:

"What can we bring to the Lord to make up for what we've done? Should we bow before God with offerings of yearling calves? Should we offer him thousands of rams and tens of thousands of rivers of olive oil? Would that please the Lord? Should we sacrifice our firstborn children to pay for the sins of our souls? Would that make him glad?" (6:6-7).

What about you? What would your gift be? Would you think about giving a large lump sum to your church? Would you consider making a promise? *I'll read my Bible every night before bedtime, and I'll go to church every Sunday, Lord. Maybe I'll even join a men's breakfast group.* Do you think that would appease him? Is that what God wants? Let's let Micah answer the question for us.

"No, O people, the Lord has already told you what is good, and this is what he requires: to do what is right, to love mercy, and to walk humbly with your God" (Micah 6:8).

Do you want to make God happy? Do you want to know what he wants in place of your money or gifts or offerings? He wants your heart. Your life. Your mercy toward others. Your humility before his throne. God wants from you the same thing that he gives to you. He pours himself out for us, and he wants us to pour ourselves out for others. He gives unconditional love, and he wants us to selflessly love others. He walks with us, and he wants us to walk with him.

God doesn't want to break your bank; he wants to have your heart. He doesn't want your gifts, he wants you. God doesn't need a present, he wants devotion. And that's something that each of us have to give.

REFLECTION
What gifts, presents, and promises have you given to try to appease God?
Why not give him the one thing he most wants?
Why not give him yourself?

WHOM CAN YOU TRUST?

As for me, I look to the Lord for his help.   Micah 7:7

WHOM CAN YOU trust completely? Is there anyone in your world on whom you can depend without reservation? Many of us have a wife or husband who comes to mind. I trust my wife implicitly, without reservation. But what if I turned my back on her and left? What if I forsook our marriage vows and moved on? As loving and forgiving as she is, I'm sure I could push her too far and fall out of her good graces. Of course, I don't intend to ever let that happen, but the possibility for pain and disappointment exists in every human relationship.

Maybe you come from an unbelieving family, and your siblings don't understand your faith. Can you trust them with your heart? Can you turn to them in a crisis? Is there anyone on earth without the capacity to let you down under the right set of circumstances? According to Micah, the answer is no.

> "If you have placed your trust in Christ alone for salvation by grace through faith, you are a true tribulation saint."
>
> *The Mark, 337*

"Don't trust anyone—not your best friend or even your wife! For the son despises his father. The daughter defies her mother. The daughter-in-law defies her mother-in-law. Your enemies will be right in your own household" (Micah 7:5-6). Micah understood that people are people, no matter how close you are to them. We are flawed and often unforgiving. Our love may be genuine and true and deep, but it is not entirely without condition. Turn your back on your friend, and it won't be long before he'll turn his back on you.

But God is not that way. "As for me, I look to the Lord for his help," says Micah. "I wait confidently for God to save me, and my God will certainly hear me" (7:7). People have turned their backs on God time and again, yet he has never given up on us. We have let him down over and over and over, and each time he retaliates with forgiveness. We spit in the face of his Son, and he embraces us with his love and redemption.

If you think you can fall out of God's graces, think again. If you think you can push him so far that he'll never accept you back, you're wrong. If you believe his love has an ounce of condition attached to it, just look at the story of humanity.

So let me ask again. Whom can you trust completely? Only God.

REFLECTION
How can you and I trust God for the things we need? Have you accepted his unconditional forgiveness and love? If not, go to him today.

GODLY STRENGTH

*I can do everything with the help of Christ who gives
me the strength I need.*   Philippians 4:13

GEORGE FOREMAN first won the World Heavyweight Championship boxing title in 1973 at the age of twenty-three. He was at the top of his game and in his prime when he defeated Joe Frazier that fateful day in Jamaica. A year later he lost his title to Muhammad Ali in their infamous bout in Kinshasa, Zaire, known as the "Rumble in the Jungle."

Foreman retired a few years later to pursue the career he'd always dreamed of. He became the pastor of a small church in Houston, Texas. Members said he was as fiery and powerful in the pulpit as he was in the ring. He used part of his boxing money to establish a youth center in Houston, and his church did its best to cover the rest of the expenses. But it wasn't long before financial resources dried up. The church struggled to keep the center alive. In 1987 Foreman surprised everyone by announcing his plans to save the youth center from bankruptcy. "I'm going to be heavyweight champion again," he said.

In spite of the jokes and jeers from the media and late-night comedians, Foreman set himself on a strict regimen of training. He had to start at the bottom, fighting little-known boxers and working his way back up the ranks. Though he was older, he'd never lost his ability to land an explosive punch and bring his opponent down, so his climb was quicker than expected. Before long, Foreman had become a serious contender for the top belt. After seven years of work, he finally had a shot at the title. In 1994, at the age of 45, Foreman shocked the world by knocking out Michael Morrer to regain the World Heavyweight Championship title. He was the oldest man in history to do so. He used the money he made to save the center. The comedians were no longer laughing. From the beginning, Foreman attributed this feat to his faith in God and his belief that the Holy Spirit would supply him with the strength he needed.

"It doesn't matter what people say about you," Foreman said after the fight. "Look in the mirror and never put yourself down. Give yourself time and anything can be accomplished."[5]

"I can do everything with the help of Christ who gives me the strength I need," writes Paul (Philippians 4:13). When God sets a task on your heart, all you have to do is believe that he can help you carry it out. His power is sufficient for all our needs in any given situation.

REFLECTION
*What is the big dream God has placed in your heart? What is keeping
you from believing that God is able to see it through?*

JULY

TODAY'S READING
Galatians 6:6-10

TRUE SACRIFICE

So don't get tired of doing what is good.   Galatians 6:9

A MOTHER WAS preparing pancakes for her two young sons, Kevin and Ryan. The boys began arguing over who would get the first pancake. The mother scolded them, and then took the opportunity to relay some moral truths to her children.

"What would Jesus do if he were here?" asked the mother. The boys shrugged their shoulders in unison. "Jesus would insist that his brother take the first pancake," she told them. "And then he would wait for the next one."

The boys nodded, and the mother felt confident that her lesson had taken. She turned her back and continued baking, but soon heard her oldest boy whispering to the younger one, "Ryan, you be Jesus."

It's a cute story, but at times it hits a little too close to home to be very funny. How often do you and I see an opportunity for good and instead of acting, wait for someone else to play the part of Jesus? Ever cast your eyes downward in a meeting hoping someone else will volunteer for the sacrificial jobs? Ever looked the other way when a brother in need walked past you? Ever passed the buck to a deacon when news of a needy family came your way? "I'm a little busy at the moment. Why don't you be Jesus?"

I've been guilty more than once of leaving the tough jobs to others. I know a couple who have spent years working in inner-city missions, and we've spent years supporting them. Somehow it makes me feel noble and sacrificial. At least it did until we took a trip to visit them for the weekend. I saw firsthand the way they lived and ministered to some of the most needy and helpless people in our country, and suddenly I didn't feel quite as merciful for my small contributions. *Here's a little money. Why don't you be Jesus?*

"We are each responsible for our own conduct," writes the apostle Paul. "Those who live only to satisfy their own sinful desires will harvest the consequences of decay and death. But those who live to please the Spirit will harvest everlasting life from the Spirit. So don't get tired of doing what is good. Don't get discouraged and give up, for we will reap a harvest of blessing at the appropriate time" (Galatians 6:5, 8-9). It's easy to let others be Jesus for us, but a true follower doesn't pass on that responsibility when it comes. Jesus expects more from us than we often expect from ourselves. Sacrifice means getting involved, not just getting others to do it.

REFLECTION
In what ways do you allow others to do the work of Christ for you?
How can you take more responsibility in service to Jesus?

FORGIVE AND FORGET

The Lord forgave you, so you must forgive others.   Colossians 3:13

I HAVE A FRIEND who has never forgiven me for a mistake I made years ago. It was a small infraction in my mind, but I later learned how much it hurt him. I called several times to apologize. Each time he told me not to worry about it, but I could tell in his voice that the resentment was still there. The last few times that I left messages for him he didn't return my calls. He is still angry, and I've done all I can to make up for it. He's chosen to sever our friendship, and that troubles me deeply.

> "David fell into bed. He asked forgiveness for how he had treated Guy Blod and asked God to give him special compassion for the man."
>
> *The Indwelling, 267*

There's nothing quite as painful as having someone carry a grudge against you. Except maybe carrying a grudge against someone else. No matter how you slice it, an unwillingness to forgive causes grief for everyone involved.

Just this morning I read of two unmarried sisters who lived together but hadn't spoken in years. They both harbored resentment for some unresolved disagreement they'd had in the past, and neither was willing to forgive. The sisters couldn't afford to live apart, so they continued living together in a tiny house. They used the same rooms, ate at the same table, used the same appliances, even slept in the same bedroom, without ever saying a word. A chalk line was drawn down the middle of each room, and both stayed within their allotted area. Each night they lay a few feet from each other, listening to each other's breathing but never speaking a word. Neither was willing to take the first step toward forgiving and forgetting the silly rift that had come between them.[1]

"If you forgive those who sin against you," Jesus tells us, "your heavenly Father will forgive you. But if you refuse to forgive others, your Father will not forgive your sins" (Matthew 6:14-15). It's hard to get around the decisiveness of these words from our Savior. Jesus doesn't mince words when it comes to the issue of forgiveness. His warning to us is as clear as it is sobering. Our forgiveness is dependent on our willingness to forgive. Our status before God is dependent upon the status of others in our heart.

I personally can't think of a transgression someone could commit against me that would be worth risking my soul over. The best approach for Christians is to forgive others the second we realize we have something to forgive. And to make sure that we've done all we can to gain forgiveness from others. It's the least we can do, after all that Christ has done for us.

REFLECTION

When have you carried a grudge in your heart? What is the grudge you are carrying now? What keeps you from making it right today?

DISTANT HEARTS

They honor me with their lips, but their hearts are far away.   Isaiah 29:13

THE TAJ MAHAL is one of the most beautiful and costly memorials ever built. It is constructed of white marble and rests on a platform of red sandstone. At each corner of the platform stands a slender prayer tower over 133 feet high. The building itself rises more than 185 feet, with a huge dome roof stretched out over the center.

The monument was built by the emperor Shah Jehan, in honor of his favorite wife. Her death devastated the Indian ruler, so he set out to build a temple to house her remains. Her coffin was placed in the center of a large piece of land, and construction of the temple began around it. The Shah insisted that no expense be spared.

But somewhere along the way the Shah found himself so engrossed in the project that he forgot about his wife. He was so busy building the temple that he forgot why he started the project in the first place. One day he bumped into a large wooden box and ordered workers to throw it out. Only later would the emperor learn that the box he'd had them dispose of was his wife's coffin.[2]

How does a person get so caught up in building a temple that he forgets his purpose for building it? You and I do the same thing every day. We don't often admit it, but we're not much different than the forgetful emperor.

Ever complained about the preacher's sermon to your wife on the drive home from church? Ever mouthed your way through the worship service with your mind a thousand miles away? Ever prayed with your kids on autopilot, reciting the same worn out phrases that you normally use at dinnertime? Most of us have. And in doing so we're no different than an absentminded ruler laying stone after stone in a temple without a thought given to its true purpose.

"These people say they are mine," God says through his prophet Isaiah. "They honor me with their lips, but their hearts are far away. And their worship of me amounts to nothing more than human laws learned by rote" (Isaiah 29:13). There's nothing quite as offensive as paying homage to God but not really meaning it. When we get so caught up in the day-to-day tasks of our faith that we forget to acknowledge the object of our faith, it's time to stop and take a good look at our priorities. God deserves more than our words. And he demands nothing less than our heart.

REFLECTION
In what ways do you honor God with your lips but not your heart?
How can you regain your original passion for him?

PASSING BLAME

*People ruin their lives by their own foolishness and then
are angry at the Lord.*   Proverbs 19:3

EVER WONDER about some of the excuses people give to insurance companies when they try to explain their accidents? I'm sure the employees have a good laugh at our expense. One company received this note on their questionnaire: "The telephone pole was approaching fast. I was attempting to swerve out of its path when it struck my front end."

Another read, "As I approached the intersection, a stop sign suddenly appeared in a place where no stop sign had ever appeared before. I was unable to stop in time to avoid the accident."

Still another, "The guy was all over the place. I had to swerve a number of times before I hit him."

Some of the funniest excuses come from motorists who are able to avoid other cars but seem to have trouble missing innocent bystanders. "A pedestrian hit me and went under my car," wrote one. "To avoid hitting the bumper of the car in front, I struck the pedestrian," wrote another. But my favorite comes from a woman who explained, "The pedestrian had no idea which direction to go, so I ran him over."[3]

> "I must tell you sadly that many of you will make that choice. You will choose sin over God."
>
> *Desecration, 228*

It's amazing how quick we are to blame others for the mistakes we make. We're so busy making excuses that we seldom take time to think through what we could have done differently. And we're even less likely to try and learn from our failures. It's easier to simply deny them and move on.

"People ruin their lives by their own foolishness and then are angry at the Lord," notes King Solomon, the author of Proverbs (19:3). Somehow it seems easier to blame God when life doesn't go our way than to try and reevaluate our poor choices. When our portfolio shrinks, we wonder why God allowed it to happen. Never mind that a dozen people told us to stay away from risky high-tech stocks. Our children rebel and turn away from God, and we wonder why he wasn't keeping a closer watch over them. We tend to forget the times we spent complaining about the pastor over Sunday dinners or the days we went without talking to them about the Lord. We all make choices in life—some good and some bad. And if we're going to take credit for our successes, we need to take responsibility for our failures as well.

REFLECTION
*Are you in the habit of blaming God for your mistakes?
Begin today taking responsibility for your poor choices.*

MAKING WISE CHOICES

Lot . . . pitched his tents near Sodom.   Genesis 13:12, NIV

LOT HAD A HISTORY of making poor choices, and God was continually bailing him out of crises. He was a good man, but his foolish decisions got him into a lot of trouble.

Lot was the nephew of Abram who traveled with him from Egypt through the land of Negev and Bethel and Ai. The two had many flocks and herds, and the trip was a grueling and slow one. Their herdsmen were getting in each other's way and getting on each other's nerves, so Abram and Lot decided to separate. Abram gave Lot his choice of parcels in the region. "If you want that area over there, then I'll stay here. If you want to stay in this area, then I'll move on to another place," he told Lot (Genesis 13:9). As usual, Abram took the high road and let God work out the details. But Lot saw it as an opportunity to get the choice property. He looked out over the plains of the Jordan Valley and saw the plush and fertile ground. Water was in abundance, just as he remembered from the beautiful gardens of Egypt. It was the perfect place to live. Except for one big problem. It was right next to Sodom.

Everyone knew about Sodom. It was the city that had forgotten God. It was brimming with evil men doing unspeakable things. A detestable place to live. *But what beautiful land*, he thought. *Think of the fortune I can make.*

So Lot pitched his tents near Sodom. He chose good soil over good sense. He moved his family next to the most wicked city in the region and put down roots. Sodom was a great place to live if you could just overlook the evil. Get past the constant temptation to sin and turn away from God, and you'd have yourself a perfect place to raise a family. That was Sodom. *Did I mention how good the soil was?*

You and I make similar choices every day. We decide where we want to live, whom we want as neighbors, where we want our kids to attend school. We choose our careers and the best places to pursue them. We pick our friends, and watch which friends our children pick. We decide where we want our family to go to church. All of these decisions have a bearing on our future. Our choices matter. It makes a difference where we choose to pitch our tents. My criteria is simple: I want life-giving friends and a God-centered church. A place where my faith and family will not only survive but thrive.

REFLECTION
What choices have you made when it comes to your friends and your family's spiritual climate? Is your faith thriving where you've planted it?

A FRIEND TO THE WORLD

No, my friends. Don't do this wicked thing.   Genesis 19:7, NIV

LOT MAY have been a righteous man, but that didn't keep him from making foolish choices. His heart was in the right place, but his mind seemed to be in neutral. He loved God, but he lacked resolve. And this truth was readily revealed when God decided to destroy Sodom. Abraham convinced God to spare Sodom if he could find just ten righteous men, but even that didn't buy it a stay of execution. Lot was the only one God could find worth saving. So he sent two angels to rescue Lot from the destruction. As the angels were staying in Lot's house, the men of the city gathered outside his door. "Where are the men who came to spend the night with you?" they shouted out to Lot. "Bring them out so we can have sex with them" (Genesis 19:5).

And listen to Lot's first response. "'Please, my brothers,' he begged, 'don't do such a wicked thing'" (Genesis 19:7). Lot's biggest problem shows in his first words to the city's depraved residents. He called them his "brothers." They were his friends—his running buddies. They were not only his neighbors but also the people he hung out with. His support group. Lot lived as a friend to the world, yet somehow he never became a light in the midst of it. He saw the wickedness around him, and it no doubt grieved his heart, but he didn't do anything about it.

> "The choice is hers, not ours. But it is painful to see someone you care for make a decision that will cost her her soul."
>
> *Apollyon, 375*

Here's a question that's always bothered me: If Lot was so on fire for the Lord, why couldn't God find another righteous man in Sodom? Where were the converts? Where were the people to whom he witnessed—the men who saw the strength of his faith and wanted to be like him? The people he brought into a relationship with his Lord? Where were the fruits of a righteous man living in the midst of Sodom? The answer is simple and sobering. There were none. Lot hadn't influenced his culture; he simply tried to remain faithful in spite of it. He kept his faith to himself and grieved inwardly about the evil around him. His heart still pined for God, but his resolve left little to brag about.

Many of us find ourselves in similar circumstances. We live largely in a culture that is hostile toward the things of God. We've determined not to let the culture change us, but how much have we done to change our culture? Are we a friend to the world or a beacon to the lost? Are we pitching out tent near Sodom, yet lacking the resolve to make a difference?

REFLECTION

In what ways are you influencing the culture in which you live?
Do you have the resolve to make a difference?

WHAT LOT FORGOT

I have two virgin daughters. Do with them as you wish.   Genesis 19:8

THE BIBLE is filled with disturbing stories of people doing thoughtless and wicked things to each other. One of the unique elements to Scripture is that it shows people with all their flaws and inconsistencies—even good and decent people. God could have pulled his punches, but he chose not to. He could have shown us the successes of his people and remained silent about their failures, but he didn't. He exposes his servants in all their shame as well as their glory. God holds David up as a man after his own heart—a man who ruled Israel with integrity and wisdom. But David also sins greatly. And God records every vile detail for posterity. Abraham is a man who displays unbelievable trust and obedience in his life, but he also slips—more than a few times. He is flawed, and God isn't afraid to show us that truth. God's heroes aren't perfect, but he loves them anyway. That's the message he wants us to get.

In spite of that fact, there's one story I can't quite get past. There's one "righteous" man in Scripture whom I'd like to see God take behind the woodshed. Lot did something that completely contradicts my sense of goodness. When the wicked men of Sodom stand outside Lot's door demanding to have sex with the two visiting angels, Lot says the unthinkable. "Look—I have two virgin daughters," he tells them. "Do with them as you wish, but leave these men alone, for they are under my protection" (Genesis 19:8).

Lot offers his daughters to be molested in the place of God's angels. In his effort to show how noble he is before God, he succeeds only in showing how careless and contemptible he is as a father. It isn't enough that he puts his family in harm's way by pitching his tents near Sodom. He tops that by displaying the true depth of his thoughtlessness. Lot forgets his most basic and primary role as a husband and a father—to protect and care for his family. Next to our relationship with God, our family members should be our most critical concern. If they can't depend on us to look after them—physically, morally, and spiritually—then whom can they trust?

A lot of men today are guilty of this same sin. They may not be as blatant, but when the pressure is on, they quickly abandon their family responsibilities. How many husbands have left their wives at the first sign of trouble? How many are so wrapped up in their own concerns that they leave their children to fend for themselves morally? If you want to see the true character of a man, watch how well he protects his family. How safe is your family?

REFLECTION
*Do your children feel safe under their father's protection? What can you
do to see that they are protected from the world's evil?*

FINDING MERCY IN SODOM

You have been so kind to me and saved my life.   Genesis 19:19

ASK A HUNDRED people what God's message was in destroying Sodom and Gomorrah, and ninety-nine of them will likely give you the same answer: It was his judgment on homosexuality. It was God showing his utter contempt for sexual perversion and immorality.

It's not hard to see why we would think that, and there's some truth to the idea. God does detest sins of the flesh because they reveal the state of the heart, and he makes no secret in Scripture how he feels about this particular perversion. But is that really the primary message behind the destruction of Sodom and Gomorrah? Is that why God saw that the event was recorded in Scripture in such detail? Maybe so, but perhaps God wanted us to take a closer look at Lot's choices. Lot was the focus of God's rescue mission, and his story was the one told in detail. The fate of Sodom and Gomorrah was simply the backdrop behind Lot's unfolding moral dilemma.

Lot made a bucketful of bad choices in his life, and that's why he found himself and his family in such a fix. He pitched his tent near Sodom, knowing the possible consequences. He became a friend to the world, living in the midst of perversion yet doing little to make an impact on his culture. Yet in spite of all this, God saw something in Lot worth rescuing.

> "'Thank you, God' was all he could say, and he said it over and over."
>
> *The Indwelling,* 111

I don't see it, and you probably don't either, but God did. Something in Lot's heart touched the Father and caused him to have compassion. And that is the point of the story.

Could Scripture bring any better message to those of us who have disappointed God? Could the Bible offer any more comfort to us in the midst of our failures? Could God be any more gracious in light of our propensity for foolish choices?

I'm quick to point a judgmental finger at Lot and his family, but that's only because no one has ever scribbled my sins into the margins of their Bible. When it comes to poor choices and bad judgment calls, I've certainly logged my share. And God has stepped in and rescued me on occasion just as he had to do with Lot. You and I can be grateful that we serve a God of second chances. And third and fourth and fifth. . . . We can rest easy knowing that in spite of ourselves, God is faithful and true and forgiving.

REFLECTION
When did God rescue you from the consequences of your poor choices? What lessons did you learn?

ACCEPTING GOD'S WAYS

The Lord is close to the brokenhearted.   Psalm 34:18

YOU DON'T usually have to look far to find a heart that has been deeply wounded. I found several this morning by simply skimming through yesterday's paper.

One particular article caught my attention. Beside it was a picture of a beautiful twenty-four-year-old girl named Leah, and the story highlighted her life as a struggling single mother. The writer told of Leah's two boys and the baby on the way. Her life has not been an easy one, but she's done the best she could. With loving parents and a healthy outlook, Leah's future seemed brighter than her past. Recently she enrolled in a GED program in an effort to make a better life for herself and her children. But that was before Leah got shot in the head by a man she barely knew.

As she lay in the hospital on life support with no brain activity and no hope of recovery, her nine-year-old boy held her hand and sang to her: "You are my sunshine, my only sunshine. . . ." Crowded around her bed were her sister, her two brothers, her two sons, and her grieving parents. Tears flowed freely among them. When visiting hours came to a close, her oldest boy said good-bye and kissed his mother on the cheek. "If you're here in the morning, I'll come see you," he told her. Sometime during the night Leah passed away. "It's hard to see all of your children's hearts broken in one day," Leah's mother said through tears. "Especially when one is dying."[4]

How do you explain God's goodness and mercy to a mother who is about to bury her child? What do you say to a nine-year-old boy who has just kissed his mother good-bye for the last time? What can you do to bring comfort to a family during such a dark and confusing hour of their lives? The truth is, sometimes God doesn't make sense, and there's little we can do about that fact but accept it. We can't always understand God, but we can always trust him.

"Just as the heavens are higher than the earth, so are my ways higher than your ways and my thoughts higher than your thoughts," God tells us (Isaiah 55:9). Even in the most baffling moments of life, God is in control in spite of how it may seem. The best that you and I can do is to simply let God be God and believe that he cares deeply. That his plan is still in place. That heaven is watching, and God is still on his throne. It's not our place to figure out the profound mysteries of life, so we shouldn't waste our time trying. Someday we will all understand. That's a promise you can trust in.

REFLECTION
What brings you the most comfort during times of sorrow? How should we respond to others during times of loss and heartache?

REACHING OUT

Love your neighbor as yourself.   Romans 13:9

AN ELDERLY WOMAN lived alone in her small house in a suburb of Worcester, Massachusetts. Her neighbors didn't know much about her except that she rarely looked up as she walked each morning to the mailbox and back. She lived a quiet life, always keeping to herself. No one ever came to visit, not even her family. Many on the street couldn't even tell you her name.

One day a neighbor noted to another one that he hadn't seen the woman in a while and wondered if something might be wrong. They contacted the police, and the police called the woman's brother. He said he hadn't talked to her in a while, but he thought she might be living in a nursing home, so they called the post office and had her mail delivery stopped.

Soon the woman's lawn started getting out of control, so one neighbor paid her grandson to mow it. The boy put the house on his route and came regularly to keep the neighborhood looking decent. When winter came, a pipe on the front of her house froze and cracked, sending water spewing down to the curb, so the man next door called the utility company and had her water and electricity shut off.

Three years went by before police got another call—this one from a bank manager. The woman's account had been inactive for some time, and no one seemed to be able to reach her. The police went to her house and found her lying on the floor of her kitchen. She'd been dead for four years. Neighbors were shocked when they heard the news but not terribly surprised. "My heart bleeds for her," said the woman across the street, "but you can't blame a soul. If she saw you out there she never said hello to you."[5]

How could someone live a life of such isolation that no one would even miss her when she died? Where was the one neighbor who cared enough to build a friendship? Was there no family member thoughtful enough to call? It's a tragedy that a woman would push the world away and live a life of seclusion, but even worse is that those around her would allow her to do so. Paul writes, "For the commandments . . . are all summed up in this one commandment: 'Love your neighbor as yourself'" (Romans 13:9). No one should ever live and die in such loneliness. As followers of Christ we have a responsibility to reach out to the lonely and hurting. To be a friend to the friendless.

REFLECTION
Who is one person you're aware of that lives in loneliness?
How would God have you reach out to him or her?

A TUG OF WAR

The thief's purpose is to steal and kill and destroy.   John 10:10

A FAMILY was camping by a lake somewhere deep in the southern part of Louisiana. The father was busy pitching the tent while his wife began setting up the stove and building a small fire. Their boy had already dragged his small canoe down to the water and rowed out toward the middle of the lake to explore.

Suddenly the mother and father heard a loud splash, followed by a short scream. The mother immediately ran toward the water to see her boy bobbing in the lake beside his capsized canoe. She didn't worry too much, since she knew her son could swim. The father laughed, the mother chuckled, and the boy began swimming to shore. As the boy made it to the water's edge, the mother reached her hand out to help him. He grabbed hold and at that instant heard a loud splash behind him and felt something grab hold of his right ankle, sending him crashing face-first into the water. The mother held on, and to her horror she saw that a huge alligator had followed the boy to shore and had him by the right ankle.

> "Satan will kill them at the end of three and a half years, and their bodies will lie in the street of the city where Christ was crucified."
>
> *Left Behind*, 313

Suddenly she realized that she was in a tug-of-war with a six-foot-long, four-hundred-pound sea monster. She gripped her boy's arm with both hands and pulled with all her might, while the alligator clamped down harder on his ankle. Her boy screamed helplessly in the middle.

The scene that this horrified mother found herself in seems a perfect analogy for the spiritual battle that many of us wage each day for our families. We hold our children tightly by one hand, while the enemy fights and pulls on the other end, trying desperately to drag them into his lair. He is a four-hundred-pound monster with gnarly teeth and superhuman strength, and often we feel like ninety-pound housewives struggling against his power. We know that he has only one goal in mind—to drown and devour his prey. "The thief's purpose is to steal and kill and destroy," says Jesus (John 10:10). And in the midst of it, we fight to see that the evil one doesn't win the battle.

The end of our story in Louisiana was a happy one. The mother hung on for dear life, and the father reached them just in time to beat the monster back into hiding. Today the boy has two scars to remind them of the episode—a large gash in his ankle, and five small indentations in his right wrist. They came from his mother's fingernails. Other than that the boy is fine. This shows once again that the enemy doesn't have a chance against a determined and loving parent.

REFLECTION
How often do you feel as if you're losing your battle with the enemy?
Pray today for the strength to hang on and win the battle with Jesus' help.

FULLNESS OF LIFE

My purpose is to give life in all its fullness.   John 10:10

BEFORE HER DEATH, Ann Landers spent several decades dispensing daily advice in newspapers throughout the country. She answered people's questions on every conceivable topic—from marriage to children to relationships to health problems. She was quick-witted and decisive and was seldom caught without an answer. But one time a question left Ms. Landers somewhat speechless. A reader asked her simply, "Do you believe in heaven and hell?"

Lander's reply was surprising. "It's a subject I haven't given much thought," she said.[6] The self-appointed guru to the masses had never considered one of life's most pressing and critical questions. It's hard to fathom, but it's true. And it speaks volumes about why so many people live their entire lives never seriously investigating the claims of Jesus and the consequences of dying without him. We're so caught up with living day to day in this life that we never stop to think about the afterlife. We spend our days in pursuit of a full life yet never discover the fullness of life eternal.

Dr. Nelson Bell once said, "Only those who are prepared to die are really prepared to live."[7] If you haven't settled the question of eternal life, you've settled for a poor substitute for life at best.

"The thief's purpose is to steal and kill and destroy," says Jesus. "My purpose is to give life in all its fullness" (John 10:10). The enemy is hard at work keeping people in the dark. He hates us all and wants to kill us, and the way he does that is by keeping us away from the truth of Jesus. He keeps our mind on the here and now, focused on the problems at hand, so that we never take time to consider the future. He succeeds in winning our soul when he can keep us from thinking about the reality of heaven and hell. But Jesus comes to set us free. To give us the answer to the only question that really matters. He brings more than a full life— he brings the fullness of life eternal.

REFLECTION
What does it mean to have fullness of life? How has the enemy worked to keep you in the dark spiritually? Pray that Jesus will open your eyes to the truth.

RUNNING THE NUMBERS

Who do you say I am?   Matthew 16:15

IF YOU LIKE physical probabilities, consider this one: Imagine that the entire state of Texas is covered in silver dollars, each laid side by side and stacked two feet deep. Somewhere in the midst of all these coins is a marked one, perhaps with a small *s* on one side. You have no idea where the coin is among this sea of silver dollars.

Now take a man and blindfold him. Send him out into the state, and tell him he can travel as far as he wants in any direction. His job is to find the coin. The catch is, he has only one try. He must pick it up on the first attempt. So what are the chances that he can do so?

Dr. Peter Stoner is a probability expert who put it to the test, and he came up with this number: 1 in 100,000,000,000,000,000. That's one followed by 17 zeros. In effect it is a physical improbability. In other words, it couldn't happen in a billion lifetimes. The chances are so minute that it reduces itself to the realm of impossibility.

> "I had discovered, strictly from an academic approach, that nearly 30 percent of the Bible (Old and New Testaments together) consisted of prophetic passages."
>
> *The Mark, 142*

This is the same number you get when you apply another problem of probability. It is the exact probability of Jesus fulfilling only eight of the sixty major prophesies written about him in the Old Testament. The chances of him fulfilling just eight of these prophecies are so remote that it is considered a scientific impossibility. Any physicist on the planet would tell you that it couldn't happen. There is absolutely no chance that he could do it.

Yet he did. More than that, he fulfilled all sixty major prophecies. Each and every foretelling of Jesus in the old manuscripts nailed it to a tee. And those are just the major prophecies. To take it to a level beyond the stratosphere of comprehension, he also fulfilled 270 other prophetic references to his life. No matter how you look at it, the chances of Jesus not being the Messiah is a mathematical and scientific impossibility.[8]

It's not as if God didn't prove his point. It's that so many are unwilling to see it.

REFLECTION
How does this truth about prophetic fulfillment change the way you look at Jesus? In what ways does it strengthen your faith?

THE SPIRIT'S CALM

The Holy Spirit helps us in our distress. Romans 8:26

CHUCK SWINDOLL tells of a time years ago when he got a call at the office that his daughter, Charissa, had been in an accident at school. As a cheerleader, she was practicing with her squad and had taken a long fall from the top of a human pyramid. They told him she had hit the back of her head on the ground and was unable to move. Swindoll jumped into his car and started toward the school, having no idea what to expect. On the way he began to pray fervently for wisdom, strength for Charissa, skill for the paramedics, anything he could think of. He writes: "As I drove and prayed, I sensed the most incredible realization of God's presence."

He reached his daughter to find that she could not feel anything below her shoulders. Something in her back had snapped, just below her neck. Everyone near was certain she had done irreparable harm, yet Swindoll remained calm. Somehow the Spirit helped him in that time of desperate need. "With remarkable ease, I stroked the hair away from her eyes and whispered, 'I'm here with you, sweetheart. So is our Lord. No matter what happens, we'll make it through this together. I love you, Charissa.'"

Over the days to come the Holy Spirit continued to give Swindoll and his daughter a supernatural measure of calmness and assurance. Though the prognosis was grim, their faith remained strong. "God the Holy Spirit filled me," writes Swindoll, "took control, gave great grace, calmed fears, and ultimately brought wonderful healing to Charissa's back. Today she is a healthy, happy wife and mother of two, and the only time her upper back hurts is when she sneezes!"[9]

What Chuck Swindoll experienced during that time is exactly what Jesus promises the Holy Spirit will bring into the life of his followers. He promises to bring wisdom and comfort and faith beyond that which we are capable of on our own. He promises to give supernatural strength during times of distress, and counsel in times of confusion. The Spirit's presence is a great and powerful thing to experience. And it's something available to all believers.

REFLECTION
When have you experienced the presence of the Holy Spirit in a powerful way? How did it make you feel?

THE SPIRIT'S TRANSFORMING POWER

When the Holy Spirit has come upon you, you will receive power. Acts 1:8

BEFORE THE DEATH of Jesus, the disciples were certain they had the strength they needed to remain faithful. They had witnessed the boldness of Christ and believed they could emulate his authority. "I am ready to die for you," Peter said the day before he denied Jesus three times (John 13:37). "Even if everyone else deserts you, I never will" (Mark 14:29). But within hours his resolve had dissolved in fear and panic. He denied Jesus, just as the Lord had predicted.

Except for Judas, all eleven disciples shared that same desire. They longed to remain faithful and thought of themselves as fiercely loyal to Jesus. But when the chips were down, they all ran into hiding. On their own power they were unable to stand against the spiritual temptations they faced. They cowered in fear at the first sign of trouble. "When the Holy Spirit has come upon you, you will receive power," Jesus promised them (Acts 1:8). The Holy Spirit would give them the resolve to remain true to God and faithful to their convictions. He would bring a sense of supernatural authority to their lives—the ability to resist evil, to discern the truth, to wage war in the spiritual world as well as the physical one. He would give them faith and wisdom and knowledge that they could never find through their own devices.

And that's exactly what he did. When Jesus went and the Spirit came upon them, the disciples demonstrated his power forcefully and preached boldly in the streets. The once-cowering Peter was now filled with the Holy Spirit, and he began to preach so convincingly that thousands were saved in just the first few days of his ministry. He began to heal people of their infirmities, just as Jesus did. He cast out demons and took authority over the forces of evil. So great was his power that people brought the sick into the streets in hopes that Peter's shadow would fall over them as he walked past (see Acts 5:15). The Spirit of God had transformed the disciples from mere men into supernatural warriors for the Kingdom.

That same Spirit rests inside the heart of every believer today. He brings with him the power to transform us beyond our wildest dreams. He breathes into us the power to stand up against evil, the strength to resist Satan's lies, the boldness to speak decisively on God's behalf, the supernatural wisdom and discernment that we need, the resolve to become great warriors for the Kingdom. Where we are weak, he brings strength!

REFLECTION
In what ways have you experienced the Spirit's transforming power?
What areas of your life do you need to surrender to him more fully?

THE SPIRIT'S TESTIMONY

I will send you the Counselor—the Spirit of truth. He will come to you
from the Father and will tell you all about me.   John 15:26

DO YOU EVER wonder if you're saved? Have you ever lain awake at night staring at the ceiling, thinking of the sins you've committed and the evil thoughts you've had and wondering how you could possibly be called a child of God? Ever lost your temper and then later felt bad about it, causing you to question your status in the eyes of Jesus? *If I'm saved, why am I still so flawed?*

We've all had those doubts at one time or another. We've all wondered how God could love someone so sinful and unlovable. We've all turned our back on God and later repented, praying for forgiveness and hoping desperately that we haven't gone too far and fallen out of favor. Though God tells us our sins are forever forgotten, Satan makes sure we remember them, causing fear and doubt to creep in and haunt us.

> "He felt in his spirit that he was doing what God had led him to do."
>
> *Tribulation Force,* 310

"So you should not be like cowering, fearful slaves," Paul admonishes us. "You should behave instead like God's very own children, adopted into his family—calling him 'Father, dear Father.' For his Holy Spirit speaks to us deep in our hearts and tells us that we are God's children" (Romans 8:15-16).

Satan wins when he causes us to doubt. He's angry because he can't have our soul, so he lashes out by creating uncertainty in our mind. *You're no good*, he whispers. *You're just another sinner.* When we listen to his lies, we find ourselves reeling in insecurity and fear.

So how do you squelch the pesky voice in your ear? You listen instead to the "still small voice" in your spirit. You turn away from the dark shrill of doubt and dance instead to the Spirit's song of redemption. You allow God's Spirit to speak to yours. And you rest in his wonderful words: "Nothing can ever separate us from his love. Death can't, and life can't. The angels can't, and the demons can't. Our fears for today, our worries about tomorrow, and even the powers of hell can't keep God's love away. . . . Nothing in all creation will ever be able to separate us from the love of God" (Romans 8:38-39).

REFLECTION
In what ways have you allowed doubt to keep you in fear?
How can you overcome this uncertainty in the future?

THE SPIRIT'S GUIDANCE

It won't be you doing the talking—it will be the Spirit of your Father
speaking through you.　　Matthew 10:20

ONE OF THE MOST powerful and misunderstood dynamics of the Holy Spirit is his ability to speak to us and guide us in our daily life. He gives us wisdom and direction when we need them. I've experienced his guidance numerous times in my life, and it never ceases to amaze me.

A few years ago I desperately needed guidance. I had been praying about a critical decision that I needed to make on behalf of my family. For eight months I prayed for help, yet no answer seemed to come. One Thursday evening I stayed up late into the night pleading for some kind of direction. I wrote my thoughts out on my computer, journaling an answer that I would willingly accept if God would only show me that that was his will for us. Then I appealed to God to somehow let me know.

Sunday morning came, and I woke up earlier than usual. I was wide-awake and immediately felt the Lord speaking to my spirit. He was telling me to attend an early service at a church across town. This wasn't our regular church, so his request didn't make any sense to me. But God persisted, so I explained the feeling to my wife and went. When I arrived, I was shocked to see a good friend of mine—Wes, a man that I had known for several years. I sat beside him, and he seemed extremely nervous. Wes told me that he, too, had been roused from his sleep by God that morning and prompted to attend the early service of this church. Wes went on to explain that God had laid a specific message on his heart the previous night—a message for me. He had told his wife of it and had planned on sharing it with me the next time we saw each other, yet he had no idea it would be so soon. The message made no sense to him, yet it was very clear, he told me. You can imagine my anticipation.

When Wes spoke the words that God had put on his heart, they literally sent chills down my spine. He repeated word for word the answer that I had written on my computer four days earlier. The words that I had recorded and prayed over. He spoke three full sentences, exactly as I had written them. I was speechless. God had given me an answer, and he had done it in the most powerful way possible.

"When the Spirit of truth comes," Jesus says, "he will guide you into all truth" (John 16:13). God may surprise us, but he won't let us down.

REFLECTION
How has God prompted you in your spirit? What would you pray to ask him
for a prompting? How should you respond when the prompting comes?

MARTHA AND ME

There is really only one thing worth being concerned about. Luke 10:42

I CAN RELATE to Martha. If I were planning a party, she'd be the one I'd ask to help put up the decorations and set the table. She'd be the person I called to help me put the invitations together, to decide on a caterer, to hang the balloons and make a banner. Martha knows that everything needs to be just right. I'm the same way. I'm into details. I like to have things ready when the company shows up. When there's work to be done, there's no time for sitting around—that's my motto.

When Jesus showed up at Martha's door, she did what I would have done. She started getting everything ready. She put the meat in the oven and started setting the table. She brought out the fine china and the crystal vases. She swept the floor and shook out the rugs. Everything had to be just right. Jesus was here for dinner!

But her sister, Mary, had other plans. Mary didn't share Martha's need to please, so she sat with Jesus. He was telling stories, and Mary didn't want to miss a word of them. She knew the house was a mess, but she also knew that Jesus wouldn't be there long, so she forgot about the cleaning and plopped down at his feet. *What nerve*, Martha thought to herself. *Doesn't she know there's work to be done?*

Finally, Martha had to speak up. "Lord, doesn't it seem unfair to you that my sister just sits here while I do all the work? Tell her to come and help me" (Luke 10:40). *That's right, Jesus,* I'm thinking. *Tell her that cleanliness is next to godliness. Tell her about the importance of hospitality and diligence. Teach her the merits of hard work and preparation—of giving your best to the Lord. Make her get up and help.*

But that's not what Jesus did. "My dear Martha," he said, "you are so upset over all these details! There is really only one thing worth being concerned about. Mary has discovered it" (Luke 10:41-42). Jesus took Mary's side. He said that Mary was the one who had the right idea. She did nothing but listen and was praised; Martha did everything but listen and was chastised.

The Lord's priorities are not the same as ours. Jesus isn't as concerned about our lace tablecloths and clean kitchens as we are. He's concerned with the state of our heart. He's more interested in the time we spend at his feet, reflecting on his words and resting in his presence.

REFLECTION
Are you more like Martha or Mary? What would Jesus say about the time you spend at his feet?

NEVER SATISFIED

Lord, show us the Father and we will be satisfied. John 14:8

I HAVE A FRIEND who is not a believer, but he loves to talk about religion. He knows many of the stories in the Bible—especially the Old Testament. He's a history buff who has studied the account of Israel through the ages and sees the Bible as a great reference. As a hobby, he watches historical documentaries on PBS and the History Channel, and he collects bits of information like a boy would collect trading cards. He's often told me how fascinated he is by the accuracy of the old biblical manuscripts. I tell him that's because God doesn't lie and the Bible is his inspired Word. He nods but seldom responds.

> "At one time I was one of those puzzled ones. . . . Yet when I began an incisive and thorough examination of these passages with an open mind and heart, it was as if God revealed something to me that freed my intellect."
>
> *The Mark,* 141–42

I've told him the story of Jesus and shared the gospel with him several times, but he's more interested in talking about the history of it all. I've showed him the numerous fulfilled prophesies about Jesus recorded in the Old Testament and then pointed out the accuracy of the events as Jesus fulfilled them. Not one prophecy of the coming Messiah went unrealized. Not once was the Bible wrong. Though he sees it, he still refuses to believe.

Just last week we were discussing Jesus, and I asked him why he had such a hard time accepting him as God's Son. He thought for a minute and said, "I just need more proof. If God is real, why doesn't he just show himself?"

Once again my heart sank. How much more could God have done to show that Jesus was his Son? How many more fulfilled prophecies would it take to convince the world of Jesus' credibility? How many miracles before we finally believe?

Even the disciples of Jesus struggled with this issue. "Lord, show us the Father and we will be satisfied," Philip said to him (John 14:8). He'd seen the countless healings and miracles of Jesus. He'd followed Jesus as he taught from city to city. He knew that Jesus was the Messiah they'd been waiting for, yet still he wanted more proof. No matter how much proof God gives us, there will always be those who want more. I think my friend knows Jesus is the real thing—somewhere deep in his heart. He just can't seem to admit it. I'm praying that someday he will.

REFLECTION

Where are you looking for more proof of God's authenticity? What is keeping you from believing what you've already seen to be true?

PRAYERS OF THE RIGHTEOUS

"The earnest prayer of a righteous person has great power."   James 5:16

TED HAGGARD, a best-selling author and the pastor of our church, has been known to say that he believes in "long private prayers and short public ones." I've always shared this belief, though I've never been able to sum it up so succinctly. Like most of us, I've found myself more than a few times held hostage by long-winded prayers from well-intentioned people. I say that with respect, but honesty. It almost seems as if some people believe that the way to get God to respond is to filibuster the pulpit until he does. If we say it enough times in enough different ways, maybe he will listen.

How many times have you heard someone talk about the effective prayers of Elijah? We read about it in the book of James. "Elijah was as human as we are, and yet when he *prayed earnestly* that no rain would fall, none fell for the next three and a half years! Then he prayed for rain, and down it poured" (James 5:17-18, italics mine). It was the earnestness of his prayers that made the difference, we say. And the word conjures up visions of furrowed brows and long, grueling days of pleading. We imagine him on his knees beside his bed, beating his chest and pouring out his request to God. But is that the message of the text? Is that what James meant?

I wanted to find out, so I looked up Elijah's prayer. It's found in 1 Kings 17:1. "As surely as the Lord, the God of Israel, lives—the God whom I worship and serve—there will be no dew or rain during the next few years unless I give the word!" That was it. Sounded more like a statement than a prayer, but it was enough to hold the rain for over three years. I don't question that the prayer was earnest, and I'm sure there was more to it than the writer recorded, but the point is valid just the same. It wasn't the earnestness of the prayer that got God's attention; it was the righteousness of the man praying. Elijah didn't need to scrunch his face and wear out his vocabulary to bring about God's will. He lived a faithful and obedient life, and God took notice.

"The earnest prayer of a *righteous* person has great power and wonderful results" (James 5:16, italics mine). A righteous life is something God always honors.

REFLECTION
How does your life before God affect the tone of your prayers? What is the correlation between God's response and your obedience?

PROMPTED TO PRAY

And continue to pray as you are directed by the Holy Spirit.   Jude 1:20

DOES GOD wake you up in the middle of the night as he sometimes does me? Does he nudge you awake from a perfectly good dream at two in the morning and then keep you wide-awake? Does he bring a friend or family member to mind almost out of the blue? Maybe someone you haven't heard from or thought of for quite a while? Does he urge you to pray for them? If so, are you obedient?

At times I will receive notes or e-mails from friends who say that they've been praying for me. Often they will say that God put it on their hearts to pray for me as I write or study or travel, and they just wanted to write and let me know of their prayer covering. I received just such a letter earlier this week, and it lifted my spirits in a powerful way. I covet these prayers. Just knowing that God is urging people to pray for me gives my heart a renewed sense of joy and purpose. It tells me that God is interested in what I do and that he wants my life to remain obedient and my writing to remain on track. There is nothing my friends could do to invigorate my soul more than to cover me in their prayers. And there is nothing God could do to make me feel more loved.

When the Spirit prompts us to pray, it is a powerful testament to God's active participation in our life. Several months ago my wife felt compelled to pray for her parents. She knew that they were traveling at the time, so she prayed earnestly for their protection. The sense that her prayers were needed was a strong one, and she was obedient to it. Only later did she learn that her parents had narrowly escaped an accident on the highway, and it happened at the exact time that she was praying for their protection. A car swerved into their lane and very nearly crashed head-on into their car. It missed them by inches, leaving them shaken, but unhurt. Was it my wife's prayer that made the difference? As a Christian I don't believe in luck— good or bad—so I'm convinced that it did.

"Prayer starts with God," says Lloyd John Ogilvie. "It is his idea. The desire to pray is the result of God's greater desire to talk with us. . . . He is the initiator."[10] Throughout Scripture we see God's desire to engage with his people. He wants to speak to us, and he wants us to speak back. When you are prompted to pray, know that the dialogue has begun and the ball is in your court. It's your turn to speak back—even if it's two in the morning.

REFLECTION
How do you normally respond when God prompts you to pray?
How does it make you feel when he prompts others to pray for you?

TWO THIEVES

We deserve to die for our evil deeds, but this man hasn't
done anything wrong.   Luke 23:41

THE PLACE was called Golgotha, Aramaic for "The Skull." It was chosen as the perfect setting for an execution. The crosses could easily be seen from the heavily traveled highway outside the walls of Jerusalem. Romans ruled by intimidation, and public executions sent a clear message to the criminals within their midst. Offend Caesar and you die in humiliation and pain.

This is where they hung Jesus on a cross, between two common thieves. This was no accident—just another method of discrediting the man who claimed to be the Messiah. *He lived among sinners, so let him die among them,* Pilate might have thought. Pilate also ordered that a sign be made and nailed to the cross above him. It read: "Jesus of Nazareth, the King of the Jews." He had it written in three languages so that no one would be left out of his little joke. The leading priests were offended by the placard. "Change it from 'The King of the Jews' to 'He said, I am King of the Jews,'" the priests said to Pilate (John 19:21). But he refused, saying, "What I have written, I have written" (19:22).

> "Do not be afraid,
> for I know that
> you seek Jesus."
>
> *Nicolae, 160*

Even one of the criminals by his side scoffed at Jesus. "So you're the Messiah, are you? Prove it by saving yourself—and us, too, while you're at it!" (Luke 23:39). Somehow his anger seemed out of place. Why would he care? What would cause him to lash out at one of the few people who understood the pain that he himself was suffering? Could it be that he wanted to believe? Could he have seen Jesus preach, watched him heal others of their afflictions, lingered behind as the crowds followed him through the countryside? Maybe he hoped that Jesus was the Messiah he'd been waiting for. But now here he was, dying among common thieves.

But the man on the other side of him saw a different Jesus. Somehow he got it. For some reason, in the middle of all the lies and accusations, while the whole world was turning its back on the Savior, this man saw through the chaos and turned his face toward him. Jesus' disciples scattered, his followers shook their fists at him, and the Jewish leaders were certain they had carried the day. Yet somehow this man saw through it all and believed. Hanging on a cross, nearing his last breath on earth, he saw what the entire world had missed and said, "Jesus, remember me when you come into your Kingdom" (Luke 23:42). And the answer Jesus gave is the same he gives to all who believe: "I assure you, . . . you will be with me in paradise" (23:43).

REFLECTION
When did you call out to Jesus to save you? If you have not done so,
what is keeping you from taking that action? What steps can you
take today to resolve that decision?

PICKING A WINNER

But Daniel made up his mind not to defile himself.   Daniel 1:8

HOW WOULD YOU define a winner? If you had to pick someone out of a crowd and hold him up as an example of what it takes to get ahead in life, what would you look for? What would it be that sets that person apart?

King Nebuchadnezzar decided that he knew winners when he saw them, and those were the kind of people he wanted around him. He didn't want any slouches serving in his court, so he commanded his chief palace official to bring him the best and brightest he could find from among the Jewish royal family and nobility. "'Select only strong, healthy, and good-looking young men,' he said. 'Make sure they are well versed in every branch of learning, are gifted with knowledge and good sense, and have the poise needed to serve in the royal palace'" (Daniel 1:4). Then when his guards rounded them up, he instructed them to treat the young men like kings. They were to eat the best foods and drink only the finest wines from his own kitchens. They were to be taught Babylonian history and literature by the greatest professors around. They were to "be all that they could be," and serve as a reminder to all Babylon what kind of people the king admired. These were the winners in the eyes of Nebuchadnezzer.

Among the ones chosen was a young man named Daniel, but he wasn't about to let it go to his head. He saw himself as a child of God, not a protégé of the king, so he immediately set himself to a different standard. "Daniel made up his mind not to defile himself by eating the food and wine given to them by the king. He asked the chief official for permission to eat other things instead" (1:8). Much of the food the king wanted them to eat was forbidden by Jewish law, so Daniel convinced his handler to let him and his four friends eat only vegetables and water. "At the end of the ten days, see how we look compared to the other[s]" Daniel told him (1:13). The king's attendant agreed and soon saw that they were healthier than the rest.

Because of Daniel's obedience, God gave him a special measure of wisdom and knowledge as well as the gift of interpreting dreams and visions. In the eyes of God, Daniel was a winner. It wasn't because he was strong or intelligent or good-looking. It was because of his loyalty to his King. His willingness to stand up for his beliefs. His obedience to his God in spite of the pressure and temptation to go along with the crowd.

REFLECTION
Have you ever come under pressure to bend your principles?
How did you react? How did God bless your response?

A GOD AMONG THE PEOPLE

No one except the gods can tell you your dream, and they do not
live among people.   Daniel 2:11

WHAT IS THE DIFFERENCE between God and the many false gods people worship? How does our Lord differ from Baal or Dagon or the many other idols that people put their faith in during the time of Daniel? How does he differ from Muhammad or Buddha or the many gods that people bow down to today?

The differences are too numerous to list, but there's one that stands out starkly. And even those who worship these many gods are forced to admit it when backed into a corner. False gods don't live among the people. But our God does.

When King Nebuchadnezzar had a dream that disturbed him deeply, he called in his sorcerers, astrologers, enchanters, and magicians to find out what it meant. These are the people he'd always turned to for such things—the ones who claimed divine wisdom from their gods. But this time the king would make them prove themselves. He'd had enough of their words—he wanted action. So he put them to the ultimate test. He not only wanted them to interpret his dream, he wanted them to tell him what he had dreamed. It should be an easy request for a powerful god, he reasoned. "This is an impossible thing the king requires," they told him. "No one except the gods can tell you your dream, and they do not live among people" (Daniel 2:11).

> "How wonderful it is that we can come as children into the presence of God himself, the creator of everything, and call him our Father."
>
> *The Remnant,* 230

When the chips were down, the king's spiritual advisors had to make an embarrassing admission. "I'm sure our gods could do it, O King, but we . . . we . . . don't really know them all that well. In fact, we've never really talked to them." That's the problem with serving a false idol, I suppose. They're never around when you really need them.

Daniel, on the other hand, served a different kind of God. When Daniel was ordered to be killed along with "all the wise men of Babylon," he heard the story of the king's dream and after prayer said, "Take me to the king, and I will tell him the meaning of his dream" (Daniel 2:12, 24). With God's help, he not only told the king what he dreamed, but he told him what it meant. Because Daniel served a God who is not only all-knowing but accessible. A God who lives among his people. Because of it, the wise men were spared death, and the king of Babylon bowed down to the one true God.

REFLECTION
In what ways have you experienced the nearness of God? What are the
times you feel him with you as you go through your day?

TODAY'S READING
Daniel 2:19-23

GIVING GOD THE CREDIT

*That night the secret was revealed to Daniel in a vision. Then Daniel praised
the God of heaven.*   Daniel 2:19

WHAT DO YOU DO on the heels of God's mercy and provision? You praise
him for his kindness.

Daniel understood that principle. When king Nebuchadnezzar had a horrible dream, God not only told Daniel what the dream was but he provided the interpretation. Because of it, the king spared the lives of his advisors—the once
wise men, who had come inches from becoming dead men. Daniel's intervention in the matter was the only thing that saved all of them from the king's wrath.

When God revealed the king's dream to Daniel, the first thing he did was
bless God for his goodness. The king could wait for the interpretation; Daniel
had more important matters to attend to first. "Praise the name of God forever
and ever, for he alone has all wisdom and power. . . . He reveals deep and mysterious things. . . . I thank and praise you, God of my ancestors, for you have given
me wisdom and strength" (Daniel 2:20-23).

The secret to Daniel's wisdom and strength was that he never forgot where it
came from. He knew that if it weren't for God he would have no reason to boast.
And because of it, he boasted only in God's power, never in his own ability.

There are times when I find myself pretty impressed with the things I do. Just
this morning I received a call from an agent, singing my praises for some work I
had done for him. I felt the compliment going to my head and quickly had to remind myself that I had little to do with it. God is the strength and wisdom behind all I do. In my heart I know that, though I'm tempted so often to take credit.

I have a simple prayer that I pray each morning before I write. *Father, I have no
way of knowing who will read the things I write today, but you do. Guide my thoughts
and fingers, and speak to that person through me. Make me an instrument of your will.*
It's a prayer that I depend on him to answer daily, because on my own I have
nothing to say that's worth reading. With all my heart I believe that. Daniel's humility before God gave him strength beyond his wildest imagination. Our humility before God will do the same for us.

REFLECTION
*In what ways do you give God the glory for things he does through you?
How do you feel his strength as you move in his will?*

AN ARROGANT SPIRIT

I, by my own mighty power, have built this beautiful city.   Daniel 4:30

ON THE HEELS of God's mercy and provision, Daniel praised God for his goodness. He knew the true source of his strength and wisdom. Because of it, God showered blessings upon his servant Daniel.

But what about King Nebuchadnezzer? What did he do on the heels of God's provision? He praised himself. He took the credit. He looked out over Babylon and saw the great wealth and riches of the kingdom, and it made his heart soar with pride. So he started patting himself on the back.

"Just look at this great city of Babylon! I, by my own mighty power, have built this beautiful city as my royal residence and as an expression of my royal splendor" (Daniel 4:30).

While Daniel dropped to his knees in praise when God brought good things into his life, the king took to the highest roof and bragged. Daniel gave credit to God; the king took it all for himself. You'd be hard-pressed to find a more stark contrast. And what was God's response to the arrogant king?

"While he was still speaking these words, a voice called down from heaven, 'O King Nebuchadnezzar, this message is for you! You are no longer ruler of this kingdom. You will be driven from human society. You will live in the fields with the wild animals, and you will eat grass like a cow'" (Daniel 4:31-32).

Mark this down because it is a law of the universe: God will not be mocked. God doesn't allow foolish and arrogant words to go unpunished. He's not fooled by our fancy titles and our bloated ego. He knows that we depend on him for every breath we take, and he sees that, sooner or later, we recognize that truth.

Don't make God have to step in and humble you. Don't make him have to bring you down to size the hard way. Don't test him with your haughty heart and proud eyes. See your blessings for what they are—gifts from the Lord that come only because of his goodness. And give him the glory. Keep your life in perspective, and God will keep you in his shelter of blessing.

REFLECTION
In what ways do you struggle with a proud and boastful heart? When did you last pray that God would reveal any hidden spirit of arrogance within you?

MERCY AFTER JUDGMENT

*Now I, Nebuchadnezzar, praise and glorify and honor the King
of heaven.*   Daniel 4:37

WHEN YOU SEE God's hand of judgment, you can be sure that mercy is not far
behind. And the more severe the punishment, the greater the relief.

God promised to punish Nebuchadnezzer for his arrogant spirit, and within
an hour of his words the prophecy was fulfilled. The king was driven from society
and into the fields surrounding Babylon. As his servants looked on in horror,
their king lost his mind and began living like an animal. "He ate grass like a cow,
and he was drenched with the dew of heaven. He lived this way until his hair was
as long as eagles' feathers and his nails were like birds' claws" (Daniel 4:33).

> "He is righteous and
> a God of justice, and
> it is not in his nature
> to allow sin to go
> unpunished or
> unpaid for."
>
> *The Mark,* 148

Nebuchadnezzer refused to humble his heart, so God
humbled it for him. He literally humiliated the great king in
front of his subjects. He stripped the king of his power as well
as his dignity and then left him that way for seven years, just
as he said he would do. Only when the king looked up to
God and repented did God release him from judgment. His
sanity returned, and his heart submitted to God's splendor.
"Now I, Nebuchadnezzar, praise and glorify and honor the
King of heaven. All his acts are just and true, and he is able to
humble those who are proud" (4:37).

God's judgment was swift and severe, and so was his
mercy. He restored the king to his throne a much better man
than he was before. God wasn't after Nebuchadnezzer's throne or his kingdom.
He didn't want his gold and silver. He didn't want the king's servants or his
power or anything else in his vast empire. All he wanted was the king's humility.
He wanted his heart. He wanted the king to know that all blessings, big and
small, come to us only through the grace of the One who created it all in the beginning.

Don't leave the story without grasping that message. Don't go away with the
wrong impression of God and what he wants from us. We don't serve a God
who's hell-bent on wrath. We serve a Savior who desperately longs for our heart.
Arrogance leaves no room for such a wonderful God, so he can't put up with it.
It's a message that is so simple, yet critical. We must not let anything come between us and the wonderful blessings God has in store. Let us keep our heart pure
and gracious and true, and allow him to reign. Be humble. And give God the
glory for everything!

REFLECTION
*When have you found yourself under God's judgment for a proud heart?
How can you ensure that your heart stays true to him in the future?*

SLOW TO ANGER

The Lord is slow to get angry, but his power is great, and he never lets the guilty go unpunished.   Nahum 1:3

LIFE DOESN'T ALWAYS seem fair. There are times when it seems like some people get away with anything and everything. They've learned how to work the system, so they cheat and steal and lie and never seem to get caught.

Our family lost a great deal of money to such a person just a few years ago. We invested in a man's company only to find out a short time later that his entire business was a scam. Without warning, his doors closed and the money suddenly disappeared. Along with hundreds of other investors, we were left in shock, wondering how it could have happened. The man was brought under investigation, and within weeks his fraud became apparent, yet there was little we could do. Even the courts seemed helpless against his evasive tactics. Throughout the whole legal process he lived like a king, though his lawyers claimed he had no income and no net worth. He bought new cars, threw parties for his friends in his million-dollar home, and took his family on cruises. All the while we saw decent people, who had lost much of their retirement to his sham, struggle daily just to pay their bills. Nothing about it seemed fair.

At times like these we wonder, *Why doesn't God do something about it?* We know he could, yet he lets it go on. The people of Judah must have wondered the same thing. At the time of Nahum's prophecy they'd been under the Assyrians' thumb for several generations, longing for God to bring justice, yet he remained silent. Nahum came to Ninevah, the capital city of Assyria, about 120 years after Jonah warned them of God's wrath. The Ninevites repented when they heard Jonah's warnings but quickly slid back into their evil ways. Judah was the object of their evil, and the people were tired of being pillaged and plundered at the hand of Ninevah and its wicked king.

And what was Nahum's message? That God may be slow to anger, but he always settles accounts. The wicked may have their day, but God will have the final word. And when he does, his judgment will be decisive and severe.

That's a comforting thought to those who try hard to stay in God's will and do the right thing. To those of us who daily try to please God by having an obedient spirit and a contrite heart but who seem to get trampled on by the evil Assyrians of the world. But to those who cheat and steal and lie—those who live like they can't get caught—it's a sobering bit of truth to assimilate.

REFLECTION
When have you felt the sting of persecution by those who are evil and disobedient? How does God want you to pray in this situation?

THE PROBLEM OF BACKSLIDING

Where can anyone be found who has not suffered from
your cruelty?   Nahum 3:19

THERE WAS A MAN who continually rededicated himself to the Lord. The people in his church had grown weary of his constant backsliding and repenting. It seemed that every few weeks he was back at the altar, once again asking for God's forgiveness and favor. He always said the same thing: "Lord, take the cobwebs out of my life."

One day he came forward and uttered the well-worn phrase as he stood beside his pastor, and the pastor responded with a prayer of his own: "Lord, instead of doing that, would you please just kill the spider?"

Maybe that was Ninevah's problem. When Jonah warned them of God's judgment and wrath, they turned from their evil ways. They asked God to take the cobwebs out of their lives. But the spider was still alive. Ninevah's repentance was sincere, otherwise God would not have spared them, but their faithfulness was short-lived. When Nahum came to them 120 years later, they were back to their old tricks, as vile and evil as ever.

Remorse doesn't always lead to obedience. Guilt and shame don't always manifest themselves in a changed lifestyle. Regret doesn't always turn a person from his evil ways. Satan is a sly and elusive foe, and he doesn't turn loose of people easily. In fact, it is on the heels of repentance that we often feel the enemy's pull most powerfully. Like an alcoholic trying to free himself from liquor, we find that the allure is greatest when we are sober. It's easier to fall *back* into sin than it is to fall into sin in the first place.

Snake handlers understand this principle well. Those who work to milk the venom out of the fangs of poisonous snakes know that the most dangerous part of the process is letting the snake go afterward. That's when the serpent is angry and vengeful. They say that more people are bitten turning loose of the snake's neck than when grabbing it.

It's the same way with repentance. Even the most sincerely remorseful souls will struggle to remain faithful after giving themselves over to God. And that's why we need to be vigilant. That's when we most need the help and support of others. That's when we need to stay in the Word and stay in prayer and meditate on God's goodness. Because backsliding does happen, but it doesn't have to happen to us.

REFLECTION
When have you struggled to remain faithful to God? What triggered
the struggle? Commit today to take the steps needed to remain obedient
for the long haul.

A BLAZE OF GLORY

Then the godly will shine like the sun in their Father's Kingdom.
Matthew 13:43

CORONERS GET a lot of strange requests for funerals. Some people don't want to simply be buried in the ground after they die; that's a bit boring and old hat for them. So a lot of unusual ideas have come around through the years. Some want their remains to be sprinkled into the sky from an airplane or scattered over the ocean from a high cliff. Others have asked that their ashes be poured into the gas tanks of their favorite car or simply kept in a vase on the mantel. But Brian Kelly had a request that topped them all.

Kelly lived in a suburb of Detroit and found out he was going to die from complications to surgery on his intestines. After giving him a few days to grieve, his family asked how he'd like to be buried. Kelly's idea surprised them all, but they promised him they would do it.

Kelly worked at a firecracker shop in Osseo, Michigan, and he'd always loved seeing the fireworks go off. So he asked that his remains be rolled up into a twelve-inch round shell and shot into the air. The owner of the shop agreed to cooperate, so on Friday, August 12, 1994, at a fireworks convention near Pittsburgh, Kelly's request was granted. In one glorious display, the shell was shot from a cannon. Two silvery comet tails trailed behind as it ascended into the night sky. When it exploded, it sent red and green stars in all directions, each screaming outward, then floating gently to the earth. Kelly's send-off was anything but boring. He literally went out in a blaze of glory.

> "That was Jesus' guarantee that though he was leaving his disciples, one day he would return. The world had not seen the last of Jesus the Christ."
>
> *The Remnant,* 228

As exciting as it was, though, it is nothing compared to what believers have to look forward to at the return of Jesus. "Our bodies now disappoint us," says Paul, "but when they are raised, they will be full of glory. They are weak now, but when they are raised, they will be full of power. They are natural human bodies now, but when they are raised, they will be spiritual bodies. . . . It will happen in a moment, in the blinking of an eye, when the last trumpet is blown" (1 Corinthians 15:43-44, 52).

Now there's a day to look forward to!

REFLECTION
How do you imagine the day of Jesus' coming? How does it help you to get through the daily struggles of life to know that someday we will all be with Jesus?

GOD'S SPARK

Lord, you light up my darkness.   2 Samuel 22:29

THE FALL of the great Roman Empire left Europe in utter chaos. It ushered in the beginning of the Dark Ages—history's most desperate days. Barbarians came to rule the day through fear and intimidation. Brutal bands of illiterate Germanic tribes sprang up and went to war with each other. People scattered across the land, making their homes in crude huts among tiny bands of exiles. It seemed as if Europe were destined for a future of barbarism.

But there was one small ray of hope that shone above it all: the church was determined to hold its ground. Instead of conforming to the crude culture, the medieval church rallied in quiet opposition. While the world fell into depravity, the church held her moral position. While others abandoned literature and learning, the church opened schools and became the gatekeeper of knowledge. Thousands of monastic orders were set up across Europe as a sanctuary from the chaos and confusion. They were characterized by discipline, creativity, and spiritual training.

In France these monasteries ran schools and opened up their doors to orphans, widows, paupers, and slaves. They cared for the sick and needy.

In Ireland the monks set to work clearing the forests, plowing the fields, and growing food. They fasted and prayed and lived disciplined and orderly lives.

In England they fought illiteracy and violence. They held together the roads and infrastructure as best they could. And they began copying and distributing manuscripts to keep history and their faith alive.

Eventually the Dark Ages began to give way to the light. The church's diligence and discipline had succeeded in holding back the night until the West could emerge from her darkest hour. Vestiges of civilization began to pop up and thrive, and a renewed period of culture emerged.

"O Lord, you are my light," cries David, "yes, Lord, you light up my darkness. In your strength I can crush an army; with my God I can scale any wall" (2 Samuel 22:29-30). In a world of chaos and darkness, the light of God will always shine through. Although at times it may seem to reduce to a flicker, it is still very much alive. And it will always succeed in holding back the night.

REFLECTION
In what ways do you feel like a tiny flicker in the middle of a dark culture? What does God promise to those who call on his name? How does this knowledge lead you to pray?

AUGUST

HEAR AND OBEY

Anyone who listens to my teaching and obeys me is wise.   Matthew 7:24

SEVERAL YEARS AGO a group of scholars met together to discuss the accuracy of Christ's words in the Gospels. The group decided that the best approach to their task would be to color-code the text, based on the level of authenticity. Red would mean that the statement was "authentic," pink would mean it was "probably authentic," and black would mean it was "not authentic." They decided to vote individually, then tally the results and code the text accordingly. Proud of their creativity, the scholars went to work.

The Beatitudes and the Sermon on the Mount took the greatest beating. "Blessed are the peacemakers" was quickly voted down. There's certainly nothing about peacemaking that would bring much blessing, so the idea must not be authentic, reasoned the scholars. "Blessed are the meek" went down as well. In the end only three of Jesus' twelve assertions were deemed authentic. The rest just didn't make the cut, according to the scholars. And they had barely begun working their way through the Gospels.

You and I can sit back and laugh at the exercise because we see it for what it is. The Bible has weathered numerous attacks from the liberal elite, yet it always stands the test of time. There will always be those who want to seek God on their own terms. Apply the parts you like and ignore the ones you don't—that's how you reconcile your own agenda with the Word of God. Especially when the commands become too hot to handle.

But we would never do that. We believe that God's Word is inspired and authentic to the core. We hold the Bible up as our perfect standard—the words we live by. We would never water it down or ignore the teachings of Jesus.

Or would we? How many times have you passed by a brother in need to get to an appointment? How many little white lies have you told, thinking that no real harm was done? How often have you gone to bed angry with your spouse? Ever listened to gossip about a brother? Ever spread it around yourself? Ever lusted in your heart?

It's not that we don't all struggle with our sinful nature. We do. It's just that we're so easy to dismiss our sin and focus instead on the more blatant sins of others. You and I may never color-code our Bible the way some liberal scholars have done, but we still have a way of picking and choosing the teachings we're willing to obey. Our actions speak as loudly as our words in the eyes of God.

REFLECTION
Are there teachings of Jesus that you've chosen to ignore? What does today's passage have to say about "wise" and "foolish" builders?

JUDGING OTHERS

Stop judging others, and you will not be judged.　　Matthew 7:1

THE LATE FRED ROGERS spent his life teaching and comforting children everywhere. His children's television program, *Mr. Rogers' Neighborhood*, became an American icon through the years, touching kids from several generations. But most people don't know that Mr. Rogers originally wanted to become a preacher. He attended seminary and was a dutiful student of Scripture.

Once during those years he was attending a small church with his wife. The two were on vacation and decided to visit with some friends. Rogers was in the middle of a homiletics course at the time, and during the sermon he found himself ticking off every mistake he thought the preacher was making. The pastor must have been eighty years old, Rogers thought, and should have retired earlier, judging from his ability in the pulpit.

> "She couldn't expect unbelievers to live like believers, and so she was left without the option to judge them—only to love them."
>
> *Armageddon, 232*

The sermon ended, and Rogers quickly turned to a friend of his sitting nearby. He intended to make a critical comment about the sermon but caught himself. To his surprise, his friend was crying. Before he had a chance to say anything, his friend leaned over and whispered, "He said exactly what I needed to hear." Rogers later wrote of the incident, "That was really a seminal experience for me. I was judging and she was needing, and the Holy Spirit responded to need, not judgment."[1]

"Stop judging others, and you will not be judged," said Jesus. "For others will treat you as you treat them. Whatever measure you use in judging others, it will be used to measure how you are judged" (Matthew 7:1-2). It's a sobering teaching when you really think about the implications. I wonder how quick I would be to pronounce judgment on someone else if I knew that I would have to bear whatever sentence I hand down? How willing would I be to condemn them? How swiftly would my gavel hit the table? We'd all be more lenient, I think.

And what about those who like to make decisions about who is and who isn't going to make it into heaven? Those self-appointed keepers of the truth who are convinced that their denomination or movement is the only true church? What do the words of Jesus say to them? Will they be given the sentence that they handed down so quickly to others? God didn't appoint us judge over the souls or lives of others. He reserved that job for himself. Ours is to love our brothers and sisters and trust Jesus for our salvation. And to help others do the same.

REFLECTION
Have you been guilty of judging the motives or fate of others?
How would Jesus have you respond in light of today's reading?

A BOOK'S COVER

God does not judge by external appearance.   Galatians 2:6, NIV

DODIE GADIENT was a fifth-grade schoolteacher who decided one day to take a vacation. She'd been teaching her students about the wonderful landmarks throughout the country and decided to see them for herself. So she hopped into her truck with a camper in tow and launched out on a drive across America.

Just outside of Sacramento, while rounding a curve on I-5, the water pump on her truck started blowing steam. Dodie tried to pull over, but her large camper still took up half the lane. Cars backed up for miles and angry drivers honked in irritation as they slowly edged around her, but no one stopped to help. Leaning against the trailer, Dodie was near tears when she began to pray. "Please, God, send me an angel . . . preferably one with mechanical experience." Within a few minutes a huge Harley drove up and parked in front of her. A large tattooed man with black hair and a full beard stepped off of it. He was sporting a black leather jacket with "Hell's Angels" emblazed on the back. Dodie froze with fear.

Without saying a word, the man glanced at Dodie and went to work on her truck. Within minutes he had flagged down a large truck and convinced the driver to tow them to a safer spot away from traffic. Then he calmly opened the hood and started removing the broken water pump. Before long he had the truck put back together and running smoothly. Dodie summoned the courage to tell him thanks and then carried on a brief conversation. Before leaving the man looked her straight in the eye and said, "Don't judge a book by its cover. You may not know who you're talking to." With that he smiled and drove away.

Some people have a bad habit of crawling out of the boxes we put them into. Just when we think we have them labeled right, they do something to prove us wrong. I'm just as guilty as anyone of placing motives and attaching blame based on the little information I have. And I'm sure others have been quick to do the same with me. But that's a shallow way to live and an unhealthy pattern to get into. "God does not judge by external appearance," Paul tells us (Galatians 2:6, NIV), and neither should we. People deserve the benefit of our doubt. And we deserve the benefit of theirs.

REFLECTION
Who is the person in your life you are judging based on his or her appearance? What do you think of the people you know who have a different race or skin color? How would God have you respond to them?

ONLY ONE WAY

No one can come to the Father except through me. John 14:6

TONY CAMPOLO spends a lot of time on airplanes, and he often uses the opportunity to talk to others about Jesus. Sometimes people listen, and other times they don't; but Campolo never tires of sharing his faith.

One stormy night he was on a plane from California to Philadelphia. The man next to him, certain that he knew better than this Christian preacher, said to Campolo, "I believe that going to heaven is like going to Philadelphia. You can get there by airplane, by train, by bus, by automobile. There are many ways to get to Philadelphia." The man sat back smugly in his seat, sure that he had won the argument. I'll let Campolo tell you about the rest of their conversation.

> As we started descending into Philadelphia, the place was fogged in. The wind was blowing, the rain was beating on the plane, and everyone looked nervous and tight. As we were circling in the fog, I turned to the theological expert on my right. "I'm certainly glad the pilot doesn't agree with your theology," I said.
>
> "What do you mean?" he asked.
>
> "The people in the control booth are giving instructions to the pilot: 'Coming north by northwest, three degrees, you're on beam, you're on beam, don't deviate from beam.' I'm glad the pilot's not saying, 'There are many ways into the airport. There are many approaches we can take.' I'm glad he is saying, 'There's only one way we can land this plane, and I'm going to stay with it.'"[2]

"You may rest assured that if you are a believer and have placed your hope and trust in the work of Jesus Christ alone for the forgiveness of sins and for life everlasting, your name is in the Lamb's Book of Life."

The Mark, 149

We've all known people who refused to believe that Jesus is the only way to heaven. However, Jesus says, "No one can come to the Father except through me" (John 14:6). Scripture clearly explains time and again that there is only one way for a soul to get to heaven, and that is through faith in Jesus as our Savior.

God makes it easy to find salvation. We're the ones who make it seem so difficult.

REFLECTION
Do you know anyone who is seeking another road to heaven? What is another approach you could use to try and reach that person?

IN OR OUT?

Anyone who puts a hand to the plow and then looks back is not fit
for the Kingdom of God.   Luke 9:62

JESUS HAS little patience for hypocrites. As you read through the Scriptures, you get the distinct message that he has more respect for those who reject him and live in sin than those who say they accept him but live according to their own desires. He would rather we be in or out but not in-between.

"Anyone who isn't helping me opposes me," Jesus said to the religious leaders of his day, "and anyone who isn't working with me is actually working against me" (Matthew 12:30).

Last fall our family went on a bus tour of Germany and Austria. There were a number of people on our tour bus, and we depended on each other to keep up with the group. One morning our tour guide gave us all instructions about where and when to meet the next morning. My wife and I somehow misunderstood where the group was supposed to meet, and we were waiting in the back of the lobby. We finally realized that we were in the wrong place and ran to the bus to see everyone else sitting in their seats waiting on us. We began apologizing to the rest of the group, but it was obvious that they were not happy. I didn't blame them. They were ready to go, and we were holding them back from their agenda.

That's what it's like when you have people in the faith who don't share the group's enthusiasm for Christ's mission. Their apathy holds back the rest and slows down the trip for everyone. It would be better to simply get off the bus than to constantly keep the driver waiting.

"Anyone who puts a hand to the plow and then looks back is not fit for the Kingdom of God," Jesus says in Luke 9:62.

"Don't pretend to follow me while keeping your eye on the world," he is saying to us. Jesus wants us to be honest about our dedication to him. Either we're committed, or we're not. Either we're in, or we're out. Either we love him, or we don't. Get on the bus, or get off. Sitting on the fence is not an option in God's economy.

REFLECTION
How are you trying to live in two worlds at the same time? What would
Jesus have to say to you about the way you are living?

A WINNABLE WAR

I have given you authority over all the power of the enemy.   Luke 10:19

IF YOU FIND yourself constantly losing the battle against temptation, then something is desperately wrong. If Satan is getting the upper hand in your life, consistently getting you to fall into sin, maybe you need to change your approach to spiritual warfare. The enemy is a cunning and skillful foe, but he is no match for the Holy Spirit that lives within each and every believer. The only way Satan can win the battle is for Christians to stifle the work of the Spirit.

The Holy Spirit empowers us as believers to overcome the forces of evil as well as our sinful nature. Before we accepted Christ as Savior we had no power to combat temptation, but now we do. We have a force greater than ourselves living within us and helping us in our weaknesses. And if we are falling into sin often, it means that we are squelching the work of the Spirit.

"I have given you authority over all the power of the enemy," Jesus says in Luke 10:19. The power that Jesus gives to us as his followers is all we need to overcome Satan. When we walk in the Spirit, we have the ability to stay focused and resist evil. When we fall, it is because we are trying to do it on our own.

The beauty of spiritual warfare is that it is a battle we can win every time. It's a war that God fights on our behalf. And with the Holy Spirit's help, we *can* overcome.

REFLECTION
How are you doing in your struggle against temptation? What should you do to invoke the power of the Holy Spirit in your behalf?

SOMETHING TO REJOICE IN

Rejoice because your names are registered as citizens of heaven.
Luke 10:20

JESUS TOLD his disciples, "Don't rejoice just because evil spirits obey you; rejoice because your names are registered as citizens of heaven" (Luke 10:20).

He knew that the Holy Spirit would give them such power over Satan and his demons that they would be tempted to glory in their ability to defeat evil. So he reminded them ahead of time not to lose their focus. "Don't rejoice just because evil spirits obey you," he told them, "rejoice because your names are registered as citizens of heaven."

"There is something to cheer about," he was telling them, "but it has nothing to do with you and what you do on earth. Rejoice in the promise of heaven. Rejoice because you're going to spend eternity with God."

> "Suddenly he stopped and leaned against a fence. 'Captain, these are the times when I long for heaven.'"
>
> *Assassins,* 355

We, too, have a tendency to forget what is truly important. We tend to get so caught up in our daily routine that we forget how short life on earth really is. We're so intent on doing great things for God, on beating back the enemy, on making an impact on the world, that we seldom take time to just sit back and reflect on our true reward. Because of God's wonderful grace and mercy, we have a home waiting for us when we pass from this life to the next. Jesus is there making the final preparations. The angels are setting up the banquet table, polishing the golden gates, getting their harps tuned and ready. Heaven is being built and decorated just for us— for God's people.

It's hard to fall for Satan's lies when your mind is filled with thoughts of eternity. I wonder how often we would sin if we kept our eyes focused on heaven? How many battles would the devil win against an army marching toward its reward in the hereafter? It's amazing how quickly your perspective changes when your heart and mind are set on eternity.

"Rejoice because your names are registered as citizens of heaven."

REFLECTION
*How often do you take time to reflect on heaven? Why not begin
today to look upward instead of inward?*

WHAT DOES GOD SEE?

*O Lord, you have examined my heart and know
everything about me.*   Psalm 139:1

WHEN THE LORD looks into your heart, what does he see? When he gazes into the corners of your soul, what does he uncover?

"O Lord, you have examined my heart and know everything about me," says King David (Psalm 139:1). David understood that he could not keep a secret from God. There is nothing he doesn't know about us. No sin is hidden. No evil thought is shielded from his eyes. No corner of our heart and mind is safe from the gaze of our Lord.

"You know when I sit down or stand up," David continues (139:2). God sees every move we make. When we sit at the computer, he is there. He sees the e-mails we send and the ones we receive. He knows the things we put before our eyes. He's aware of the things we read, the letters we write, the jokes we snicker at, the figures we pencil into our tax forms. When we watch television, he is right there beside us. He sees what we watch, what we laugh at, what we put into our mind. When we stand and walk, he knows where we go. He sees the places our legs take us.

"You know my every thought when far away," says David (139:2). God is aware of the things we think about. He knows when our mind wanders to thoughts of lust and greed and envy. He sees our proud and haughty heart. Nothing is hidden from God. And sometimes what he sees breaks his heart.

But God also sees our pure thoughts. He sees when our mind is set on him and his Word, when we think thoughts of heaven, when we worship with our heart and our life, when we think on lovely and admirable things. He knows when our remorse is real and our repentance is genuine. And because of Jesus, he is willing to forgive all the other things he sees and accept us in spite of our sin.

When God looks into our heart, it's up to us to determine what he will see. We have the ability to please or to hurt him. To accept his love or reject it. To break his heart or to make him proud to be called our Father.

REFLECTION
*When God looks into your heart, what things there make him happy?
What things in your heart make him sad? How can you cleanse yourself
of those habits and attitudes that break God's heart?*

ADOPTED BY GOD

You should behave . . . like God's very own children,
adopted into his family.　　Romans 8:15

RUBY AND HER HUSBAND tried for five years to have children of their own. Eventually it seemed like God was saying no to them, so they began looking into adoption. It didn't take long before the counselor found them a beautiful baby boy who needed a family. The two adopted him, and then to their surprise, Ruby became pregnant a few months later. She had a bouncing baby boy just a year younger than her adopted one.

> "He wants you to know and believe beyond a doubt that your sins and iniquities he will remember no more. He has separated you from the guilt of your sins as far as the east is from the west."
>
> *The Indwelling,* 111

One day when the boys were eight and nine years old, a friend came to visit. The woman looked at the children playing in the yard and asked, "Which boy is yours, Ruby?"

"Both of them," Ruby replied with a smile.

"No, I mean which one is adopted?" the friend persisted.

Ruby looked at the boys for a minute, then gazed back at her inquisitive friend and said, "I've forgotten."[3]

"You should behave . . . like God's very own children, adopted into his family—calling him 'Father, dear Father,'" Paul tells us. "For his Holy Spirit speaks to us deep in our hearts and tells us that we are God's children. And since we are his children, we will share his treasures—for everything God gives to his Son, Christ, is ours, too" (Romans 8:15-17).

What is the difference between a biological child and one who has been adopted into the family of God? In the eyes of our Father, there is none. We are full brothers and sisters of Jesus. We share in his glorious inheritance. God willingly brings us into his family and lets us sit at the table beside his one and only Son. He doesn't remember our bloodline any more than he remembers our sins. He only knows that we needed a home, and he gave us one. That's what it means to be children of God.

Thank you, "Father, dear Father!"

REFLECTION
What does it mean to you to be able to call God "Father"? What can you do to express your gratitude and joy for this holy adoption?

A SPIRIT OF ANGER

Your anger can never make things right in God's sight. James 1:20

ROAD RAGE appeared to be at its peak in the mid-1990s. All over the country, news stations were reporting on senseless acts of violence and rage. Some called it an epidemic.

Such an event unfolded one day during rush hour on Chicago's Northwest Tollway. A white Cadillac driven by an ex-convict was riding too close to the bumper of a passenger van. The van driver slowed down to irritate his tailgater. It worked. The Cadillac driver passed him in a fit of anger, throwing an indecent gesture his way as he went by. The van driver sped up, and soon the two were side-by-side, yelling and swerving toward each other.

The battle escalated until the ex-con decided he'd had enough. He pulled out a handgun and fired at the van, sending the bullet through the side of it and into the head of a little girl seated quietly in the backseat. She lived, but she will never be the same. Today she is blind in one eye, partially deaf, and severely impaired mentally. The ex-con is back in jail, and the girl's father lives every day with the terrible pain of regret.[4]

James tells us, "My dear brothers and sisters, be quick to listen, slow to speak, and slow to get angry. Your anger can never make things right in God's sight" (James 1:19-20). At its core, anger is little more than our attempt to take control of a situation that only God's wisdom can manage. Fredrick Buechner sums it up well: "Of the seven deadly sins, anger is possibly the most fun. To lick your wounds, to smack your lips over grievances long past, to roll over your tongue the prospect of bitter confrontations still to come, to savor to the last toothsome morsel . . . in many ways it is a feast fit for a king. The chief drawback is that what you are wolfing down is yourself. The skeleton at the feast is you."[5]

The problem with anger is that it does no good to anyone. Anger is a diversion from the love that God wants all of his children to have for each other.

> "What a revolutionary Jesus turned out to be. Buck was fascinated with the character. . . . *If you want to be rich, give your money away,* he told himself. *That's the gist of it. If you want to be exalted, humble yourself. Revenge sounds logical, but it's wrong. Love your enemies, pray for those who put you down. Bizarre.*"
>
> *Tribulation Force,* 40

REFLECTION
Do you struggle with anger? How would God have you combat this problem? Have you prayed to be delivered from your anger?

SPIRITUAL FOOD

You must crave pure spiritual milk so that you can grow into the fullness
of your salvation.   1 Peter 2:2

MICHEL LOTITO has a strange and unhealthy appetite. For some reason he likes to eat metal. I've watched him do it on television, and it's an unusual sight, to say the least. In the past thirty-five years or so, Lotito has eaten over a dozen bicycles, seven shopping carts, a metal coffin, a cash register, a washing machine, a television, and hundreds of feet of chain.

He still remembers the first time he ate a bicycle. "I started with the metal and moved on to the tires," he recalls. "It was really difficult to stay that extra day to finish off the rubber. Metal's tasteless, but rubber is horrible." Since then it's gotten easier for him.

None of that compares, however, to Lotito's biggest meal. He ate a Cessna airplane. That's right, Michel ate an entire plane. Over twenty-five hundred pounds of aluminum, steel, vinyl, Plexiglas, and rubber. It took him several years to get it all down, since he could only eat about two pounds a day, but he finished the whole thing. Doctors have warned Lotito about the harm he's doing to his digestive system, but he refuses to stop. Imagine what the inside of his stomach must look like![6]

You'd see much the same thing if you looked inside the hearts of a lot of people. Twisted metal of sin, steel of anger and vengeance, vinyl sheets of lust and envy, rubber wheels of greed and regret. What you'd see in a person's heart are the things that he or she has put into it. John warns us, "Stop loving this evil world and all that it offers you, for when you love the world, you show that you do not have the love of the Father in you. For the world offers only the lust for physical pleasure, the lust for everything we see, and pride in our possessions. These are not from the Father. They are from this evil world" (1 John 2:15-16).

If you want to have a healthy and innocent heart before God, you begin by watching what you digest. You develop an appetite for wholesome spiritual food. "You must crave pure spiritual milk," says Peter, "so that you can grow into the fullness of your salvation. Cry out for this nourishment as a baby cries for milk, now that you have had a taste of the Lord's kindness" (1 Peter 2:2-3). What goes into our heart stays in our heart. And it directly affects the health of our soul.

REFLECTION
What type of spiritual appetite do you have? What is the best way
to keep your soul healthy and your diet wholesome?

STRANGE IDOLS

*Instead of worshiping the glorious, ever-living God, they worshiped
idols made to look like mere people.*   Romans 1:23

"GOD SHOWS his anger from heaven against all sinful, wicked people who push the truth away from themselves," says the apostle Paul. "For the truth about God is known to them instinctively. God has put this knowledge in their hearts. . . . They can clearly see his invisible qualities—his eternal power and divine nature. So they have no excuse whatsoever for not knowing God" (Romans 1:18-20).

In spite of the evidence and the fact that creation screams out the truth of God's existence, that the Scriptures have proven their own authenticity, that the fulfilled prophecies easily bear out the accuracy of God's Word, there are still people who choose not to acknowledge or obey God. In spite of his warnings to those who would deny him, people still turn their hearts away in defiance.

Sometimes it seems that people will do almost anything to keep from acknowledging Jesus as their Savior. Even when faced with undeniable evidence, they refuse to believe. "They knew God, but they wouldn't worship him as God or even give him thanks," continues Paul. "And they began to think up foolish ideas of what God was like. . . . Claiming to be wise, they became utter fools instead. And instead of worshiping the glorious, ever-living God, they worshiped idols made to look like mere people, or birds and animals and snakes" (1:21-23).

> "As a brilliant and reasonable man, you will not be able to refute the evidence I have for Jesus as Messiah."
>
> *Apollyon, 90*

Just this morning I read of a church in Denver made up of die-hard Elvis Presley fans. They don't just listen to his music—they actually worship him. The congregation is called the *Church of the Risen Elvis*, and they hold regular meetings, where they sing songs of worship, raise their hands and chant his name, even pray to him for guidance and protection. They revere the king of rock and roll as their god, and are convinced that the spirit of Elvis watches over them.[7]

I admit that I like "The King's" music, but I certainly wouldn't put my faith in him. I trust instead in the One who created us all—the one true God, who has made himself known to every person on earth.

REFLECTION

*Have you put your faith in God for your salvation? In what ways have
you denied him and put your trust in lifeless idols?*

A PASSIONATE CHURCH

A deep sense of awe came over them all.   Acts 2:43

FRIEDRICH NIETZSCHE, the German existentialist philosopher, once wrote of a madman who charged into the marketplace of a medieval town. The man leaped onto the steps of the cathedral and cried out to the crowd, "I want a requiem mass! I want a requiem mass!"

"Who has died?" the people asked him.

"God is dead!" the madman answered. The crowds immediately began to mock and condemn the man for his statement of blasphemy, and when they finished, the man retorted, "If God is not dead, then why have the churches become mortuaries?"

It's a good question for all of us, isn't it? God is certainly alive and well, but you would have a hard time telling it by some of the church services I've seen. Recently a friend of mine told me of a service he had attended. Throughout the entire service attendees sat motionless, seldom smiling, never once appearing to enjoy themselves. The songs were stale, the prayers dull and lifeless, and the sermon unemotional. My friend said it was more like attending the funeral of an unbeliever than worshiping a risen Savior.

The church we attend is an exciting place to be. Our worship is lively and meaningful, the pastor is alive and engaging, and people exude a love for God and each other. My kids can't wait to get to church on Sunday mornings. For our family, worship is the most enjoyable part of our week. And that's how church is supposed to be!

Listen to how Luke describes the church of the first century: "All the believers met together constantly and shared everything they had. . . . They worshiped together at the Temple each day, met in homes for the Lord's Supper, and shared their meals with great joy and generosity—all the while praising God and enjoying the goodwill of all the people. And each day the Lord added to their group those who were being saved" (Acts 2:44-47). Life is too short and faith is too precious to be spent in a dead, lukewarm church. If you've found yourself in such a place, my advice would be to run and not look back. Find a life-giving church made up of a passionate group of believers. Find the kind of church that Jesus would attend.

REFLECTION
Have you lost the passion you once had for Jesus? What are some concrete things you can do to recapture your excitement for Christ?

MADE FOR A PURPOSE

The Lord has made everything for his own purposes.   Proverbs 16:4

ON MY DESK is a small tape recorder. It's one of the most useful tools I own. In my career I do a lot of writing for other people, and I use this recorder to conduct interviews and gather notes and quotes. I also use it to dictate my thoughts for future use. This simple tool saves me a great deal of time and energy and is invaluable to my writing.

But what if someone had never seen a tape recorder before? What if he picked it up and played with it for a few minutes, maybe pushed a button or two, but never figured out what purpose it served? He might decide that it would make a good paperweight or a bookend but beyond that have little use for it. In his hands it would do little more than collect dust. And that would be a shame.

You and I know that this little recorder was created for a purpose. A very specific purpose. Years ago someone saw the need for a tool exactly like this one and set out to create one. It was made intentionally to fulfill a very unique role in the world, and because of it, millions of people today are able to record their thoughts on tiny tapes. It's an ingenious little gadget.

You and I were created for a specific purpose as well. Before we were born, God saw something he needed to accomplish, and he set out to create someone to fulfill that need. He gave us the unique gifts and tools we needed to carry out his plan, even before we were formed in our mother's womb.

> "Buck had been given a second chance; he was here for a purpose."
>
> *Soul Harvest, 7*

He had a specific plan in mind for each and every one of us—a plan that was birthed before we were conceived. And his desire is to see us fulfill that divine destiny. "'I know the plans I have for you,' says the Lord. 'They are plans for good and not for disaster, to give you a future and a hope'" (Jeremiah 29:11).

Try to imagine the day of your birth. Do you think God looked down from heaven at this tiny new baby and thought to himself, *I wonder what I'm going to do with this one? I wonder what talents this one is going to have?* Of course he didn't. That's as absurd as thinking that someone would invent a tape recorder and then wonder what it does. God created us because he needed us for something special, something unique and exciting and divine. He created us for a purpose—each and every one.

REFLECTION
What might God have had in mind when he created you?
What do you love to do? How can that be used for God?

237

WHEN WE REJECT OUR PURPOSE

Everything I plan will come to pass, for I do whatever I wish.   Isaiah 46:10

I SPENT twenty years in the business world when I should have been writing. I believe the Lord called me to write as a boy in high school, but because of fear and doubt and opposition, I instead set out to create my own future. Throughout my time in business, I often felt God prodding me to accept the plans that he had for me, but for a number of reasons I continued to turn a deaf ear. I finally believed the Lord and left the world of business in a leap of faith, trusting that he would take care of my family and me. He has not let us down.

Today I often wonder what blessings I forfeited by rejecting the Lord's call on my life at a young age. What books was I supposed to write while I was busy making my own plans? What great things did he have in mind for me while I was skipping along on the wrong road? It's not something I dwell on, but it is something I think about from time to time. Though my rebellion was a subtle one born more from doubt and fear than willful disobedience, I'm well aware that there are things I've missed out on because of it. And that thought makes me sad.

Every day I see people that I believe are rejecting God's call on their lives. I know one man who pastors a church, yet he should be teaching in a university. When I shared this thought with him, he said with a smile, "You wouldn't believe how many people have told me that." Then he explained to me that as a boy he always envisioned himself as a college professor. He acknowledges that his talents are better suited for the world of academics than for pastoring a church, yet somehow he continues in his job. It's so clear that God has other plans for his future, yet he refuses to embrace them.

God fulfills his plans in spite of our rebellion. The books God wanted me to write during my years in business were written by someone else. Another professor is teaching the class that God had in mind for my pastor friend. "Everything I plan will come to pass, for I do whatever I wish," God says through his prophet Isaiah (46:10). It's not that God isn't powerful enough to get his will accomplished; it just saddens him to see his children reject their divine calling. And we may never know what blessings we forfeit by failing to embrace God's purpose for us.

REFLECTION
*What do you sense God's plans are for your future? Pray and ask him
to reveal his true purposes for you.*

DISCOVERING YOUR PURPOSE

Our purpose is to please God, not people. He is the one who examines the motives of our hearts. 1 Thessalonians 2:4

WHAT DIVINE PLAN did God have in mind when he created you? What role does he want you to play in his great and masterful purpose for all humanity? Why did he equip you with your specific gifts and talents? Isn't that what we all desire to understand?

God doesn't always tell us what he is doing, but he always works to prepare us for it. One of the ingredients of faith is a willingness to follow God on a "need to know" basis (when we need to know, he will tell us). We trust that God knows what he is doing, even when we don't. Our job is simply to let God be God and to focus instead on his specific plan for our life. We don't need to understand the whole game of chess. We simply need to be in the right spot on the board when he wants to move us.

But how do we know what role he has in mind for us? That's something that God readily reveals if we seek the answer. We may not understand his ultimate plan for our life, but we can know his plan for us today. If you are seeking God's purpose for your life, there are four good places to start. These suggestions are neither inspired nor exhaustive—just a good place to begin.

First, settle in your heart the truth that you were created for a purpose. If you believe that your existence is accidental and your purpose undefined, you will never be able to grasp God's divine plan for you.

Second, recognize your unique gifts and talents. Understand your personality traits, your aptitudes, and interests. What do you do better than anyone you know? Write these things out if you need to.

Third, articulate the desires of your heart. What are you passionate about? What makes you happy, angry, sad, or exasperated? What have you always wanted to accomplish in life yet never felt equipped to carry out?

Fourth, seek God's guidance with all your heart. Pray that he would bring his will into focus. When you read his Word, pray that he would lead you to confirming passages of Scripture. Listen for the voice of the Holy Spirit. Watch the circumstances around you to see what God is trying to tell you. Seek his will for your life, and you will find it.

REFLECTION
*How has God responded in the past when you sought to find his will?
Why not seek him now, and believe that he will answer?*

EMBRACING GOD'S PURPOSE

*God causes everything to work together for the good of those who love God
and are called according to his purpose for them.*   Romans 8:28

SNOW WHITE and the Seven Dwarfs was one of the first full-length animated movies ever released. Walt Disney sent it to theaters in 1937, and at the time it was like nothing that had ever been seen. Skeptics had been saying that Disney's vision would never make it to the big screen. The task seemed gargantuan by any filmmaker's standards, but Disney was committed to seeing it through. The finished movie contained over a million drawings by artists, and took several years to complete. Each picture flashed onto the screen for a mere one-twenty-fourth of a second. As you watched the film, it seemed so simple and seamless that you never stopped to think about the work that went into making it all come together.

> "At the words of God, Buck dropped face first into the grass and wept. God's very thoughts would come to pass, and his purposes would stand. No one could come against the anointed ones of God until God decided it was time."
>
> *Apollyon, 144*

Our life is put together the same way. From our vantage point, our days may often seem aimless and unsure, but God is making a divine movie. Each frame has been carefully crafted to fit into his plan for us. Nothing is an accident. Each day he brings people and experiences into our life that play a part in the picture he is making. Each moment we live we see his brush stroking across the canvas of our life. He knows what he is doing, even though we don't.

Sometimes we fight against his strokes. We move away and try to keep his hand from defining who we are. Instead of embracing his will, we reject it and try to go our own way. But he keeps working, trying to create in us the beautiful painting he has in mind for our future.

In eternity we will all be able to sit back and see the movie of our life. Some will view a film that is incomplete. They will be able to see what God had in mind, but the finished product never quite came to the fullness he envisioned. Others will see a film that is complete but didn't live up to the storyboard. The plots took too many turns and twists to make much sense. But those who embraced God's vision will sit back and watch with tears in their eyes and a lump in their throat. "So that's why you did that," they will say with wonder. And God will smile and say, "Thank you for letting me paint."

REFLECTION
*In what ways are you fighting against God's brush strokes on your life?
What fears keep you from trusting him and allowing him to work?*

RESTORED TRUST

Restore to me again the joy of your salvation.   Psalm 51:12

EVERY DAY we hear of friends who are going through tough times. We know people who have lost a great deal of money due to the downturn in the stock market. Friends have lost jobs in layoffs and corporate bankruptcies. Others are going through health problems. Just last night we prayed for the family of a man who had died from heart failure, leaving three small children for his wife to raise alone.

Often in the midst of these dark days we call out to God for help. We ask him to get us through our troubles and to restore the things we've lost. We plead with him to restore our fortune, our health, our business, our marriage, and our sense of peace. And we believe that God has the power to do so, yet often he remains silent.

Sometimes it is because we are asking the wrong question. Maybe what God wants to do is to restore *us*. To redeem our heart, not our money. To rebuild our relationship with him, not our bank accounts or portfolios.

Several years ago our family went through an extremely trying situation. Some poor investments had taken away much of our retirement money, and at the time it felt extremely unfair. We had to drastically change our plans for the future. We reminded the Lord that we had been faithful with our tithes and offerings, that we had worked hard at staying obedient to him, that the plans we had made came through a great deal of prayer and petition, and that we were certain we were in his will. We struggled to understand what God was trying to teach us and began to pray earnestly that he would restore the money we had lost. We claimed the promise of Joel 2:25, believing that God would restore to us "the years the locusts have eaten" (NIV), yet he only allowed things to get worse.

Then one day as I was praying, God spoke to my spirit saying, *What I want to restore is your trust in me.* Suddenly the money we had lost seemed irrelevant. I had allowed our distress to shake my faith in God as our provider. I had forgotten that he knew exactly what he was doing, even though things seemed out of control. He is now rebuilding our retirement account, but more important, he has restored our peace of mind. Our future is always secure in God's hands; it's our trust in that truth that needs refreshing from time to time.

REFLECTION
How do you handle trying situations? Do you find yourself pulling away from God or drawing nearer to him? How does God want us to respond?

GOD HAS NEVER FAILED

Once I was young, and now I am old. Yet I have never seen
the godly forsaken.   Psalm 37:25

ONE OF THE MOST arrogant statements a person can make is to say, "God has failed me." It is the haughtiest thought of a person's mind. It is the most conceited sentence a tongue can utter.

Yet most of us have thought or said it at one time or another—if not through our words, at least through our actions. When trying times come, we slump into our sulking chair and fold our arms across our chest, thinking, *How could God have let this happen? Doesn't he know I had a plan? Isn't he paying attention? How could he fail me like this?*

> "God, our Father, we come to you weak and frail and wounded. So many here have lost so much, and yet we are grateful to you for your grace and for your mercy."
>
> *The Mark, 362*

We're certain we know what's best for our future, and when God doesn't cooperate, we're quick to remind him how out of line he is. If only he could see things our way, he'd understand. At least that's how it seems from our point of view. But is God really so out of touch? Do we really think he isn't paying attention?

"The steps of the godly are directed by the Lord," said King David. "He delights in every detail of their lives. . . . Once I was young, and now I am old. Yet I have never seen the godly forsaken, nor seen their children begging for bread" (Psalm 37:23, 25).

There have been literally billions of people on the planet since the days of Adam, and God has never failed one of them, yet somehow we convince ourselves that he has forgotten our predicament. What message does that send to God about the level of our trust?

God's power is most evident when it seems that our life is most out of control. When we are the weakest, he is the strongest. When we need him most, he is nearer than ever. Even when it seems that life has left us alone, God is right beside us, holding us in the palm of his mighty hand. The worst we can do during these times of trial is to blame God and fight him for control. The best we can do is to let go and believe his promises.

REFLECTION
When is the last time you felt like God had forsaken you? Has he ever let you down in the past? Pray that he will help you trust him in the midst of your troubles.

MAKING CHOICES

Choose today whom you will serve.   Joshua 24:15

YOU AND I make choices every day. At work we decide how we're going to conduct ourselves. When someone tells a coarse joke at the water cooler, we can either listen and laugh along with the crowd, or we can quietly slip away and not take part. In our dealings with clients we make decisions about what we're going to say or do to get their business. When a boss asks a question, we can either be truthful or evasive.

At home we decide how we're going to act around our children and our spouse. We decide what we're going to watch on television. When shows insult our faith or tempt us to sin, we can either change the channel or ignore it and watch. And we decide which TV stations we will allow to come into our home.

We decide which books to read, which sites to visit on the Internet, which places we allow ourselves to go, which magazines we subscribe to, which friends and neighbors we align ourselves with. Every day we make decisions that affect our life, our faith, our family, and our relationships. And the decisions we make say a lot about the state of our heart.

"Choose today whom you will serve," said Joshua (Joshua 24:15). It is a decision that every man and woman has to make. And it can be broken down into two primary life choices.

First, God asks us to make the biggest decision of all—to choose whom we are going to serve for the balance of our life. Are we going to live for ourselves or give ourselves over to God's will? Are we going to worship the things of this world or the God of the universe? Are we going to put our faith in Jesus for salvation or trust our instincts? Whom are we going to serve from this day forward?

If our decision is to follow God, then he asks one more thing of us—to decide to die to ourselves daily. To wake up each morning and set our heart on his will. To make a daily decision about how we're going to act, what we're going to say, how we're going to treat our friends and family, what kind of example we're going to set, how we're going to live out our faith—not tomorrow or the next day but today. Dying to self daily is a foundational principle of Christian discipleship.

REFLECTION

Have you decided whom you are going to serve from this day forward?
What does it mean to die to yourself daily?

THE WISDOM OF GOD

Call to me and I will answer you and tell you great and unsearchable things
you do not know.   Jeremiah 33:3, NIV

DO YOU EVER feel completely inadequate for a task? Have you ever been entirely overwhelmed by a project that needed completing? Ever felt yourself in desperate need of supreme guidance? During those times, where do you turn?

I find myself in those situations often, and it's a frightening place to be. It's more than a little humbling to be asked a question that you don't know or to try to give advice when you're at a complete loss for words. When we need God's help, we usually need it in a big way. And he has the amazing ability of coming through for us, almost always at the last moment.

"I would ask that all pray during the broadcast that the Lord give me his wisdom and words."

The Remnant, 317

"Call to me and I will answer you and tell you great and unsearchable things you do not know," God says to us through the prophet Jeremiah (33:3, NIV). His promise is to provide supernatural wisdom and help during those times of our greatest weakness. It's a promise that Christians should cling to daily.

I was less than fifteen days into this devotional when it struck me how inadequate I was for the task. What wisdom could I possibly have to offer people to help them along their daily walk with Christ? What gives me the right to speak for God on a daily basis? The simple truth is, I could no more complete such a task on my own than I could build a cold fusion machine in my basement. Without God's supernatural guidance, I have no chance of creating a book that both glorifies God and encourages his people.

What about you? Ever been called on to do something for God that left you speechless? Ever sat across the table from a friend in crisis and had no idea what to say that would bring comfort or guidance or wisdom? Ever been at a loss when it comes to your kids? If so, have you felt a surge of knowledge flow into your brain at just the right moment? Have you given advice that surprised you? What you're feeling is the Holy Spirit guiding your thoughts and words. What you're experiencing is the power of God and his promise for supernatural wisdom. When we are weakest he is strongest. When we need help, we can be sure that he is there.

REFLECTION
What task have you faced that felt overwhelming? What did you pray
when you asked God for wisdom and guidance?

GOD IS IN CONTROL

Watch and be astounded at what I will do!   Habakkuk 1:5

DOES IT EVER seem as though God isn't paying enough attention to what's going on in the world? Do you ever see something bad happen to a good person and wonder why God doesn't step in and stop it? Have you ever noticed how unfair life can seem?

We've all wondered at one time or another why God allows evil to run so rampant in the world. We long for him to put an end to it. We even pray fervently that he will, yet still he often remains silent.

Habakkuk struggled with that same dilemma. Year after year he watched as the nation of Judah wallowed in sin and wickedness, and he pleaded with God to do something about it. Like us, Habakkuk knew that God was a just God who promised that sin would not go unpunished. "How long, O Lord, must I call for help?" Habakkuk laments. "Must I forever see this sin and misery all around me? Wherever I look, I see destruction and violence. I am surrounded by people who love to argue and fight. The law has become paralyzed and useless, and there is no justice given in the courts" (Habakkuk 1:2-4).

Habakkuk saw what you and I see every day. He saw criminals getting away with their crimes. He saw rich people taking advantage of the poor. He saw bosses cheating their workers and workers padding their time sheets. He saw sin and corruption going unchecked and unpunished. Judges were unjust. Law keepers were unlawful. Even the priests couldn't be trusted. What Habakkuk saw in Judah might as well have been a page out of today's newspapers.

And what was the Lord's response? "The Lord replied, 'Look at the nations and be amazed! Watch and be astounded at what I will do! For I am doing something in your own day, something you wouldn't believe even if someone told you about it'" (1:5).

It's as if God told Habakkuk, "Don't ever think I'm not in control. I know what's going on, even when it seems like I'm not watching. I see the wickedness. I see the injustice. I know what's going on. You can't even fathom the depth and width of my authority, so don't even try." With God you have to believe that something is happening even when it seems it isn't. He is in control even when you and I can't see it.

REFLECTION
Is it comforting to know that God is in control of the world in spite of the wickedness? What should be our response when we see others in sin?

IDOLS WITHOUT TONGUES

What have you gained by worshiping all your man-made idols?   Habakkuk 2:18

I'M GUESSING you don't have a man-made idol in your home that you worship the same way that you worship God. You probably don't have a statue of Buddha on an altar in your den or a likeness of Dagon on your shelf. Most believers wouldn't dream of insulting God so directly. But does that mean you don't bow down to an idol or two in your life? I'd venture to say that almost all of us do.

Maybe your idol is a red Porsche that sits covered in your garage. You spend more time waxing and polishing it than you do in private prayer. In God's eyes, wouldn't that qualify? Maybe your idol is your career. The things you've accomplished. A house that you've painstakingly decorated room by room until everything is exactly as you like it. I know some people who worship their particular church beliefs or doctrine. Though they would scoff at the thought, the true object of their devotion is the man-made rituals they practice. They've tried to make God in their image.

> "There is one God and one mediator between God and man, the man Christ Jesus."
>
> *Apollyon, 287*

Chances are good that each one of us can think of at least one thing we've done or made or acquired that borders on idolatry. God has some sobering words about the things we bow down to. "What have you gained by worshiping all your man-made idols? . . . You ask speechless stone images to tell you what to do. Can an idol speak for God? They may be overlaid with gold and silver, but they are lifeless inside. But the Lord is in his holy Temple. Let all the earth be silent before him" (Habakkuk 2:18-20).

Do you want to know the difference between the idols we make and the God we serve? Man-made idols have nothing to say. We're the ones who have to do all the talking and explaining. But God neither needs nor wants our words. He doesn't need us to defend his authority. We didn't create him; he created us. And then he told us, "You be silent and let me do the talking."

That's the difference between a counterfeit and the real thing. That's the difference between an almighty God and a cheap substitute. One has no voice, while the other is the only voice we'll ever need.

REFLECTION
What is the idol that you worship? How does God feel about your devotion toward this man-made idol? How would he have you deal with this problem?

RESTING IN GOD'S SOVEREIGNTY

Even though the fig trees have no blossoms, and there are no grapes on the vine; . . . yet I will rejoice in the Lord!   Habakkuk 3:17-18

HOW MUCH do you trust God?

Take a few moments to think before you answer. I'm not talking about a surface-level faith based on knowledge or experience. I'm talking about gut-level trust and devotion. The kind of trust that runs so deep and long that it borders on absurdity. The kind of belief in God's goodness that defies logic and overrides every other human emotion. The kind of faith that remains true even when the world seems to be spinning helplessly out of control. The kind of trust that Habakkuk had.

In his darkest hour, in the moment of his deepest fear, Habakkuk cries out to God, "Even though the fig trees have no blossoms, and there are no grapes on the vine; even though the olive crop fails, and the fields lie empty and barren; even though the flocks die in the fields, and the cattle barns are empty, yet I will rejoice in the Lord! . . . The Sovereign Lord is my strength!" (3:17-19).

So let me ask again: How much do you trust God? How deeply convinced are you that he is in complete control of everything that happens to you? that he has not turned his back on you, no matter how dark and confusing life becomes?

If you lost your job and all your worldly possessions, would you still praise God as your provider? If you lost your sight, would you still proclaim him a God of vision? If you lost your home, would you still call him your fortress and shelter? If you lost your health, would you preach of his healing power? If your child died, would you sing of his goodness? If your spouse died, would you declare him a God of mercy?

These are tough and honest questions that you and I need to settle once and for all in our heart. I want to come to a place in my life where I can stand beside the mighty prophet Habakkuk and say, "In spite of what happens to me, in spite of the pain and uncertainty, I trust you, God. You and you alone are my strength."

It's easy to trust God when thing go well. But can we trust him when they don't?

REFLECTION
Spend some time reflecting on today's question. How much do you trust God? What prayer does God want you to pray in light of your answer?

THE PROVISION OF GOD

For the Lord will go ahead of you, and the God of Israel will protect
you from behind.   Isaiah 52:12

THERE IS NO room for coincidence in God's economy. When we are walking in the Spirit and moving in God's will, we can be certain that whatever happens to us is part of God's design. There is no such thing as luck. And when God directs our steps, we can do little more than stand in amazement at his miraculous intervention.

I've heard hundreds, even thousands of stories about God's supernatural provision, yet still I find myself in awe of him. I read one such story just this morning. It happened to an evangelist named John Robb. He was at a week-long seminar in Moscow, where he spent much of his time passing out Bibles to Muslims. A few days before his departure he ran out of Bibles and had only some tracts to give away. During his last day in Moscow, he ran into a man named Mirza—a Muslim doctor. Robb told Mirza about Jesus and gave him a tract. The man seemed intrigued, but the conversation was short.

The next day Mirza showed up at Robb's hotel room, just as he was leaving for the airport. He said he came by to simply express his appreciation, but Robb could tell that his Muslim friend was interested in hearing more about Jesus. *Lord, what I'd give for a Russian New Testament right now*, Robb prayed silently as they spoke. Not ten seconds later a knock came at the door. It was a Russian Gideon missionary with a box full of New Testaments. They had just been given permission to place the Bibles in every room. The missionary stood with a New Testament extended toward Robb, almost as if to say, "Is this what you needed?" He gave the Bible to his new friend and said good-bye before rushing to catch his flight.[8]

"For the Lord will go ahead of you, and the God of Israel will protect you from behind," says the prophet Isaiah (52:12). Though it may often feel as if we're on our own, God is always beside us. When we are moving in his strength, he is guiding our steps and watching from behind. We are never alone.

REFLECTION
When have you experienced the miraculous provision of God during a time of need? Do you allow God to direct your steps on a daily basis?

WHEN GOD SCOLDS

There is so much more we would like to say about this. But you don't seem to listen, so it's hard to make you understand.   Hebrews 5:11

HAVE YOU EVER sat in church behind a couple of bratty kids? I did, just a couple of weeks ago. I was out of town and sitting in on a Sunday morning service, and two rows ahead of me were a couple of boys who were bouncing off the ceiling. Every person in the vicinity was distracted by their antics. I lost count of how many times their father told them to sit still and be quiet, but they refused to listen. Throughout the service they continued to jump and squirm and pinch each other. And they were old enough to know better—that's what was most irritating.

At one point the father was scolding the older of the two, and the boy simply closed his eyes and pressed his hands tightly over his ears. Though he knew he was wrong, he didn't want to hear about it. He refused to listen.

Aren't we a lot like that sometimes? Aren't there times when we know God is telling us to straighten up and act like Christians, and we respond by closing our eyes and covering our ears? We read a Scripture that convicts our spirit, yet we choose to simply keep reading and shut out the convicting thoughts. A pastor gives a word that seems as if it were meant just for us, and we nod introspectively but forget about it by the time we get home. God's Spirit whispers a word of caution into ours, and we shrug it off and go our merry way.

> "Rayford wasn't sure he wanted the blinding light of God in his mental mirror. . . . He could cover his ears and hum as he did as a child when his mother tried to scold him."
>
> *The Indwelling, 50*

The writer of Hebrews faced this same attitude among the first century Jewish Christians and addressed it head-on in his letter. "There is so much more we would like to say about this. But you don't seem to listen, so it's hard to make you understand. You have been Christians a long time now, and you ought to be teaching others. Instead, you need someone to teach you again the basic things a beginner must learn about the Scriptures. You are like babies who drink only milk and cannot eat solid food" (Hebrews 5:11-12).

They were acting like bratty children, so that's how the writer of Hebrews chooses to treat them. They refused to listen like adults, so he doesn't talk to them like adults. At times I wonder what a letter to us might sound like. When God scolds his people, he means business. When he speaks, it's our responsibility to listen—and to respond accordingly. Anything less is an insult to our heavenly Father.

REFLECTION

How do you respond when God convicts your spirit? Is there anything in your life that he is scolding you about today?

SOLID SPIRITUAL FOOD

Solid food is for those who are mature.   Hebrews 5:14

HAS GOD had you on a diet of milk for too long? Have you been slow to cut your teeth in Christian service or to grow out of childish needs and desires? Have you been a follower of Christ for long enough to know better, yet still find yourself being treated like a baby Christian?

"Solid food is for those who are mature," says the writer of Hebrews, "who have trained themselves to recognize the difference between right and wrong and then do what is right" (5:14). When we find ourselves on a diet of milk, it is because God knows we are not yet ready for solid food. His desire is to wean us off of baby food and to set real meat and potatoes on our table, but he won't do so until we choose to grow mature and ready.

A solid diet is made up of things that strengthen our faith and lead others to Jesus. Jobs that take spiritual muscle and knowledge to perform. Responsibilities that are not for the faint of heart or the squeamish. God gives big assignments to those who prove that they can handle the pressure. And with these assignments come great rewards.

But also they bring great temptation. When God sends disciples to work, the enemy is close by, waiting to trip them up. The greater the task, the harder he works to bring them down. The steeper the road, the more stones thrown along the path to make us stumble. That's why God is careful how he doles out his spiritual steaks and potatoes.

So how do you convince God that you are ready for solid food? You begin by learning to "recognize the difference between right and wrong." You hone your skills of discernment. You hide God's Word in your heart until you know instinctively what to do when temptation comes your way. You learn the enemy's strategy—how he plays on the weakness of his prey, how he lies and cheats and steals, how he hides around the corner to catch us unaware. You learn the difference between God's will and Satan's schemes.

And once you know the difference, you "do what is right." You make a choice not to sin. You stare the enemy down and turn a deaf ear to his lies. You choose God's will over your own. You remain obedient even to the point of pain and embarrassment. When you develop the strength to chew and digest solid food, God will serve it to you.

REFLECTION
What hinders God from trusting you with solid spiritual food? Pray today that he would prepare you for greater service and responsibility.

WAITING ON THE LORD

We wait in hope for the Lord.   Psalm 33:20, NIV

ARE YOU WAITING in hope for God? Can you sense your heart longing for his touch, pondering his ways, dreaming of eternity? Is your spirit yearning to be one with God's Spirit?

There is a way to know if your mind is more fixed on heaven than it is fixated on the things of this world. There's a good litmus test that we can take. Believers who truly understand the beauty of the world awaiting us in the afterlife are more consumed with thoughts of eternity than with earthly indulgences. They find themselves lying awake at night dreaming of streets of gold. They relish the words of the psalmist: "I will live in the house of the Lord forever" (Psalm 23:6). Their prayers take on a new fervency and passion. They long for Jesus to return and take them home.

"I wait quietly before God, for my hope is in him," says King David (Psalm 62:5). David was consumed with thoughts of heaven. He immersed himself in God's glory. He waited for God, and put his complete trust in his Lord's promises. His heart beat to the tune of God's glorious song of salvation.

I often find small pieces of paper on the nightstand beside my wife's pillow. They are notes she makes when she can't sleep, and they are almost always filled with scribbled thoughts about God and heaven and eternity. She writes poems and songs and simple phrases that come to her mind in the night. They are beautiful words of comfort and worship, and it embarrasses her to hear me say that. But more than anything they reflect the state of her heart before God. It is her soul waiting for the Lord, and these random notes are her way of trying to capture this divine longing in words.

"I lie awake thinking of you," writes David, "meditating on you through the night. I think how much you have helped me; I sing for joy in the shadow of your protecting wings. I follow close behind you; your strong right hand holds me securely" (63:6-8).

There is a way to know the state of your heart before God. Just look at the thoughts that fill your mind during times of quiet reflection. When all is silent and the lights are out, does your soul wait for God?

> "The dust settled, and quietness wafted over the assembled. . . . Chaim slowly rose and addressed the people. 'As long as you are on your knees, what better time to thank the God of creation, the God of Abraham, Isaac, and Jacob?'"
>
> *Desecration, 289*

REFLECTION

Do you feel that your heart is right before God? Are you heavenly minded or earthly focused? What is God saying to you through these psalms of David?

WELCOME HOME

What is faith?   Hebrews 11:1

SEVERAL WEEKS ago my wife went on a women's retreat for the weekend. The kids and I had a surprise planned for her, and we couldn't wait to get busy on it. We dropped her off at the church building on Friday afternoon, and that's when the giddiness started. We had it all worked out. As soon as we got home, we started to clean the house. Not just to pick up, but to really dig the dirt out of the corners—the kind of deep cleaning that you usually do in the spring. We also did the wash and even cleaned off the desk and shelves in her office.

Next we went to an office supply store and bought her a new computer. Her old one had been around since dinosaurs ruled and was starting to make all kinds of frightening sounds and glitches, so it was time to send it into retirement. Her new one was bright and shiny and fast. We set it up on her desk and then took turns guessing what she would say when she saw it. We couldn't wait for her to get home.

Her surprise didn't disappoint us. The kids were thrilled at their mother's delight. They took her around the house, room by room, making sure she saw the work we had done while she was away. And for a day I was "Husband of the Year."

I think that's what Jesus must feel as he oversees the construction work in heaven. I imagine him walking through the streets of gold, making sure everything is just right, setting up our new homes and making sure the pillows are all fluffed and ready. He smiles and tries to envision what we will say when we get home. "Won't they be surprised?" he says to his angels. "Just wait until they see this!"

As for our part, what do we have to do to take part in the festivities? What does it take for us to be there among the saints in heaven? We have to believe in the promises of Jesus. It's that simple.

"What is faith?" asks the writer of Hebrews. "It is the confident assurance that what we hope for is going to happen. It is the evidence of things we cannot yet see" (Hebrews 11:1). We know that Jesus is God's Son. Scripture bears out that truth again and again. The only thing left to believe is that his promises are certain. We trust that when we get to heaven he'll open his arms wide and say, "Welcome home! Let me show you what we've done with the place!"

REFLECTION

When you reflect on heaven, how do you envision it? Have you accepted the truth that Jesus' promises are real?

WARNING SIGNS

When the Son of Man returns, you will know it beyond all doubt.

Luke 17:24

THE MIGHTY Mississippi River is a body of water that gathers from over 40 percent of the continent's lakes and tributaries. Sixty-three thousand tons of soil collects along its banks each day. The power of such a river is mind-boggling.

That truth becomes even more sobering when you consider the river's surroundings. The Mississippi is held back by a series of levees designed by scientists and engineers. These levees average twenty-five feet high and run for over twenty-two hundred miles along both sides of the river. They are the only things keeping the mighty Mississippi from flooding the area for miles around. Confident that the levees would hold, people have planted cotton and built a community right in the middle of the floodplain now known as the Mississippi Delta. Today over eight million people live in the delta, many oblivious (or apathetic) to the danger. At least four times in recent history, the Mississippi has overtaken the levees: 1882, 1927, 1973, and most recently in the summer of 1993.

Each time the people were warned. As you look through archives you find that in February of 1993, just a few months before the Mississippi's last rampage, an article was featured in *Smithsonian Magazine* warning residents that a catastrophe was inevitable. "What the river has written in the mud again and again is simple," states the writer, "'Someday soon.'" That day came just a couple of months later, and it was the worst recorded flood in Mississippi history.[9]

> "Horrible as these judgments will be, I urge you to see them as final warnings from a loving God who is not willing that any should perish."
>
> *Tribulation Force, 64*

It's easy to point a finger at the people who live in the delta, but what about those who choose to ignore the warnings of Scripture? The signs are just as clear and the danger just as imminent. Yet the consequences of our apathy are much, much greater. "The Lord himself will come down from heaven with a commanding shout," records Paul, "with the call of the archangel, and with the trumpet call of God. First, all the Christians who have died will rise from their graves. Then, together with them, we who are still alive and remain on the earth will be caught up in the clouds to meet the Lord in the air and remain with him forever" (1 Thessalonians 4:16-17). Jesus left no mystery. "Someday soon," he tells us. It's a matter of when, not if.

REFLECTION

What warning signs do you see that Jesus may return soon? What have you done to heed the warnings and ready yourself for his imminent return?

DEADLY WATERS

Be careful! Watch out for attacks from the Devil.   1 Peter 5:8

THE GREAT white shark is a cunning and skillful predator. It goes to great lengths to strategize its attacks before striking. One shark expert studied the habits of great whites off the coast of central California and found that year after year they would return to a specific area to look for victims. A particular shark would return to the exact spot each day and stalk its prey by swimming three to ten feet off the bottom of the ocean, always in a place about thirty feet deep. He said this shark would wait in the same area for over three weeks before finding the perfect opportunity to strike.

A diver named James Robinson found out this truth firsthand. At the age of forty-two, Robinson was diving for sea urchins in a spot that he had been frequenting for months. Each day he returned to the same spot to dive, going through the same ritual. He would gather his urchins, then tread water beside his boat while taking off his gear. He'd done it hundreds of times and never felt unsafe. Until one day a shark decided to strike. With lightning speed the shark shot up from the depths and clamped down on Robinson's leg. Crew members were able to grab hold of his suit and pull him to safety, but it was too late. The shark had his leg, and Robinson died a few hours later.[10]

You get the sense that Satan must have taken a lesson from sharks. Their methods are uncannily similar, and the results are about as devastating. Like the shark, our enemy carefully stalks before striking. He knows just the right time to attack. And when he does decide to bite, his strike is quick and decisive and deadly.

"Be careful!" warns Peter. "Watch out for attacks from the Devil, your great enemy. He prowls around like a roaring lion, looking for some victim to devour. Take a firm stand against him, and be strong in your faith" (1 Peter 5:8-9).

And where can we most expect Satan to attack? Anywhere he can, but most often when we swim in the shallow waters of temptation. When he finds us treading in an ocean of enticement and lust and potential sin. If you want to keep Satan at bay, stay out of shark-infested waters. If you want to stay alive, don't tempt the enemy to strike.

REFLECTION
What habits or places put you in the greatest temptation?
What can you do to see that you stay out of harm's way?

SEPTEMBER

LIVING SACRIFICES

*I plead with you to give your bodies to God. Let them be a living
and holy sacrifice.*   Romans 12:1

GOD GAVE everything to save us, and he wants us to give everything to serve
him. When Jesus laid down his life on the altar for us, he set an example of what
being a true follower looks like. If we love him, we will lay our life on the altar as
he did. We will give ourselves wholly to the work of God's Kingdom. We will forsake all other earthly pleasures in order to serve God and lead others into his
arms.

We call ourselves Christian "disciples" without ever giving much thought to
what that idea implies. A disciple is one who follows in the footsteps of his master. He goes wherever his master goes, says what his master says, does what his
master does, and lives as his master lives. With every part of his being he tries to
imitate his master's actions and obey his commands. There is nothing a true disciple would not do for the one he follows.

There is a radical and revolutionary element to the Christian faith that most
of us never really embrace. So many followers make Christianity a part of their
lives without ever letting it transform their lives. Yet Christ calls us to a complete
and total renovation of the heart and lifestyle.

"I plead with you to give your bodies to God," Paul tells us. "Let them be a living and holy sacrifice—the kind he will accept. When you think of what he has
done for you, is this too much to ask?" (Romans 12:1). Jesus went to the cross on
our behalf; the least we can do for him is to obey his teachings and to live a life
that is worthy of his name. That's the message that Paul was pleading on behalf
of our Savior. He was asking us to lay aside our own agendas and to put all our
energies into pleasing God and allowing him to guide us.

"Don't copy the behavior and customs of this world," Paul continues, "but let
God transform you into a new person by changing the way you think. Then you
will know what God wants you to do" (Romans 12:2). True discipleship takes
sacrifice and commitment beyond which most followers are willing to give. Not
every believer will strive to reach this level of service to the Master. But those who
do will feel his strength and power beyond all human comprehension. Commit
today to becoming a living sacrifice for Jesus.

REFLECTION
*Would Jesus consider you a disciple in the truest sense of the word? What
do you need to do in order to allow him to transform your heart and mind?*

THE CARNAL MIND

To be carnally minded is death.   Romans 8:6, KJV

IS IT POSSIBLE to be "carnally minded" yet still be considered a Christian? Can such a person still be saved? Sometimes Scripture answers our hard questions more definitively than others, and this one is as sobering as it is plain.

The phrase "carnally minded" means literally, "the mind of the flesh." And the Greek word for "mind" is more comprehensive than we might think. It refers not only to our thoughts but also to the actual seat of our passions. It encompasses our fears, our joys, our sorrows, and all the mental and emotional faculties we possess. In effect, Paul is referring to the carnality of the heart and soul—to be immersed in thoughts and concerns of the flesh. A carnally minded person is one who sets earthly goals by human means and then sets out to reach them through worldly measures. They look to inner strength to resolve problems and overcome fears.

> "I thought I had a great life. I even went to Bible college. In church and at school, I said the right things and prayed in public and even encouraged people in their Christian lives. But I was still a sinner."
>
> *Left Behind,* 196

From a human standpoint these appear to be admirable traits. Don't we all admire someone with "inner strength"? Aren't we all supposed to strive for such a life? The world would tell us yes, but God's Word says otherwise.

Make a trip to any mainstream bookstore, and you'll find row upon row of self-help books and resources. Books that promote self-worth, self-reliance, and personal fulfillment abound. They promise to reveal the secret to happiness and wealth and well-being, and almost always do so through a doctrine of self-actualization. Many are well-written books that seem to make a lot of sense on the surface. Christians frequent these shelves almost as often as unbelievers. From a human standpoint their guidance seems solid and helpful. But the problem is, much of the advice you find is "carnally minded." It is a human's view on how to solve the human problems. And in the end, such views lead only to spiritual destruction.

To be "carnally minded" is to depend on yourself rather than God. It is a lifestyle of looking inward instead of upward. It may sound good, but it doesn't solve the greatest dilemma of all—our eternal fate.

REFLECTION
In what ways are you looking inward to solve your problems instead of looking to God? What steps do you need to take to change this habit?

THE SPIRITUAL MIND

To be spiritually minded is life and peace.   Romans 8:6, KJV

RACHEL BARTON was a child prodigy. She's a violinist who first appeared on the public scene at the age of eight, when she played solo with the Chicago Symphony Orchestra. Her performance was one that few would forget, bringing tears to the eyes of the audience. The violin she played that day was an Amati, worth over three hundred thousand dollars. It was on loan from a local benefactor for the concert.

She had that same violin slung over her shoulders on January 16, 1995, as she commuted home on the train from a recital. The train stopped, and as Rachel exited, she somehow got caught in the door when it closed behind her. To the horror of all nearby, the train started to move with Rachel dragging behind it. Bystanders screamed for the engineer to stop, but by the time he heard them she had already been dragged for several hundred yards, her legs dangling beneath the train. When it was over, her left leg had been severed below the knee and her right leg seriously damaged.

She would have died had it not been for the quick actions of a few rescue workers. They stopped the bleeding using their belts as tourniquets and then quickly got Rachel to a hospital. Eight surgeries later, Rachel was on the road to recovery. After a few months she held a press conference. As the reporters gathered around, Rachel sat in her wheelchair wearing a bright red dress and a glowing smile. Everyone was surprised to see her so cheerful after what had happened to her, but the girl seemed undaunted. She talked more about her daily violin practice than about her accident.

"In the years to come," she told them, "I hope to be known for my music, not my injuries."[1]

That's the kind of attitude that Paul had in mind when he encouraged the Roman Christians to focus on spiritual thoughts, instead of carnal ones. "To be carnally minded is death, but to be spiritually minded is life and peace" (Romans 8:6, KJV). Being spiritually minded means to set our thoughts on things higher than fleshly concerns. It means to forgo worrying about the state of our earthly body and to concern ourselves instead with the music of our soul.

Those kinds of thoughts lead to "life and peace." They not only bring a life of eternal happiness and fulfillment but peace to the soul during our days on earth as well.

REFLECTION
Do you have the peace that comes from being spiritually minded?
In what ways are you struggling to stay focused on eternity instead
of fixated on earth?

THE MASTER POTTER

When a potter makes jars out of clay, doesn't he have a right to use the same lump of clay to make one jar for decoration and another to throw garbage into?   Romans 9:21

A MAN ONCE wrote about watching a potter mold a lump of clay. The potter took a lump of clay and rolled it into a tight ball, then placed it onto his old wooden wheel. He sat down in front of it on a wobbly little stool and started the wheel spinning. His hands gently caressed the clay, molding it gently between his fingers. Before long an exquisite goblet began rising from the middle of the wheel. The observer writes:

> Suddenly the stone stopped, and the potter removed a piece of grit. His seasoned fingers detected the unpliable aggregate. The stone spun again, allowing him to smooth out the former lodging of the grit. Suddenly the stone stopped again. He removed another hard object from the goblet's side, leaving a mark in the vessel. The particles of grain within the cup resisted his hands. It would not respond to his wishes. Quickly the potter squashed the form back into a pile of clay. Instead of the beautiful goblet, the artisan formed the material into a crude, finger bowl.[2]

Sometimes the creation a potter sets out to create doesn't cooperate as he would like it to, which forces him to settle for something less. The same holds true for you and me. How often have we resisted the Master Potter's hands as he works to make us into a beautiful and useful instrument of his will?

"We are the clay, and you are the potter. We are all formed by your hand," says the prophet Isaiah (64:8). God has big plans for each and every one of his creations, but for him to accomplish those plans, he needs our pliability. When we fight his hands on our life, we force him to change his plans for our future. How much better to allow him to work and to become all that we can in the Potter's mighty hands?

REFLECTION
In what ways have you felt God shaping and molding you? How have you resisted his attempts? What can you do to remain pliable and ready?

STAYING YOUNG

Let the children come to me. . . . For the Kingdom of God belongs
to such as these.   Mark 10:14

THIS PAST WINTER my kids and I spent an afternoon outside building a snowman, and for a time I felt more like a fellow playmate than their father. As usual, the task eventually turned into a snowball fight, and before long we were all running through the yard, pelting each other with snow. I laughed like a giddy schoolboy, and for a while I was ten again.

The same thing happens every time I take my kids to play laser tag. If you're not familiar with it, laser tag is a game that's played with guns that shoot red beams of light. About thirty people are turned loose in a huge warehouse, where they scramble and shoot each other with large laser guns. It's my kids' favorite thing to do, and we often take them on birthdays and special occasions. While suiting up to play, I always feel a bit out of place. My wife and I are often the only adults in the room—with about twenty-nine kids from eight to eighteen—but I don't let it bother me. Once the game starts I feel like I'm no older than they are. For twenty minutes I'm the tallest ten-year-old on the planet. Laser tag has a way of bringing out the kid in me.

> "How young Tsion appeared! Buck knew him to be a youthful middle age anyway, but sitting there rocking and crying he appeared young as a child."
>
> *Nicolae, 204*

I think the reason I relate to kids so well is that I can remember being their age. Someone once said that age is merely a state of mind, and I think he's right. We are only as old as we feel when we allow ourselves to feel old.

There's a reason Jesus has a heart for children. He sees in them what he hopes to see in every one of us. He sees innocence and passion and hopefulness. He sees himself. "Let the children come to me," he says. "Don't stop them! For the Kingdom of God belongs to such as these" (Mark 10:14). So how do we remain as children in the eyes of God? How do we keep from growing old and stale in our Christian walk? We remember the days that our faith was young and fresh. We forget our age, put aside our sagging joints and religious cynicism, and let our mind wander back to a time when our faith was vibrant and new. And then we allow that feeling to become the norm.

REFLECTION
How do you keep from feeling "old" spiritually? In what ways
are you still a child in the faith?

OVERCOMING SPIRITUAL BURNOUT

He gives power to those who are tired and worn out;
he offers strength to the weak. Isaiah 40:29

WE'VE ALL experienced spiritual burnout at one time or another. We've all gone through days, weeks, or months of feeling far from God. We may not doubt his goodness or mercy; we just don't feel as close to him as we once did. We become dry and tired and lonely. Our prayers become stale, and our worship seems forced and empty.

In the middle of this project I went through a short period of spiritual burnout. It started with a bout of the flu a couple of months ago. I spent a week getting over my sickness and on the heels of that felt completely exhausted spiritually, emotionally, and physically. Hard as I tried, I couldn't shake it. Writing became a chore, not a joy, as it usually is. Thankfully I had the opportunity to get away for a long weekend with my son. We went to a men's conference in the mountains, where we attended a number of great classes and spent our free time fly-fishing in the Arkansas River. I came home utterly revived and ready to get back to work.

Spiritual burnout comes to us when we least expect it, and often when we can least afford to feel far from God. These are times when we most need to feel God's hand on our shoulder and hear his gentle whisper in our heart. Oftentimes it is a sign that we are pouring ourselves out more than we are allowing God to fill us. It comes when we spend more time focusing on the things we are doing for God than we do reflecting on the Source behind our ministry. And the cure for burnout is to allow God to renew our strength with his.

"He gives power to those who are tired and worn out," says the prophet Isaiah; "he offers strength to the weak. Even youths will become exhausted, and young men will give up. But those who wait on the Lord will find new strength" (Isaiah 40:29-30).

During times of spiritual burnout, the temptation for most of us is to chase after the Lord. We cry out to him and wear ourselves thin trying to get him to revive our spirit. Maybe what we should do instead is to wait on him. To stop chasing and start relaxing. To rest in his presence and allow him to work. To meditate on his Word. To get away and listen. The best approach to finding revival from God is to simply linger in his presence. A few days of fly-fishing may be just what you need!

REFLECTION
When is the last time you experienced spiritual burnout? How does God
work to revive you during these times?

MESSAGE TO THE SEVEN CHURCHES

This letter is from John to the seven churches in the province
of Asia.   Revelation 1:4

WHAT WAS John's purpose behind the seven letters to the seven churches in
Asia? What did God have in mind when he included these messages in his prophetic book of Revelation? A number of scholars have come up with good ideas
on the subject, and most have a lot of merit. My thought is that there are many
conclusions we can draw and even more applications to our present life. Like all
Scripture, God's message is relevant to all of us, regardless of the time in which
we live.

Still, there is a reason God included these particular letters to these particular
churches. His Word is not random. He had a reason for both the order and the
content of these seven messages. And theologians have debated these reasons for
years. One commentary speculates that John simply took the churches in geo-
graphical order when he wrote the letters. If you look at a map you see that this
could be true—the churches are all located in a circular pattern around the province of Asia, in the same order that John recorded them. Interesting thought, but
it still doesn't explain why God chose these seven churches.

Here's a thought to consider—not my own, but the most interesting theory
I've run across. Perhaps the messages to the seven churches reflect seven dispensations of time. Could it be that God used these letters to the churches as a symbolic recap of Jewish history? Maybe God is using his words to each of these
churches as a reminder of seven unique periods of history in which God dealt
with his people. There is ample evidence in the text to support this idea. And here
is what the outline looks like:

Ephesus represents the time of paradise—the days of Adam and Eve in the
Garden of Eden. *Smyrna* represents the patriarchal age—the time of Abraham,
Isaac, Jacob, and Joseph. *Pergamum* is symbolic of Israel's days in the wilderness.
Thyatira denotes the monarchy period and God's covenant with David. *Sardis* sig-
nifies the time of God's prophets and his dealings with Israel's unfaithfulness.
Philadelphia characterizes Israel's return from exile. And *Laodicea* denotes the
time of the Pharisaical rule—the days of Jesus' rejection from the Jews.[3]

It's a lot to take in, but for the next seven days we'll explore this idea further.

REFLECTION
In Revelation 1:20 John refers to seven stars, seven lampstands, and seven
churches. In Scripture seven signifies completeness. Why is this important
to the message of Revelation?

CHURCH AT EPHESUS

You have forsaken your first love.   Revelation 2:4, NIV

GOD'S MESSAGE to the church at Ephesus brings us back to the beginning of humanity and the origins of our fall from God. The letter could have been written directly to Adam. But it speaks to each one of us.

"You have forsaken your first love," God laments (Revelation 2:4, NIV). Adam forsook his first love for his second one. He allowed Eve to turn his head and heart away from the One who created them both. How often do you and I do the same? "Remember the height from which you have fallen!" God continues. "Repent and do the things you did at first" (2:5, NIV). One minute humanity lived in perfect unity with God, but through the sin of Adam, we were torn from his presence. It is history's greatest fall. When Adam turned away from his first love, it cut a chasm in the universe between the Creator and his creation—a chasm that could only be bridged through the ultimate sacrifice from Jesus. The Cross was the only thing that could fix our problem. That's why God sent his Son. That's why he died. It's the only thing that gives us hope.

"He who has an ear, let him hear what the Spirit says to the churches. To him who overcomes, I will give the right to eat from the tree of life, which is in the paradise of God" (2:7, NIV).

Because of Jesus we can once again partake in the glory of the Garden. He invites us to come back to paradise with him—to eat of the tree of life that Adam lost. To once again live in complete unity with our first love. It is an invitation extended to every man and woman on earth, and all we have to do is accept it.

God's message to the church at Ephesus is powerful and unambiguous. "Don't commit the sin of Adam," he is saying. "Don't turn away from me the way that he did. Don't forsake your first love."

And if we heed his warning, God's tree of life is ours for eternity.

> "Buck wanted to humble himself, to communicate to his Creator and Savior how unworthy he felt, how grateful he was. 'All I can do,' he whispered huskily into the night air, 'is to give you all of me for as long as I have left.'"
>
> *Tribulation Force, 347–48*

REFLECTION
*In what ways have you forsaken your first love?
What can you do to return to God?*

CHURCH AT SMYRNA

Don't be afraid of what you are about to suffer.   Revelation 2:10

"I KNOW about your suffering and your poverty," God says to the church at Smyrna. "I know the slander of those opposing you. . . . Don't be afraid of what you are about to suffer" (Revelation 2:9-10). The message was aimed at Smyrna, but you can see how God's mind might have drifted back to the early believers. The patriarchs of our faith were the first to suffer for God's Kingdom. They were the ones who readily obeyed when God sent them.

Abraham, the original patriarch of our faith, followed God at great personal sacrifice. Though he was a wealthy man, he lived his life as a wanderer. He had no land of his own—only a promise from God. Isaac was a child of promise, but he was also a child of persecution. He was asked to leave the country by jealous friends and relatives and constantly persecuted by Ishmael.

"The Devil will throw some of you into prison and put you to the test," God warns the church at Smyrna (Revelation 2:10). Thinking of the patriarchs, we may be reminded of Joseph. He was sold into slavery by his own brothers and purchased by Potiphar to serve in the king's palace. Though God blessed everything Joseph did, he was eventually thrown into prison for something he didn't do. Falsely accused by Potiphar's wife, Joseph was bound and chained, forced to suffer as a common criminal (see Genesis 39).

"Remain faithful even when facing death, and I will give you the crown of life," God says. "Whoever is victorious will not be hurt by the second death" (2:10-11). The period of the patriarchs was defined by faithfulness and obedience in the face of great opposition and risk. The fathers of our faith suffered on our behalf, and God is reminding us that their example is worthy of our notice.

The people in the church at Smyrna had the kind of faith that God blesses. Their faith was reminiscent of the great patriarchs and stands as a testament to us all. There may come a time when we are faced with that same level of opposition and trial. Our faith may one day be tested to the same degree as theirs. Some of us may be imprisoned; others may be martyred in the name of Christ. The world will turn against us, as it did with our forefathers. When that day comes, are we ready to stand strong and true? Do we have what it takes to suffer on behalf of Jesus? If we do, we have nothing to fear and everything to gain.

REFLECTION
When is the last time your faith was tested? How did you respond? What steps should you take to see that your faith is ready for any persecution you may face?

CHURCH AT PERGAMUM

Everyone who is victorious will eat of the manna that has been hidden away in heaven.   Revelation 2:17

THE CHURCH at Pergamum had the same problems that Israel went through in the wilderness. They struggled with the same issues of unfaithfulness and doubt and spiritual infidelity. Some in their midst reverted to idol worship, just as the Jews did in the Old Testament. And God's wrath against them and his words of warning seem surprisingly similar. John's letter to the church at Pergamum is symbolic of Israel's days of wandering in the wilderness. It is pertinent to us as well.

"I know that you live in the city where that great throne of Satan is located, and yet you have remained loyal to me," God says to the church in Pergamum (Revelation 2:13). The church sat in the center of a city dominated by four idolatrous cults. It wasn't easy to be a Christian in such a perverse and evil culture.

"I have a few complaints against you," God continues. "You tolerate some among you who are like Balaam, who showed Balak how to trip up the people of Israel. He taught them to worship idols by eating food offered to idols and by committing sexual sin. In the same way, you have some Nicolaitans among you—people who follow the same teaching and commit the same sins" (2:14-15).

The desert was another one of Satan's playgrounds. During Israel's days of wandering, many in their midst continued to worship the idols of Egypt. At the first sign of doubt they melted their jewelry into a gold calf and bowed down to it. They gave their bodies to each other in sin and perversion. Pergamum's sin was the same as Israel's, and God's message brought a similar warning.

> "People by the thousands filled into the new pool to submerge themselves and to drink directly from the wide spring in the middle. Manna covered the ground, and Rayford was nearly woozy from its refreshing taste."
>
> *The Remnant,* 107

He also brought the same hope of redemption. "Everyone who is victorious will eat of the manna that has been hidden away in heaven. And I will give to each one a white stone, and on the stone will be engraved a new name" (2:17). To those who remain faithful, God promises to bring eternal nourishment. In the desert he provided manna for the body; you and I are given manna for the soul. For those who abstain from the temptations of Satan and remain true to God, a white stone will be presented. And on that stone will be printed a new name.

REFLECTION

How strong is your faith in the midst of an evil and perverse culture? How can you remain faithful instead of bowing down to the gods of our day?

CHURCH AT THYATIRA

You are permitting that woman—that Jezebel who calls herself a prophet—
to lead my servants astray.   Revelation 2:20

THE CHURCH at Thyatira allowed itself to be influenced by its culture. It was a blue-collar city, home to cloth makers, cloth dyers, and simple potters. The merchants were basically secular, with no focus on a particular religion. The church struggled to retain its zeal for the Lord and did little to influence its culture.

"I have this complaint against you," God says to them. "You are permitting that woman—that Jezebel who calls herself a prophet—to lead my servants astray. She is encouraging them to worship idols, eat food offered to idols, and commit sexual sin. I gave her time to repent, but she would not turn away from her immorality" (Revelation 2:20-21).

Jezebel was the wife of King Ahab, Israel's most evil and corrupt ruler. Could it be that God was reminding those in the church at Thyatira that what they were experiencing had been lived out before in another time and place in history? Jezebel worshiped Baal and even set up an altar to him in Samaria. In her evil clutches, King Ahab did more to anger God than any king in Israel's history. Together the two turned Israel's heart away from God and toward paganism (see 1 Kings 18).

God's warning to Thyatira is a timeless one. "I am the one who searches out the thoughts and intentions of every person. And I will give to each of you whatever you deserve" (2:23). Every time and culture has its Jezebels to deal with, and you can't let her bring you down. That's the message God was sending to Thyatira—and to us as well. An evil culture can corrupt any one of us, and we need to be on our guard.

But for those who stand strong against temptation, there is great reward. "To all who are victorious, who obey me to the very end, I will give authority over all the nations. . . . They will have the same authority I received from my Father" (2:26-28). Those of us who stand against evil influences will some day become rulers in our own right. We will rule alongside Jesus in the Father's eternal Kingdom. We will become the royal offspring that God always longed for.

REFLECTION
In what ways do you struggle against the evils of "Jezebel"?
What can you do to remain strong until Jesus' return?

CHURCH AT SARDIS

They will walk with me in white, for they are worthy.   Revelation 3:4

WHAT WAS the message that God's prophets brought to Israel? What was the primary intent behind their numerous warnings to God's people?

The Bible dedicates over four hundred pages to the prophetic period in Israel's history, and each one is filled with words of caution and encouragement to the Jews. In a thousand ways God spoke to his people, yet the message he brought each time through every single prophet can be summed up in one simple phrase: *Turn from your sin, and I will redeem you.*

God's one desire on earth is to restore people to himself. It is his consuming thought—his intent for all humanity, from Adam through today. This was the message he gave to the church at Sardis, and the message he gives to each and every one of us: "Your deeds are far from right in the sight of God. Go back to what you heard and believed at first; hold to it firmly and turn to me again. Unless you do, I will come upon you suddenly, as unexpected as a thief" (Revelation 3:2-3).

> "He is gracious. . . .
> He is merciful,
> slow to anger, and
> abundant in loving-
> kindness. He relents
> from doing harm."
>
> *The Remnant, 229–30*

All nations will face a day of judgment—from Israel to Sardis to America and beyond. All people will face the day when Jesus comes like a thief in the night. And on that day those who kept the faith will be restored. "They will walk with me in white, for they are worthy," God continues. "All who are victorious will be clothed in white. I will never erase their names from the Book of Life" (3:4-5).

God's prophet Isaiah uses similar language: "All of us have become like one who is unclean, and all our righteous acts are like filthy rags" (Isaiah 64:6, NIV). God also brings the same hope of eternal restoration for those who will turn back to Jesus. "Behold, I will create new heavens and a new earth. The former things will not be remembered, nor will they come to mind. But be glad and rejoice forever in what I will create, for I will create Jerusalem to be a delight and its people a joy" (Isaiah 65:17-18, NIV).

God's message to Sardis is the same as his message to us. "Though your sins are like scarlet, they shall be as white as snow" (Isaiah 1:18, NIV).

REFLECTION
*When did you turn from your sin and ask God to redeem you?
If you haven't done this, what is keeping you from accepting
God's promise of salvation today?*

CHURCH AT PHILADELPHIA

I have opened a door for you that no one can shut. Revelation 3:8

WHEN ISRAEL was allowed to return to Jerusalem after being exiled by the Babylonians, their greatest desire was to rebuild the Temple. To the Jews the Temple represented their connection with God. It was the lifeline of their faith. To a Jew the Temple was everything. There is no way to overstate its importance to Israel's way of life and the heritage of their nation. Rebuilding it was equivalent to restoring them to God.

Understanding this fact, you get a little better glimpse of the significance of God's message to the church at Philadelphia. The letter to Philadelphia can be seen as symbolic of Israel's return from seventy years of exile at the hands of the Babylonians, and in this letter Jesus says to the church, "All who are victorious will become pillars in the Temple of my God, and they will never have to leave it" (Revelation 3:12).

Imagine a Jew being told that God was going to make him a "pillar" in the Temple. Not only would God allow him to enter into the Temple, he would become an integral part of it. He would share space in its foundation. God would mold him into the framework of the pillars upon which it stood. To a Jew there would be no greater gesture of love and acceptance into God's holy family. "You want to rebuild the Temple, but I want to make you my temple." That's the message God was sending.

"I will write my God's name on them, and they will be citizens in the city of my God—the new Jerusalem that comes down from heaven from my God. And they will have my new name inscribed upon them" (3:12).

Today people are still searching for God's holy temple. Many are still wandering in exile, longing to somehow find their connection with God. As they glance into the heavens, they wonder how they will ever find him. He seems so far away, and we seem so small and insignificant. The chasm feels insurmountable. But God tells us we don't have to wander any longer. That's the beauty of the gospel. Because of Jesus, you don't need a temple to find God. All you have to do is call out to him, and he will make his temple in your heart. He will give you a new home and a new name. Your eternal fate will be sealed and secure. And no one can take that away from you.

REFLECTION
Are there times when you feel far from God and insignificant in his sight?
How does his promise to the church in Philadelphia change the way you feel?

CHURCH AT LAODICEA

Since you are like lukewarm water, I will spit you out
of my mouth!   Revelation 3:16

WE SPEND a lot of time criticizing the Pharisees. Sit in on almost any Bible study on the life of Jesus, and someone will inevitably bring up the hard-hearted, stiff-necked Jewish leaders who gave Jesus such a hard time during his days on earth. We love to laugh and jeer at their expense. And why not? They're an easy target. Jesus condemned them as much as we do. They rejected Jesus as their Messiah as well as God's promise of restoration in the process. They are the kind of people that none of us wants to be like.

Yet how often are we as guilty as they were?

"I know all the things you do," Jesus says to the church at Laodicea, "that you are neither hot nor cold. I wish you were one or the other! . . . You say, 'I am rich. I have everything I want. I don't need a thing!' And you don't realize that you are wretched and miserable and poor and blind and naked" (Revelation 3:15-17).

Ever felt pretty proud of yourself? Ever felt content with your nice job and your great paycheck? Ever looked out your window at your nice car parked in front of your nice house in your cozy neighborhood and think about how well you've done for yourself? *I started with nothing, and now look at all I've accomplished,* you say in your heart. *And they thought I'd never amount to anything. If they could only see me now!*

Israel has no monopoly on Pharisees. I've been one myself on occasion, and I'm sure Jesus is just as disgusted today as he was back then. "I am the one who corrects and disciplines everyone I love," Jesus says to the Laodiceans. "Be diligent and turn from your indifference" (3:19).

A haughty heart and a lukewarm faith have a tendency to go hand in hand. When we think we don't need God is when we need him the most. When we feel most self-sufficient is when we are the most needy. The church is filled with hard-hearted believers who are convinced that they stand tall in the eyes of God. But what Jesus wants is those with contrite spirits who understand their brokenness. People who understand the depths of their sin and the heights of their own insufficiency. People who trust Jesus for their salvation, not their own ability to overcome. That was Jesus' message to the Pharisees and God's message to the church at Laodicea.

REFLECTION
When have you been guilty of pharisaical thoughts and actions?
How would Jesus have you pray in light of today's study?

A HOLY AMBUSH

He will convince the world of its sin, and of God's righteousness,
and of the coming judgment.   John 16:8

HAVE YOU EVER been ambushed by the Holy Spirit? Have you ever experienced a time when you were simply minding your own business and God's Spirit caught you by surprise, bringing deep conviction to your heart? Has he ever brought you to your knees in repentance when you least expected it?

I've had that happen several times in my life, and each is embedded securely in my memory. Each instance made a marked impression on my life and had a lasting impact on my service to Christ.

I once took my wife to a lecture hosted by a visiting evangelist. We'd heard this man's tapes, and my wife thought it would be nice to hear him speak in person. I was just along for the ride, mostly as a courtesy to her, as I didn't have anything better to do that evening. Before the night was over, I found myself under tremendous conviction regarding a judgmental attitude I had allowed to fester inside my heart. The feeling came out of nowhere. The evening's lesson had nothing to do with my sin. Nothing was said that would bring this spiritual transgression to my mind. It was clearly and completely a warning message from God regarding the state of my heart. Out of nowhere I had been ambushed by the Holy Spirit.

> "He would have you not wallow in regret but rejoice in his forgiveness."
>
> *The Indwelling,* 111

God's Spirit plays many roles in our life, and he embodies many different traits and dimensions. But this one is perhaps the most life changing. When the Spirit convicts you of your sin, he does it quickly and definitively. And he seldom lets you off very easily. Jesus says of his Holy Spirit, "When he comes, he will convince the world of its sin, and of God's righteousness, and of the coming judgment" (John 16:8). Conviction is a sword that he wields often and well, and he doesn't take prisoners.

What about you? Ever been there? Ever been victim to a holy ambush? Ever been brought to your knees in repentance over a haughty heart or a lying tongue? Has God's Spirit ever stabbed you with guilt regarding something you said or did or thought? Maybe some sin you weren't even aware of, like a propensity toward pride or anger or selfish ambition? Or perhaps one that you knew all too well but never intended to deal with? An adulterous heart, maybe, or a habit of gossip? If so, then you understand that he means business. You know how brutal his conviction can be. God will deal with our sins now or later. Why not let him do it now?

REFLECTION
How have you felt the conviction of the Holy Spirit? What action have
you taken in response to that conviction?

NO MORE RUNNING

Where are your accusers?   John 8:10

"WHERE ARE your accusers?"

Those were the first words Jesus said to the woman who was caught in the act of adultery. It was the first thing she heard when the Savior's loving eyes met hers.

It's a story you've no doubt heard before. The Pharisees had been wearing out their welcome trying to get Jesus to admit he was a fraud. They'd spend days trying to trick him, arrest him, or make a fool of him, yet each time he foiled their plans. His divinity was more than their anger could handle, but they were determined not to give up. So one day they burst through a closed door to catch a downtrodden woman, then threw her at the feet of Jesus.

"This woman was caught in the very act of adultery," they said to him. "The law of Moses says to stone her. What do you say?" (John 8:4). As you read between the lines, you can almost sense their delight. *We've got him now*, they thought. *He'll never get out of this one.*

But Jesus wouldn't be Jesus if he didn't know exactly how to answer them. "All right, stone her," he told them. "But let those who have never sinned throw the first stones!" (8:7). Then he stooped down and calmly went back to writing in the dust with his finger. One by one the Pharisees slipped away. Jesus was left alone with the adulterous woman. He rose to his feet, looked her in the eye, and uttered the most unlikely words imaginable. "Where are your accusers?"

They both knew she was guilty. The woman didn't need a jury to tell her she had done wrong. Her sin had weighed heavy on her heart most of her life, and she had no reason to believe that would change now. Sinners know they are sinners, even when there's no one around to tell them. But Jesus saw past her sin—he saw what she could become. He saw a broken woman in need of forgiveness, and that's the branch he extended.

"There are no accusers here," he was telling her. "I forgive you. Now all you need to do is stop sinning, and everything you've done will be forgotten. You can stop running now and start living." Who wouldn't accept an offer like that?

REFLECTION
When have you been beaten down by sin and the world's accusations?
Do you need a hand of forgiveness? Why not reach out to Jesus today?

FORGIVENESS ISN'T CHEAP

If you forgive those who sin against you, your heavenly Father will forgive you. Matthew 6:14

I LOVE WATCHING my kids grow older, but I do miss the big birthday parties we used to throw when they were little. Today they've decided they're too old for cartoon plates and napkins, but when they were young, we would pull out all the stops. We'd invite a bunch of their little friends and gorge on Mickey Mouse cake and vanilla ice cream. I think I had more fun than they did.

I remember one bash we threw when my son was four or five years old. My wife had hung balloons and banners all over the kitchen and bought matching plates, napkins, and tablecloth. We even had matching hats with a little rubber band under the chin to hold it in place. The kids quickly got into the spirit of things.

> "He basically says that if we forgive others, God will forgive us, but if we don't forgive others, neither will God forgive us."
>
> *The Mark,* 160

But one kid wouldn't wear his hat. I don't know if he was bratty or just in a bad mood, but I remember being irritated at his unwillingness to cooperate. I was in charge of the pictures, and everyone else was wearing a hat. I tried to coax him into slipping it on, just for one quick snapshot, but he shook his little head and refused. I should have let it go, but I didn't. Eventually I took the hat and strapped it onto his head. "You can come to the party, but only if you wear the hat," I told him, half joking and half because I was the adult. He didn't like it, but I got my picture.

A lot of us have the same attitude as my little friend when it comes to our Christian faith. We want what Jesus has to offer, but we want it on our terms. "I'll eat the cake and ice cream, just don't make me wear any silly hats." The trouble is, it's his party, and he sets the rules.

"If you forgive those who sin against you, your heavenly Father will forgive you," Jesus tells us. "But if you refuse to forgive others, your Father will not forgive your sins" (Matthew 6:14-15). Salvation is free—Jesus hasn't changed his mind on that offer. But that doesn't mean it comes cheap. It doesn't mean we can mock the host of heaven and take advantage of his good graces. Jesus understands that the kind of contrite heart that would cause us to ask for his forgiveness would be more than willing to do the same for others. He's just explaining that principle to us. "You can come to the party, but only if you wear the hat." That's what Jesus tells us.

REFLECTION

Whom are you struggling to forgive? What would God have you do in light of today's lesson?

WORKING OUT SALVATION

Continue to work out your salvation with fear and trembling.
Philippians 2:12, NIV

"THEREFORE, my dear friends . . . continue to work out your salvation with fear and trembling," Paul writes to the Christians at Philippi. And the sentence has since become the perfect life-verse for every legalistic Christian on the planet. Any time a believer who struggles with the grace of God gets hold of a convert, this is the passage he turns to. Every follower who can't quite accept the fact that salvation comes as a free gift from God proves his point by quoting this line from Paul. It's the proof-text of every works-based religious movement around.

The trouble is, that's not what Paul means. You and I know it, because the rest of his letters easily bring that truth to light. And like all Scripture, if you take this verse in context, it explains exactly what he's saying.

"Therefore, my dear friends, as you have always obeyed—not only in my presence, but now much more in my absence—continue to work out your salvation with fear and trembling, *for it is God who works in you* to will and to act according to his good purpose" (Philippians 2:12-13, NIV, italics mine).

The "works" Paul talks about have little to do with us and everything to do with God. It is God who worked out our salvation, and it is God who is working out his purposes within us. Paul's admonishment is to continue obeying so that God can work. Salvation is free, but discipleship is costly. When a potter puts his hand to the clay, the clay had better be ready for a little pain. A little "fear and trembling" is in order. "This is going to hurt a bit," the Potter says, "so you might want to bite down on something."

Paul wasn't changing his view on grace; he was preparing believers for the inevitable cost of following Jesus. Any other interpretation of the text is a perversion of Scripture. But that doesn't mean we're off the hook. What we become once God saves us depends on our level of obedience and tenacity. God has great plans for our future, but in order for him to carry them out, he needs our cooperation. He needs our faithfulness. He needs us to continue trusting and allowing him to work.

REFLECTION
*In what ways have you felt God working out his purposes through you?
How can you increase your level of obedience in order for him to work?*

TWO STORIES

I am the Lord, and I will free you from your slavery.   Exodus 6:6

LOOK AT THE MESSAGE God sent Moses to give to the Israelites enslaved in Egypt:

"I am the Lord, and I will free you from your slavery in Egypt. I will redeem you with mighty power and great acts of judgment. I will make you my own special people, and I will be your God. And you will know that I am the Lord your God who has rescued you from your slavery in Egypt. I will bring you into the land I swore to give to Abraham, Isaac, and Jacob" (Exodus 6:6-8).

God promised Israel the one thing they most wanted—freedom. He promised to deliver them out from under Pharaoh's iron fist and into a land they could call their own. What he held out was Israel's greatest desire in life. And how did they respond?

"Moses told the people what the Lord had said, but they wouldn't listen anymore. They had become too discouraged by the increasing burden of their slavery" (6:9).

The Israelites had before them two different realities to choose from. One was what God wanted to do for them and through them. The other was the reality of their bondage. One was the promise of freedom and hope of God's faithfulness. The other was the feel of chains on their feet. God was asking them to decide which of these two realities they would embrace, and they chose the chains. They chose the reality they could see.

Just like the Israelites, you and I are faced with two realities every day. There are two stories that we can choose to believe. One is the plan that God has for our future—what he wants to do in and through us. The bondage that God wants to deliver us from. The other reality includes the circumstances of our life. It includes the chains that we see—the lack of resources, talent, ability, or faith. The smallness of our situation. The shattered dreams and broken promises of our past. The walls of fear and doubt that enslave us.

And we have to decide which of those two realities we will allow to define our future. What are we going to believe? Where are we going to put our trust? Which story are we going to embrace as our own? One story leads to freedom. The other brings only more bondage. And the decision is one that sits before each and every one of us.

REFLECTION
Which of these two realities have been defining your life? How can you go about embracing the story of God's purpose?

TWO CHOICES

God will generously provide all you need.   2 Corinthians 9:8

IF YOU DIDN'T know better, you'd think the apostle Paul worked for Norman Vincent Peale. Some of his writings seem to come right out of the *The Power of Positive Thinking*. Look at this one from his second letter to the Corinthian church:

"God will generously provide all you need. Then you will always have everything you need and plenty left over to share with others" (9:8).

Or this one from his letter to the church at Philippi:

"I have learned how to get along happily whether I have much or little. I know how to live on almost nothing or with everything. I have learned the secret of living in every situation, whether it is with a full stomach or empty, with plenty or little. For I can do everything with the help of Christ who gives me the strength I need" (Philippians 4:11-13).

> "'Eating directly from God's table,' he told Abdullah, 'was something I never expected in this lifetime.'"
>
> *The Remnant*, 107

Either Paul was a hopeless optimist, or he knew something that most people don't. You and I know it was the latter. Paul defined his reality by God's power, not his own abilities or shortcomings. And that made all the difference in how he perceived his circumstances. He knew that his future was in God's hands, not his enemies'. He saw the bigger picture. He understood that poverty was just another opportunity to see God's miraculous hand of provision. Paul trusted in God's sovereignty more than he feared his own weaknesses.

Ever known someone like that? Ever had a friend who always seemed to be able to rise above his situation? Ever known someone who had a hard life but never let it get her down? People like this always seem to be able to see the rainbow through the clouds. They always know the sun will rise the next morning. No matter how bad things get, they always focus on the light at the end of the tunnel—even when they can't see it. These are the kind of people that God is looking for. That's what God wants from his followers. He wants us to rise above our own doubts and frailties and see the bigger picture. To see that he is mightier than our circumstances. To believe that all things are possible through God.

REFLECTION

When it comes to your future, are you a hopeful optimist or a hopeless pessimist? How would God have you pray in light of today's lesson?

TWO IDENTITIES

I stand in the very presence of God.   Luke 1:19

HAVE YOU EVER said something you really wished you could take back? Ever thrown out a phrase that you'd give anything to be able to retract? If so, then I'm sure you can relate to Zechariah.

When an angel appeared to Zechariah to tell him that he would be having a son, he was completely caught off guard. At the time Zechariah was in the sanctuary burning incense to the Lord. He was an old man and had long since given up praying for a son. The last thing he expected to see was an angel of the Lord prophesying his future.

"Don't be afraid, Zechariah! For God has heard your prayer, and your wife, Elizabeth, will bear you a son! And you are to name him John. . . . He will be great in the eyes of the Lord. . . . He will precede the coming of the Lord, preparing the people for his arrival" (Luke 1:13-17). You and I know his son as John the Baptist. But Zechariah wasn't sure what to think of this encounter. He said the first thing that popped into his mind: "I'm an old man now, and my wife is also well along in years" (Luke 1:18).

Zechariah said what you and I might have said in the same circumstance. He knew that having babies was a young person's job, and when you get old, you put away such foolish dreams. He probably couldn't even remember the last time he'd prayed for it. *I think you've got the wrong person*, he thought to himself. And that's when he uttered the phrase that could be taken as lacking faith, the phrase that he'd have given anything to be able to take back: "I'm an old man now." Zechariah wasn't trying to be disrespectful, just practical. But the reality he saw didn't set too well with the angel.

"I am Gabriel!" the angel shot back at him. "I stand in the very presence of God. It was he who sent me to bring you this good news!" (1:19). And because of Zechariah's doubt, the angel struck him dumb on the spot. Zechariah was unable to speak again until his son was born. The angel probably did it for his own good. It was the only way to keep him from speaking out even more curses on himself.

Zechariah defined his identity by his circumstances. The angel defined his identity by the One he served. The only question left on the table is for you and me. How are we going to define our identity? Who are we going to be in the eyes of the Lord? How are we going to see ourselves in light of God's power and glory? How we answer that question makes all the difference for our future.

REFLECTION
How do you see yourself in God's great plan? How does it help you to see your identity as a child of God?

SPEAKING OUT BLESSINGS

A good person produces good words.   Matthew 12:35

IMAGINE BEING GIVEN the greatest gift of your life and not being able to tell anyone about it. What would it be like to receive a blessing from God so great that you couldn't contain your excitement and then have to keep it to yourself? That's what happened to poor old Zechariah.

When the angel of the Lord told him he would be having a son—not just any son, but John the Baptist, the foreteller of the Savior—Zechariah didn't know how to receive the news. He doubted the angel's words. "I'm an old man now," he said. And his lack of faith caused the angel to strike him dumb. "Meanwhile, the people were waiting for Zechariah to come out," Luke records, "wondering why he was taking so long. When he finally did come out, he couldn't speak to them" (1:21-22).

The angel figured that if Zechariah couldn't stop speaking out curses on his life, then maybe it would be best for someone to stop it for him. He quieted the old man's tongue and told him he'd have to stay that way until his son was born.

The object lesson for you and me is pretty clear. There is power in the words we say, both good and bad. What comes out of our mouths affects the state of our heart. The things we say have an impact on the direction of our future. If we speak out messages of gloom and despair and doubt, we are doing little more than bringing those destinies about. What we say influences how we see ourselves, and it limits what God can do through us.

But when we speak words of blessing and faith, we are allowing God to shower us with that kind of future. We are spreading seeds of hope, not hopelessness. "A good person produces good words from a good heart," says Jesus, "and an evil person produces evil words from an evil heart. . . . The words you say now reflect your fate" (Matthew 12:35, 37).

We can choose the words that come out of our mouth. We can quiet the doubt before it reaches our lips. We have the ability to bite our tongue when negative thoughts come to our mind. We also have the ability to speak blessings in their place. How we choose to speak says volumes about the depth of our faith. And a person in God's will chooses carefully.

REFLECTION
Are you in the habit of speaking out curses or blessings?
Why not begin today developing positive speech habits?

THE GOD OF ZEPHANIAH

And the Lord himself, the King of Israel, will live among you!   Zephaniah 3:15

WHAT KIND of God were you raised with? The God of wrath? The God of judgment? The God of destruction and punishment? A jealous God who hates disobedience and pursues insubordinates with a passion? The God whom Israel feared?

Or were you raised with a God who loves you and walks with you daily? A God who lives in your heart and whispers gentle messages in your ear? A God who would die for you? A God who *did* die for you?

It's not surprising that so many people can read the same Bible and come away with so many differing views of the Creator. Scripture describes God in all of these ways—and many, many more. One could paint a thousand pictures of God and then find a passage to qualify each one of them. "Can you solve the mysteries of God?" Zophar asks. "Can you discover everything there is to know about the Almighty?" (Job 11:7). If God is anything, he is beyond our ability to comprehend.

"Sing with me the song of Moses, the servant of God, and the song of the Lamb."

Desecration, 362

So how does God want you and me to view him? What kind of picture does he most want us to paint on the canvas of our heart? God wants us to see him as the prophet Zephaniah described him. "The Lord your God has arrived to live among you. He is a mighty savior. He will rejoice over you with great gladness. With his love, he will calm all your fears. He will exult over you by singing a happy song" (Zephaniah 3:17). We have a God who sings and delights over us, a saving God who resides among us, a God whose love is so compelling that it brings us to silence in his presence. A Redeemer who accepts us as we are and stands by us, no matter what.

The Bible includes sixteen books of prophecy, each chronicling God's dealings with Israel. Ask most people to describe the theme of these books, and they would talk of God's judgment and wrath against his people. Israel continued to fall into sin, provoking God to anger. Yet as you read through these sixteen books, you discover that the vast majority of them ends in redemption. In spite of Israel's unfaithfulness, God continued to bring them back. He loved them and walked with them in spite of their wickedness. And he does the same for you and me.

A God who is near. A God who quiets us with love. A God who sings over us. Hard to imagine, but it's true.

REFLECTION
What was the view of God in your childhood home? How does the view of a God who sings over you (Zephaniah 3:17) change the way you see yourself in God's eyes?

IN GOD'S PRESENCE

The Lord your God has arrived to live among you.   Zephaniah 3:17

SOME NATIVE AMERICANS went to great lengths to usher boys into manhood. Their rites of passage were as significant as they were frightening. On the night of a boy's thirteenth birthday, he would be blindfolded and taken far from camp, deep into the dense, dark forest. There he would be left alone to survive the night. The darkness of the forest can frighten even the bravest warriors; imagine what it must have felt like to a young boy. Animals howling, snakes crawling, and spiders, rats, and bugs rustling the leaves beneath his bare feet. Even the wind took on new terror as it whistled through the trees in the pitch-blackness of night.

After hours of grueling terror, the boy would fight to keep his eyes open as the dawn began to break. Suddenly the world around didn't seem so frightening anymore. The boy could see the forest as it really is. Flowers blooming, trees swaying in the wind, furry animals scurrying about looking for food. Then, to his utter surprise, he would see the most comforting sight of all. There standing beneath the trees, just a few yards away, would be his father. He'd been there all along. The boy who had spent an entire night in worry had had nothing to worry about after all. The frightened warrior had no reason to fear.

"Do not be afraid, for I am with you," God promises Isaac (Genesis 26:24). Jesus utters that same sentiment to us: "Don't be afraid, little flock" (Luke 12:32). When we're convinced that we're all alone in a dark forest, Jesus reminds us that he is standing right by our side, watching, waiting, protecting. Like a shepherd keeping watch over his flock. Like a father keeping watch over his frightened son.

So how would the story differ if our Native American friend had known that his father was there in the forest with him all along? Obviously, he would no longer have been frightened. He probably would have nestled into the leaves and gotten a good night's sleep while his father kept vigil. His fear was born from thinking he was alone. And that's where our stories differ.

We have no reason to fear the darkness. We can rest easy knowing that God is in control and Jesus is standing nearby. We can rest easy, even during the darkest hour of night, because we are never alone. So why do we still fear? That's what God is wondering.

REFLECTION
*What fears do you struggle with? What would God have you
do with those fears in light of today's reading?*

QUIETED BY LOVE

With his love, he will calm all your fears.   Zephaniah 3:17

IT HAPPENED during the reign of Cyrus, king of Persia. The Persian army ruled the land with an iron fist, maintaining the king's authority and position with ease. But one solitary rebel roamed the land. He was a man who fought to keep his autonomy, and his antics exasperated the king and his army at every turn. His name was Cagular—a lone and mighty warrior. One day the king put together a band of men to capture Cagular and bring him to justice. They were to capture not only Cagular but his wife and children as well. The king was out for revenge. The men set an ambush and captured the great warrior, then rounded up his entire family. Cagular and his wife were then brought before King Cyrus, bound in chains.

Standing face-to-face in the throne room, Cyrus looked at the rebel with contempt. "Cagular," he said, "if I were to spare your life, what would you do?" Without pause Cagular answered, "King, I would serve you the rest of my days." The king pondered his answer, still not satisfied.

"What would you do if I spared the life of your wife?" the king asked him. Cagular answered, "Your Majesty, if you spared my wife, I would die for you." The king was so taken by this response that his heart softened and he released Cagular and his family. More than that, he made an alliance with Cagular, putting him in charge of his troops along the southern border of Persia.

Later that night Cagular and his wife were reflecting on their brush with death before the king. Cagular asked his wife, "Did you see the marble and the solid gold throne that Cyrus sat on?" His wife looked at him with wonder. "I didn't see any of that," she said. "I saw only the face of the man who said he would die for me."[4]

Is there any truer measure of pure love than this? Can a man possibly show greater devotion and trust than when he is willing to give his last breath for another? Is it possible to take loyalty to greater heights and depths? Jesus said, "Greater love has no one than this, that he lay down his life for his friends" (John 15:13, NIV). Then within days of making that statement, he did that very thing. Jesus allowed himself to be nailed to a cross in our place. He died so that you and I could live forever. When you think of love, his should be the first face you see.

REFLECTION
In light of Jesus' sacrifice, how should we serve others? In what ways can we give our life for others?

A GOD WHO SINGS

He will exult over you by singing a happy song.   Zephaniah 3:17

HERE'S SOMETHING I've never admitted in public: I cry at weddings. It's not a very manly confession, but it's an honest one. In fact, I'm not sure I've ever been to a wedding that didn't bring a tear to my eye. I've been to my share of them, and they've all been special in their own way, but none has made an impression on me quite like the last one we attended. It was a few months ago in Texas. The girl was barely out of her teens, a beautiful bride all in white. The boy was tall and skinny, more nervous than any groom I've seen. As he stood at the altar next to the minister, you could almost hear his knees knocking. The poor kid looked terrified. Until his beautiful bride appeared at the back of the church. The music changed, and suddenly his whole demeanor calmed. His eyes lit up, and his smile relaxed. His gaze never left hers. The moment was priceless, but nothing compared to what was coming.

> "All we can do is trust in your promise that we shall one day see our dear brother again in the land where sorrow shall be turned to singing."
>
> *Assassins, 58*

After the two said their vows, the young man surprised his bride by taking her hand and facing her. Accompanied by a guitarist, he began to sing. His voice quivered and shook and broke, but he was determined to get through it.

Tomorrow morning if you wake up / and the sun does not appear / I, I will be here / If in the dark / we lose sight of love / hold my hand and have no fear / 'cause I, I will be here / I will be here / when you feel like being quiet / when you need to speak your mind / I will listen / and I will be here / when the laughter turns to crying / through the winning, losing and trying / we'll be together /'cause I will be here . . . [5]

The brave young man couldn't carry a tune in a basket, but that didn't stop him from singing every line of the song to his young bride. By the time he finished, everyone in the church was blinking back tears. When you love someone deeply, you want to sing over them, even at the risk of looking silly. We were moved, not because of the song or his voice, but because we knew that at that moment this young man would have done anything to show his bride how much he adored her.

That's the picture I have of God. I envision him dancing and rejoicing and singing over his children.

REFLECTION
Does it bring you comfort to imagine a "singing God"? Does it change your view of worship to know that he sings along with you?

HARDENED HEARTS

The Lord hardened Pharaoh's heart once more, and he would
not let them go.　　Exodus 10:27

WHO HARDENED Pharaoh's heart? Was it God, or was it Pharaoh himself who did it? When Scripture records the story of Moses and Aaron going before Pharaoh, asking him to free the Israelites, sometimes it says that Pharaoh hardened his heart, and other times it says that God hardened Pharaoh's heart. So which was it?

We can all understand how Pharaoh could have hardened his heart because we've all known hard-hearted people. Stubbornness is common among humans. But to hear that God hardened his heart somehow affronts our sense of fairness. We don't want to believe that God would override a man's free will in order to make a point. It's hard for us to hear that someone could be used as a puppet by the Creator, with no choice in what he says or does. If God hardened Pharaoh's heart, then whatever happened to free will?

None of us can claim to know the answer definitively, and the truth is, God doesn't have to answer to us for anything he chooses to do. But I have a theory on the subject—one that is best told through a simple analogy. If you went to Texas in the middle of summer and laid a stick of butter on the sidewalk, with the scorching Texas sun bearing down on it, what would happen? Within minutes it would be completely melted. But what if you took that same sidewalk and laid a lump of soft clay on it instead? You know the answer. It would soon become hard and unyielding.

The same hot sun that melted the butter hardened the clay. And you can't blame the sun for what happened in either case. The result had to do with the makeup of the element on the sidewalk. They each reacted to the heat based on the stuff that they were made of. The sun simply did what it always does—it shone brightly.

Maybe the same is true with Pharaoh's heart. What caused it to harden in the face of God's power had more to do with what Pharaoh brought to the table than with God's intervention. Pharaoh hardened his heart the same way many today do when faced with the reality of Jesus. They see the evidence but refuse to listen. It's what we have filled our heart with that makes the difference.

REFLECTION
How do you react when God brings judgment and discipline into your life?
What have you allowed into your heart that causes it to harden toward God?

AFRAID TO BELIEVE

Despite all the miraculous signs he had done, most of the people
did not believe in him.   John 12:37

PHARAOH WASN'T the only person in Scripture who hardened his heart in the face of God's power. He wasn't the only one who allowed his heart to be so filled with anger and stubbornness that it refused to soften to the sovereignty of God.

Years before Jesus came to earth, Isaiah prophesied that the Jewish leaders would refuse to believe in him. John records, "Isaiah also said, 'The Lord has blinded their eyes and hardened their hearts—so their eyes cannot see, and their hearts cannot understand, and they cannot turn to me and let me heal them.' Isaiah was referring to Jesus when he made this prediction" (John 12:39-41).

In spite of the many miracles that Jesus performed, and in spite of the evidence he presented regarding his divinity, the Jewish leaders refused to believe. They hardened their hearts in the light of his glory. They blinded their eyes to the truth of his testimony. And even sadder, a number of those who did believe in him were afraid to admit it.

"Many people, including some of the Jewish leaders, believed in him. But they wouldn't admit it to anyone because of their fear that the Pharisees would expel them from the synagogue. For they loved human praise more than the praise of God" (12:42-43).

Could anything be sadder than that? Can you imagine seeing the gates of heaven open right in front of you but being afraid to enter because of what someone might think? How would it feel to live an eternity without God because you feared a moment of embarrassment in front of your friends? It's a sobering thought. And it's exactly what many Jews allowed to happen.

> "Rayford knew the prophecy—that people would reject God enough times that God would harden their hearts and they wouldn't be able to choose him even if they wanted to."
>
> *Armageddon, 17–18*

What about you? Ever know anyone like that? Ever have a friend abandon the truth of Jesus for fear of rejection from his or her friends? Ever seen people walk away from heaven because they didn't want to look silly in front of their family? It happens every day. Fear of peer pressure causes people to turn their backs on God. They see the evidence but refuse to listen. Their fate is the saddest imaginable.

REFLECTION
Whom do you know who believes in God but still rejects the truth of Jesus?
Pray that God would soften their hearts and allow you to reach out to them.

LOVE THROUGH SERVICE

He now showed the disciples the full extent of his love.   John 13:1

HOW WOULD you go about showing someone the full extent of your love? What would you do to prove your undying affection for a friend? How would you show your husband how much you care for him? What would you do to show your wife how completely committed you are to your relationship?

Would you buy them something expensive? Something thoughtful and costly—something you knew they wanted? Would you try to express your love in words? Maybe write a carefully crafted poem or a letter in an attempt to capture your feelings on paper? Would you look them in the eye and tell them how much you love and cherish them? Maybe you would shout your love from the rooftops. Isn't that the ultimate sign of absolute adoration?

Jesus didn't do any of those things to show his disciples how much he loved them. But what he did do said volumes. It happened just before the Passover celebration, while Jesus was in the upper room with his disciples. He knew that this would be the last time they were all together before his death. "He now showed the disciples the full extent of his love," records John (13:1). And how did he do it?

"He got up from the table, took off his robe, wrapped a towel around his waist, and poured water into a basin. Then he began to wash the disciples' feet and to wipe them with the towel he had around him" (John 13:4-5).

Jesus did the unthinkable. The King of the universe did what no king would ever stoop to do. The Creator got down on his knees before his creation and washed the dirt off their feet. It was a job reserved for the lowliest slave in the household. You could scour the earth and not find a more menial and humiliating task to perform. In an effort to show his disciples the full extent of his love, Jesus did it by exposing the full depth of his humility.

When he finished, he put on his robe and joined them at the table. Then he said to them, "Since I, the Lord and Teacher, have washed your feet, you ought to wash each other's feet" (13:14). Through this simple but great object lesson, Jesus was teaching his disciples what true love was all about. Love isn't just about gifts or words or even uncontrolled emotion; it's about service. Love is about meeting a person's most basic needs. It's about humbling yourself and doing what needs to be done.

REFLECTION
How can you show the extent of your love to someone close to you?
How have you tried to show your love in the past?

THE BODY

This is my body, given for you. Do this in remembrance of me. Luke 22:19

WHEN WE PARTAKE in Communion in remembrance of Jesus, what are we remembering? What is it about him that we focus on? If you are like me, you usually use the opportunity to set your thoughts on the Cross and the bodily sacrifice that Jesus made on our behalf. You fix your thoughts on the Crucifixion and the day that Jesus paid the ultimate sacrifice for humanity.

But maybe Jesus had a bigger thought in mind. When you look at the words spoken by Jesus in the upper room, you can't divorce them from the other events that took place.

Jesus began by washing his disciples' feet. He humbled himself before them, meeting their most basic need, and then told them that they should emulate his example by serving others. "Do as I have done to you," he tells them (John 13:15).

He followed up that act by confronting Judas. In front of the others he exposed the one who was to betray him. The one whose heart was hard and whose mind was set on money. He also predicted that Peter would betray him. Jesus dealt with the sin among them before breaking bread with his disciples.

He then gave a word of encouragement: "Love each other. Just as I have loved you, you should love each other. Your love for one another will prove to the world that you are my disciples" (13:34-35).

It was on the heels of these acts that he took the bread and held it up in front of them. "This is my body, given for you," he says. "Do this in remembrance of me" (Luke 22:19). Could it be that what Jesus had in mind with these words had a wider application than we place on it? Could he have been saying to them, "You know who I am. You've heard my words. You've seen my acts of service and love. You've heard my words of warning, reprimand and encouragement. You know my heart. Now do the same."

When Jesus says, "Do this . . ." maybe he means, "Do all of these things. . . ." Maybe when we remember the body of Jesus during Communion, we should focus as much on his life as we do on his death. Maybe we should center our heart on his words and actions as much as on the Cross. Remembering Jesus means living like Jesus.

REFLECTION
In what ways does it honor Jesus when we emulate his actions? How does it change your view of Communion to focus on his life as well as his death?

OCTOBER

TODAY'S READING
Luke 22:20, 29-30

THE CUP

This wine is the token of God's new covenant to save you.   Luke 22:20

ASK MOST PEOPLE what the cup of wine represents during Communion, and they will say the blood of Jesus. But that's not the only analogy he used. He also said that the cup represents the new covenant. Let's look at his words:

"After supper he took another cup of wine and said, 'This wine is the token of God's new covenant to save you—an agreement sealed with the blood I will pour out for you'" (Luke 22:20). Granted, both Matthew and Mark record his words a little differently, but the spirit is the same. What the cup represents is the covenant that was fulfilled at the spilling of Jesus' blood at Calvary. It is a symbol of Jesus' death, but more than that, it is a symbol of what his death did for each and every one of us. It represents the fulfillment of God's promise to redeem the world from sin. It's a subtle difference but a distinct one.

> "A covenant of peace is only as good as either side's keeping its word."
>
> *Desecration, 148*

When we raise a glass in remembrance of Jesus' covenant, we are doing more than reflecting on his death; we are recommitting our life. We are remembering the salvation that his blood ushered into the world. We are connecting with the greater picture of redemption.

A covenant is a two-way street. Jesus is the author of the covenant, and we are the recipients. He holds out the promise of a better life and an eternal hope, but we have to accept it. And when we do, we are committing ourselves to the covenant. We are promising to remain faithful and true. And each time we lift the Communion cup we are reiterating that promise.

"Just as my Father has granted me a Kingdom," says Jesus, "I now grant you the right to eat and drink at my table in that Kingdom" (22:29-30). When we partake of the bread and the cup at the Communion table, we are doing more than remembering the sacrifice of Jesus; we are reflecting on his life and the covenant that his life brought to fruition. We are observing a small piece of heaven on earth. Communion is more than an act of symbolism; it is an agreement to share in the sacrifice of Jesus. An acceptance of our role in God's new covenant for humanity. And that's something that should never be taken lightly.

REFLECTION
How have you embraced your role in God's new covenant? How often do you reflect on the promise of heaven that Jesus brought at the Cross?

WHEN GOD WAITS

Why are you crying out to me? Tell the people to get moving!
Exodus 14:15

THERE ARE a lot of *why* questions that we lift up to God. Every day people are looking to heaven and crying out in frustration. "Lord, why aren't you doing something about this? Why is this happening to me? Why isn't anything happening? Why aren't you helping me with this problem?" We saturate the airwaves with the *why* questions of life.

I'm convinced that God has one answer for almost every one of those questions. He says, *I'm just waiting on you.*

When Moses and the Israelites stood on the edge of the Red Sea watching the Egyptian army close in on them, they cried out to God in fear. They began praying that God would somehow rescue them. They lamented over their dilemma and pleaded with the Lord to intervene. And look what God said when he answered them. "Why are you crying out to me? Tell the people to get moving!" (Exodus 14:15). To paraphrase, God told them, "I'm just waiting on you."

Too often we spend our days waiting for a miracle. When trouble comes, we cry out to God for help. When things don't move fast enough, we blame God for taking his time. When our faith is weak, we wonder why God has forsaken us. And all the while God is saying to us, *I haven't gone anywhere. I'm just waiting on you.*

And what is it that God is waiting for? Often he is waiting for us to lay aside our own agenda and trust him. He is waiting for us to deal with the hidden sins in our heart, to be obedient to his Word, to love more, to fear less, to believe without doubt, to soften our heart, to draw nearer, to seek his will. Whenever God waits, he waits for a purpose.

And when we finally come to our senses and do the thing that we know he wants us to do, he moves with a vengeance. The Red Sea parts, and things start to happen. When our faith motivates us to act, we will be astounded at what God can accomplish.

REFLECTION
Does God seem silent on an issue in your life?
What is he waiting on you to do?

SOWING DISCORD

Those who are peacemakers will plant seeds of peace and reap
a harvest of goodness.   James 3:18

HAVE YOU EVER broken a commandment of God in order to get your way? Have you ever ignored the teachings of Jesus because they interfered with a prior agenda? I have. Probably more than a few times.

Years ago I served as editor of a church newsletter. It was during a time of tremendous turmoil within this particular church family. People were embroiled in conflict over some divisive issues. Most of the things that people were fighting about were rather petty and insignificant, but at the time they seemed daunting. Camps began to form and polarize on both sides. I saw it as a war between the conservatives and the progressives, and being a man who likes to move forward, I put myself in the progressive camp. Our newsletter quickly began to reflect that view.

Each issue we published was filled with articles and viewpoints that pleaded the case of progressiveness. As editor I had the power to print what I agreed with and to refuse what I didn't. I never set out to create an agenda-based paper; it just slowly began to happen. I was simply doing my part to bring perspective to the many debates being brought out among the members of our congregation. In my mind I had the noble role of pointing out sacred cows and laying them to rest. My positions were accurate, articulate, and convincing. Surely God was pleased.

Then one day while preparing a lesson to teach, I happened upon some pesky passages of Scripture. I'd read them before, but not from the business end. Not when they were aimed at my own agenda.

"There are six things the Lord hates—no, seven things he detests," begins the Proverbs writer. And it's the last one that got my attention: "a person who sows discord among brothers" (Proverbs 6:16, 19). In one fell swoop God heaped coals of conviction right in the middle of my bald spot. *Could that be me? Could it be that I'm the problem? Am I causing more trouble than I'm fixing?*

"But Lord, you know I'm right," I argued. "You know my arguments hold water." But God wasn't interested in my arguments. *Sometimes you can be right and still be wrong,* he said to me in my spirit. *It's a matter of the heart.*

REFLECTION
In what ways have you broken God's laws in order to maintain your own
agenda? What self-serving traditions are you guilty of maintaining?

DEFIANT SIN

They are fully aware of God's death penalty for those who do these things, yet they go right ahead and do them anyway. Romans 1:32

YOU PROBABLY haven't met many criminals as bold and defiant as Charles Taylor. Judge James Fleetwood certainly hadn't. Taylor was brought before his courtroom accused of robbing a shoe store at knifepoint. The only thing the robber took was a pair of tan hiking boots, worth about $69. The clerk identified Taylor as the one who did it, but the young man continued to deny it. He wasn't anywhere near the place, he said.

Throughout the trial, Taylor continued in his loud and obnoxious manner. He leaned back in his chair and propped his feet up on the table in front of him during most of the day. The boy seemed almost too confident and cocky.

Halfway through the trial the judge looked over at Taylor and did a double take. He noticed that Taylor was wearing a pair of tan hiking boots, just like the ones described by the clerk. *Surely he wouldn't be that brazen,* the judge thought. *Nobody is that stupid.*

But the judge's curiosity got the best of him, and he called a deliberation. He had an FBI agent call the shoe store and get the size and lot number of the stolen boots. They were size 10½ from lot 1046. The judge checked the boots that Taylor was wearing, and—you guessed it—they were size 10½, lot 1046. Taylor was found guilty and sent back to jail. This time in his stocking feet.[1]

> "I believe we are called to see this as a picture of the sad fact that sin and rebellion have their consequences. There are scars."
>
> *Apollyon*, 330

With some people it's hard to tell what's worse—their brazenness or their stupidity. They're so busy reveling in their own cockiness that they can't even see their sins. Those are the kinds of people that Paul had in mind when he wrote these words to the Roman church: "When they refused to acknowledge God, he abandoned them to their evil minds and let them do things that should never be done. Their lives became full of every kind of wickedness, sin, greed, hate, envy, murder, fighting, deception, malicious behavior, and gossip. . . . They are fully aware of God's death penalty for those who do these things, yet they go right ahead and do them anyway" (Romans 1:28-32).

Nothing is quite as frustrating to God as sinners who sin in the face of their own Judge—people who know the consequences of their actions but do them anyway. His penalty is not something to take lightly. When his gavel comes down, it comes down hard. And definitively.

REFLECTION
What defiant sin are you harboring in your heart?
How does God see your brazenness?

THE ARMOR OF GOD

Put on all of God's armor so that you will be able to stand firm against all strategies and tricks of the Devil. Ephesians 6:11

DURING HIS LIFE, Harry Houdini had a standing challenge that he could escape from any jail cell within an hour. Several jails took him up on his offer, and he always succeeded—until one day a small town in the British Isles accepted Houdini's challenge. They had just constructed what they thought was an escape-proof jail cell, and they wanted to put it to the test. Houdini entered the cell and immediately went to work. He pulled out the instruments he had smuggled in and began trying to trip the lock. An hour passed, and he still hadn't got it open, but he didn't give up. He worked feverishly on the lock as the clock continued to tick. After two grueling hours—an hour past his deadline—Houdini finally withdrew his file from the lock and leaned against the door in exhaustion. To his amazement, the cell door swung open.

He was ready to give up when he discovered that the door had been open the entire time. The jailors had tricked the great magician by closing the jail door but never bolting the lock. He was free all along; he just didn't know it.[2]

Satan has the same strategy, doesn't he? His greatest weapon is to make us think that we are trapped, when in reality the cell door is always open. The devil is a master of illusion, and his most effective trick is to dupe believers into thinking that they are ensnared, when in reality Christ has freed us from Satan's deceptive locks. The only power he holds is the power we allow him to have.

"Put on all of God's armor so that you will be able to stand firm against all strategies and tricks of the Devil," Paul tells us (Ephesians 6:11). The armor of God is not intended to shield the body from arrows but to shield the heart and mind from deception. This war is one not of the flesh but of the spirit. The battleground is within us, not in front of us. Satan can't bind us, so he tricks us into making us believe the cell door is locked.

"We are not fighting against people made of flesh and blood, but against the evil rulers and authorities of the unseen world, against those mighty powers of darkness who rule this world, and against wicked spirits in the heavenly realms" (6:12). When you're fighting against an unseen enemy, the battle can be tricky. And having the right armor in place is crucial.

REFLECTION
In what ways has Satan deceived you into believing you are bound to sin? How can you work to free your heart and mind from this deception?

THE BELT OF TRUTH

Stand your ground, putting on the sturdy belt of truth.   Ephesians 6:14

"YOU WILL KNOW the truth, and the truth will set you free," says Jesus (John 8:32). But what will the truth set us free from?

First of all, it sets us free from the snares of deception. When people know the truth, they can't be taken in by a lie. When a person knows what is real, he won't be fooled by counterfeits. You can't convince people to believe in something that they know in their hearts and minds is false. An art critic who has studied the works of Picasso for years will be able to recognize one of his paintings at a glance. He'll look at the strokes and flair of the painting and know instinctively if they hold true to Picasso's style. He'll recognize by the colors and shapes whether it is something that Picasso would have done. He knows an original from a fake, and he can't easily be fooled.

So it is with someone who understands the teachings of Jesus. She understands the Master's heart and soul, and she'll know a false teaching when she hears one. She'll pick out a counterfeit doctrine at a glance. She won't easily be taken in by a lie, or duped into believing a spiritual falsehood.

> "I feel so new to this, so ignorant of the truth. I know the gospel, but it seems I need to know much more if I'm going to be a bold evangelist."
>
> *Soul Harvest, 234*

The truth will also set you free from guilt and shame. When you've held tightly to the truth, you don't have to worry about a lie coming back to haunt you. You're not bound by the fear of being found out. You don't spend your nights lying awake wondering what words of deception might trap and ensnare you. You are free to live with a clean conscience and an innocent heart.

Finally, the truth sets you free from judgment. When you trust in the truth of Jesus, you have no more fear of death—physical or spiritual. You know his promises to be true and his words to be life-giving. You can no longer be bound by Satan's lies.

"Stand your ground, putting on the sturdy belt of truth," writes Paul (Ephesians 6:14). The belt of truth is the strap that holds together the entire armor of God. It is what supports the rest of the uniform and holds it all in place. The truth is the most critical garment a believer can wear. Without it, everything else would fall away and Satan would have an open target to your heart. So take the truth of Christ, and latch it firmly around your waist. Let it set you free!

REFLECTION

Have you secured your life by the truth of Christ? In what ways are you still bound by fear and guilt and shame due to falsehood in your life?

THE BREASTPLATE OF RIGHTEOUSNESS

Stand your ground, putting on . . . the body armor of God's
righteousness. Ephesians 6:14

"GOD MADE HIM who had no sin to be sin for us," writes Paul, "so that in him we might become the righteousness of God" (2 Corinthians 5:21, NIV). Through his death on the cross, Jesus exchanged our sins for God's righteousness. He conquered sin so that sin would no longer be the covering of our heart. In Paul's words, we have actually "become the righteousness of God."

How sad that we so often take that truth with such disregard. If we understand what God has done in and through us in order to cleanse our heart, would we still treat it with such disrespect? Would we still be so apathetic toward the things we expose our heart and mind to? When the blood of Jesus lines the walls of your heart, you have an obligation to guard it carefully. And God's righteousness is the only breastplate that can do so.

And what are we protecting our heart from? The things that vie for our heart's affections and turn us away from God. You and I know well what those things are and how Satan uses them. I experienced just such an assault this past weekend.

I dropped my son off at church for a special youth event and had an hour or so to kill before picking him up, so I decided to take a drive in the country and pray. The winding roads proved to be a perfect place to clear my mind and focus on God as I lifted up some concerns and petitions. But soon I found myself on a road surrounded by huge, beautiful houses with perfect lawns and large circular driveways. I found myself dreaming of what it would be like to live in such a place—to have a mansion with a large library and a huge cherry desk in the center to practice my craft. To have more money than I knew what to do with. To be able to travel around the world on a whim. To maybe have a vacation home in Hawaii, and a loft in Austria. To have . . .

You get the picture. In short, I found myself lusting after the things of this world. The things that look good and promise happiness yet have little value in God's economy. I found my heart unguarded and under assault, and for a moment I drifted into the sin of lust and envy. Satan is a good aim, and even the slightest opening in our armor gives him a shot at our heart. The key to protection is to keep the righteousness of God girded tightly at all times and in all places.

REFLECTION
How does it affect your view of yourself to know that your sin has been traded for God's righteousness? How can you guard your heart with that truth?

THE SHOES OF READINESS

For shoes, put on the peace that comes from the Good News, so that you will be fully prepared.　　Ephesians 6:15

I HAVE A PAIR of shoes that don't fit. They're nice shoes, and I can't seem to make myself get rid of them. They're the right size, and when I first put them on, they seem fine. But if I keep them on for more than an hour or so, they start to rub against the sides of my toes and pinch them. The arch is in the wrong place, so the bottom of my feet start to ache. Before long I am miserable and have to take them off.

I didn't know this fact when I first bought them. I picked them up the day before leaving on a business trip. I knew that I would be doing a great deal of standing and walking, and I wanted a good pair of shoes for the task. Little did I know that these shoes would wear blisters on my feet and make the trip a nightmare. By the time I arrived home, my feet were sore and swollen and blistered in several places.

A critical part of any good soldier's wardrobe is a pair of comfortable and good-fitting shoes. God's army is on the move, and his soldiers need to stay ready at all times. The banner we carry is emblazoned with the Good News of the gospel, and it's important that we carry it proudly and high. And that we're able to keep up with the great General as he leads us into battle.

Tight shoes make for sorry soldiers. You can't keep your mind on battle when you spend your days looking for a place to sit down and rest your feet. It's hard to keep from stumbling along the road when your shoes don't fit properly. That's why God offers the perfect footwear for those who follow him. They are made from the peace of Christ, sewed with threads of God's good news. They were fashioned from the finest cloth heaven could find and tailored by the Savior himself. They are guaranteed to keep your feet warm and dry and stable. As long as you wear them, your steps will be sure and your gait unfettered.

The enemy will try to make you stumble, so be on your guard. Watch your step. Keep your eyes peeled. And make sure your shoes are tied and secure. It's a long journey, and good shoes make all the difference.

REFLECTION
*When have you been prone to stumble along the road to battle?
How can you better protect your feet with the shoes of readiness?*

THE SHIELD OF FAITH

*In every battle you will need faith as your shield to stop the fiery arrows
aimed at you by Satan.*   Ephesians 6:16

A SAFARI HUNTER was once stopped in his tracks by a curious scene in the jungle. A bird was dancing around her nest of eggs as a huge snake made its way toward them up the trunk of the tree. The bird screeched and flailed in vain as the hungry snake drew closer by the second. Her eggs were in mortal danger. Suddenly the bird flew away, as if running from the snake. But within a few seconds she returned with a small leaf in her mouth. She reached the nest just as the snake was about to strike. Quickly the mother bird draped the leaf over her eggs and then flew away to a nearby branch. The hunter was shocked to see the snake hesitate. It froze as if it had encountered a deadly foe. Slowly it recoiled from the nest and went away.

> "Buck needed a miracle, but his faith was weak. He knew it shouldn't be. He had seen enough from God in three and a half years that he should never again doubt for an instant."
>
> *The Indwelling, 85*

The hunter was puzzled by this curious scene and later asked some natives about it. They laughed and explained that the leaf the mother bird used to cover her eggs was poisonous to the deadly snake. The serpent knew instinctively to back away. The shield was small and flimsy, but it was the one thing that the snake most feared.[3]

"In every battle you will need faith as your shield to stop the fiery arrows aimed at you by Satan," writes Paul (Ephesians 6:16). It's naïve to believe that the enemy is a dormant foe who minds his own business. He is a cunning and crafty adversary who will do anything to catch us off guard and bring us down. His arrows are sharp and sure, and his aim is deadly. He attacks when we least expect it and will try to devour the thing that we most cherish—our relationship with God.

Faith is the shield that keeps his arrows at bay. It is the guard that we hold before us to protect us from the fire of his wrath. Without it, we have no hope of survival.

And what is this life-saving faith made of? It consists of a deep belief in God's promises and a trust in his words of truth. We believe that God's purposes are higher than our frailties. We trust that even in the midst of battle, his will is being fulfilled. We have faith that someday the war will end, and we will be brought home to eternal glory.

REFLECTION
When did your faith withstand the blows of the enemy? When was your faith not strong enough? How can you allow God to strengthen your shield for battle?

THE HELMET OF SALVATION

Put on salvation as your helmet.   Ephesians 6:17

EVER HAVE an argument between your head and your heart? Ever know in your heart that something is real, only to have your mind tell you it's not? Ever questioned a fact because of a feeling? Then you understand why Paul encourages us to "put on salvation" as a "helmet" (Ephesians 6:17).

Paul is warning us to guard our mind against thoughts of doubt and confusion. He is encouraging us to shield our head from Satan's bombarding arrows of uncertainty and disbelief. He is telling us to keep our thoughts in line with what our heart already knows to be true.

Eve forgot this simple lesson when approached by the serpent in the Garden of Eden. "Did God really say you must not eat any of the fruit in the garden?" the sleazy snake asked her. Eve explained that there was only one tree that God told them not to eat from, and the serpent persisted in trying to confuse her. "'You won't die!' the serpent hissed. 'God knows that your eyes will be opened when you eat it. You will become just like God, knowing everything, both good and evil'" (see Genesis 3:1-4). Eve fell for his lies and ate the fruit. And so began humanity's great fall from grace.

Did Eve really believe that she would become like God? How was she so easily duped into believing something so absurd? Her greatest sin was letting her head win the argument with her heart. She already knew who the Creator was, and she was well aware that she wasn't on the same par; yet somehow she allowed Satan to confuse her. It only took a second, and it only took a little doubt, but the result was deadly.

The enemy hasn't changed his methods much. Mostly because he hasn't needed to. People still fall for the oldest trick in the book. "Did God really say that? Surely you won't die if you take just a little bite." Our heart knows better, but his words sound so convincing. We allow ourselves to be taken in by confusion and doubt.

The helmet of salvation does more than keep our mind shielded from doubt. It keeps us centered on what's really true. It reminds us of the grace that brought us into God's garden in the first place. It covers our head with eternal thoughts, not self-serving ones. It is our greatest weapon against Satan's oldest tricks.

REFLECTION
*What lies has Satan whispered into your ears? What does it mean
to you to put on the helmet of salvation?*

THE SWORD OF THE SPIRIT

Take the sword of the Spirit, which is the word of God.   Ephesians 6:17

"FOR THE WORD of God is living and active," says the writer of Hebrews. "Sharper than any double-edged sword, it penetrates even to dividing soul and spirit, joints and marrow; it judges the thoughts and attitudes of the heart" (4:12, NIV).

When was the last time you felt the blade of God's sword pierce your heart? Can you remember a time when the steel ripped your conscience to conviction, bringing you to your knees in repentance? Can you still feel the piercing sting of remorse? Did the blade make an indelible mark on your spirit? If so, then you understand the power of God's Word. You know why the writer of Hebrews would describe it as a "double-edged sword." You also understand why it would be the only weapon we need against Satan and the fury of hell that he brings to battle.

> "I thanked God over and over for his Word, for his truth, for answering my prayer and revealing himself to me."
>
> *The Mark,* 116

"Take the sword of the Spirit, which is the word of God," writes Paul (Ephesians 6:17). It is the only piece of armor on his list that isn't meant for defense. The belt of truth, the breastplate of righteousness, the shoes of readiness, the shield of faith, and the helmet of salvation—all are meant to protect the heart, mind, and soul. All are intended to keep the soldier alive and fresh and ready for battle. All are critical pieces of armor in the fight against evil.

But the sword of the Spirit is different. It doesn't protect; it maims. It isn't passive; it's active. It is intended for combat—a weapon for frontline spiritual warfare.

When the Holy Spirit led Jesus into the desert, the enemy came to do battle. "If you are the Son of God, change these stones into loaves of bread," Satan taunted him. And Jesus charged forward with the Word of God. "The Scriptures say, 'People need more than bread for their life; they must feed on every word of God.'"

Two more times Satan mounted an attack, and each time Jesus wielded the sword of the Spirit (see Matthew 4:1-11).

Never underestimate the power of God's mighty Word. Hide it in your heart, and wield it with confidence and authority. Satan will not be able to withstand its fury.

REFLECTION
What can you do to know God's Word well enough to wield it as a weapon? How can you better prepare yourself for spiritual battle?

COVERED BY PRAYER

*Pray at all times and on every occasion in the power
of the Holy Spirit.* Ephesians 6:18

ALL THE SPIRITUAL armor in the world won't keep you safe from the enemy without the covering of prayer. You can take up the full uniform of God's protective covering in your war against Satan, but unless you are plugged into Jesus, you'll likely fall to the enemy's sword.

Imagine a soldier enlisting in the army and being issued all the tools he needs. He gets a uniform that identifies which troop he belongs to. He gets his weapons and supplies and protective artillery. He's dressed for war and ready to go.

Now imagine his commander sending him out onto the battlefield alone. He has no radio and no backup troops. No one tells him what his mission is or where he is supposed to go. He simply assumes he'll fight the enemies wherever he finds them. So he goes with no instruction, no communication with his superiors, no training, and no fellow soldiers by his side. How absurd does that sound? Would any commander do such a thing? Would any soldier survive the ordeal? Of course he wouldn't.

It's just as absurd to think that we could go to war with Satan without daily communication from our Commander and the support of our fellow troops. We need to know our assignment, and we need help in carrying it out. We need the camaraderie that comes from being part of God's army. We need the spiritual, physical, and emotional support of our fellow soldiers in Christ.

"Pray at all times and on every occasion in the power of the Holy Spirit," Paul reminds us. "Stay alert and be persistent in your prayers for all Christians everywhere" (Ephesians 6:18). A good soldier is one who stays in touch with his commander, who follows orders, and who knows that he is part of a unit. He supports others and allows others to support him.

I have a group of friends who pray for me regularly. When working on a writing project, I keep them informed of the progress and tell them when I am struggling. I know that I can depend on them to lift me up when they pray. I can feel their prayers as I write. They also depend on my prayers for them. The bond we share comes from being co-soldiers in Christ, and it is as strong a connection as I've ever experienced. Everyone on a battlefield needs that kind of support and camaraderie. Without it we could never survive.

REFLECTION
*Do you stay in touch with your commanding officer daily?
Are you getting the support you need from your fellow troops?
Are you giving them the support they need?*

KEEPING GOD'S HOUSE

Why are you living in luxurious houses while my house lies
in ruins?   Haggai 1:4

GOD SEES how you keep your house. Do you see how you're keeping his house?

God sees how you live for yourself. Do you see how you live for God? He knows how much time you spend educating yourself for your job. But how much time have you spent educating yourself about God? He sees the effort you put into earthly relationships. Have you put that same effort into your relationship with him?

There is our house, and there is God's house. And God sees the time and effort we put into each one. Our house represents those things we do for ourselves. It is often characterized by self-love and indulgence. We fill it with all the things we think we need to feel secure and independent. The halls are garnished with PhDs and achievements, high-powered friendships, and impressive stock portfolios. The rooms are lined with books we've read or written and souvenirs of trips we've made around the world.

God's house represents those things we've done solely for him. Within its rooms are the times we've spent seeking to draw nearer. The prayers we've lifted up on behalf of others. The souls we've reached out to. The quiet and painful sacrifices we've made in God's service. Our humility before the throne. Our obedience in the most trying of circumstances. The condition of our heart.

Only God can see inside these two separate homes, and he knows the effort we put into keeping them. "Why are you living in luxurious houses while my house lies in ruins?" God asks Israel through the prophet Haggai (1:4). The question could have just as easily been posed to you and me. The Israelites were so busy with their own concerns that they never bothered to rebuild God's Temple. Too often you and I allow God's temple in our heart to lie in ruins as well. The homes we build for ourselves seldom go without, but God's home is frequently sparse and barren.

God sees how you keep your house. Let him see that you keep his house with the same zeal and effort.

REFLECTION
Are you giving God an adequate share of your time, energy, and resources?
How would he have you live in light of today's reading?

IN NEED OF REVIVAL

So the Lord sparked the enthusiasm of . . .
the whole remnant of God's people.   Haggai 1:14

SO HOW DO WE GO about rebuilding the Lord's temple? When we realize that we haven't spent the time we should have taken tending to God's home in our heart, how do we go about turning things around? What does it take to begin a revival in our spirit?

Those are questions the Israelites had to deal with once the message of Haggai brought them to conviction. God was angry that they had allowed his Temple to lie in ruins, and he sent his prophet to warn them of his anger. Israel got the message and set out to obey the Lord's command. But what would it take to rebuild it?

It would take an empowering by God's Spirit. The Israelites began by repenting of their sin and worshiping God with all they had. They pleaded for his help, and he didn't let them down. "I am with you," the Lord told them. Then he "sparked" the spirits of Zerubbabel, Jeshua, and "the whole remnant of God's people" (Haggai 1:13-14). The Temple was rebuilt but only because God empowered Israel to do it.

Revival must begin with God—otherwise it will fail. Rebuilding God's home takes supernatural intervention from God himself. If we want to reignite our soul for Christ, we start by looking to God's holy fire.

> "Dozens waited to tell their stories, to say where they had been on their spiritual journey. . . . Their stories were moving and hardly anyone left, even when the clock swept past noon and forty or fifty more still stood in line."
>
> *Left Behind*, 220

Like Israel, we begin with true repentance and worship. We turn our heart away from sin and toward the Cross, acknowledging our helplessness before the throne and God's sovereignty over our life. We praise God for who he is, not for what he can give us. Then we go to God in prayer, pleading for empowerment. Asking him to spark our spirit and to give us the strength and wisdom to rebuild his temple.

Too often we believe that spiritual revival can be orchestrated through our own efforts. We think we can "will" ourselves into a deeper relationship with God. But revival only happens when our spirit taps into his. He is the One who reinvigorates our heart and reignites our soul. It begins through conviction and obedience to his will, but it always ends with God.

REFLECTION
When was the last time you pleaded for spiritual revival from the Lord?
Do you need to go before the Lord today in humility and worship,
pleading for spiritual revival?

WHEN DOES LIFE BEGIN?

You saw me before I was born.   Psalm 139:16

SO WHEN DOES life begin? It's one of the most debated legal questions of our day. The dispute has spread so wide and far and created so much division, that the U.S. Supreme Court has been forced to weigh in on it. Every state has had to deal with the issue when passing and enforcing laws. Every country has had to decide where it stands on the matter of what to do with a life inside of a mother's womb.

When does life begin? Only when we answer this critical question can we know how to answer the abortion debate.

For believers the question takes on a different form. We need to ask ourselves, *Where does God stand on the issue?* And that question is dealt with definitively in Scripture.

"You watched me as I was being formed in utter seclusion, as I was woven together in the dark of the womb. You saw me *before I was born*. Every day of my life was recorded in your book. Every moment was laid out before a single day had passed" (Psalm 139:15-16, italics mine).

According to God's holy Word, life begins at conception. Your life began before your mother and father knew they were going to have a child. Your days were numbered before you were a twinkle in your daddy's eye. God knew your soul before he decided to place it into a body.

The debate on life is really nothing more than a question on the authority of God. If you believe that God created us and that Scripture is his inspired Word, the question has already been answered. There is nothing left to talk about. God weighed in on the debate before it ever became a debate. We simply have to ask ourselves whether we're going to take his Word as truth or continue arguing our opinions.

How much easier to simply leave it to God to answer the big questions of life and concentrate instead on trusting what he says.

REFLECTION
What has confused you about the question of when life begins?
Why not allow yourself to take God's Word as your standard?

A BOLD PRAYER

Search me, O God, and know my heart.   Psalm 139:23

"SEARCH ME, O God, and know my heart," prays King David in Psalm 139. "Test me and know my thoughts. Point out anything in me that offends you, and lead me along the path of everlasting life" (Psalm 139:23-24).

Is there a bolder prayer that we can possibly lift up to the Savior? Is there a greater act of submission and humility that we can show? Is there a petition that pleases God any more than this one?

The greatest thing a disciple can ask of his master is to take a microscope to his or her life and see if there is any unhealthy thought or habit that needs to be dealt with. To have him look deep into our heart and soul and detect any hint of offensive behavior. To show us whatever might be keeping us from a greater level of servanthood.

David understood that in order to grow closer to God he needed to be rid of hindrances to the relationship. He knew that the way to God's heart was through surrender and sacrifice. He understood that God could only do through him what he allowed God to do within him. He wanted no hidden sins or agendas in his heart that might keep him from fulfilling God's purposes.

What about you? How deep into God's will do you want to go? How close do you want to get to God's heart? How serious are you about wanting God's glory fulfilled in your life? Are you willing to pray the boldest of prayers? Are you willing to let God reach inside of the deepest parts of your being and reveal any hidden sins or agendas? Are you ready for such a relationship with the only One who can change you? If so, why not pray this prayer today?

Father, search my heart. Expose the crevices of my inmost being. Shine your light into the cavity of my soul and see if there is anything there that offends you. Test my thoughts, my words, my motives, and my actions. Reveal any hidden sins or agendas. Show me what I need to change, and then do whatever it takes to help me do so. I give you complete and unreserved access to my mind and heart. Shape my character so that I can draw nearer to you. In Jesus' name, amen.

REFLECTION
As you pray this prayer of true discipleship, spend some time meditating on the words and listening for God's voice. Allow him to speak to your spirit and reveal his will.

SURRENDER IN WORSHIP

*Accept my prayer as incense offered to you, and my upraised hands
as an evening offering.*   Psalm 141:2

"I WANT MEN to pray with holy hands lifted up to God," the apostle Paul writes in his first letter to Timothy (2:8). His words appear to be more of a command than an encouragement, yet we seldom take them as such. Any other statement made so definitively in Scripture would be taught as a direct mandate, yet this one is often passed off as a suggestion at best. "There's nothing wrong with lifting your hands—it's just not my style of worship," we say. And we keep our hands in our lap and our emotions in check, never once feeling guilty or disobedient.

> "Bruce suggested they pray on their knees—something each had done privately, but not as a group. Bruce brought his chair to the other side of the desk, and the four of them turned and knelt."
>
> *Tribulation Force, 240*

I was raised in a conservative church and was well into my thirties before I ever saw people lift their hands to God in worship or prayer. I remember feeling uncomfortable the first time I sat in a service where the worship was free and expressive. It was an awkward experience. I've since come to completely embrace the joy and freedom of singing and praying to God with abandon. I no longer feel the need to remain staid and serious when expressing my love for Jesus. I no longer worry about what those around me might think. I've come to understand the beauty of Paul's command to Timothy and the reason he told his young protégé to have everyone lift holy hands to God when they pray.

It takes tremendous humility to bow before your King and to open your arms in reverence. It takes courage to surrender yourself so openly to God's majesty and authority over your life. When you open your hands before him, you are saying, "Here I am Lord! I stand before you in complete and total surrender. My heart and life belong completely to you. I hold nothing back. I'm not embarrassed to submit myself to your glory. My hands are free from sin and open to your bidding."

"Accept my prayer as incense offered to you," says King David, "and my upraised hands as an evening offering" (Psalm 141:2). David understood that an abandon of the heart begins with an abandon of the body. When you hold back your emotions, you hold back a critical part of your life and spirit. David wasn't afraid to dance and sing before God, no matter who might be watching, and we should have that same attitude. We should be willing to worship God with all our heart, mind, strength . . . and body.

REFLECTION
How have you let others set the tone for how you worship? Do you have the courage and humility to pray with open hands and bended knee before God?

A CONTROLLED TONGUE

Take control of what I say, O Lord, and keep my lips sealed.
Psalm 141:3

"IF YOU CAN'T say anything nice, don't say anything at all," goes the old axiom. And like a lot of great sayings, this one hits the nail right on the head. The phrase didn't come out of Scripture, but it could have.

"Take control of what I say, O Lord, and keep my lips sealed," writes King David (Psalm 141:3). He knew that left to his own devices, he would inevitably say the wrong thing most of the time, so he asked God to take charge. "If I can't make myself shut up, please do it for me," he basically says to God. It's a good thought for you and me as well.

"And I tell you this," says Jesus, "that you must give an account on judgment day of every idle word you speak. The words you say now reflect your fate then; either you will be justified by them or you will be condemned" (Matthew 12:36-37).

Have you ever considered that your fate is dependent largely on your tongue? Ever thought that the words you speak control your destiny? Ever imagined that such a small thing could have such a large impact on your future? The tongue can create more problems, start more fights, break up more relationships, and cause more trouble than any single part of your body. Wars have been started, marriages have ended, children have been damaged, and lives have been lost all due to a few simple but careless words spoken in haste. Is there another weapon on the planet with such power and might?

Words can also do more good than any other tool. The right words can heal relationships, bring countries together, save the hearts of children, and solve the biggest problems of humanity. A kind word carefully spoken can do more good than all the intentions on earth. And more important, sincere words from a contrite heart can bring us back to God forever.

Allow God to control your tongue, and he will use it to shape your future. Let him stop you from speaking at the wrong times, put words in your mouth at the right times, and you've made him the author of your fate. Put your mouth under God's control, and see how he uses it to reshape your heart and life.

REFLECTION
When did you allow your tongue to cause problems in your life? What is the first step you need to take in allowing God to control your words?

DO YOU BELIEVE?

Do you believe that I am able to do this?   Matthew 9:28, NIV

RONALD PINKERTON found himself in a frightening situation. He was in a glider and somehow caught a burst of unexpected wind. It carried him to a height of over forty-two hundred feet before turning him loose. Suddenly Pinkerton was descending too quickly and began to lose control of his plane. Out of nowhere a powerful blast of air sent his glider plummeting toward the ground. Here's how he records the ordeal:

> I was falling at an alarming rate. Trapped in an airborne riptide, I was going to crash! Then I saw him—a red-tailed hawk. He was six feet off my right wingtip, fighting the same gust I was. . . . I looked down: 300 feet from the ground and still falling. The trees below seemed like menacing pikes.
>   I looked at the hawk again. Suddenly he banked and flew straight downwind. Downwind! If the right air is anywhere, it's upwind! The hawk was committing suicide.[4]

Everything Pinkerton knew about flight told him that the hawk was making a grave mistake. It went completely against his better senses. Yet he also knew that hawks were masters of the sky and that this one must understand something that he didn't. Pinkerton had no other options, so he did the unthinkable.

> I followed the hawk. One hundred feet. Suddenly the hawk gained altitude. For a split second I seemed to be suspended motionless in space. Then a warm surge of air started pushing the glider upward. I was stunned. Nothing I knew as a pilot could explain this phenomenon. But it was true: I was rising.[5]

Pinkerton was forced to look past his own instincts and experiences and trust in something other than himself. Sometimes you and I have to do the same thing. Faith demands that we abandon our own judgment and follow Jesus.

"Do you believe that I am able to do this?" Jesus asks two blind men who were asking to be healed (Matthew 9:28, NIV). There was nothing in their life experiences that would make them think that such a miracle could be performed. It didn't make sense, but they reached out to him in faith, and that's exactly what he did.

What is it in your life that you need Jesus to do? Do you believe that he is able to do it?

REFLECTION
*When was the last time you reached out to Jesus in blind faith
and asked for a miracle? What was the result?*

APPROACHING MOUNT ZION

You have come to Jesus, the one who mediates the new covenant
between God and people. Hebrews 12:24

HAVE YOU EVER known someone who lived with an insecure faith before God? They want to believe that they are saved, but they struggle with a nagging sense of doubt and worry. Everything they know about Jesus tells them that their sins are covered by his blood. They know the promises of Scripture, and they've put their trust in Christ for salvation. Yet still a feeling of fear remains.

Maybe it's because they are approaching God on the wrong mountain.

Israel approached God at Mount Sinai, and they had good reason to be afraid. "Be sure they are ready on the third day," God commanded Moses, "for I will come down upon Mount Sinai as all the people watch. Set boundary lines that the people may not pass. Warn them, 'Be careful! Do not go up on the mountain or even touch its boundaries. Those who do will certainly die!'" (Exodus 19:11-12).

> "Jesus has already paid the penalty. The work has been done."
>
> *Nicolae,* 314

That's how many people see God today. They're afraid to draw near for fear of his wrath. But Jesus ushered in a new covenant, and with it, a new relationship with God.

"You have not come to a physical mountain, to a place of flaming fire, darkness, gloom, and whirlwind, as the Israelites did at Mount Sinai. . . . No, you have come to Mount Zion, to the city of the living God, the heavenly Jerusalem, and to thousands of angels in joyful assembly. . . . You have come to Jesus, the one who mediates the new covenant between God and people, and to the sprinkled blood, which graciously forgives instead of crying out for vengeance as the blood of Abel did" (Hebrews 12:18, 22, 24).

God has not changed, but the relationship we are able to have with him has. Those who have put their faith in Jesus no longer have to approach God with fear and trembling. We no longer have to struggle with a sense of insecurity before his throne. Because of Jesus, we can approach God from Mount Zion—a mountain built on grace and covered with the blood of Jesus. It's not a mountain of fire and earthquakes but of relationship, peace, and safety. A place of refuge, not wrath.

REFLECTION
Which mountain have you been approaching God from? How does
today's message change your view of God?

SECURE IN SALVATION

I will not be afraid.   Hebrews 13:6

A COUPLE ONCE confided in me that they had spent the first ten years of their faith worried about their salvation. Reading the Bible for them was more of an exercise in guilt than an expression of love for Jesus. A passage would convict them of sin, and they would cry out to God for forgiveness. They would often get together in the evening hours and repeat the Lord's Prayer together, just to make sure that they were in good standing with the Lord. They even took turns baptizing each other in their large bathtub in hopes that God would see the sincerity of their repentance. They put their faith in Jesus, but they still lived with a nagging sense of insecurity before the Lord.

Perhaps you understand what they were going through. Maybe you struggle with some of those same feelings. Maybe you, too, lie awake at night, wondering if you've done all the right things. Hoping you haven't somehow displeased God and made him turn his back on you. Dreading the day that you will stand before Jesus in judgment.

If so, take heart. And then learn to relax in the arms of Jesus. Forget your fears, and find comfort instead in the words of the writer of Hebrews: "For God has said, 'I will never fail you. I will never forsake you.' That is why we can say with confidence, 'The Lord is my helper, so I will not be afraid'" (13:5-6).

For those who trust in Jesus for their salvation, there is no more fear to deal with. God's promises are real and irrevocable. The blood of Jesus is the only covering your sins need. Your salvation is secure with Jesus on your side.

Fear and insecurity are simply Satan's attempts to drive a wedge between God and his people. If he can get us to doubt God's promises, he's just one step away from getting us to doubt God himself. If he can keep us in worry, he can keep us from living the full life that Jesus intends for us. Don't let yourself fall prey to Satan's evil agenda. Trust the promises of Jesus and live with joy and certainty. Have faith that your fate is securely sealed forever.

REFLECTION
How has Satan made you doubt your standing before God?
How can you remain secure in your salvation?

FINAL EPITAPHS

Solomon has abandoned me.   1 Kings 11:33

HOW WOULD YOU like to be remembered after your death? Have you considered what the epitaph on your gravestone might read?

You can learn a lot about a person's life from reading what people wrote about them after they died. It's sobering to see what people come up with when faced with the task of summing up an entire lifetime in just a few words.

One headstone in Ribbesford, England, marking the grave of a woman named Anna Wallace, reads: "The children of Israel wanted bread, and the Lord sent them manna. Old clerk Wallace wanted a wife, and the Devil sent him Anna."

Not the final words Anna expected, I'm sure. But as always, those she left behind got the last word.

You have to cringe and wonder when you see the gravestone of a man from Plymouth, Massachusetts, named John McMahon. It says: "He Was a Failure As a Husband and Father."

How would you like that as your legacy?

But the saddest epitaph of all isn't found on a tombstone; it's found in the pages of Scripture. When faced with the task of memorializing the wise king Solomon, God had some sobering words. "Solomon has abandoned me and worshiped Ashtoreth, the goddess of the Sidonians; Chemosh, the god of Moab; and Molech, the god of the Ammonites. He has not followed my ways and done what is pleasing in my sight. He has not obeyed my laws and regulations as his father, David, did" (1 Kings 11:33). Solomon was buried in the city of David, and in spite of all the good things he did, he will forever be remembered as the king who turned his back on God.

How sad to live a life in God's blessing and favor only to turn away from him late in life. To die completely estranged from the One who most loved him. Can you imagine a sadder way to end your life? Can you think of a worse epitaph to be remembered by?

We would all do well to ask ourselves a simple question: If God were to write my obituary, what would he record?

REFLECTION
Reflect on how you would most like to be remembered by those around you.
Are you living a life worthy of such a legacy?

A LIFE WORTH REMEMBERING

Asa did what was pleasing in the Lord's sight.   1 Kings 15:11

Not all epitaphs are as sad as the one given to king Solomon by God. Some people have a great sense of humor about their death.

Dr. James Dobson once asked his mother what she'd like to have written on her gravestone, and she jokingly answered, "I Told You I Was Sick!"

Spend some time browsing through cemeteries, and you'll be surprised at some of the funny things people have recorded on their gravestones. Johnny Yeast was buried in Ruidoso, New Mexico, and his gravestone reads: "Pardon Me for Not Rising." Bonnie Anderson had a similar sense of humor. Her grave is in Los Angeles, California, and the headstone reads: "I Don't Want to Talk about It Now."

But one of my favorite headstones is that of Thomas Murphy, in Vancouver, British Columbia. His simply says: "Sh-h-h."

You get the feeling that some people aren't as worried about death as the rest of us. It's a good sign when you can leave life on a laughing note. Maybe that's a sign of someone who understands that death is just a passageway to a better life. Those who know that their eternal fate is secure in God's hands.

> "Rayford had no fear of death itself or of the afterlife. Providing heaven for his people was a small feat for the God who now manifested himself miraculously every day."
>
> *The Remnant, 2*

King Asa was such a person. He became king of Judah after his father, Abijam, died. His first order of business was to undo the evil policies of his predecessors. Asa was a man who feared God and understood that life was too short to waste in sinful pursuits. He had his sights set on eternity, and it kept his life in perspective. At the end of Asa's life, God gave him a glowing final epitaph: "Asa did what was pleasing in the Lord's sight, as his ancestor David had done. . . . Asa remained faithful to the Lord throughout his life" (1 Kings 15:11, 14).

Now that's a legacy worth leaving. Imagine getting to the end of your life and hearing God say about you, "He remained faithful to me throughout his life." Who wouldn't want that kind of letter of reference waiting for them at the pearly gates? God loves to honor those who have honored him with their lives. Such lives do not go unnoticed—in heaven or on earth.

REFLECTION
How did king Asa honor God in today's reading?
Are you living in a way that honors God?

FINDING BY LOSING

If you try to keep your life for yourself, you will lose it.   Mark 8:35

HAVE YOU NOTICED that the most miserable people you find are those who live only for themselves? They are seldom fun to have as friends and are usually the unhappiest people on the planet. No one wants to be around them.

They are the people who think only of their own happiness. Everything they do is about them. They live to protect their personal interests and agendas. When making a decision, they think only of the consequences to their own life and circumstances. When setting their schedule, they set it according to their own wants and needs. In business transactions they think only of how the deal will impact their financial situation. They are selfish and single-minded.

Self-centeredness is a cancer that eats away at the core of a person's heart and completely sucks the joy out of life. It kills relationships quicker than any other human condition and usually repels those who are closest. There's nothing quite as sad as that person who becomes isolated from friends and family because of his or her selfish ambitions.

Worst of all, self-centeredness tears us away from God. Jesus says, "If any of you wants to be my follower, . . . you must put aside your selfish ambition, shoulder your cross, and follow me. If you try to keep your life for yourself, you will lose it. But if you give up your life for my sake and for the sake of the Good News, you will find true life" (Mark 8:34-35).

Those who live only for themselves live in vain. But those who put their own interests and desires aside for the good of Jesus find true life. The only road to happiness is to live for something greater and nobler than yourself. To become a giver, not a taker. To live for Jesus, not our own desires. To pour ourselves out in God's service, not to wear ourselves out trying to get our own way.

That's the kind of disciple that Jesus is looking for.

REFLECTION
Would those closest to you characterize you as "selfless" or "self-centered"?
In what ways are you living for yourself instead of God?

UNKNOWN SOLDIERS

If you give up your life for my sake . . . you will find true life.   Mark 8:35

LAST YEAR during a business trip to Washington, DC, I had the chance to see the Tomb of the Unknown Soldier at the Arlington National Cemetery. I have a picture of the tombstone in a photo album. The inscription beneath it reads: "Here Rests in Honored Glory an American Soldier Known but to God." Beneath the shrine lies the remains of an unidentified soldier from World War I, but the marker stands as a tribute to the thousands of unknown soldiers who have lost their lives serving this country.

Seeing the memorial makes you wonder about the person buried beneath. You try to imagine who he was, what he was like, how he died, and what sort of sacrifices he made for his country before paying the ultimate price. You reflect on all the soldiers who have died in battle without recognition. You wonder what it must be like to give everything for a cause and then die in anonymity. It's one thing to die and be remembered as a hero, but it's another thing to live and die as a hero and have no one know your name.

As Christians, we are called to make that same level of commitment. The Christian faith may hold that same fate. Many followers of Christ live their lives in quiet service to God, daily sacrificing on behalf of Jesus, and they will pass away without ever being recognized for the things they did. They are the unknown soldiers for Christ.

Ever spend a sleepless night praying for someone who needs Jesus? Ever spent a day in prayer and fasting for someone going through a trying time in their lives? Ever give sacrificially to a cause even though you could have used the extra money yourself? Then you know what it's like to be an unknown soldier. You know that true service often comes without thanks or acknowledgment.

Every day people give quietly and thanklessly to the cause of Christ, and many will die without fanfare. No one may know about the things they did in service to their King. But that doesn't mean they will go unrewarded. God knows their sacrifice. He knows the names of every soldier in his service, and he has no intention of letting them go unnoticed. His may be the only praise they ever receive, but that's okay. Because it's the only praise that truly matters.

REFLECTION
*Are you willing to be the unknown soldier in the body of Christ?
In what ways have you served Christ in anonymity?*

ONE QUESTION

This is my beloved Son, and I am fully pleased with him. Matthew 3:17

LARRY KING has made a career of asking the tough questions. Those who know him understand that he considers himself a confirmed agnostic. He's made no attempt to conceal his doubts about God. But one time the tables were turned, and the questions were aimed at him. Bryant Gumbel interviewed the famous interviewer and concluded his program by asking King, "What questions would you ask God if he were a guest on your show?"

King answered without missing a beat. "Do you have a Son?" he said.

Larry King understood that if you're going to deal with the question of God's existence, you have to deal with the person of Jesus. You can't separate the two. Jesus claimed to be One with the Creator of the universe, and the Bible points to Jesus as God's only Son. It's a package deal. Believe in one, and you must believe in the other.

"After his baptism," records Matthew, "as Jesus came up out of the water, the heavens were opened and he saw the Spirit of God descending like a dove and settling on him. And a voice from heaven said, 'This is my beloved Son, and I am fully pleased with him'" (3:16-17). There are many today who claim a belief in God, yet haven't quite settled the divinity of Jesus in their hearts. They see the wonder of creation and instinctively understand that it points to a grand Creator. God's existence is real to them. Yet they haven't taken the time to investigate the claims of Jesus. Their faith is sincere but not yet complete because the question of salvation pivots on the person of Jesus, not on belief in God. Even Satan knows that God is real, but that won't save his soul.

"I am the way, the truth, and the life," says Jesus. "No one can come to the Father except through me" (John 14:6). Apart from the person of Jesus there is no salvation. It's that simple. Believing in a Creator won't lead you to him. Acknowledging his works won't save your soul. Only Jesus can lead us to the gates of heaven.

For all that Larry King gets wrong, he got this one right. The most critical question that any of us could ask God is, "Do you have a Son?" We know the answer. The only question left is, Are we going to trust him?

> "My wife said she prayed for me every day that I would find Jesus Christ before it was too late. . . . I still have the letters in which she warned me that I might die before finding the one true God, or that Jesus could return for those who loved him, and I would be left behind."
>
> *Assassins,* 102

REFLECTION
What do you think of the person of Jesus? If you haven't dealt with him, why not begin today investigating his claims further?

TRUE HUMILITY

Moses was more humble than any other person on earth.   Numbers 12:3

DID YOU HEAR about the guy who won an award for being the humblest person on the planet? They took it away because he accepted it.

That's how humility is, isn't it? If you think you've got it, you probably don't. At least that's how we often look at it. But if that's the standard, where does it leave Moses?

In Numbers 12:3, Scripture records, "Moses was more humble than any other person on earth." We nod in agreement because we've seen his humility played out in the pages of the Bible. But then we realize that it was Moses who wrote these words about himself. It was his own pen that recorded the glowing reference for generations to come.

So what gives a man the right to make such a claim? Who made Moses the "king of humility"? Why does he think he deserves such an honor? Because it wasn't his idea, it was God's. God is the One who laid the words on his heart and gave him the title. God saw Moses for who he was, and because of it, he developed a special relationship with his most humble servant.

"Even with prophets, I the Lord communicate by visions and dreams," God says. "But that is not how I communicate with my servant Moses. He is entrusted with my entire house. I speak to him face to face, directly and not in riddles! He sees the Lord as he is" (12:6-8).

This is how God responds to true humility. This is how he sees a man who lives in complete dependence and brokenness before him. This is what gives Moses the right to call himself the most humble man on earth. He was allowed to see the Lord, but only because the Lord first saw his humble heart.

If you want to see God for who he is, you approach his throne in humility. No haughty heart has ever pleased him. No humble spirit has ever gone unnoticed.

REFLECTION
*Would God consider you to have a humble spirit? In what ways
do you struggle with pride and haughtiness?*

A HOME NOT OUR OWN

When the world hates you, remember it hated me
before it hated you.   John 15:18

RIGHT NOW there is a war going on outside my bedroom window.

It started about three weeks ago when a handful of pesky wasps decided to make their nest in one corner of our house. Our home is made of cedar, and they found a small opening in the frame just above our bedroom window. I can't get to the nest, but I see the wasps come and go. I've done everything I can to discourage them. I've poked at the hole with a long stick, swatted them with a broom, sprayed them with the water hose and depleted several cans of wasp killer, yet still they persist.

They've suffered a lot of persecution at my hands over the last few weeks. Many have died to protect their mission, yet still they seem undaunted. I don't plan to give up because if I leave them alone, the nest will only get bigger. And I don't want my children to get stung. Still, I respect their perseverance in the face of persecution. And down deep inside, I wonder if I have the same level of resolve and commitment.

> "Now I was an outcast in my own home. My men were devout enough Jews to resist Carpathia, but they were not ready for Messiah. . . . I had had enough of their rejection and ridicule."
>
> *Armageddon,* 349

You and I have a lot in common with those wasps. We, too, are in the business of making our home in the corner of a house that doesn't belong to us. We, too, are pesky and unwelcome visitors in a place that isn't ours. We're the ones who bring a sense of threat to the house's owners.

"When the world hates you," Jesus says, "remember it hated me before it hated you. The world would love you if you belonged to it, but you don't. . . . Since they persecuted me, naturally they will persecute you" (John 15:18-20). It's tough living where you're not welcome. But it's comforting to know that the battle is not in vain. Those in the world are threatened by us for good reason. Our presence brings with it the sting of conviction. This is their home, and we don't belong here. And the greater our numbers grow, the more menacing we become to their way of life.

This is our lot in life, and it's a noble one. Someday we will have a home of our own in a place reserved just for us. That's why we persist in spite of the resentment and persecution.

REFLECTION

When was the last time you felt unwelcome and persecuted because of your faith? How does today's lesson give you greater comfort and strength?

CHANGING YOUR TASTES

I will refuse to look at anything vile and vulgar.   Psalm 101:3

HAVE YOU NOTICED that the closer you get to God, the less appealing the things of this world become? Isn't it true that the more you learn about God's will for your life and the deeper you go into his Spirit, the less interested you are in worldly endeavors or possessions? Many of the things that once held your attention now seem boring and useless. The little sins and vices that you once took for granted and felt were rather harmless now feel like weights around your neck. The jokes you used to chuckle at don't seem funny anymore. The movies you used to watch have completely lost their appeal. Some of the celebrities you used to admire are people that you now pity. You notice things that you never noticed before. Your heart is broken over things that you never gave a second thought before. You find yourself more sensitive to sin, more in tune to goodness, and less likely to be taken in by Satan's lies and deceit.

That's how discipleship is supposed to be. As you grow closer to your Master, you grow further from the world. Your heart changes, and your interests change with it. Your vision becomes clearer than ever. With King David, you find yourself saying, "I will refuse to look at anything vile and vulgar" (Psalm 101:3). And that's a sign that you are on the right track.

Often I will happen upon a movie on TV that I remember watching in my twenties. *I love this movie,* I'll think to myself. *I haven't seen it in years.* I'll settle in to watch it, and within minutes find myself completely repulsed by the language or the vulgar behavior of the characters. The film's message insults my faith and my intelligence. I begin to wonder how I could have developed fond memories of such an immoral film. I discover that my tastes have changed as I have grown closer to God.

That's what happens when God's Spirit takes hold in your heart. That's when you know that you are becoming more in step with Jesus. And that's a good thing to strive for. I would be worried if my taste for worldly things was the same today as it was in my youth. I would have to wonder about the depth of my faith if I hadn't grown more sensitive to sin through the years. If my appetite for earthly pleasures hadn't matured, it would mean that my Christian walk was stagnant and immature as well.

This is the truest test we have of Christian growth. It is the surest way to tell if we are drawing nearer to Christ or simply coasting through life.

REFLECTION
Do you find yourself growing more sensitive to sin? What is it in your Christian walk that has made the most difference?

WHEN SATAN SIFTS

Satan has asked to have all of you, to sift you like wheat.   Luke 22:31

EVER FEEL LIKE you've been run through the ringer? Ever get to the end of the day and collapse in bed, glad to finally have a minute's peace and dreading the next morning when you know you'll have to get up and deal with it all again? Ever found yourself caught in the whirlwind of life and work and worry, wondering when (and if) it's ever going to end?

If so, then you can be sure that what you are experiencing is but a fraction of what Satan would like to do with you. Rest in the fact that your trials are nothing compared to what the enemy intended for you. If he had his way, you'd have been dead long ago—and so would I.

"Simon, Simon," says Jesus to his apostle Peter, "Satan has asked to have all of you, to sift you like wheat. But I have pleaded in prayer for you, Simon, that your faith should not fail" (Luke 22:31-32). The enemy couldn't wait to get his grimy paws on Jesus' followers, but Jesus tightened the leash. Satan wanted to destroy them all, but Jesus only allowed him to taunt them. The devil wanted a banquet, but all he got was a handful of crumbs.

Interesting that Satan had to ask God's permission, isn't it? Many Christians are in the business of fearing Satan as much as they trust Jesus. Their prayers are more consumed with thoughts of "binding the enemy" than they are in praising God. They spend more time worrying about spiritual strongholds than they do listening for God's voice. But Satan isn't worth the effort we spend on him. He is under God's authority just as we are. He can do no more harm than God allows him to do.

That's not to say that we won't feel his hand at work. God allows him to sift us from time to time, just as he did Peter and the apostles. But it is always on God's terms and for God's purposes. When temptations and trials come our way, it is because God wants to teach us something. When Satan's hand comes against us, it is because Jesus is at work. When life gets stressful and confusing, it is only because God decided to allow the stress and confusion. And knowing that truth makes all the difference in how we react to it. It changes our perspective to know that God is in control, even when it seems that he isn't.

REFLECTION
How do you normally react during times of turmoil and stress? Does it change your perspective to know that God allows those times to happen for a reason?

SEEKING HEALTH AND WEALTH

"Have you noticed my servant Job?"   Job 1:8

"HAVE YOU NOTICED my servant Job?" God said to Satan. "He is the finest man in all the earth—a man of complete integrity. He fears God and will have nothing to do with evil" (Job 1:8). Most of us can only dream of such a glowing endorsement. Especially from the One who can see right into the core of our heart. And Satan's response shows that he understands something about the human heart as well.

> "I will do what you want, go where you send me, obey you regardless."
>
> *Tribulation Force, 348*

Satan the Accuser replied, "Yes, Job fears God, but not without good reason! You have always protected him and his home and his property from harm. You have made him prosperous in everything he does. Look how rich he is! But take away everything he has, and he will surely curse you to your face!" (1:9-11).

Job's integrity brought him into the favor of God, and because of it, he lived a sheltered life. That was Satan's argument. "Of course he's good," Satan was saying. "Because that's what you pay him for. But cut off his salary, and see how long that lasts." God allowed Satan to do just that. He took away his wealth and his children, yet still Job remained faithful. But Satan wasn't through. Again he came to the Lord to test Job further.

"Skin for skin," says Satan, "he blesses you only because you bless him. A man will give up everything he has to save his life. But take away his health, and he will surely curse you to your face!" (2:4-5). Again God allowed Satan to test Job. This time he took away his health. Still Job remained faithful. "Should we accept only good things from the hand of God and never anything bad?" he says to his wife (2:10). In spite of all that had happened, he still trusted God.

There is a corner of religion today that can't seem to wrap their theology around the story of Job. They see all matters of trial and trouble as a sign of God's displeasure. "Give generously, and God is bound to make you wealthy," they preach. "Obey him, and he is obligated to keep you healthy." The theory is not a new one—it originated with Satan in the first two chapters of Job. And it doesn't hold water today any more than it did back then. Job didn't serve God for what he could get out of him, and we shouldn't either. Sometimes bad things happen to very good people, but that doesn't mean that God isn't watching. And it doesn't necessarily mean that we have sinned or displeased him. We live in a fallen world, and sometimes Satan is allowed to test our faith. But by God's strength, we can all overcome.

REFLECTION
How often do you find yourself blaming God when bad things happen? How can you remain obedient in spite of trials and troubles?

NOVEMBER

MAINTAINING INTEGRITY

Are you still trying to maintain your integrity?   Job 2:9

A FAMOUS PREACHER was once asked by a fellow clergyman, "Have you ever stared into the face of Satan?"

Without missing a beat, the preacher answered, "No, but I'm married to his sister!"

Sometimes I wonder if that's how Job must have felt. At a time in his life when he most needed love and support, his wife gave him nothing but grief. He'd lost his wealth, his cattle, his children, and his health, and as if that wasn't enough, his wife came at him with both barrels. "Are you still trying to maintain your integrity?" she asks him. "Curse God and die" (Job 2:9).

For what little we know about Job's wife, we're pretty certain of one thing: Most men are thankful they're not married to her. Imagine having her at your family reunion each year. (For some it may not be much of a stretch!)

And what is the "integrity" that she wanted Job to give up? Integrity simply means that he was "integrated" with God. The two were of one mind and heart. Job's relationship with God was complete and whole. The Lord was an integral part of his being, and he knew that trials were not going to change that truth. Job was able to remain faithful to God, because God was woven into the fabric of his being.

The greatest fear of someone who is integrated with God is that somehow that bond will be lost or broken. When the prophet Isaiah saw his sinfulness in light of God's holiness, he cried out, "Woe to me . . . I am ruined!" (Isaiah 6:5, NIV). His integrity had been compromised, and he saw himself losing his oneness with God. It was the thing he most treasured—the one thing he couldn't bear to live without. Isaiah's integrity was more than a character trait; it was his lifeline. So it was with Job.

When hard times come, it's easy to lose perspective. We may be tempted to turn away from God and compromise our integrity. The bond we have with Jesus may suffer. Those closest to us may have thoughts of doubt and uncertainty. A lot of sin is born in the throes of a storm. But don't let it happen. Don't give in to the temptation. Don't "dis-integrate" in a moment of darkness. Reach instead toward the One who shapes eternity. Trust in God, no matter what.

REFLECTION
How does your "oneness" with God hold up in the middle of trials and temptation? How can you work to strengthen your faith and integrity?

JOB'S GREATEST FEAR

What I always feared has happened to me.   Job 3:25

"PERFECT LOVE expels all fear," writes John (1 John 4:18). God is the perfect love he spoke of, and the more of God we have, the less we have to fear. Write it down; it is a universal principle that will never change.

Job enjoyed a closer relationship with God than anyone else at the time. He was God's most faithful servant. So do you think he had any fears? Was there anything that Job lay awake at night worrying about? Was there any thought that brought a cold sweat to his brow?

Just one. When Satan was allowed to bring Job to the very end of himself, he was forced to face it head-on. "What I always feared has happened to me," he says. "What I dreaded has come to be" (Job 3:25).

In spite of Job's faithfulness to God, in spite of his complete trust in God's provision, in spite of his unmatched integrity and relationship with God, there was one thing that Job feared. Somewhere in the back of his mind he wondered if God might take it all away some day. His biggest fear was that somehow God would remove his hand of blessing. And now that this fear appeared to have become a reality, he struggled for the first time to hold on to his faith.

> "Rayford told Mac how he had landed at O'Hare after the disappearances . . . and had his worst fears confirmed. 'Irene and Raymie were gone.'"
>
> *Soul Harvest,* 106

There is a fear that resides deep inside the innermost part of each and every one of us. Somewhere, hidden deep in the crevasses of our humanity, we all suspect that maybe God isn't as good as we want him to be. We all struggle with this hint of doubt, even if it is ever so slight and even though many of us may never have to face it head-on.

Job was brought to the very edge of himself, and it forced him to deal with this hidden demon of doubt. The thing he most feared had come to pass, and now he had to decide whether he would give in to his fear or transcend it and continue to trust God. Could he still believe that God is good, even when God seemed so very, very bad? Was God still God, and was God still good, even when nothing but adversity rained from heaven?

This is why God allowed Satan to test him. This is the lesson that Job needed to learn. He needed to face the fear that haunted him most in order to overcome it. In the end Job passed the test. And that same grace is available to us as well.

REFLECTION
What is your greatest fear? Has God ever tested your faith by allowing this fear to come to pass?

DEFINING GOD'S GOODNESS

I have no peace, no quietness. I have no rest.   Job 3:26

GOD HAS BLESSED my different careers through the years, and we've been able to live in relative comfort as a result. But I well remember the time when that wasn't the case. A lot of the years were spent struggling to build a business and make ends meet. God always provided, but they were still tough times. Today we know that God is the source of all we have and all we do, and that brings a great deal of comfort. But it also brings a measure of fear.

I still remember a day not so long ago when I was sitting in my office praying. For some reason I developed a nagging sense of concern deep in my spirit. Somehow it didn't feel like we deserved the good things God had given us. It didn't feel right. Deep in my heart I wondered if he wasn't going to take it all away. I knew that he could and feared that someday he would. He was the One who had showered us with blessings, and he could just as easily turn off the faucet.

You can relate, can't you? I know you've been there. Somewhere deep in your spirit you've found yourself wondering if you really deserve the good things God has given you. Sometimes late at night you lie awake looking at the ceiling. Your nighttime prayers drift into thoughts of doubt and concern. You know your sins, and you know that he knows. You don't feel worthy, and you wonder if he doesn't agree. Your greatest fear is that God will someday turn off the faucet and walk away. And where will that leave you?

Job was the most righteous man on earth, yet even he struggled with this universal fear of humanity. His greatest concern in life was that someday God would take it all away. Through Satan's hand Job's greatest fear came to pass, and he was left to stare his demons directly in the face. Job had to make a decision that each and every one of us has to make. He had to settle a critical issue in his heart once and for all. How was he going to define God's goodness? Was he going to trust God only in times of blessing? Or could he transcend his fears and say that God is good even in times of total chaos and despair?

God's goodness and mercy is determined by who he is, not by what happens to us. His dominion over the world and authority over our life should never be measured by the amount of blessing he chooses to give. God is not accountable to man. And until each one of us settles this truth in our heart, we will always struggle with a sense of foreboding fear. We will never be able to love God as he loves us—without condition.

REFLECTION
Can you relate to Job's struggles? How have you struggled yourself?
Pray that God would help you trust him in spite of your trials.

HALF & HALF THEOLOGY

How much less are mere people, who are but worms in his sight?   Job 25:6

A FRIEND of mine often jokes that he's certain half of his theology is wrong; he just doesn't know which half. That's true with most of us, though we don't always like to admit it. And it's certainly the case with Job's three friends.

At the lowest point in his life, Job had to suffer the advice of three armchair theologians—Eliphaz, Bildad, and Zophar. They'd been watching his plight from a distance and were certain they had his problems figured out. They weighed his situation, put their heads together, and approached Job with their solution to his quandary. It's not as if they didn't mean well. Their concern was genuine. But somehow their advice missed the mark. And God wasn't too impressed with what they had to say, even though most of their advice was true—at least technically.

"God is powerful and dreadful," says Bildad the Shuhite. "He enforces peace in the heavens. Who is able to count his heavenly army? . . . How can a mere mortal stand before God and claim to be righteous? . . . God is so glorious that even the moon and stars scarcely shine compared to him. How much less are mere people, who are but worms in his sight?" (Job 25:2-6).

You have to admit that Bildad had a point. God is glorious and all-powerful, and compared to him we might as well be worms writhing around in the dirt. But there is a fuller picture of God in Scripture.

"He will rescue the poor when they cry out to him," writes the psalmist. "He will save them from oppression and from violence, for their lives are precious to him" (Psalm 72:12, 14). On the one hand, it is true that we are but maggots in comparison with God. On the other hand, didn't he create us in his own image? He chose to breathe his Spirit into ours and bring us into his divine presence. We may be worms, but we're not worms in God's eyes. He sees us as precious children, and he loves us as he loves his own Son. Bildad may have been only half wrong, but the half that was wrong made all the difference.

Be careful when you decide to speak for God. Choose your words carefully when dishing out advice on behalf of the Savior. God doesn't like it when we put words in his mouth.

REFLECTION
*How do you see yourself in the eyes of God? Is it comforting
to know that you are precious in his sight?*

SOURCE OF TRUE WISDOM

Sometimes the elders are not wise.　　Job 32:9

OG MANDINGO once wrote, "Experience is overrated by old men who nod wisely and speak foolishly."

That describes Job's three friends pretty well, doesn't it? During his time of suffering they came to him brimming with advice and condemnation. You can almost picture them stroking their beards and nodding in approval at each other as they spoke. The three were so full of themselves that they professed to know exactly what God was doing. They nodded wisely but spoke foolishly.

Standing to one side through the entire conversation was young Elihu. He'd been listening to their words and waiting for his turn to speak. When he saw that the three had nothing else to say, he decided to step forward. "I am young and you are old, so I held back and did not dare to tell you what I think. I thought, 'Those who are older should speak, for wisdom comes with age.' Surely it is God's Spirit within people, the breath of the Almighty within them, that makes them intelligent. But sometimes the elders are not wise. Sometimes the aged do not understand justice. So listen to me and let me express my opinion" (Job 32:6-10).

> "Only God bestows such wisdom, Director."
>
> *The Mark, 80*

Imagine the look on the old men's faces when they heard that. I'm not sure what the Hebrew word for *whippersnapper* is, but I'm sure that's what they were mumbling. *Kids today. . . . No manners at all!*

In the end it was Elihu who had the best take on Job's problems. Job's three friends claimed that Job was suffering because of sin, but it took Elihu to point out that Job's only sin was complaining about his suffering. He explained that not all trouble is meant to punish us; sometimes it's meant to strengthen us. He encouraged Job to look at his time of trial from a different perspective—that maybe God had a greater purpose than any of them could possibly comprehend. His speech was one of the wisest in all of Scripture. In spite of his young age, Elihu showed himself to be a man of true depth and understanding.

Elihu knew that wisdom doesn't come from having gray hair; it comes from being plugged into the heart of God. His words show that he had more than a knowledge about God—he had an understanding of his nature and being. He *knew* God. And that's what brought true wisdom to his lips.

REFLECTION
Do you feel that you have more knowledge about God than an intimate understanding of his heart? What do you think makes the difference?

THE LAST VOICE

Then the Lord answered Job from the whirlwind.   Job 38:1

WHEN ALL is said and done, the only thing that really matters in life is what God thinks. When all the dust is settled, when the last stone has been turned, when the final chorus has been sung, when the last float has passed in the parade, you still don't have the full picture. Not until God weighs in. Not until God steps up and settles the matter once and for all.

For thirty-seven chapters into the book of Job we've been hearing people express their opinions. We've heard from Job and his unsupportive wife. We've listened to the half-truth ramblings of Job's three friends, Eliphaz, Bildad, and Zophar. We've heard the wise counsel of the young Elihu. But through the whole thing God remained silent. He let them talk while he stayed in the shadows listening to what they had to say. Then when all the words were over, he finally opened his mouth.

"Then the Lord answered Job from the whirlwind," Scripture records. When it came time for God to speak, he began by summoning the forces of nature. From all corners of the globe he called the winds into submission and brought forth the power of a whirlwind—power that can be contained by no man or woman—only God. Out of this thunder from heaven, God brings the last word on Job's dilemma. When he finally speaks, he speaks definitively. And you can bet every ear was listening. A few knees were no doubt knocking as well.

We spend a lot of time in life spouting our thoughts and opinions. Most of us feel like experts in at least one area, and we're seldom afraid to speak our mind. We're pretty certain of what we believe about God and his ways. We think we understand him and are usually quick to explain him to others. But there is an important truth that each of us needs to remember. All of life comes down to this one unchanging principle. After all the talking, all the philosophizing, all the opinions, all the sermons, all the thoughts about who God is and why he does what he does, there is only one thing that really matters.

The last voice any of us will ever hear will be the voice of God. He will always get the last word. He will settle every argument. He will quiet every complaint. He will leave no lingering doubts about who he is and who we are in the grand scheme of things.

REFLECTION
When do you find yourself questioning God's authority over your life?
What does the message of Job have to say to you?

ANSWERING TO GOD

*Who is this that questions my wisdom with such
ignorant words?*   Job 38:2

DOES IT FEEL to you that Job had good reason to complain? Do you have a hard time blaming him? Does it seem as if God was a little hard on him after all he had been through?

God allowed Satan to test Job to a degree that most of us will never experience. Satan took away his farm and his livelihood. He killed his animals, his servants, and his children. He took away Job's health, causing boils and disease from head to toe. Job went from a blessed man to a cursed one in a matter of days, losing everything he had worked so hard to attain—everything that God had given him. Who wouldn't be angry and confused in such a situation? Who wouldn't wonder aloud why God had turned his back? Who wouldn't question God in such dire circumstances?

> "He paced, a hand over his mouth, praying silently. Ming and Chloe had tried to reason with him, reminding him that God was sovereign, but he could not make sense of what he had done."
>
> *Desecration,* 118

It's hard for me to blame Job because I've questioned God a few times myself. And my life has never seen the kind of turmoil that he faced. I've been angrier with God for far less than he, and somewhere in the back of my mind I want to believe that I had the right. I want to think that my words were justified. That I deserved some kind of answer for my woes.

But as Job found out, God doesn't answer to us for the things he does. It isn't our place to pass judgment on the One who will ultimately judge us all. "Who is this that questions my wisdom with such ignorant words?" God says to Job. "Brace yourself, because I have some questions for you, and you must answer them" (Job 38:2-3).

It seldom occurs to us while we're questioning God's wisdom and railing against his ways that he might someday part the clouds and give us an answer. It's easy to doubt God when you don't have to face him. It seems safe to complain about his provision when you don't see him standing over your shoulder. But God gave Job and his friends a crash course in the concept of "omnipresence," and you can bet that they all watched their words more carefully from then on.

Things don't always go our way in life, and during times of confusion it's easy to blame God. But someday we will have to give account for our careless words and lack of faith. The best we can do during those times is to remember the lesson of Job and to bite our tongue before it gets us into even more trouble.

REFLECTION
We have Jesus to cover our sins at judgment, but what will be the effect of our careless words of doubt? How do they affect us during our life on earth?

REMEMBERING WHO'S FIRST

Where were you when I laid the foundations of the earth?   Job 38:4

A RUSSIAN PHILOSOPHER once said to his friend, "The most important thing a man can learn is that he is second."

His friend thought for a minute and said, "No. The most important thing a man can learn is what's first."

There is a point that God wants to get each of us to believe before he will truly bless us. He wants us to understand this critical and universal truth: *He is God, and we are not.* God needs us to understand intimately who we are in the grand plan of creation. And more important, he needs us to realize who he is. Before we can really come to terms with ourselves, we must first come to terms with God.

We are second. God is first. Period.

It is when we forget this unchanging truth that life gets confusing and chaotic. That's when it's time to take a step back and reevaluate our words and motives. Job was a righteous man—the most righteous in all the earth. But in the midst of his period of trial and testing he forgot who he was and who God was. So God took some time to remind Job, as he does with each one of us when we get confused.

"Where were you when I laid the foundations of the earth? Tell me, if you know so much. Do you know how its dimensions were determined and who did the surveying? What supports its foundations, and who laid its cornerstone as the morning stars sang together and all the angels shouted for joy? Who defined the boundaries of the sea as it burst from the womb, and as I clothed it with clouds and thick darkness? For I locked it behind barred gates, limiting its shores. I said, 'Thus far and no farther will you come. Here your proud waves must stop!'" (Job 38:4-11).

God reminded Job who he was, not because he had a need to brag, but because Job had a critical need to remember. The only thing that will set life straight during times of confusion and doubt is to put yourself and your troubles in the right perspective. The only cure for a worldly mind-set is to be reminded of who God is and how temporal life is. And the only thing that will bring us back to God in times of sin is an understanding of our unworthiness in the face of God's power and holiness.

REFLECTION
How often do you lose perspective of who God is? How has he worked to remind you during those times? What would help you remember this truth daily?

EXPERIENCING GOD

*I had heard about you before, but now I have seen you with
my own eyes.*   Job 42:5

HOW MUCH of your life has been spent hearing about God? How many hours of sermons have you sat through learning about the way God works and the way he has dealt with people? How many times have you sat around the dinner table discussing God with your friends? talking about his mercy, wrath, holiness, direction, and ultimate intentions? listening to others proclaim their understanding of his will and ways? How many days of your life have been spent in search of the truths about God?

Now, how much of that time would you trade for a moment of seeing him with your own eyes? How much more could you learn if you could experience God firsthand? if you could stand in his presence and listen to him speak?

I'm convinced that we've all spent too much time talking and hearing about God and far too little standing in silence before him. We're so busy debating his ways that we never take the time to experience them. We're so caught up in questions and answers about God's holiness and mercy that we've never allowed him to show us just how holy and merciful he really is.

"Be silent, and know that I am God!" he tells us (Psalm 46:10). "Be silent before the Lord, all humanity," proclaims the prophet Zechariah (2:13). Standing in God's presence, Job replies in total humility, "I will put my hand over my mouth in silence. I have said too much already. I have nothing more to say" (Job 40:4-5).

How many of us have said too much already? How many of us continue to talk long after we have nothing more to say? How much more could we gain if we simply learned to stand still and quiet in the presence of God?

"I had heard about you before, but now I have seen you with my own eyes," says Job. "I take back everything I said, and I sit in dust and ashes to show my repentance" (42:5-6).

When we see God, it changes everything. It silences our heart and soul in a way that nothing else can. It makes every word we've ever spoken and everything we've ever heard about God seem foolish. It is the only way we will ever truly come to know him.

REFLECTION
*How much time do you spend in silence before God? How often
do you take time each morning to listen instead of talk to him?*

HEAVEN'S GLORY

O Lord, our Lord, the majesty of your name fills the earth!
Your glory is higher than the heavens.　　Psalm 8:1

WHERE DO YOU GO to see God? Where do you look to experience his glory? How do you get in touch with his greatness? How do you keep your life in perspective and remind yourself who God is and who you are in the grand scheme of things?

The glory of God isn't hard to find. In fact, you have to work hard at ignoring it. You have to make a conscious decision to shut out the heavens and the power of creation in order to lose sight of God's hand in your life. When you stand at the base of a mountain range and see the peaks towering high into the heavens, you wonder how you could ever forget God's power. When you nestle your toes into the coastal sand and gaze at the vast ocean, watching the waves crest and fall as far as the eye can see, you have a hard time imagining that you ever doubted God's unlimited might and authority. When you hold a rose in your hand, feeling the softness of the petals, allowing the fragrance to invade your senses, you find yourself in complete and total awe of God's creativity.

> "God had become more than a force of nature or even a miracle worker to Buck, as God had been in the skies of Israel that night."
>
> *Left Behind,* 441

I see God everywhere I look. This morning some deer came to graze in the back of our house, and I spent a few minutes watching them. Once again I found myself in total wonder of their beauty and grace. They move with such effortless elegance. They can leap with power and precision and run as swiftly as a horse. They are creatures of unbelievable magnificence yet are but one simple example of God's amazing design.

"The heavens tell of the glory of God," writes the psalmist. "The skies display his marvelous craftsmanship. Day after day they continue to speak; night after night they make him known. They speak without a sound or a word; their voice is silent in the skies; yet their message has gone out to all the earth, and their words to all the world" (19:1-4).

Don't let a day go by without allowing yourself to see God. Don't go to bed until you've experienced his glory. Don't allow yourself to go through even one day of life without basking in his presence and the marvel of his creation.

REFLECTION
Where is it that you go to experience God's glory? How can we teach ourselves to see God's power even in the smallest things of life?

POWER IN HUMILITY

Your king is coming to you . . . riding on a donkey.   Zechariah 9:9

NOT SO LONG AGO I attended a special worship service at a church. As part of the service two people from the congregation were asked to pray for guidance and direction. A young man went first. With a loud voice he shouted his prayer into the microphone. He quoted commanding phrases and claimed authority in the name of Jesus. "Show us your might and power," he cried in a loud voice, raising his fist high in the air. "Bring us to victory in our hour of need!" His prayer was sincere and brought a great deal of applause from the congregation.

But what happened next surprised us all. A young woman walked on stage and took the microphone to pray. Before beginning, she knelt on the floor. Her prayer was short and quiet and humble. She never raised her voice or asked for power. She reverently prayed for wisdom and humility. By the time she finished, a spirit of submission had fallen on the crowd. It was a remarkable thing to witness.

There is tremendous power in humility. The moment of our greatest strength comes at the hour of our most genuine brokenness before God. We are never nearer the throne of victory than in the depths of submission.

The prophet Zechariah foretells the coming Messiah: "Rejoice greatly, O people of Zion! Shout in triumph, O people of Jerusalem! Look your king is coming to you. He is righteous and victorious" (9:9). Zechariah paints a picture of power and authority—a scene that Israel longed to see. An event that Israel had been waiting thousands of years to witness. They prayed for the day that their King would come to claim his throne and lead them to victory. But they never imagined the manner in which he would come. It's the end of Zechariah's sentence that perhaps confuses them: "Yet he is humble, riding on a donkey—even on a donkey's colt" (9:9).

A donkey for a chariot? A smelly colt to carry their King to his throne? A God riding on a common mule? What kind of victory ride is that? What kind of King is this anyway?

He's a King who knows that power is not about noise and pretension but about humility. He's a Messiah who understands the strength of brokenness. He's a God who came to redeem the world, not to go to war with it.

REFLECTION
In what ways does your life display the kind of gentleness and meekness that Jesus reflected? Are you humble when you come before the throne?

WHEN GOD IS SILENT

Since they refused to listen when I called to them,
I would not listen when they called to me. Zechariah 7:13

DO YOUR PRAYERS seem to go unanswered? How many times have you lain awake at night pleading for God's peace and provision, only to wake up the next morning feeling empty? Have you prayed for wisdom, only to find yourself more confused by the day? Have you prayed for guidance, only to find yourself more lost? Have you longed to hear God's voice, yet found him to remain silent?

I can answer yes to each one of those questions. I've gone through periods in my life when my prayers seemed to fall on deaf ears, and my requests were ignored. I've struggled to hear God's voice yet heard nothing. And deep in my heart I usually knew the reason.

"Since they refused to listen when I called to them, I would not listen when they called to me, says the Lord Almighty" (Zechariah 7:13).

When God turns a deaf ear to us, it is usually because we have done the same to him. When we live in defiance and disobedience to his commands, he often turns away. It's not that he doesn't hear our pleas; he simply knows that silence is what we most need. Through God's silence we are reminded how much we need his voice.

> "Buck turned to Rayford. 'As wonderful as that prayer time was, I didn't get any direct leading about what to do.'"
>
> *Tribulation Force,* 243

When my prayers seem empty and useless, it is usually because I have ignored God's direction in the past. He has set a task before me, but I have chosen not to obey. My defiance isn't overt, but it is real. I may not outwardly deny his directive, but inwardly I know my rebellion. And because of it, God chooses to move away until I obey.

You may have experienced the same thing in your life. Maybe you're experiencing it now. You've prayed fervently for help or healing or direction, only to find yourself more confused than ever. You know that God could help you because you've seen his hand in the past, but still he doesn't come. If so, then maybe it's time to take your eyes off your request and look instead at your heart. Do you have sin hiding among the crevices? Have you ignored a command or mandate from God? Have you ignored his voice? If so, that's where you need to begin looking for God's answer.

REFLECTION
How do you respond when you hear God's voice? Do you respond to him the same way you hope he will respond to you?

SEEDS OF BLESSING

I am planting seeds of peace and prosperity among you.   Zechariah 8:12

HAVE YOU EVER looked at the silence of God as the seeds of peace and prosperity? When God turns away, does it feel like he's laying the groundwork for blessing? Does it occur to us that sometimes unanswered prayers are God's way of pulling weeds and tilling the soil—of working the ground for a future harvest?

When the Israelites turned a deaf ear to God's commands, he responded by turning a deaf ear to their prayers. He remained silent when they most needed his help. And through his silence the people were scattered "as with a whirlwind among the distant nations, where they lived as strangers" (Zechariah 7:14). Soon their land became desolate and barren. "The land that had been so pleasant became a desert," reports the prophet Zechariah (7:14). And God allowed it to happen for a reason. He knew that the people needed to be broken before he could repair them. Had he answered their prayers and propped them up in their defiance, their rebellion would have only grown worse.

The Israelites turned back to God, and he again heard their prayers. And his blessings rained down even greater than before. "For I am planting seeds of peace and prosperity among you. The grapevines will be heavy with fruit. The earth will produce its crops, and the sky will release the dew. Once more I will make the remnant in Judah and Israel the heirs of these blessings" (8:12).

God doesn't remain silent out of anger or retribution but out of love. When we remain in sin and disobedience, his primary interest is to see us restored. He yearns to bless us, but he refuses to enable us. He knows that unchecked defiance only leads to greater defiance. His discipline is purposeful and loving and needed. And through his silence he is planting the seeds for future blessing.

When you feel far from God, don't ever think that he is far from you. When your prayers have gone unanswered because of sin hidden in your heart, don't think that God isn't aware of your pain. He knows that you need him, and he's waiting to bring you home. And through your obedience, he plans to open the skies of heaven and "release the dew."

REFLECTION

How does it change your prayers to know that God is waiting to bless you?
What should be your response when he is silent?

A SOURCE OF BLESSING

Don't be afraid or discouraged, but instead get on
with rebuilding the Temple!   Zechariah 8:13

THE WORST THING about sin and disobedience is that it can so easily immobilize us in regret. When we think we've disappointed God, it's often all we can do to get up in the morning and keep moving forward. We wallow in our failure, wondering how God must feel about us. Our prayers tend to be filled with thoughts of remorse and regret. We plead with God for forgiveness long after he's forgotten our transgression.

I once knew a woman who had had an abortion as a teenager. At the time she was young and scared and didn't know the Lord. Those around her convinced her that it was the only option. She had lived with the guilt of that decision for over twenty years and had never been able to forgive herself. During times of sharing with other Christians she would often bring up the event and discuss her past sin. She wondered aloud what her child might have looked like and how things might have turned out had she not had the abortion. She was consumed with remorse. Even though others tried to comfort her and convince her that God had long since forgiven her, she still struggled with guilt and shame. And through her guilt she remained spiritually immobilized.

> "When regret crept in, when he felt ashamed of the husband and father he had been, he merely prayed for forgiveness for having been so blind."
>
> *Tribulation Force, 225*

"Among the nations, Judah and Israel had become symbols of what it means to be cursed," God says through his prophet Zechariah. "But no longer! Now I will rescue you and make you both a symbol and a source of blessing! So don't be afraid or discouraged, but instead get on with rebuilding the Temple!" (8:13).

The people's sin against God was great, but not nearly as great as God's forgiveness. On the heels of their repentance God not only forgave them but blessed them beyond their wildest dreams. Then he told them to forgive themselves and move on. They were once a symbol of "curses," but God made them a symbol of blessing. Not only that; he made them a *source* of blessing. Through God's forgiveness Israel would become an avenue through which he would forgive others. And what greater purpose could a people serve?

If you've found yourself immobilized because of past sins, then give your past, your sins, and your everyday life to God. When you find yourself discouraged because of your unfaithfulness, focus instead on God's grace and mercy. Don't allow yourself to wallow in guilt. Let him instead make you a source of blessing to others.

REFLECTION
What does it mean to be a source of blessing to others? How can you become a symbol of God's grace and mercy?

NEVER GIVE UP

They went out in the boat, but they caught nothing all night.   John 21:3

IS THERE ANY task or project in your life that you are about to give up on? Have you been working on a plan for so long that you're tired of waiting on the results? Is there something you've been praying about that seems to have grown stale and old? Some prayer that God doesn't seem to be answering? Some idea that you were sure was God's will but now seems futile?

If so, maybe you should think twice before abandoning it. Maybe you're simply fishing on the wrong side of the boat.

Jesus' disciples once went fishing and spent all night without so much as a nibble. Over and over they cast their nets into the sea, each time coming up empty. They were good fishermen, and they knew the right spots to fish. They had brought in boatloads of fish in the past with the same techniques, yet somehow this time it just wasn't working. Until Jesus showed up.

> At dawn the disciples saw Jesus standing on the beach, but they couldn't see who he was. He called out, "Friends, have you caught any fish?"
>
> "No," they replied.
>
> Then he said, "Throw out your net on the right-hand side of the boat, and you'll get plenty of fish!" So they did, and they couldn't draw in the net because there were so many fish in it. (John 21:4-6)

Just when they were ready to give up, their venture turned fruitful. Just when they thought they would go home empty-handed, they started reeling in fish by the bucketfuls. And what made the difference? They cast where Jesus told them to cast. They got clearance from God. They didn't give up, even when the water seemed empty and the fishing seemed like a waste of time.

There may be someone in your life you've been praying for. Maybe someone who needs the Lord. Maybe someone who needs to come back to the Lord. Maybe you're praying for direction, help, healing, wisdom, or strength. If so, don't give up. Don't let your impatience turn to indifference. Continue fishing, and listen for the words of Jesus.

REFLECTION
What is the task that you most feel is God's will yet seems most fruitless?
What would your ardent prayers for a fruitful outcome sound like?

BEAUTY FOR ASHES

To all who mourn in Israel, he will give beauty for ashes.   Isaiah 61:3

IN GREEK MYTHOLOGY Phoenix was a beautiful, lone bird that soared the skies of Arabia for over 600 years before being consumed in a raging fire. After a time it rose from the ashes in even greater glory and splendor to begin a longer and more brilliant life of freedom and grace. In Greece, Phoenix is a symbol of restoration and immortality.

I'm not a fan of mythology, but I do like the idea this fable represents. Its symbolism could have been torn from the pages of Scripture.

"To all who mourn in Israel, he will give beauty for ashes," writes the prophet Isaiah, "joy instead of mourning, praise instead of despair. For the Lord has planted them like strong and graceful oaks for his own glory" (61:3).

From the ashes of Israel's sin, God promised to raise them up in even greater glory and splendor. Their season of mourning would turn to an eternity of dancing. Their despair would turn to worship. They would rise from the pit of death to be restored as God's holy people.

That promise was fulfilled in Jesus. Death has been conquered. The fire has been extinguished. The Phoenix has risen from the ashes once and for all time.

Have you allowed Jesus to turn your mourning into joy? Have you let him take away the despair and turn it into praise? Have you embraced your future in Christ as a strong and graceful oak—a symbol of his glory? Have you let Jesus trade his beauty for your ashes?

So often we wallow in the ashes of our sin. We roll in the dust of our failures and misfortunes. We allow ourselves to be covered with the soot of Satan's lies and the dirt of our own sinful nature. We live in regret and shame over past sins and pitiful habits. We struggle in the mire of our own self-doubt. But God never intended us to stay there. His intent is to free us!

Rise from the ashes and embrace your future!

REFLECTION
In what ways have you wallowed in the ashes of sin? How is it possible to embrace God's restoration? What ashes do you need turned into beauty?

HEAVENLY MATERIAL

Now anyone who builds on that foundation may use gold, silver, jewels, wood, hay, or straw.   1 Corinthians 3:12

IF IT BURNS UP in the fire of judgment, whose work is it—yours or God's? Which things will stand the test of time? Which will disappear and be left in ashes?

> For no one can lay any other foundation than the one we already have—Jesus Christ. Now anyone who builds on that foundation may use gold, silver, jewels, wood, hay, or straw. But there is going to come a time of testing at the judgment day to see what kind of work each builder has done. Everyone's work will be put through the fire to see whether or not it keeps its value. If the work survives the fire, that builder will receive a reward. But if the work is burned up, the builder will suffer great loss. (1 Corinthians 3:11-15)

You and I build our life with a myriad of materials. Every day we create things and set them before the world. We construct ideas and opinions. We erect works and projects and mighty plans. We raise towers of achievement and success, often in the name of God. But how much of it will survive the flames of judgment?

> "'The Lord will reward you,' [Tsion] said."
>
> *Armageddon, 347*

Builders can choose the material they use to build. They can use gold, silver, or jewels. Or they can use wood, hay, or straw. One set represents the substance of eternity—the works of God. The other represents the fabric of earth—the works of people. One group endures the fire, the other turns to ashes.

A lot of what we do is done out of self-indulgence. Much of our money goes toward earthly matters. Much of our time is spent in pursuit of things that will burn up in the light of eternity. I grieve over that truth about my life, and I work daily to change it. I've spent enough time building my own agenda; I want to spend the balance of my life in pursuit of God's agenda.

And what are those things that will last? Which works are built of gold, silver, and jewels? The times we spend shaping our children in the ways of God. The hours of prayer for others. The moments of service to those in need. The times of quiet reflection and obedience to God. The seeds of salvation we sow into the lives of the lost. The words of love and encouragement we bring to those who are hurting. In short, the time we spend loving God, loving others, and reflecting God's goodness.

REFLECTION
What are some of the temporal tasks you tend to spend too much time on?
Which of your works are sure to stand the test of time?

SPIRITUAL REVIVAL

Go out and stand before me on the mountain.   1 Kings 19:11

ELIJAH WAS one of God's greatest prophets, but he was still human. He still suffered from discouragement and spiritual fatigue. When the pressure built up, he struggled to maintain his strength before God.

It was on the heels of his greatest spiritual victories that he found himself in the pit of despair and confusion. Elijah defeated the prophets of Baal and then summoned a mighty rain from the sea to show God's power to the evil King Ahab. Jezebel swore to have him killed when she learned what he had done, so he fled. He ended up under a tree in the desert, praying that God would take his life. God's prophet learned the price of obedience to the Lord. People don't always like what God has to say, and those who speak for him take the brunt of the world's wrath.

God understood Elijah's confusion. He put him into a deep sleep and then sent angels to minister to him. He brought food and water and physical restoration to his prophet. Then he had Elijah travel to Mount Sinai, where he could meet with him face-to-face. "Go out and stand before me on the mountain," the Lord tells Elijah (1 Kings 19:11).

Have you ever been so beaten and discouraged that all you want to do is lie down and die? Have you ever found yourself saying with the prophet Elijah, "I have had enough, Lord. . . . Take my life" (1 Kings 19:4)? Have you ever felt so persecuted and weary that you didn't think you could go on? If so, then maybe you need to meet God on the mountain.

It is often on the heels of our greatest spiritual highs that we find ourselves in the depths of discouragement. Most mountaintops feed directly into valleys, and that's usually where we find ourselves when we come down. The higher we go, the farther we can fall. The Lord understands this truth, and he is there to prop us up when we need him most. He will refresh our heart and spirit. And he will meet with us to renew our vision. All he needs is for us to go to him.

If you don't have a mountain, a prayer closet will do just as well. God met with Elijah on the peaks of Sinai, but he'll meet with you in the depths of your heart. Go to him today, and allow him to revive your body and spirit.

REFLECTION
How do you normally deal with spiritual discouragement?
How would God have you handle these times in the future?

WHEN GOD SPEAKS IN THE WIND

The Lord was not in the wind. 1 Kings 19:11

THE LORD SENT Elijah to the top of Mount Sinai to meet with him. He told his prophet to go there and wait. "And as Elijah stood there, the Lord passed by, and a mighty windstorm hit the mountain," Scripture records. "It was such a terrible blast that the rocks were torn loose, but the Lord was not in the wind" (1 Kings 19:11).

Sometimes God speaks to us in the whirlwind, and sometimes he doesn't. There are times when God deals with us through the power of a tornado, and times where he doesn't see the need.

God came to his servant Job in the wind. Job questioned God's goodness and complained about his lot in life. When God had had enough of Job's foolish words and whining spirit, he decided to show him more of himself. "Then the Lord answered Job from the whirlwind," records Scripture (Job 38:1).

When God decides to speak to you in the wind, you know you've gone too far. When he summons his wrath from the four corners of the globe in order to make his point, you'd better be holding onto something. Because when God comes in the whirlwind, that usually means he's irritated.

"They have planted the wind and will harvest the whirlwind," warns the prophet Hosea (8:7). The Israelites had turned their backs on God and once again embraced the sins of the world, giving their devotion to false gods and worldly pleasures. "My fury burns against you," God tells them. "How long will you be incapable of innocence?" (8:5).

Has God ever come to you in a whirlwind? Have you ever lived in such high and mighty rebellion and disobedience that he was forced to blow you back to earth? Ever felt the gale-force winds of God's wrath wailing against your spirit? Ever made God angry enough to send a tornado into the middle of your life?

This isn't the way God wants to speak to his people, so don't make him. He'd rather not have to get our attention by summoning a hurricane. But he will if that's what it takes. It's entirely up to us.

REFLECTION
Can you remember a time when God spoke to you through the fury of the whirlwind? What did you learn from that experience?

WHEN GOD SPEAKS IN THE EARTHQUAKE

After the wind there was an earthquake, but the Lord was not in the earthquake.   1 Kings 19:11

"AFTER THE WIND there was an earthquake, but the Lord was not in the earthquake" (1 Kings 19:11). When Elijah went to meet with God on the mountain, a mighty whirlwind passed by, but that's not how God chose to speak to him. Elijah had done nothing to incur God's anger and wrath, so he saw no need. After the wind, God sent an earthquake. But again, that's not how he chose to address his faithful prophet. The mountains shook, but the Lord was not in the earthquake.

That doesn't mean that God won't speak through an earthquake. And when he does, you don't want to be standing idly by.

"For in my jealousy and blazing anger, I promise a mighty shaking in the land of Israel on that day," the Lord says through his prophet Ezekiel. "All living things . . . will quake in terror at my presence. Mountains will be thrown down; cliffs will crumble; walls will fall to the earth. . . . Thus I will show my greatness and holiness, and I will make myself known to all the nations of the world. Then they will know that I am the Lord!" (38:19-23).

> "An earthquake is coming, and it is not symbolic. This passage indicates that everyone, great or small, would rather be crushed to death than to face the one who sits on the throne."
>
> *Nicolae, 327*

Just as the earthquake followed the whirlwind in front of Elijah, God's judgment always comes on the heels of his anger. God's wrath usually leads to discipline. And discipline always comes for the purpose of redemption. When God comes to you in the earthquake, you can be sure that what you are feeling is his hand of discipline on your life. And you can be just as sure that he is doing so in order to restore you to himself.

It is more than a little significant that history's greatest moment of redemption was accompanied by an earthquake. Jesus had been in the grave for three days, and with the guards standing outside the tomb, God orchestrated his most powerful and final act of restoration. All of creation had been waiting for this moment—the moment when Jesus would rise from the grave and redeem his people once and for all time. "Suddenly there was a great earthquake, because an angel of the Lord came down from heaven and rolled aside the stone and sat on it" (Matthew 28:2).

God shook the very foundations of the earth in judgment in order to usher in a new age of redemption. And with that act, brought ultimate restoration to his people.

REFLECTION

How do you respond when God's hand of discipline comes upon you?
Does it help to know that his purpose is restoration?

WHEN GOD SPEAKS IN THE FIRE

After the earthquake there was a fire, but the Lord was not
in the fire.   1 Kings 19:12

ELIJAH STOOD on Mount Sinai waiting for the Lord to come and speak to him. As he waited, a whirlwind passed by, but God was not in the whirlwind. When the winds died down, God sent an earthquake, but he was not in the earthquake. "After the earthquake there was a fire," Scripture records, "but the Lord was not in the fire" (1 Kings 19:12).

God had spoken before from a fire. When Moses stood on this same mountain many years earlier, he saw a bush engulfed in flames. When he went to see what was happening, the Lord spoke to him from the fire. "'Do not come any closer,' God told him. 'Take off your sandals, for you are standing on holy ground'" (Exodus 3:5).

Fire represents the holiness of God. It symbolizes his power and purity among an impure people. When God speaks to us from his holy fire, he is showing us the very essence of his character and glory. Like the fire, God is intense and dynamic and powerful. His holiness cannot be touched or approached without fear and trepidation.

"Be very careful never to forget what you have seen the Lord do for you," Moses says to the Israelites. "Do not let these things escape from your mind as long as you live! And be sure to pass them on to your children and grandchildren. Tell them especially about the day when you stood before the Lord your God at Mount Sinai. . . . You came near and stood at the foot of the mountain . . . and the Lord spoke to you from the fire" (Deuteronomy 4:9-12).

God's holiness is not something to take lightly. When you've seen God in all his glory, you don't easily forget the encounter. God didn't speak to Elijah in the fire, but Elijah may have expected him to. This is how he spoke to Moses and to the Israelites. God led Elijah to the same mountain, maybe even to the same spot. Yet as the fire passed, God's voice didn't come. He had something greater in mind for Elijah. Something that was perhaps a foreshadowing of what was to come. Something that you and I can readily relate to.

God spoke to Elijah in a gentle whisper. Some translations call it a "still, small voice." He spoke to Elijah as one friend to another.

REFLECTION
Have you ever felt the holiness of God around you during times of worship
or prayer? How do you react when in the presence of God's glory?
How should we react?

A GENTLE WHISPER

And after the fire there was the sound of a gentle whisper.   1 Kings 19:12

ONE OF GOD'S greatest miracles is the way he works silently in the hearts of his people. The way he speaks to our spirit, nudging us to do right instead of wrong. The way he communicates with us through the gentle whisper in our soul. God speaks to us as he spoke to Elijah on the mountain.

There are times in my life when I don't obey. Times when I ignore his teachings and my better judgment. I defy God and live for myself, even though I know better. During those times God sends a whirlwind to warn me that he's angry. It's his shot over the bow to let me know that I am on dangerous ground. His raging whirlwind is my red flag, and if I don't heed it, I can expect an earthquake to follow.

I've lived long enough to have survived a few of God's earthquakes, and it's not a fun place to be. When God's anger is raised, his hand of discipline often follows. And when the Lord shakes your foundation, you know you've been shaken. You also know that his purpose is to bring you back. Sometimes you have to tear down a few walls to remodel, and that's what God often does with us.

> "Rayford suddenly heard a voice, as if someone were in the car with him. The radio was off and he was alone, but he heard."
>
> *Apollyon, 296*

But these times of turmoil don't last forever. When God's discipline has brought us back into submission, he usually follows it by giving us a glimpse of his glory. He sends his fire to pass before us and lets us see his holiness. It is God's way of reminding us who he is and who we are before him.

God is never closer than when he speaks through a gentle whisper. His Spirit speaking softly into ours. Guiding us. Teaching us. Mentoring us. Drawing us nearer to his ways. "My sheep recognize my voice," Jesus says (John 10:27).

God's whisper is heaven's greatest love song.

REFLECTION

How much time do you spend listening for God's gentle whisper? Why not commit to spending time each day in quiet meditation?

WORKING INSTEAD OF WATCHING

Why are you standing here staring at the sky?   Acts 1:11

I KNEW A WOMAN once who was convinced that Jesus' return was right around the corner. She was sure that we were living not only in the last days but in the last few minutes. She stopped going to work, didn't bother to pay her bills, and even cancelled a hair appointment. That was about fifteen years ago.

At the time she had just finished reading a book that predicted the return of Jesus by a specific date. She gave me a copy, and I found a dozen flaws within the first few chapters, but that didn't faze my friend. She was still so convinced that her life came to a complete stop. When the date came and went without fanfare, the author revised his thoughts and published an addendum to the book predicting a new date and time a few years down the road. My friend bought his pamphlet as well and decided to go back to work. At least for a while. I've since lost touch with her.

When Jesus was taken up into heaven in a cloud, a crowd stood by and watched. The angels saw them with their jaws dropped open and said to them, "Men of Galilee, why are you standing here staring at the sky? Jesus has been taken away from you into heaven. And someday, just as you saw him go, he will return!" (Acts 1:11).

In spite of the angels' words, people have been watching the sky ever since. We're often so mesmerized by the thought of Jesus' return that we spend more time gazing than we do preparing the way. I think if we listened closely, we could still hear the angels saying to us, "Why are you standing here staring at the sky when there's still so much work to be done?"

Is there anyone on your street who doesn't know Jesus? If so, then don't just stand there.

Are there any people in your city who don't have food or shelter this evening? If so, why are you staring at the sky?

Have you drawn as close to God as you could be? stored up all the heavenly treasures you want? righted all the wrongs within your sphere of influence? If not, then haven't you got work to do? As Christians, we're all excited about Jesus' return, but until then there are things he needs us to be doing.

REFLECTION
*How are you preparing for the return of Jesus? What do you need
to do that you haven't yet done?*

A CINDERELLA SAVIOR

They were like sheep without a shepherd.   Matthew 9:36

IT HAPPENED several years ago at Disney World. A crowd had gathered inside Cinderella's Castle to get a glimpse of the princess's arrival. Children everywhere craned their necks to see when she would appear through the gates of the castle. Several bounced on their father's shoulders in anticipation.

Suddenly she appeared. Cinderella. The girl who played her was perfect for the part—young and blonde and beautiful. Her smile lit up the crowd as she passed through the middle of them, waving and shaking hands.

Far to one side a young boy stood beside his older brother with his head bowed. He only glanced at the beautiful princess, not daring to draw near. His face was disfigured, just like his shattered self-image.

By accident Cinderella happened to catch a glimpse of the boy out of the corner of her eye. He looked away, but she didn't. She immediately began making her way toward him, parting the crowd slowly as she walked. When she reached the young boy, she bent down until they were at eye level. Gently she kissed him on the cheek. She took his hand, whispered into his ear, smiled, and then returned to middle of the crowd.[1]

It was a simple but beautiful act. And a perfect illustration of how Jesus sees you and me. "Wherever he went, he healed people of every sort of disease and illness," records Matthew. "He felt great pity for the crowds that came, because their problems were so great and they didn't know where to go for help. They were like sheep without a shepherd" (9:35-36).

Jesus doesn't see us as we are—sinful and disfigured people. He sees us for what we need. We need a Savior. We need help. We need a kiss on the cheek and a gentle touch. We need a kind word of compassion. We need someone loving and forgiving to hold our hand and show us how much we are worth.

We need Jesus. That's why he came. And that's why we love him so.

REFLECTION
When have you felt ugly and disfigured because of your sin? Do you find comfort knowing that Jesus sees past your transgressions and into your heart?

FOREVER FAITHFUL

If we are unfaithful, he remains faithful.   2 Timothy 2:13

THIS MAY SOUND more judgmental than I mean it to, but some preachers don't belong in the pulpit. Any pulpit, any church, any time. They'd do us all a favor if they'd put on a pair of jeans and take a job in construction. Maybe then they'd learn to build something up instead of always tearing things down.

I heard one such preacher on the radio just the other day. In his opinion, none of us is pulling our weight. The church is lazy and overfed. Christians are all hypocrites. Preachers aren't preaching the truth anymore. Dads are distant, and moms only care about their careers. Kids are out of control and hell-bent. We eat too much, sleep too much, make too much, spend too much, work too much, and give too little.

I'm thinking, *Maybe we're just listening to too many radio preachers!*

It's not as if I can't see his point. I know we have a lot of changing to do. I'm not in denial. I've been let down by Christians more times than I care to admit. I've seen sin and laziness in the church.

> "We believe that he who called us is faithful."
>
> *Soul Harvest,* 317

I've helped shape a church budget, and I'm aware of the lack of financial support. I know Christian kids can be brats, and Christian parents can be distant. We're far from perfect individually, and collectively we don't love each other as we should. Any preacher looking for a good sermon on sin doesn't have to look past his own congregation.

But I also know that God's faithfulness has never depended on the faithfulness of his people. His love has never hinged on our ability to love each other. His salvation has never been reserved for the most obedient among us. God is faithful, even when we aren't.

The most beautiful part of God is that he is so much greater than our weaknesses. He takes the ugliest part of our character and covers it with the most pristine corner of his beauty. Where we are weak, he is strong. That's what makes him God. "If we are unfaithful, he remains faithful, for he cannot deny himself," records Paul (2 Timothy 2:13).

The only thing I contribute to my salvation is the sin that makes it necessary. In spite of all my flaws and inconsistencies, God accepts me anyway. And he does the same for you. He cannot and will not deny himself.

REFLECTION

When have you struggled with a negative attitude toward other believers? How does today's lesson help you have more tolerance for the church's shortcomings?

TEXTUAL EVIDENCES OF GOD

All Scripture is inspired by God.   2 Timothy 3:16

IF YOU STARTED reading the Bible from the beginning, chances are you'd skip over the fifth chapter of Genesis. It's the genealogy of Noah and appears to have nothing of practical value to us. But if you believe that "all Scripture is inspired by God and is useful to teach us" (2 Timothy 3:16), you have to believe that every word in the Bible is significant.

Let me show you something from this little chapter that you've probably never heard. You need a Hebrew dictionary to find it, but it's there. And it's one of the most awe-inspiring confirmations of the authenticity of Scripture that you'll ever discover. There's a lot here, but stay with me, and I promise it will be worth your while.

The genealogy begins with *Adam*, the first man. And his name simply means "man." His son was *Seth*, which means "appointed." Eve gave him this name because she felt he was appointed as a replacement for Abel. Seth named his son *Enosh*, which means "mortal" or "frail." Perhaps he was a sickly child. He gave birth to *Kenan*, which means "sorrow." Kenan must have wanted a more positive name for his son, so he named him *Mahalalel*, which means "the blessed God." Later it was common for Jews to use the Lord's name within the names of their children. Mahalalel had a son and named him *Jared*, which is a verb meaning "shall come down." And Jared gave birth to *Enoch*, whose name means "teaching" or "commencement." Enoch named his son *Methuselah*, which was a strange name for a child. It literally means "his death shall bring." Many scholars believe that Enoch was given a prophecy about the Flood and was promised by God that the Flood would not come until his son was dead. And if you add up the years in Scripture, you find that the Flood happened the same year of Methuselah's death. Methuselah gave birth to *Lamech*, whose name means "despairing." His son was *Noah*, which means "to bring comfort." So what does all this mean? Let's put the words together and see what message God was giving through this simple record of Noah's lineage.

"*Man appointed mortal sorrow. Blessed God shall come down teaching (that) his death shall bring (the) despairing comfort.*"[2]

There it is. The gospel of Jesus, hidden within the lines of Scripture.

REFLECTION
What about today's devotion makes you want to dig deeper into Scripture?
What does it say about God when we see textual evidences
of his hand at work within the lines of Scripture?

AWAITING OUR DAY

We who are still alive and remain on the earth will be caught
up in the clouds to meet the Lord in the air and remain
with him forever.   1 Thessalonians 4:17

THE STORY IS TOLD of an old missionary couple returning to the States after many years of thankless service in Africa. They happened to be on the same ship to New York as President Theodore Roosevelt, who was returning from a big game hunt in Africa. As the ship pulled past the Statue of Liberty and into the dock, huge crowds were gathered to welcome him home. The press was out in full force, and thousands of people had come to get a glimpse of the president.

In the middle of the chaos, the aged missionary couple fought their way through the crowds with their large suitcases in tow. Silently they hailed a cab and made their way to a cheap hotel. The missionary sat on the bed and said to his wife, "It just doesn't seem right. We gave our lives to Christ to win souls for the Kingdom in Africa, and when we arrive home there is no one here to meet us. The president shoots a few animals and receives a royal welcome."

His wife sat beside him on the bed and said softly, "That's because we're not home yet, dear."

"The Lord himself will come down from heaven with a commanding shout," writes Paul, "with the call of the archangel, and with the trumpet call of God. First, all the Christians who have died will rise from their graves. Then, together with them, we who are still alive and remain on the earth will be caught up in the clouds to meet the Lord in the air and remain with him forever" (1 Thessalonians 4:16-17).

> "While he was determined not to miss anything in New Babylon, he knew he needed sleep. He sat back down and settled in, hoping, praying he would again be transported to the very portals of heaven."
>
> *The Indwelling, 262*

It may seem at times as if our work for Christ is going unnoticed. There's not a lot of fanfare for obedient servants. They don't throw many parades on behalf of prayer warriors. There aren't many award ceremonies for loyal followers. Faith doesn't bring a lot of praise on this earth. But that's only because our trip is not yet over. We haven't arrived home quite yet.

Our day will come, you can be sure. And when it does, the ceremony will last for an eternity.

REFLECTION
When do you find yourself getting tired and discouraged in your Christian walk? How does it bring comfort to know that heaven is your real home?

NEW CREATIONS

Those who become Christians become new persons.   2 Corinthians 5:17

LAST NIGHT I saw a new baby just a few weeks old. His mother cradled him carefully in her arms as those around doted on the fragile little angel. Everyone wanted to hold him for just a moment. It was a precious sight. And seeing his tiny hands and feet made me long for the days that my children were little. I'm glad that they are growing so strong and tall, but I've always had a soft spot for babies.

Childbirth is one of God's greatest miracles. In a sense it is God's way of sharing the joy of creation with the people that he created. It is the one time in life when we can feel what it's like to hold in our arms a person made in our own image.

But even that doesn't compare with the miracle that happens at our second birth—the moment that we are born again. The second that God re-creates what he has already created. The process that happens to us when we give our life to Jesus. Paul describes it well: "What this means is that those who become Christians become new persons. They are not the same anymore, for the old life is gone. A new life has begun!" (2 Corinthians 5:17).

When we trust in Jesus, he gives us new eyes. We no longer see things through worldly vision but through heavenly faith. We begin to see people the way that God sees them—as helpless and hurting souls in need of a Savior.

He gives us new hands. Hands of compassion, not selfish ambition. Hands that help, instead of hinder. Hands that build up, instead of tear down. Hands of hope and strength and character.

He gives us new feet. Feet of purpose and persistence. Feet that suddenly have a path to follow and a destination to aim for. Feet that lead others away from death and dead-end lifestyles and toward a glorious future with Christ.

He gives us renewed strength so that we will no longer grow weary. New hope so that our life has purpose. New love so that his love can flow through us. New joy so that others will see his face.

Most important, he gives us a new heart. A heart that beats to his will, not our own. A heart that longs for heaven and leaves earthly worries far behind. A heart that yearns for God's nearness.

REFLECTION

How have you felt yourself grow into a new creation in Christ?
In what ways do you still need to grow in Christian maturity?

GOD'S GREATEST MIRACLE

God so loved the world that he gave his only Son.   John 3:16

WHAT WOULD you say was God's single greatest and most significant miracle? If you had to choose between all the mighty things God has done from the beginning of the world until now, what would you list as his crowning achievement?

Most people might point to Creation. The fact that he created the world and the universe from nothing and life from dust. The way he set the stars and planets in motion, perfectly placing the galaxies in the sky. We look at the expanse of the universe and stand in awe of God's power and authority, and we imagine that this must certainly be God's greatest accomplishment.

But is that how God would answer the question? What do you think he would say when asked about his greatest miracle? Just a quick glance through the pages of Scripture gives us enough insight to see the answer.

The story of Creation is dealt with in the beginning of Genesis. It starts at Genesis 1:1 and ends ten paragraphs later at Genesis 2:4 with the words "This is the account of the creation of the heavens and the earth."

And what is the message behind the balance of God's Word? From that verse forward until the last word of Revelation, what story is God telling? What miracle gets the most press in God's great Book?

The redemption of God's people. God's plan to restore humanity to himself after the fall of Adam. God's strategy to save people from their sin and bring them safely home to paradise.

If the Bible is an example of God's priorities, then the redemption of humanity is easily his greatest miraculous feat. And why wouldn't he see it that way? Look at what it cost him. The Creation cost God six days. Man's redemption cost him his only Son. Creation took a little time out of his calendar. Redemption ripped through the core of his heart. Creation took some words and breath. Redemption took his Son through the bowels of hell and back.

So what is God's greatest miracle? That would be you and me.

REFLECTION
How should you live in light of God's greatest miracle? What will you say to God to show your love and appreciation?

A DIVINE RESCUE

He rescued me because he delights in me.   Psalm 18:19

I OFTEN TELL people that when I grow up I want to be like my son, David. They usually smile because they think I'm joking, but the fact is, I really do want to be just like him. His relationship with Jesus is real and genuine and deep, and I couldn't be more proud. Today he is considered one of the spiritual leaders in his church youth group. Pretty amazing when you consider that he's basically shy, and we just began attending our church about a year ago. In fact, I still remember the first youth event he went to just a few weeks after we started attending.

The event was a citywide carnival hosted by the church youth group. There were games and dunking booths and sporting events and about five hundred crazy kids running all over the parking lot. My son didn't know a soul, but he wanted to go in hopes of meeting some new friends. I told him I'd stick around for the first ten minutes or so to make sure he was okay. Everywhere you looked kids were laughing and hanging onto each other, but David was all by himself. My heart cracked a little more with each passing minute.

> "They prayed for his strength, for peace, for comfort in his grief. They prayed for supernatural contentment when that was humanly impossible."
>
> *Assassins, 70*

My ten minutes came and went, yet still I couldn't bear to leave. I sat on the curb praying that God would bring some friends for David to hook up with. Still he walked from booth to booth by himself. Suddenly I caught him glancing in my direction, and I waved him toward me. He quickly made his way through the crowd and sat beside me on the curb. "There's too many people here," I said. "What do you say you and I take off and get some burgers?"

His eyes grew wide, and his voice lifted with excitement. "Okay, let's go!" he said. And that's what we did. We decided over lunch that he had plenty of time to make friends later and that this would be a good day for us to just hang out together. "I wasn't having any fun anyway," he told me. I told him I knew. That's why I rescued him.

"He led me to a place of safety," writes the psalmist. "He rescued me because he delights in me" (Psalm 18:19). God saved us for the same reason that I saved David from an afternoon of screaming kids. Because he loves us and simply wants to spend time with us. Because there's nothing he'd rather do than be in our presence. Because we're his children, and he wants us by his side. Because he likes having us around. Is there any greater comfort a child can imagine?

REFLECTION
*How does it feel to know that God delights in having you around?
Does it change the way you see yourself?
How does it change your view of God?*

DECEMBER

DEEP LOVE

"I have loved you deeply," says the Lord.   Malachi 1:2

ROBERT AND FRANCES HASTY had been married for fifty-two years when Frances died. Robert loved his wife deeply, and her death was devastating to him. She was buried in Fort Worth, Texas, more than 240 miles from their home, but still Robert made the trip as often as possible to visit her grave and bring her flowers. For three years Robert made the long drive to Fort Worth at least four times a year—often on special holidays and always on Frances's birthday.

During the week of Easter in 1998, the seventy-five-year old man bought some beautiful Easter lilies for his wife's gravesite. He made the grueling trip, parked in his usual spot, and then knelt down beside Frances's gravestone. He neatly secured the lilies to her plot then began praying. He stayed longer than usual, talking with his departed bride well into the evening hours. Somehow he lost track of time.

At dusk a lone maintenance worker found Robert's lifeless body still kneeling at his wife's grave. His children were promptly called, and though they were saddened by the news, they didn't seem surprised by their father's actions. "He loved my mother deeply," said their oldest son.[1]

There is a kind of love that transcends human understanding. It is possible to love someone so much that you lose all sense of time and reasoning. You want to be near her, to talk to her, to reflect on her smile, to remember the times you spent together. You're even willing to die for your loved one.

The kind of love that Robert had for his wife was beautiful and beyond understanding, yet still it pales in comparison to the love that God has for his creation. "I have loved you deeply," God says to us through his prophet Malachi (1:2). Centuries later he would prove it by sending his own Son to die in our place.

"God so loved the world that he gave his only Son, so that everyone who believes in him will not perish but have eternal life" (John 3:16). We may never understand God's love, but that's not important. All we need to do is accept it.

REFLECTION
How long has it been since you reflected on the unfathomable love of God?
How can you show your love in return?

A GOD FOR ALL AGES

Are we not all children of the same Father?   Malachi 2:10

WHY IS THE STUDY of the Old Testament so important to our faith? Why is it so critical that we take the time to learn about the history of Israel and the way God dealt with the Jewish nation throughout the ages? How does it affect our daily life in the here and now?

A better question might be, Why was it so important to God? The books of the Old Testament account for over two-thirds of the entire canon of Scripture, so God must have had a strong purpose for including them. And he certainly didn't want them overlooked. If you've been working through this devotional from the beginning, you've no doubt noticed that we've spent a great deal of time elaborating on Old Testament passages, and that's not an accident. I'm not only fascinated by these books but also a strong believer in their significance and merit.

The Old Testament is so much more than the story of Israel; it is our story. It is the history of humanity's redemption and the answer to every question we can fathom about the roots and nature of our faith. It is through this history that we get our bearings—our spiritual "true north." Too often we speak of the "God of Abraham" and the "God of Moses"—as if the God they served was somehow different than the "God of grace" that we worship, but he is One and the same. "Are we not all children of the same Father?" says the prophet Malachi. "Are we not all created by the same God?" (Malachi 2:10).

There are branches of theology today that try to draw a distinction between the God of old and the God we serve. They teach that Israel worshiped a God of judgment and wrath but that we worship a God of grace—the same God, of course, but with a renewed personality and standard. But they've missed the point. God has always been defined by love and mercy, and he has not changed. "I am the Lord, and I do not change," God tells Israel (3:6). Could he possibly say it more plainly?

God chose Israel as the subset of all humanity. The seed of our faith traces back to Abraham—the seed of Israel. And his covenant with Abraham is not only fulfilled *through* us but remains *in* us. Ours is a story that spans the ages, from the beginning of time until now. And in order to fully grasp and embrace it, it's crucial that we take time to study it.

REFLECTION
Are you content with your knowledge of the Old Testament? If not, what can you do to remedy the situation? Why not spend as much time reflecting on God's older books as you do studying his newer ones?

THE GREAT DIVORCE

"I hate divorce!" says the Lord.   Malachi 2:16

WHY DOES GOD hate divorce? What is it about this particular human transgression that elicits such strong emotion from our Father? Why would he choose to mention this sin above so many others as an act that he literally abhors?

Could it possibly be because God feels like he's been through one himself?

"I have loved you deeply," he says to Israel through his prophet Malachi (Malachi 1:2). It is a sentiment that he relayed thousands of times in many different ways throughout the years to his beloved people, yet they continued to turn their backs on him. No matter how many times he lured his bride back, she continued to be unfaithful. In spite of his love and provision, Israel's heart wandered relentlessly. And in the end she left him and never returned.

> "Surely these had to be among those who waited too long to consider the claims of Christ. Their hearts had to have been hardened, because there was no logic in their behavior."
>
> *The Remnant, 325*

God hates divorce because he understands firsthand what it feels like. He knows the pain that comes from having a spouse leave you. He knows the bitterness of unkept promises and broken vows. He's experienced the sorrow of a fractured relationship, and it pains him deeply to see his children go through it. God doesn't look on divorced people as greater sinners but as hurting children—people who have gone through the ultimate sign of rejection. It's a pain he knows too well to easily dismiss.

Often the church treats those who have been divorced as second-class citizens of the Kingdom when it should be extending compassion to them. God never singled out divorce as the greatest sin. He sees it as one of the most hurtful acts one person can heap on another. And because of that he will always hate the idea of divorce.

Broken vows are something God understands intimately. His heart deals with them on a daily basis. Every time we turn our back on God and toward another, he feels the pain of rejection. Every soul who denies him adds another dagger to his heart. Everyone who leaves the earth without accepting his love brings the pain of Israel back to his mind. God is the ultimate jilted lover. He's been abandoned more often than you and I can fathom, yet still his faithfulness abounds. Still he remains true. Still he loves us deeply.

REFLECTION
In what ways have you hurt God by turning your heart toward another? What are some things you can do to remain faithful?

A FAITHFUL SPOUSE

So guard yourself; always remain loyal to your wife.   Malachi 2:16

A BITTER WIFE once stormed into a minister's office, seething with resentment toward her husband. She immediately began telling him of her plans to divorce her unfaithful partner. But her wrath didn't end there. "I not only want to get rid of him," she said, "I want to get even! Before I divorce him, I want to hurt him as much as he has me!"

The wise minister thought before responding, then came up with an ingenious plan. "Go home and act as if you really loved your husband," he began. "Tell him how much he means to you. Praise him for every decent trait. Go out of your way to be kind, considerate, and as generous as possible. Spare no efforts to please him, to enjoy him. Make him believe you love him. After you've convinced him of your undying love and that you cannot live without him, then drop the bomb. Tell him that you're getting a divorce. That will really hurt him."

The wife smiled widely with thoughts of revenge exploding from her eyes. It was the perfect plan. "Beautiful," she said. "Will he ever be surprised!"

The minister waited over two months to hear back from the woman, but she never returned. Curiosity finally got the best of him, so he called her and asked, "Are you ready now to go through with the divorce?"

"Divorce!" she exclaimed. "Never! I discovered that I really do love him."[2]

The wise minister understood an important principle of relationships. Feelings almost always follow actions. Love and loyalty are traits that we learn through practice and intention. We love through what we do, and eventually love becomes genuine.

"Didn't the Lord make you one with your wife?" the Lord asks the Israelites. "In body and spirit you are his. . . . So guard yourself; always remain loyal to your wife" (Malachi 2:15-16). God knows that loyalty leads to even greater love and loyalty. That if couples will remain true to each other, it will lead to happiness and a more fulfilling life. His disdain for divorce reveals the priority he puts on faithfulness. And his admonition to remain loyal is a command, not a suggestion. Marriage is a sacred covenant in the eyes of God, and it should remain so in ours as well.

REFLECTION
Do you treat your spouse with the love and respect that he or she needs?
How would God rate your loyalty in light of your actions?

CONTINUAL PRAYER

Be joyful always; pray continually.   1 Thessalonians 5:16-17, NIV

I ONCE HEARD of a deacon's meeting that was steeped in controversy. The arguing had reached a fever pitch and no matter how hard they tried, they couldn't seem to come to an agreement on some key issues. After a long and heated discussion, one of the deacons suggested, "Why don't we pray about it?" Another man took a deep sigh and said, "Has it come to that?"

Funny how often we see prayer as a last resort. When all other options have been exhausted, and no stone has been left unturned, we lean back in our chair and think, *Maybe it's time to take the matter to God. You never know; it might help.* When all else fails, we might as well pray. We don't usually articulate it that way, but our actions spell out our feelings pretty clearly.

"Even in her suffering she read and studied and prayed."

Apollyon, 332

"Be joyful always; pray continually," writes Paul, "give thanks in all circumstances, for this is God's will for you in Christ Jesus" (1 Thessalonians 5:16-18, NIV). If we see prayer as a last-ditch effort during times of trouble—something of an emergency hotline—then that's all God will ever be to us. Our relationship with him will remain distant and fearful. We'll look at him as a rich uncle that we only call when we're in desperate need of help. But that's not who God is, and it's certainly not how he wants us to see him.

God is our Father. A loving and involved parent who wants to be an integral part of our life. He cares about every aspect of our day, no matter how small.

Billy Graham tells the story of a young president of a company who instructed his secretary not to bother him during the morning hours of each day. He had a standing appointment that he refused to miss. One day the chairman of the board came to speak with him, and the secretary caught him at the door. "He cannot be disturbed," she told the chairman. "He has an important appointment."

The angry chairman wouldn't take no for an answer, so he burst through the president's door to find him on his knees beside his desk. He was praying. The chairman quietly backed out and closed the door softly. "Is this usual?" he asked the secretary. "Yes, he does that every morning," she answered. As the chairman walked away, she heard him say under his breath, "No wonder I come to him for advice."[3]

REFLECTION
How would you describe your prayer life?
How might God have you pray differently?

DEALING HONESTLY WITH SCRIPTURE

A time is coming when people will no longer listen to right teaching. 2 Timothy 4:3

YOU WOULD HAVE loved my dad. He was a constant tinkerer. One of those guys who was always out in the garage taking things apart and putting them back together again. He loved building things, fixing things, making things work, even if he couldn't get them to work the way they were supposed to. A friend used to say that my dad could "fix anything from a broken heart to the crack of dawn." That described him pretty well.

Once when I was a boy, he and I were in the yard working on one of his many projects, and he grabbed a large object out of the woodpile. He leaned it against the garage, took a step back and began studying it. I immediately recognized what it was. "It's one of those slabs they use to pick up things with a fork lift," I exclaimed, beaming. I motioned excitedly and began to explain to him how it worked. After a while he grinned and said in his deep southern drawl, "I know what it is. I'm just trying to figure out what I'm gonna do with it."

A lot of us approach Scripture that way, don't we? We spend a lot of time putting together our views and theology about God. We collect proof texts that support our beliefs and begin building our philosophy one board at a time. We get excited as our project comes together. Then one day we run across a passage that doesn't quite fit, so we lean it against the wall and look at it. *I know what it says*, we think. *I'm just trying to figure out what I'm gonna do with it.*

It may be a fun approach to working in the garage, but it's a dangerous way to deal with God's Word.

"A time is coming when people will no longer listen to right teaching," writes Paul. "They will follow their own desires and will look for teachers who will tell them whatever they want to hear. They will reject the truth and follow strange myths" (2 Timothy 4:3-4). It's always tempting to want to make the Bible say what we wish it would say. We should never underestimate the human capacity for rationalization. When a passage steps on our toes or gets a little too personal, it's easy to try and explain it away. But that approach can lead to trouble in a hurry.

The first tenet of true discipleship is a basic willingness to deal honestly with Scripture. It is a critical element to becoming a faithful follower of Christ.

REFLECTION

Do you feel that your faith is built on an honest interpretation of Scripture? How do you approach passages that don't fit your philosophy?

HARD TEACHINGS

Preach the word of God . . . and encourage your people
with good teaching.   2 Timothy 4:2

DO SOME TEACHINGS in Scripture bother you as much as they do me? Do you have a hard time dealing with some of the more personal passages in the Bible? Do they step on your toes the way they do mine? Some of the hardest teachings come from Jesus himself, and they have a way of making us all feel uneasy. Here's a good example:

"You have heard that the law of Moses says, 'Do not murder. If you commit murder, you are subject to judgment.' But I say, if you are angry with someone, you are subject to judgment!" (Matthew 5:21-22).

> "When Irene
> discovered the
> Christian radio
> station and what
> she called 'real
> preaching and
> teaching,' she grew
> disenchanted with
> their church and
> began searching
> for a new one."
>
> *Left Behind,* 125

I can deal with murder being a horrible sin, but just getting angry? We all get angry from time to time, don't we? Is it really that bad? If anger against a brother is an affront to God, then I've insulted him more than a few times.

What about this one? "You have heard that the law of Moses says, 'Do not commit adultery.' But I say, anyone who even looks at a woman with lust in his eye has already committed adultery with her in his heart" (5:27-28).

Whoa! That can't be right, can it? Just looking? The same as cheating? Surely Jesus has gone too far with this teaching, don't you think?

Let's try one more: "If you forgive those who sin against you, your heavenly Father will forgive you. But if you refuse to forgive others, your Father will not forgive your sins" (6:14-15).

We all try to be forgiving, but some people just know how to push our buttons. Surely Jesus will understand if we harbor a little ill will. Won't he?

The teachings of Scripture are not always as easy or comfortable as we'd like. Sometimes being a follower of Christ cuts into your personal agenda more deeply than expected. Sometimes being a Christian takes hard work and discipline and sacrifice. If we want Jesus to save us, we should also be ready for him to change us. Old habits die hard, but they can die. And following Jesus means following his example as well. Even when the teachings are hard ones.

REFLECTION
What are some of the teachings of Jesus that you struggle to obey?
Why not pray that he will open your eyes to areas of disobedience?

HARD SACRIFICES

And if your hand . . . causes you to sin, cut it off and throw it away.
Matthew 5:30

THE HARD TEACHINGS of Scripture often call for hard sacrifices. Sometimes Jesus does more than step on your toes. Sometimes he gets very, very personal. He calls you to do things that you never expected. He asks you to follow him through doors that you don't necessarily want to darken. He beckons you to surrender things you hold dear. To give more than you were prepared to give. To suffer more than you were prepared to suffer. To forfeit rights to which you feel entitled. To pay a higher price than you ever imagined it might cost to be a disciple.

"So if your eye—even if it is your good eye—causes you to lust, gouge it out and throw it away," says Jesus. "It is better for you to lose one part of your body than for your whole body to be thrown into hell" (Matthew 5:29).

I don't know about you, but I need my eyes. Both of them. I use them every minute of the day. Surely he doesn't expect me to give them up!

"And if your hand—even if it is your stronger hand—causes you to sin, cut it off and throw it away. It is better for you to lose one part of your body than for your whole body to be thrown into hell" (5:30).

> "Let me reassure you. The God who calls you to the ultimate sacrifice will also give you the power to endure it."
>
> *The Mark*, 146

How fast does Jesus think I could type with just one hand? There's no way I could do without both of them. Surely he wouldn't expect that.

We all know what Jesus was saying. He wasn't advocating self-mutilation but was asking for the highest level of self-sacrifice and surrender. He was telling us that if we are really serious about our faith, we will do whatever it takes to remain pure and faithful. Even when it hurts. Even when it's something we don't want to give up.

Having trouble keeping your eyes pure with a TV in the house? Do you find yourself in a constant battle to keep from watching the wrong kinds of programs? Then maybe it's time to put the television in the garage. Struggling to keep from thinking about a flirtatious young coworker? Maybe it's time you put in for a transfer. If something in your life is causing you to sin, you have an obligation to do something about it. To cut yourself free, no matter how painful. It's a hard teaching but a critical one for those who are serious about their relationship with Christ.

REFLECTION
Are you willing to make the hard sacrifices for Jesus? What sin do you struggle with most? What would Jesus have you give up to overcome it?

DISHONORING GOD

Do not be deceived: God cannot be mocked.   Galatians 6:7, NIV

THE FIRST BOOK I wrote has only one copy in print, and I'm the one who printed it. It sits on the shelf behind me in a spiral binding. It's a good book and probably would have done well had it been published. In fact, it has gone through two publishing contracts with two separate publishers yet still never made it into print. The reason for this is a bit embarrassing to admit, but I'm willing to tell it in order to make a point.

Finishing the manuscript was a great feeling, but before sending it into the publisher I decided to write a brief acknowledgement page, thanking everyone I could think of for their help during the process. I thanked my mom and dad, my wife and kids, the editor, the publisher . . . my dog, my fish. Then on the last line I wrote a few words thanking my Savior, Jesus. The exact words I wrote were: *Even now, as I lay the final garnishing on this labor of love, your leather-bound blueprints for life lay open on the desk beside me . . .* I stopped and reread the words, impressed with my creative use of the language. Then suddenly I got a catch in my spirit. I realized that the sentence wasn't true. I looked on my desk, and the Bible wasn't lying open on top of it. It was a simple thing, and I wondered if it really mattered. I chalked it up to creative license and sent in the manuscript.

For no apparent reason, the publisher cancelled my contract at the last minute. My editor apologized profusely, explaining that she had never seen this happen before. She encouraged me to seek another publisher, which I did, and within a few months I had another publishing contract. Again the manuscript went through editing and typesetting and cover design. Then a few weeks before it was to go to print, I received word that the publishing house had gone bankrupt.

As I was voicing my anger and frustration to God over my misfortune, I pleaded, *Why are you doing this to me, Lord?* At that very instant God brought a vivid picture to my mind of that day months earlier when I had penned a complete lie on the acknowledgment page of my manuscript. It seemed like such a little thing at the time, but God didn't see it that way. *I will not be mocked,* God said to me in my spirit.

That day I gave the manuscript to God and promised that I would never dishonor him with my writing that way again. The book sits on my shelf as a reminder of that promise—to make sure I don't forget this simple but critical principle. "Do not be deceived: God cannot be mocked" (Galatians 6:7, NIV).

REFLECTION
Has God ever disciplined you for dishonoring him? How did you respond?
How do you make sure that you will remember his lesson?

SEEKING GOD

Those who do what is right will see his face.   Psalm 11:7

THE DEEPEST DESIRE of every soul that has ever lived is to see God. Every man and woman who has ever walked the planet has shared this one longing. Every heart has craved to connect with the Creator. We all long to draw near to something higher than ourselves. To stand in the presence of the Deity. To embrace the one who shaped the universe.

Most people never understand this desire. They know they yearn for something, yet never quite know what it is. They feel the emptiness clawing at them from the core of their consciousness, yet they don't know how to feed it. The restlessness stirs within them. The hollowness of life eats at them, beckoning them toward something grand and significant. Something that matters. Something or someone who can explain the void deep inside their soul.

"O God, you are my God; I earnestly search for you," writes David. "My soul thirsts for you; my whole body longs for you" (Psalm 63:1).

David felt his soul yearning, and he knew that it was for God. He understood the longing of his heart. And because of it, he sought after God with everything he had. More than anything in life he wanted to see God. And this great desire became his greatest strength.

Can you say with David that you "earnestly search" for God? Does your soul literally thirst for him? Can you feel your body longing for God? Do you seek to see his face with every fiber of your being? If so then you, too, will find that this great desire will become your greatest strength.

> "How a million of them could be contained even in the vast area surrounding the great rock city was a problem only God could solve. David had learned not to wonder and question, but to watch and see."
>
> *Desecration*, 99

"Those who do what is right will see his face," says David (11:7). In his deep longing for God, David learned the secret to finding him. He understood what it was that made God want to reveal himself to us. The kind of person that God would allow to see his face. It is those who do what is right in his eyes. Those who listen for his voice and obey. If you truly want to see God, you will obey God. And he will reveal himself to you.

REFLECTION
How earnestly do you seek to see God's face?
Are you living the kind of obedient life that he wants?
In what ways can you live with greater obedience?

REVERENCE FOR GOD

Friendship with the Lord is reserved for those who fear him.   Psalm 25:14

YEARS AGO I had friends in college who liked to call God "Daddy" during their prayers. They pointed out that when Jesus prayed "Abba, Father," he was using a term of endearment. In effect, he was calling God "Dad." It was a common phrase in Jewish culture. They took this idea and made it their own. My friends had good hearts, and I'm sure God knew that. But something about their prayers made me uncomfortable. I couldn't really put my finger on it, though.

Their prayers went something like this: "Hey, Dad, this is me, Randy. You know I have this test coming up, and I could really use your help. And thanks for letting me meet Sandy. I really like her. She's pretty cool. I'm thinking of taking her out sometime. Let me know what you think. . . . Anyway, I gotta go to class, so see you later. Love you, Daddy! Talk to you later."

It wasn't as if these types of prayers were offensive to me, they just didn't feel right. There was a casualness to them that I wasn't used to. In some ways I wondered if it wasn't simply a backlash against the rigid, formal prayers that they had grown up with. And there seemed to be a sense of competition developing to see who could be the least formal. One friend decided that he would no longer bow his head or close his eyes during prayers, and others quickly took the same approach.

There's nothing inherently offensive about any of this. I've always taken comfort in the father-heart aspect of God, and I love the idea of seeing him as our Father. I'm thrilled that we are able to connect with God on a real and personal level. Yet somehow it seems that in our effort to embrace the nearness of God, we have run the risk of overlooking his holiness. While it is true that God is our Father, he is also the Creator of the universe. The maker of heaven and earth.

"Friendship with the Lord is reserved for those who fear him," writes David (Psalm 25:14). A reverence for God's deity and supremacy is critical to a deep relationship with him. He is our Father, but he is also worthy of our respect and honor. When we become too casual in our relationship with him, we tend to forget who God is. He is the God of Abraham and Isaac. The great "I AM." The One who is, who always was, and who always will be. The King of glory!

REFLECTION
As you read David's psalms to God, what type of relationship do you sense he had? Do you feel that you have the same reverence for God as he did?

RELATIONSHIP WITH GOD

With them he shares the secrets of his covenant.   Psalm 25:14

WE WILL NEVER understand the heart of God until we learn to revere the holiness of God. If we want to know him, we must first learn to honor him. "Friendship with the Lord is reserved for those who fear him," writes the psalmist. "With them he shares the secrets of his covenant" (Psalm 25:14). The hidden things of God are revealed only to those who understand his greatness in the face of our unworthiness. It is intended for those who come to him in humility and admiration.

When Jesus was invited to eat at the home of a Pharisee, a sinful woman showed up with a bottle of expensive perfume. She knelt at his feet weeping. Then she anointed his feet with her perfume and wiped them with her hair. She sat broken before him. When the Pharisee realized who she was, he said to himself, "This proves that Jesus is no prophet. If God had really sent him, he would know what kind of woman is touching him. She's a sinner!" (Luke 7:39).

While the woman wept, the Pharisee accused her in his thoughts. While she knelt at his feet, he judged. While she humbled herself in the presence of the Deity, he tried to humiliate the Divine One.

So what did she understand that the Pharisee had missed? She knew that friendship begins with honor. That forgiveness begins with brokenness. That being right with God begins with reverence for him.

Jesus said to the Pharisee,

> When I entered your home, you didn't offer me water to wash the dust from my feet, but she has washed them with her tears and wiped them with her hair. You didn't give me a kiss of greeting, but she has kissed my feet again and again from the time I first came in. You neglected the courtesy of olive oil to anoint my head, but she has anointed my feet with rare perfume. I tell you, her sins—and they are many—have been forgiven. (Luke 7:44-47)

Too often we want to sit and dine with Jesus, but we neglect to kneel before him. We want the pleasure of his company but not necessarily at the expense of our dignity. We want to talk face-to-face, yet never think to stoop and wash his feet. We want friendship with God without a healthy reverence for him. Jesus is our friend, but he is also our Lord. If we want a relationship with him, we begin by remembering who he is.

REFLECTION
How do you go about honoring God?
How would you define your relationship with him?

ETERNAL FOOD

Spend your energy seeking the eternal life that I, the Son of Man,
can give you. John 6:27

EVER NOTICE how Jesus has as way of boiling life down to the bare essentials? Every time we try to complicate things, he simplifies them for us. Whenever we want to make things difficult, he's there to remind us how easy things can be. We try to add things to the list; he scratches them off. We take three pages to write up our job description; he sums it up in a few sentences.

> "We want to be forgiven. We want to be accepted, received, included. We want to go to heaven instead of hell."
>
> *The Indwelling, 227*

"You shouldn't be so concerned about perishable things like food," says Jesus. "Spend your energy seeking the eternal life that I, the Son of Man, can give you" (John 6:27).

Jesus reduced all of life's struggles down to two basic philosophies: You can either work for perishable things or eternal ones. You can take food that spoils or food that lasts forever. You can concern yourself with temporal things or focus instead on heavenly things. It's your choice.

Food that spoils is anything that stays in the grave after we're gone. It's the money we've made, the houses we've owned, the awards we've won, the success we've achieved, the praises we've gained from others. It is all of those things we did for ourselves during our days on earth.

Food that lasts is anything that remains after we're gone. It's the spiritual legacy we leave for our children. The impact we had on the lives of others. The treasures we stored up in heaven. The eternal influence we had on a temporal world.

And how do we get this food? Where do we find meals that won't perish when our body does? How do we gain heavenly things in a rotting world? Jesus gives them to us. Eternal life is a free gift from God. It's not something we earn or buy or work to achieve. The food that lasts after we're gone lasts only because it comes from Jesus. He is not only the giver of our legacy; he is the source of it.

REFLECTION
How much time do you spend seeking eternal treasures? How do we develop a taste for food that lasts, instead of food that perishes?

THE SOURCE OF LIFE

They replied, "What does God want us to do?"   John 6:28

EVEN WHEN JESUS clearly explains grace, we tend to argue with him. He tells us how to gain salvation, and we shake our head in disbelief. He gives us the Good News, and we flip through the paper looking for the bad. *Surely there's something he's left out,* we think. *It can't be that easy.*

"Spend your energy seeking the eternal life that I, the Son of Man, can give you," Jesus told the crowd of curious onlookers. "For God the Father has sent me for that very purpose" (John 6:27). His words were clear, but their skepticism was deep.

"They replied, 'What does God want us to do?'" (6:28).

When faced with the free gift of salvation, they wondered how they should go about earning it. "We understand our need for eternal life," they were saying. "But what do we need to do to get it?"

Jesus understood their confusion, and he answered by reiterating his earlier promise. "This is what God wants you to do: Believe in the one he has sent" (6:29).

We are the ones who make it complicated. We are the ones who want to earn God's acceptance and approval. We are the ones who try to attach conditions to God's plan of redemption. But Jesus only asks one thing. That we put our faith in him. That we trust him to save us. That we believe in his promise of eternal life for all who would call on his name. That we accept the gift with love and faith and graciousness.

Try to pay for a gift, and you've done nothing but insult the giver. Try to work off its worth, and you're working in vain. A gift is free for the taking, or it is no gift at all.

Things have changed very little since the days that Jesus walked the earth. He continues to hold out the free gift of eternal life, and people continue to try to pay him for it. We're still wondering what God wants us to do. And two thousand years later, his answer hasn't changed. "Believe in the one he has sent."

REFLECTION
In what ways do you try to earn God's gift of salvation? How can you learn to embrace the unconditional grace of God?

THE DIVINE GARDENER

I am the true vine, and my Father is the gardener.   John 15:1

THE BOOK YOU hold in your hand is no doubt much neater and cleaner than it was while I was working on it. The words you're reading now first appeared on my computer screen. I spent my days writing and rewriting, then printing out the pages on my printer. Then it went to the publisher, and the painful process of editing began. Someone with a red pen and a refined eye took my precious words and worked them over. They marked and cut and corrected and highlighted and suggested changes to make the manuscript stronger. At times the process can be brutal. Writers learn early to be thick-skinned; otherwise they're likely to have a short career.

Good books don't become good by accident. It takes a lot of hard work by a lot of people to make them worthy of shelf space. The better I do my job and the better they do theirs, the more likely people are to want the finished product. And the more God will use what we do to touch the lives of others. If I want to write books that make a difference, I must learn to accept this process. I have to allow others to cut and prune and shape the words I write until they are the best that they can be.

God works in our life that same way. Like a good editor, God takes all that we have and are and works us over. He shapes and molds us into something better. He marks and cuts and highlights and trims us into something much more useful and beautiful than we could ever have become without him.

"I am the true vine, and my Father is the gardener," says Jesus. "He cuts off every branch that doesn't produce fruit, and he prunes the branches that do bear fruit so they will produce even more" (John 15:1-2).

The purpose of a good gardener is not to punish the vine with his shears but to make it the most fruitful plant it can be. He trims because all branches develop dead vines. He cuts because only by cutting can he make room for new growth. He prunes because pruning is critical to the amount of fruit a vine can bear. When he is finished, the vine is at its best. And when a vine is at its best, the gardener can use it to feed more people. The best we can do is to let the gardener work and wait for the results.

REFLECTION
How can you better prepare yourself for God's pruning? How can you tell that God is preparing you for a greater harvest? Does your life exhibit the fruit of the Spirit recorded in Galatians 5?

BEARING FRUIT

Remain in me, and I will remain in you.   John 15:4

SO HOW DOES a branch keep from being pruned from the vine? If God is the divine gardener and we are the branches, how do we make sure that he doesn't target us for trimming? How can we make sure that we survive the gardener's shears?

The answer seems simple enough, doesn't it? Most would say that the key is to "bear fruit." To produce product. To make sure that we do enough to please the gardener. To work hard, to look good, to stay in the light, and to try to keep our grapes from wilting. But Jesus had a different perspective. His formula for staying useful was to stay connected to the vine.

"Remain in me, and I will remain in you. For a branch cannot produce fruit if it is severed from the vine, and you cannot be fruitful apart from me" (John 15:4).

According to Jesus, the secret to growth is connection. The way we stay healthy is simply to stay attached. The formula for more fruit is to remain on the vine. To feed from its roots. To stay plugged into the source of all life.

> "But I fear they have been separated as chaff from wheat. Yet those of us who remain should be confident in our standing with God as never before."
>
> *Tribulation Force, 55*

How many times do we try and force ourselves to grow fruit? We think we can will our way to a better yield. We grit our teeth and read our Bible, checking off the commandments one at a time. "Let's see . . . haven't lusted this week. Haven't envied the neighbor. Certainly haven't robbed or killed anyone. I went to church, gave my tithe, said my prayers, even smiled at someone I didn't like. If that isn't fruit, I don't know what is."

The trouble is, the branch could no more grow its own fruit than a fish could live in a bird's nest. Without the vine, the branch will wilt and die. Without Jesus, you and I will suffer the same fate. A branch cannot exist apart from the vine. You and I are destined for spiritual death apart from Jesus. That's why the gardener prunes with such vigor. He will do anything to keep us plugged into his will.

"My true disciples produce much fruit," says Jesus. "This brings great glory to my Father" (15:8). So how do you know if you are plugged into the vine? What is the one test that shows if you are remaining in God's will? You see the fruit growing from within, because of your relationship with Christ. Though you had nothing to do with its growth, you benefit from the harvest. The credit goes only to the gardener.

REFLECTION

In what ways do you try to bear fruit on your own?
How can you stay plugged into the vine of Christ?

A QUIET LIFE

This should be your ambition: to live a quiet life.   1 Thessalonians 4:11

SAINT FRANCIS of Assisi once invited a young monk to travel with him to town to preach. The young monk was honored by his offer, and together the two set out for the city. They walked up and down the streets greeting people as they went. They chatted with the peddlers, played with the children, and smiled at the citizens that passed by.

After some time they returned to the abbey. The younger man seemed puzzled and said to Saint Francis, "You have forgotten, Father, that we went to town to preach."

"My son," he replied, "we have preached. We have been seen by many. Our behavior was closely watched. Our attitudes were closely measured. Our words have been overheard. It was by thus that we preached our morning sermon."[4]

Sometimes the best thing we can do to honor God is simply to live an honorable life. Too often we think that God expects us to change the world when he would be happy if we just changed our behavior. It doesn't take a great man or woman to make a great impact on society. It just takes a respected one.

"This should be your ambition," Paul writes to the Thessalonians, "to live a quiet life, minding your own business and working with your hands, just as we commanded you before. As a result, people who are not Christians will respect the way you live" (1 Thessalonians 4:11-12).

Do you want to make a difference in the world? Do you want to live a holy and pleasing life? Then be faithful to your spouse. Get to work on time, and do the best job that you can. Set an example in your neighborhood. Pay your bills on time. Live within your means. Help an elderly woman with her car. Don't cheat on your taxes. Spend time with your children. Live with integrity and honesty.

God is most pleased when unbelievers see him in the lives of believers. The world is most impressed with God when it sees his children living honorable lives.

REFLECTION
What are some ways that you can honor God with your daily life? What does it mean to live a "quiet life"? Does that reflect your current lifestyle?

A LOVING LIFE

Your love for one another will prove to the world that
you are my disciples. John 13:35

A JEWISH COUPLE was arguing over what name to give their newborn son. After days of discussion about the matter, they finally decided to call in a rabbi for help.

"What is the problem?" the rabbi asked.

"He wants to name the boy after his father," the wife said, "and I want to name the boy after my father."

"What is your father's name?" the rabbi asked the woman.

"Joseph," she answered.

"And what is your father's name?" the rabbi asked the husband.

"Joseph," he answered.

The rabbi was stunned. "Then what is the problem?" he asked.

"His father was a horse thief," the woman said, "and mine was a righteous man. How can I know my son is named after my father and not his?"

The rabbi carefully considered his answer and then said, "Call the boy Joseph. Then see if he is a horse thief or a righteous man. You will know which father's name he bears."

Calling yourself a Christian means very little if you don't act like it. A name is a label, but it is not a lifestyle. We are identified by what we do, not by what we choose to call ourselves. "Your love for one another will prove to the world that you are my disciples," says Jesus (John 13:35). And if that statement is true, the reverse is true as well. Our lack of love for each other speaks just as loudly.

People will know if we are followers of Jesus when they see Jesus in the way we act. It doesn't get any more profound—or simple—than that.

REFLECTION
Who is the brother or sister in Christ that you have trouble loving?
Pray that God would soften your heart toward that brother or sister.
Why not pray for that person today?

A SOUL WAITING

I wait for the Lord, my soul waits, and in his word I put
my hope.   Psalm 130:5, NIV

EVANGELIST JOHN GUEST was visiting Russia just weeks after the fall of the great Communist empire. He was stopped at the border by guards and asked his intentions for entering the country. A man traveling with him explained that they were there to preach the gospel of Jesus. One of the guards pulled the evangelist aside and asked if he would tell him about Jesus. Guest immediately began sharing the gospel with this man, who had never heard that Jesus had died on the cross for his sins. He gave a copy of the Bible in Russian to the large, burly guard, and as he told him about Jesus, he could see that the Holy Spirit was convicting him. The Russian gave his life to Christ, then said with tears in his eyes, "This is the moment for which my whole life has waited."[5]

> "I've been praying
> that God will save
> my soul. And when
> he does, I will
> be able to see."
>
> *Armageddon*, 16

Is there anything in your life that you've been waiting for as long as you can remember? Is there a promise or a task or a person that you've been longing for God to give you? Maybe you've been praying and waiting for the right marriage partner. You've pleaded with God to bring you the right person, to give you a sign, to bring you someone that he has been preparing just for you.

Maybe you long for a child. You've waited your whole life to be a mother or father, and now your childbearing years are nearly over, yet your efforts go in vain. You cry out to God at night, longing to hold a baby in your arms, yet he remains silent.

Perhaps you are waiting for a promise to be fulfilled. The career that you were sure God called you to. The funding for the project or vision that God put in your heart. The rebellious child that God promised to bring back to himself.

If so, then don't give up hope. Don't ever give up on the Lord. "Out of the depths I cry to you, O Lord; O Lord, hear my voice," cries king David. "Let your ears be attentive to my cry for mercy. . . . I wait for the Lord, my soul waits, and in his word I put my hope" (Psalm 130:1-5, NIV).

Never mistake the silence of God for apathy. Never allow yourself to lose hope in his mercy. Never stop praying and waiting for God to fulfill his promises. Someday you, too, will be able to say, "This is the moment for which my whole life has waited."

REFLECTION
What is the promise your soul has been waiting for? In what ways
is God preparing you for that promise or vision? Pray today for strength
and patience as you wait on God.

A SPIRIT OF DEATH

For all who are led by the Spirit of God are children of God.
Romans 8:14

"DEAR BROTHERS and sisters," begins Paul, "you have no obligation whatsoever to do what your sinful nature urges you to do" (Romans 8:12).

When was the last time you confronted your sinful nature face-to-face? Are you in the habit of reminding Satan that you are under no obligation whatsoever to him? That he no longer has a hold on you? That you have been set free from sin and death and everything else he has to offer? Have you told your fleshly urges that they don't rule you anymore? Have you let the evil one know that you are now a child of God and no longer a slave to sin?

"For if you keep on following it you will perish," Paul continues (8:13). In these words we have a definitive promise from Scripture. If we continue to follow our sinful nature, we will die spiritually. If we continue to sin, Satan wins.

"But if through the power of the Holy Spirit you turn from it and its evil deeds, you will live," Paul writes. "For all who are led by the Spirit of God are children of God" (8:13-14).

If we live according to the dictates of the flesh, Scripture promises that we will die. But if we live according to the Spirit, we will live. It's a guarantee that is as simple as it is significant.

And how do we live according to the Spirit? We allow the Spirit to put our old sin nature to death. We let God choke the life out of the evil within us. We let God do what we could never do on our own. We don't simply "fight" our nature; we let the Holy Spirit kill it. We allow the Holy Spirit to do a miracle in our life so that God can use us for his glory. We inform our sinful nature once and for all that we are no longer under its obligation. That we are free!

REFLECTION
What sin have you been struggling to overcome? Why do you think this sin has such a hold on you? What keeps you from allowing the Holy Spirit to choke it out?

A SPIRIT OF LIFE

The Spirit gives us desires that are opposite from what the sinful nature desires. Galatians 5:17

HOW DO WE allow the Holy Spirit to put our sinful nature to death? How do we let the Spirit do a miracle in our life so that we can live in freedom and joy and service to God? We know we are called to live by the Spirit instead of the flesh, but how do we go about doing that?

The short answer is this: We daily embrace the desires of the Spirit and let him worry about the rest. We focus on what God has planned for us and allow God to deal with what Satan has planned for us.

Too many times we live our life fighting against our sinful nature. We try to will ourselves into defeating sin. We grit our teeth and say, "I will no longer do that! I will not lie! I will not cheat! I will not lust! I will not give in to that temptation that haunts me!" We convince ourselves that by resolving not to sin and by struggling against our evil nature, we can somehow find our way into the spiritual realm. If we can just overcome our evil thoughts, then maybe the Holy Spirit can work through us.

But Paul reminds us that the exact opposite is true. He tells us that sin is overcome only when we dwell in the Spirit. If we set our heart and mind on the things of the Spirit, the fleshly nature will be crushed in our wake. It is when we decide to walk in the Spirit that our evil thoughts are overcome, not vice versa.

"So I advise you to live according to your new life in the Holy Spirit," Paul writes. "Then you won't be doing what your sinful nature craves. The old sinful nature loves to do evil, which is just opposite from what the Holy Spirit wants. And the Spirit gives us desires that are opposite from what the sinful nature desires" (Galatians 5:16-17).

We think that by conquering sin we will somehow find our way into a spiritual life, but it is through focusing daily on our spiritual life that sin is conquered. We don't do it on our own—the Holy Spirit does it for us. All we have to do is set our heart and mind on him, and he removes those evil desires and replaces them with heavenly ones.

Satan can only win when he succeeds in keeping us focused on the chains that once bound us. The minute our eyes look upward, he loses his grip. When we walk in the Spirit, the Spirit does all the overcoming for us.

REFLECTION
In what ways are you still trying to fight sin on your own? How can you daily focus on the spiritual realm? Begin to do that each morning.

A SPIRIT OF SONSHIP

Since we are his children, we will share his treasures.   Romans 8:17

"SO YOU SHOULD not be like cowering, fearful slaves," Paul tells us. "You should behave instead like God's very own children, adopted into his family—calling him 'Father, dear Father.' For his Holy Spirit speaks to us deep in our hearts and tells us that we are God's children" (Romans 8:15-16).

How do we know that we are truly God's children? The Holy Spirit tells us. God's Spirit whispers into our spirit that God has accepted us as his sons and daughters. He reminds us that we have been set free from sin and death and that we are now marked for eternity with him in heaven. He calms our heart and quiets our fears.

And how should we act in light of that promise? We should act as children of the King, not as slaves. We should embrace his guarantee of adoption into his family. We should no longer fear Satan or give credence to our sinful nature. We should not cower when the world scoffs or back away when faced with opposition. We should call him "Father, dear Father." And above all, we should act like children of royalty. "You are a chosen people," writes Peter, "a royal priesthood, a holy nation, a people belonging to God" (1 Peter 2:9, NIV).

> "Whatever you've done, God is like the father of the Prodigal Son, scanning the horizon. He stands with his arms wide open, waiting for you."
>
> *Soul Harvest,* 391

Imagine the son of a king deciding one day to take a stroll outside the castle. He walks past the beautiful golden doorways framing the palace, down the long marble hallway decorated on every side with priceless furniture and portraits of those who have gone before him. He sees the royal family from generations gone by. He strolls past the ornate wood and gold furniture. Down the perfectly crafted marble steps.

From this fortress of wealth he makes his way toward the dirty, grimy streets of the village. He sees the slave quarters, the poor peddlers, the abandoned children lining the streets. The harshness of life as a servant. Would he be the least bit enticed by this scene? Would he be intrigued by the lifestyle of those who live in the streets? Would he long to be in their position? Would he have even the slightest interest in abandoning his life of royalty? Of course not. He would have nothing but pity for those who didn't share his heritage. He would long only to return to his palace.

Why then would any of us find ourselves enticed by what the world offers? We are children of the King. Why not embrace our royal destiny?

REFLECTION
In what ways do you long for the poverty of servanthood? How can you keep your eyes fixed on your inheritance instead?

COHEIRS WITH CHRIST

*If we are to share his glory, we must also share
his suffering.* Romans 8:17

UNDER ROMAN LAW, a servant who was adopted into a family as a son or daughter could never be cast away but would always be a part of the family. The parents could not decide later to revoke the adoption or the new child's privileges. The inheritance would be secure, regardless of what the child did or said.

Roman lawmakers made the law so tight that no adoptive parent could find a loophole. Once the process was over, the servant who was adopted was looked on as a full son or daughter, with all the rights and privileges of a blood relative. In many ways the servant was more permanently bonded to the parents than their own flesh and blood. Even if the servant displeased the parents, he or she could still not be disowned because the law stated that once the adoption was finalized, it was permanent.

Knowing this fact, imagine yourself as a Roman citizen reading this message from Paul about being adopted into God's family. "You should behave instead like God's very own children, adopted into his family—calling him 'Father, dear Father.' . . . And since we are his children, we will share his treasures—for everything God gives to his Son, Christ, is ours, too" (Romans 8:15, 17).

When God redeemed us from sin, he didn't just save us, he adopted us. He gave us full inheritance into his family. He made us sons and daughters—heirs to the family fortune. He took us out of the squalor of slavery, cleaned us up, and then robed us in princely garments. He embroidered the family crest onto the breast of our new clothing. He sat us at the royal table and introduced us as his children. He became our Father, in every sense of the word. And Jesus became our brother. The adoption is final and irrevocable. The promise is secure.

"If we are to share his glory, we must also share his suffering," Paul continues (8:17). If Jesus is our brother, then we have a responsibility to act like royal siblings. If he is an heir, then we are heirs, and heirs stick together. What is his has now become ours. When he rejoices, we rejoice. When he suffers, we suffer with him. His priorities become ours.

Coheirs of the Kingdom. Brothers in arms. Children of the Most High!

REFLECTION
*How does it change your view of God to see Jesus as a brother?
In what ways do you share in his suffering? How have you embraced
your royal inheritance?*

DEFINED BY FREEDOM

What we suffer now is nothing compared to the glory
he will give us later.   Romans 8:18

DOES IT SURPRISE you that Paul could sit in a jail cell and write some of the things he wrote? Could you have had the same level of faith and boldness and heavenly perspective under similar circumstances?

From the depths of a cold, hard dungeon, with chains binding his hands and feet, he writes to Timothy, "God has not given us a spirit of fear and timidity, but of power, love, and self discipline. So you must never be ashamed to tell others about our Lord. . . . With the strength God gives you, be ready to suffer with me for the proclamation of the Good News" (2 Timothy 1:7-8).

From a prison in Rome he writes, "Let heaven fill your thoughts. Do not think only about things down here on earth. For you died when Christ died, and your real life is hidden with Christ in God" (Colossians 3:2-3). Some of Paul's greatest words of victory came in the middle of his most despairing and seemingly hopeless days. His weakest moments on earth led to some of his most profound thoughts about heaven.

> "Rabbi Ben-Judah's family was abducted and slaughtered! His house has burned to the ground. I pray he is safe, but no one knows where he is!"
>
> *Nicolae, 60*

Paul was able to live this way because he didn't define himself by his imprisonment. Even in chains he saw only his freedom in Christ. The walls that surrounded him could never keep him from his true destiny. The men who guarded him could never squelch his love for Jesus. Paul knew that even though he was a prisoner on earth, he was a king in heaven.

Ever know anyone like Paul? Ever have friends who never find the time to complain about their circumstances? They go through the same trials and troubles as the rest of us but somehow are able to rise above them. They are able to see past their present woes and into the future. What they know that so many of us have missed is that with God deliverance is always right around the corner. They understand that their circumstances don't define who they are but where they just happen to be at the moment.

"What we suffer now is nothing compared to the glory he will give us later," writes Paul to the church in Rome (Romans 8:18). The greatest thing about living in Christ is that you know things will only get better. Even when we are down, we know that he will soon lift us up. There is nothing we could go through on earth that could put a damper on what Jesus has planned for our future.

REFLECTION
How can we define ourselves by God's plan for our future instead
of our present sufferings? What can we learn from Paul's example?

THE LARK AND THE CANARY

He has sent me to proclaim that captives will be released.   Luke 4:18

A LARK ONCE landed on a windowsill and spied a canary in a small cage just inside the window. "Tell me, canary, what is your purpose?" the lark asked.

"My purpose is to eat seed," answered the canary.

"What for?" asked the lark.

"So I can be strong."

"Why do you need to be strong?" the lark continued.

"So I can sing," answered the canary.

"And why do you sing?"

"Because when I sing, I get more seed."

The lark seemed confused. "So you eat in order to be strong, so you can sing, so you can get seed, so you can eat?"

"Yes," said the canary.

"There is more to you than that," said the lark. "And if you'll follow me, I can help you find it. But there is one catch. You must leave your cage."[6]

"The Spirit of the Lord is upon me," says Jesus, "for he has appointed me to preach Good News to the poor. He has sent me to proclaim that captives will be released, that the blind will see, that the downtrodden will be freed from their oppressors, and that the time of the Lord's favor has come" (Luke 4:18-19).

Outside each window the beautiful lark perches quietly, beckoning each of us to leave our cage and find our true purpose. He calls to us from the perch of freedom to open our wings and fly. He promises to take us where we never imagined we could go. To show us skies more wide and wonderful than our greatest dreams. To lead us into a glorious future. But there is one catch: We must first leave our cage.

REFLECTION
*What cages of sin or fear still bind you? Why have you allowed yourself
to remain hostage? Why not allow Jesus to free you today?*

A GOOD DEATH

*He will come again. . . . This time he will bring salvation to all those
who are eagerly waiting for him.*   Hebrews 9:28

MARGARET KIM PETERSON knew that her husband was going to die soon. The diagnosis was severe and fatal. Together the two of them set out to plan his death, calmly and nobly.

They began by updating his will and meeting with a funeral director. A cemetery plot was purchased and a headstone put into place. Her husband said his final good-byes, wrote his final letters, made sure that all his final words had been said. He was ready to die. But first he wanted to visit his gravesite one last time before too much of his strength had left his body. Margaret writes of the event:

> When we visited the cemetery to see my husband's newly laid gravestone, we took a picture of him next to his gravestone. He is sitting cross-legged on the ground, looking straight into the camera, and in front of him is a flat stone with the legend, "I know that my redeemer liveth," and under it his name and the year of his birth, with a space next to it for the year of his death. It is a photograph at once macabre, and darkly funny, and soberly realistic. He is dying, and he knows it, and he also knows that his redeemer lives, and that he is soon to see him face to face. Isn't this how a Christian ought to live, and ought to die?[7]

Believe it or not, there is something more important than living a good life. It is preparing for a good death. It is knowing that we have lived in such a way that our destiny is secure long before our days on earth are over. It is seeing that our life goes on even after we draw our last breath.

This doesn't mean that we live for death—only that we understand the terminal nature of life. We're not talking about a death wish; we're talking about an eternal mind-set. When you can sit on your gravesite and smile for the camera, it says a lot about your true priorities. We are never more alive than when we are intimately aware of death. It brings a perspective like few other things can.

"Seventy years are given to us!" prays Moses. "Some may even reach eighty. But even the best of these years are filled with pain and trouble; soon they disappear, and we are gone. . . . Teach us to make the most of our time, so that we may grow in wisdom" (Psalm 90:10-12).

REFLECTION
Do you live in fear of death? How can you allow Jesus to help you embrace your glorious future? Pray today that you can begin eagerly awaiting the salvation Jesus brings.

NO OTHER NAME

There is salvation in no one else!   Acts 4:12

EVER GOTTEN a blank, cold stare when you explained to a friend that Jesus is the only way to heaven? Ever looked into eyes of anger when you confronted someone about their need for salvation? Ever had people walk away when you told them that Jesus was their only hope of salvation? I have. I've lost friends and had others grow distant because I tried to share the gospel.

The funny thing is, I've wondered about the claim myself. In fact, I've found myself confused in the past about God's plan of redemption. I, too, wondered why God couldn't find another way to save us. Was this the only way? Did Jesus really have to die so that you and I could live forever? If God is God, couldn't he find another way to do it?

Maybe you've struggled with some of those same questions. Maybe you've read the account of Jesus' death on the cross and wondered why he had to suffer. Perhaps you've sat through a production of the Passion play with tears in your eyes and doubts swimming through your mind. *Why did Jesus have to endure the cross on our behalf? Couldn't God have done it another way?*

If so, then don't be embarrassed by your questions. Jesus had the same questions. He agonized over the same concerns that you and I agonize over. The night before his death, Jesus went to Gethsemane to talk to his Father. The minute he was alone he fell down on his face. "'Abba, Father,' he said, 'everything is possible for you. Please take this cup of suffering away from me'" (Mark 14:36).

Jesus pleaded with God to find another way. He begged him to find an alternate method of redeeming humanity. He cried out for some kind of reprieve. "You can do anything, God! Can't you find another way?" he cries. And God's response to him is the same that he gives to you and me. "If there was another way, don't you think I would have found it? Don't you think I would have figured it out by now? Do you think I would allow my Son to die if I didn't have to?"

We may never understand why Jesus had to die, but we can no longer doubt that his death was necessary. We may question God's plan of salvation, but we can't argue with it. We may think we can find another way to heaven, but that doesn't make us right. "There is no other name in all of heaven for people to call on to save them" (Acts 4:12).

REFLECTION
Why do we have such a hard time accepting that Jesus is the only way to the Father? Have you struggled with doubts? What would Jesus say to you?

THE DAY OF THE LORD

Since everything will be destroyed in this way, what kind
of people ought you to be?   2 Peter 3:11, NIV

"THE DAY of the Lord will come as unexpectedly as a thief," writes Peter. "Then the heavens will pass away with a terrible noise, and everything in them will disappear in fire, and the earth and everything on it will be exposed to judgment" (2 Peter 3:10).

There will come a day when no one will ever doubt God again. There will be a time when every question is answered, when every word of disbelief is quieted once and for all. A day when every heart will understand. A day when "every knee will bow, in heaven and on earth and under the earth, and every tongue will confess that Jesus Christ is Lord" (Philippians 2:10-11).

Peter tells us that day will come like a thief in the night. It will catch many off guard and unprepared. It will leave many wishing they had more time, more chances, more opportunities to redeem themselves. But when life is over, it is over.

You and I may not live to see the day that Jesus returns, but we will all face a day of judgment. Our last day may not be "the" last day, but for us it will all be over just the same. We will all someday take our last and final breath on earth. In the words of the wise old bumper sticker, "No One's Getting Out of Here Alive." When Judgment Day comes, we will all be judged. It's the one thing in life that every one of us can depend on.

> "In spite of and in the midst of every trial and tribulation, let us continue to give thanks to God, who gives us the victory through our Lord Jesus Christ."
>
> *Assassins*, 328

In light of this inescapable truth, consider the question Peter poses: "Since everything will be destroyed in this way, what kind of people ought you to be?" (2 Peter 3:11, NIV). How do we live, knowing what we know? What kind of legacy should we strive to leave, knowing that our life will be judged by Jesus? How should we spend our time now that we know our days are numbered?

In the next verse Peter answers his own question: "You ought to live holy and godly lives as you look forward to the day of God" (2 Peter 3:11-12, NIV). In short, we should live like people who understand that life is fleeting and our days are numbered. People who know that we will someday be judged. People who know that the life we've lived doesn't just describe us; it defines our future in eternity.

REFLECTION
How would you describe your life in light of Christ's return?
Do you live like someone awaiting a day of judgment?
What does it mean to live a holy and godly life?

BUMPER STICKER THEOLOGY

God so loved the world that he gave his only Son.   John 3:16

WHICH CAME FIRST, the chicken or the egg? Quite frankly, I've never really cared. But there is a similar question that I do wonder about: Which came first, the novels or the bumper sticker?

The novels I'm referring to are the Left Behind books by Jerry Jenkins and Tim LaHaye. And the bumper sticker I'm curious about started showing up on cars about the same time. It read: "In Case of Rapture, This Car Will Be Unmanned." Of course, we all know that this was the idea played out in the first chapter of the first novel in the series. I've always wondered which came first.

A short time later another person came up with a follow-up to this bumper sticker. This one read: "In Case of Rapture, I Get Your Car." Misguided but witty. Later still an answer to that sentiment started appearing on cars: "In Case of Rapture, You Can *Have* My Car!"

You can tell a lot about a person by what he sticks on the back of his car. Some people have the opinion that less is more. Sometimes a picture or symbol says it all. A lot of Christians show their faith by placing a simple fish symbol on their bumpers. Some angry evolutionist decided to get in on the action by taking that simple fish and putting legs on the bottom, then writing the word *Darwin* across the middle. It wasn't hard to see what he meant. Recently I saw an answer to that idea. It was a small "Darwin" fish being swallowed by a larger "Christian" one. I'm not sure that the back of cars is the proper place to play out the debate, but you have to give both sides an A for creativity.

The whole thing makes me wonder: If Jesus had a car, would he have a bumper sticker? Probably not. But if he did, I bet I know what it would say. "God so loved the world that he gave his only Son, so that everyone who believes in him will not perish but have eternal life" (John 3:16).

Is there any other sentence in Scripture that so perfectly sums up what Jesus was all about? Is there any verse that so succinctly and beautifully explains the way to salvation? Are there any other words that relate the Good News in such a short amount of space? John 3:16 unfolds for us the definitive life verse of the Savior. It is all we need to know about God's glorious plan of salvation. The only bumper sticker we'll ever need.

REFLECTION
When was the last time you reflected on this powerful verse? Have you accepted Jesus' promise of salvation? Why not pray to him today?

TAKING HOLD OF ETERNITY

Hold tightly to the eternal life that God has given you.   1 Timothy 6:12

REGARDLESS of what anyone might tell you, always remember that your future is more important than your past. Where you are going matters more than where you have been. What you do from this day forward means much more than what you have already done. You may be affected by your past, but you are not defined by it. Not in the eyes of God.

"Hold tightly to the eternal life that God has given you," Paul encourages Timothy (1 Timothy 6:12).

"Don't let go of your glorious future in Christ," he's saying. "Don't let anyone take that away from you. Don't allow yourself to forget what God has done. Don't let your mind stray from thoughts of heaven." Destiny is the ultimate definer of your life, not history. That's something Paul wanted Timothy to remember.

> "The third pivotal event in history was the first coming of Jesus the Messiah. That event made possible our salvation from sin."
>
> *The Remnant, 228–29*

When you live in the light of eternity, it changes everything. It changes the way you think and act and believe. You no longer see yourself as an aimless being living day to day. You know that you are a child of destiny, awaiting a glorious throne to come. You no longer act like a worthless sinner. You live as if each moment were your last. And that thought doesn't frighten you; it exhilarates you! You no longer believe that what you do doesn't make a difference. You believe that every second and every decision makes an eternal impact on the world, as well as your destiny in heaven. You live as a child of the future, not as a slave to the past.

How did a prostitute named Rahab find herself in the lineage of Jesus? How did a humble Moabite named Ruth get her name on that same list? How did the adulterous Bathsheba come to be in the birth line of the Savior? Because God doesn't care what we've been. He only sees what we can become.

"I command you before God," Paul continues, ". . . that you obey his commands with all purity. Then no one can find fault with you from now until our Lord Jesus Christ returns" (6:13-14). God doesn't care what you've done or where you've been. He only cares about where you plan to end up.

REFLECTION
Have you firmly taken hold of the eternal life God has given you? In what ways are you still holding onto the past? Focus instead on your destiny in Christ.

A DAY OF DECISION

The ones who win this battle against the world are the ones who believe that Jesus is the Son of God. 1 John 5:5

I SAW A BUMPER sticker once that read: "The end is near. Last one out gets to turn out the lights."

At the time it made me snicker. Sometimes our attempts at humor hit closer to the truth than others. But I'm sure the irony was lost on a lot of people.

> "Cry out to the Lord in your trouble, and he will save you out of your distress. He will bring you out of darkness."
>
> *Armageddon, 247–48*

So how close are we to the second coming of Jesus? Closer than we were yesterday; that's as far as I'm willing to guess. But you have to admit that it does feel as if it could be any minute. For those who have put their trust in Jesus, that's a comforting thought. For those who are still sitting on the fence, well . . . you do the math.

The truth is, there is a very real battle being waged on earth, and millions of souls hang in the balance. The war is between good and evil, heaven and hell, God and Satan, those who believe and those who reject Jesus as their Savior. It is a battle that is being fought on fronts all over the globe.

And one that also wages in the heart of every man and woman on earth. God beckons us to join him; Satan tries to stop us. God draws us near; the enemy pulls us away. God holds out the free gift of salvation; the devil tries to distract our attention with his tricks.

This war won't go on forever. Someday the banners will be thrown down, and a victor will arise. One day we'll look up, and it will all be over. Heaven will be filled, earth will be in chaos, Satan will try to hang on to what little hope he has left, but the end will be evident to both sides. And there will be no doubt about who won. The apostle John was given a front-row seat to the whole thing, and he carefully recorded the details for posterity. "Then the Devil, who betrayed them, was thrown into the lake of fire that burns with sulfur, joining the beast and the false prophet. There they will be tormented day and night forever and ever. . . . Then I saw a new heaven and a new earth, for the old heaven and the old earth had disappeared. . . . And I saw the holy city, the new Jerusalem" (Revelation 20:10; 21:1-2).

Who are the victors of the battle? "The ones who believe that Jesus is the Son of God" (1 John 5:5). Settle in your heart today which army you choose to fight with. Decide this hour which side you want to be on. The war of the ages won't wage forever. See that you're on the winning side when the final banner is raised.

REFLECTION
Is anything keeping you from putting your faith in Jesus? Let today be the day that you make a decision for Christ once and for all time.

APPENDIX

INTRODUCTION
1. Craig Brian Larson, ed., *Illustrations for Preaching and Teaching: From Leadership Journal* (copublished by Christianity Today and Baker Books, 1993), 52.

JANUARY
1. *"Titanic Live,"* broadcast on the Discovery Channel, 16 August 1998; *PrimeTime Live.*
2. Jack Canfield and Mark Hansen, *Chicken Soup for the Soul* (Deerfield Beach, Fla.: Health Communications, 1993), 273–74.
3. Randy Becton, *Does God Care When We Suffer?* (Grand Rapids, Mich.: Baker, 1988), 30–31.
4. Ibid, 76, 79.
5. Jack Canfield et al., *Chicken Soup for the Christian Soul* (Deerfield Beach, Fla.: Health Communications), 5–7.
6. Jim Elliff, "The Starving of the Church," Reformation and Revival: A Quarterly Journal for Church Leadership 1, no. 3 (1992): 116.
7. Erwin W. Lutzer, *Your Eternal Reward* (Chicago: Moody, 1998), 105–6.
8. Joni Eareckson Tada, *Heaven: Your Real Home* (Grand Rapids, Mich.: Zondervan, 1995), 39.
9. Ibid.

FEBRUARY
1. C. S. Lewis, quoted in Larry Dixon, *The Other Side of the Good News* (Wheaton, Ill.: Victor, 1992), 45.
2. Brother Lawrence and Frank Laubach, *Practicing His Presence* (Goleta, Calif.: Christian Books, 1973).
3. Ibid.
4. Brennan Manning, *The Ragamuffin Gospel* (Sisters, Ore.: Multnomah, 1990, 2000), 18–20.
5. Ibid., 88.
6. Dietrich Bonhoeffer, *Life Together* (San Francisco: Harper & Row, 1954).
7. Story adapted from *Our Daily Bread*, March 29, 1992.
8. Dr. Lynn Anderson is a former minister and author of numerous books, including *Heaven Came Down*, and *They Smell like Sheep.*
9. Max Lucado, *The Applause of Heaven* (Dallas: W, 1990), 91–93.
10. B. W. Woods, *Christians in Pain* (Grand Rapids, Mich.: Baker, 1974), 57.
11. *Leadership*, January 19, 1993, 3.
12. Leighton Ford, *Good News Is for Sharing* (Elgin, Ill.: Cook, 1977), 16.

MARCH
1. Gary Smith, "Ali and His Entourage," *Sports Illustrated*, 16 April 1988, 48–49.
2. Paul Lee Tan, ed., *Encyclopedia of 7700 Illustrations* (Rockville, Md.: Assurance Publishers, 1979), 1213–14.
3. Tony Campolo, *Carpe Diem* (Dallas: W, 1994) 17. Additionally sourced Web site: http://www.pbs.org/.
4. Campolo, *Carpe Diem,* 16.
5. *Houston Chronicle*, 28 May 1998.
6. *American Bible Society Record*, March 1990.
7. Joseph Stowell, "The Jesus I Love to Know" (sermon, Willow Creek, Barrington, Ill., August 23, 2000).
8. George Eliot, *The Mill on the Floss* (New York: Harper, 1860).
9. *The Fellowship*, August 1990.
10. *1997 Guinness Book of World Records* (Stanford, Conn.: Guinness Media, Inc., 1997), 11.
11. Dr. James Dobson, *Straight Talk to Men and Their Wives* (Waco, Tex.: Word, 1980), 138–39.

APRIL
1. Marshall Shelley, "Two Minutes to Eternity," *Christianity Today*, 16 May 1994, 25–27.
2. Ibid.
3. Philip Yancey, "What's Heaven For?" *Christianity Today*, 26 October 1998, 104.
4. *Baptist Standard*, 3 June 1998, 12.
5. Craig Brian Larson, ed., *Illustrations for Preaching and Teaching: From Leadership Journal* (copublished by Christianity Today and Baker Books, 1993), 221.
6. Charles Colson, *A Dangerous Grace* (Nashville: W, 1994), 80.
7. Mark Buchanan, *Things Unseen* (Sisters, Ore.: Multnomah, 2002), 168–69.
8. Robert Coleman, *Written in Blood* (Old Tappan, N.J.: Revell, 1972).
9. Colson, *A Dangerous Grace*, 71–72.
10. "$3 Worth of God," quoted in Tim Hansel, *When I Relax I Feel Guilty* (Colorado Springs, Colo.: Cook, 1979), 49.
11. Charles Swindoll, *Improving Your Serve* (Dallas: W, 1981), 49–50.

12. Tony Campolo, *Seven Deadly Sins* (Colorado Springs, Colo.: Victor, 1987), 128.
13. Stephen Covey, *7 Habits of Highly Effective People* (New York: Simon & Schuster, 1989), 33.
14. Maxie Dunnam, *Jesus' Claims—Our Promises* (Nashville: Abingdon, 1985).

MAY

1. *Tyndale Bible Dictionary*, s.v. "Covenant."
2. C. S. Lewis, *Mere Christianity* (New York: Collier, 1960), 119.
3. Charles Swindoll, *Come before Winter* (Sisters, Ore.: Multnomah, 1985), 95.
4. Margery Williams, *The Velveteen Rabbit* (New York: Doubleday, 1958), 16–17.
5. Max Lucado, *Six Hours One Friday* (Sisters, Ore.: Multnomah, 1989), 81–82.

JUNE

1. J. Mack Stiles, "Ready to Answer," *Discipleship Journal,* March/April 1997, 42–43.
2. Craig Brian Larson, ed., *Illustrations for Preaching and Teaching: From Leadership Journal* (copublished by Christianity Today and Baker, 1993), 131.
3. *Moody*, October 1991, 87.
4. A. W. Tozer, *Success and the Christian* (Camp Hill, Pa.: Christian Pub., 1994), 29.
5. *1997 Guinness Book of World Records* (Stanford, Conn.: Guinness Media, Inc., 1997), 224.

JULY

1. Leslie B. Flynn, *Great Church Fights* (Wheaton, Ill.: Victor, 1976), 91.
2. *World Book Encyclopedia*, 1996, s.v. "Taj Mahal." Also in Max Lucado, *The Applause of Heaven* (Dallas: W, 1990), 131–32.
3. Ann Landers, "Freak Accidents Have Motorists Tongue-Tied," *Chicago Tribune*, 24 August 1994.
4. *Colorado Springs Gazette Telegraph*, "Farewell a Comfort after Tragic Death," 6 April 2003.
5. Vivian Marino, "In Jewelry, Looks Can Be Deceiving," *Chicago Tribune*, 23 March 1995.
6. *SBC Life*, February/March 1997, 22; *Bits & Pieces*, December 5, 1996.
7. Quote taken from author's sermon notes. Dr. Nelson Bell was a missionary, surgeon, author, and a former moderator of the General Assembly of the Presbyterian Church, U.S.
8. Josh McDowell, *More Than a Carpenter* (Wheaton, Ill.: Tyndale, 1977), 107–8.
9. Chuck Swindoll, *Flying Closer to the Flame* (Dallas: W, 1993), 71–73.
10. Lloyd John Ogilvie, *You Can Pray with Power* (Ventura, Calif.: Regal, 1983), 12.

AUGUST

1. Lisa Belcher-Hamilton, "The Gospel according to Fred: A Visit with Mr. Rogers," *The Christian Century*, 13 April 1994, 382.
2. Tony Campolo, *World Vision*, October/November 1988.
3. "A Perfect Squelch," *Reader's Digest,* September 1990, 82.
4. Eric Zorn, "In Traffic Disputes, Turn Away and Live," *Chicago Tribune*, 8 November 1994.
5. Fredrick Buechner, *Wishful Thinking* (San Francisco: Harper & Row, 1993).
6. Rosie Mestel, "I'll Have the Cessna," *In Health* (December/January 1992): 14.
7. *Christianity Today*, 25 April 1994, 44.
8. John Robb and Brenda Spoelstra, "A Miracle in Moscow," *World Vision*, August/September 1991, 13.
9. Michael Parfit, "And What Words Shall Describe the Mississippi, Great Father of Rivers?" *Smithsonian*, February 1993, 36.
10. Tom Cunneff, "The Great White's Ways," *Sports Illustrated*, 15 May 1995, 8.

SEPTEMBER

1. Michael A. Lev, "Injured Violinist Has a Special Kind of Pluck," *Chicago Tribune*, 22 March 1995.
2. Alan Nelson, *Broken in the Right Place* (Nashville: Nelson, 1994), 84–85.
3. This is only one of several views tying the Seven Churches in Revelation to seven dispensations of time. Though the origin of this particular view is unclear, it seems to hold closer to the "spirit of the text" than other views I researched and has now become my personal interpretation of this passage. Many of the thoughts I use here come from the sermon notes of Tim King, a good friend and a noted Bible scholar.
4. Bruce Larson, *Wind and Fire: Living Out the Book of Acts* (Waco, Tex.: Word, 1984), 167.
5. "I Will Be Here" by Steven Curtis Chapman.

OCTOBER

1. "The Best and Worst of Everything," *Parade*, 28 December 1997, 6–7.

2. *Bits & Pieces*, November 5, 1998, 19.
3. Kay Arthur, *Lord, Is It Warfare?* (Colorado Springs: Waterbrook, 2000), 219–20.
4. Ronald Pinkerton, *Guideposts* (September 1988).
5. Ibid.

NOVEMBER
1. Max Lucado, *A Gentle Thunder* (Dallas: W, 1995), 86–87.
2. Dr. Chuck Missler, *Learn the Bible in 24 Hours* (Nashville: Nelson, 2002), 24–25.

DECEMBER
1. *Houston Chronicle*, 11 April 1998.
2. J. Allan Petersen, *The Myth of the Greener Grass* (Wheaton, Ill.: Tyndale, 1983), 194–95.
3. Billy Graham, *How I Pray* (New York: Ballantine, 1994).
4. A. Gordon Nasby, ed., *1041 Sermon Illustrations, Ideas and Expositions* (Grand Rapids, Mich.: Baker, 1976), 186.
5. Bishop Joseph Garlington, "Getting Ready for 'Glory to Glory,'" Joseph Garlington Ministries, Pittsburgh, Pa. (audiocassette), 2002.
6. Story adapted from Max Lucado, *In the Grip of Grace* (Dallas: W, 1996), 29.
7. Margaret Kim Peterson, "A Good Death," *Christianity Today*, 22 May 2000, 65.

JERRY B. JENKINS (www.jerryjenkins.com) is the writer of the Left Behind series. He owns the Jerry B. Jenkins Christian Writers Guild (www.ChristianWriters Guild.com), an organization dedicated to mentoring aspiring authors. Former vice president for publishing for the Moody Bible Institute of Chicago, he also served many years as editor of *Moody* magazine and is now Moody's writer-at-large.

His writing has appeared in publications as varied as *Reader's Digest, Parade, Guideposts,* in-flight magazines, and dozens of other periodicals. Jenkins's biographies include books with Billy Graham, Hank Aaron, Bill Gaither, Luis Palau, Walter Payton, Orel Hershiser, and Nolan Ryan, among many others. His books appear regularly on the *New York Times, USA Today, Wall Street Journal,* and *Publishers Weekly* best-seller lists.

Jerry and his wife, Dianna, live in Colorado and have three grown sons.

DR. TIM LAHAYE (www.timlahaye.com), who conceived the idea of fictionalizing an account of the Rapture and the Tribulation, is a noted author, minister, and nationally recognized speaker on Bible prophecy. He is the founder of both Tim LaHaye Ministries and the Pre- Trib Research Center.

He also recently cofounded the Tim LaHaye School of Prophecy at Liberty University. Presently Dr. LaHaye speaks at many of the major Bible prophecy conferences in the U.S. and Canada, where his current prophecy books are very popular.

Dr. LaHaye holds a doctor of ministry degree from Western Theological Seminary and a doctor of literature degree from Liberty University. For twenty-five years he pastored one of the nation's outstanding churches in San Diego, which grew to three locations. It was during that time that he founded two accredited Christian high schools, a Christian school system of ten schools, and Christian Heritage College.

Dr. LaHaye has written over forty books that have been published in more than thirty languages. He has written books on a wide variety of subjects, such as family life, temperaments, and Bible prophecy. His current fiction works, the Left Behind series, written with Jerry B. Jenkins, continue to appear on the best-seller lists of the Christian Booksellers Association, *Publishers Weekly, Wall Street Journal, USA Today,* and the *New York Times.*

He is the father of four grown children and grandfather of nine. Snow skiing, waterskiing, motorcycling, golfing, vacationing with family, and jogging are among his leisure activities.

FRANK M. MARTIN is the author or coauthor of over eleven books, including the best-selling *One Holy Fire* —with Nicky Cruz). He has been published in numerous Christian periodicals, including *Discipleship Journal, Marriage Partnership, Evangelizing Today's Child, Image, UpReach,* and *Pray* magazines. Frank has served the past nine years as a family commentary writer for Dr. James Dobson and Focus on the Family. He lives with his wife and two children in Colorado Springs, Colorado. You can visit his Web site at www.frankmmartin.com.

IN ONE CATACLYSMIC MOMENT
MILLIONS AROUND THE WORLD DISAPPEAR

Experience the suspense of the end times for yourself. The best-selling Left Behind series is now available in hardcover, softcover, and large-print editions.

1
LEFT BEHIND®
A novel of the earth's last days . . .

2
TRIBULATION FORCE
The continuing drama of those left behind . . .

3
NICOLAE
The rise of Antichrist . . .

4
SOUL HARVEST
The world takes sides . . .

5
APOLLYON
The Destroyer is unleashed . . .

6
ASSASSINS
Assignment: Jerusalem, Target: Antichrist

7
THE INDWELLING
The Beast takes possession . . .

8
THE MARK
The Beast rules the world . . .

9
DESECRATION
Antichrist takes the throne . . .

10
THE REMNANT
On the brink of Armageddon . . .

11
ARMAGEDDON
The cosmic battle of the ages . . .

12
GLORIOUS APPEARING
The end of days . . .

FOR THE MOST ACCURATE INFORMATION VISIT
www.leftbehind.com

ABRIDGED AUDIO Available on three CDs or two cassettes for each title. (Books 1–9 read by Frank Muller, one of the most talented readers of audio books today.)

AN EXPERIENCE IN SOUND AND DRAMA Dramatic broadcast performances of the best-selling Left Behind series. Twelve half-hour episodes on four CDs or three cassettes for each title.

GRAPHIC NOVELS Created by a leader in the graphic novel market, the series is now available in this exciting new format.

LEFT BEHIND®: THE KIDS Four teens are left behind after the Rapture and band together to fight Satan's forces in this series for ten- to fourteen-year-olds.

LEFT BEHIND® > THE KIDS < LIVE-ACTION AUDIO Feel the reality, listen as the drama unfolds. . . . Twelve action-packed episodes available on four CDs or three cassettes.

CALENDARS, DEVOTIONALS, GIFT BOOKS . . .

FOR THE LATEST INFORMATION ON INDIVIDUAL PRODUCTS, RELEASE DATES, AND FUTURE PROJECTS, VISIT

www.leftbehind.com

Sign up and receive free e-mail updates!